NOBILITY AND KINGSHIP IN MEDIEVAL ENGLAND

Nobility and Kingship in Medieval England is a major new account of the relationship between Edward I and his earls, and of the role of the English nobility in thirteenth-century governance. Re-evaluating crown–noble relations of the period, Spencer challenges traditional interpretations of Edward's reign, showing that his reputed masterfulness has been overplayed and that his kingship was far subtler, and therefore more effective, than this stereotype would suggest. Drawing from key earldoms such as Lincoln, Lancaster, Cornwall and Warenne, the book reveals how nobles created local followings and exercised power at a local level as well as surveying the political, governmental, social and military lives of the earls, prompting us to rethink our perception of their position in thirteenth-century politics. Adopting a powerful revisionist perspective, Spencer presents a major new statement about thirteenth-century England; one which will transform our understanding of politics and kingship in the period.

ANDREW M. SPENCER is a British Academy Post-Doctoral Research Fellow and Junior Research Fellow at Corpus Christi College, Cambridge.

The series *Cambridge Studies in Medieval Life and Thought* was inaugurated by G.G. Coulton in 1921; Professor Rosamond McKitterick now acts as General Editor of the Fourth Series, with Professor Christine Carpenter and Dr Jonathan Shepard as Advisory Editors. The series brings together outstanding work by medieval scholars over a wide range of human endeavour extending from political economy to the history of ideas.

This is book 91 in the series and a full list of titles in the series can be found at:
www.cambridge.org/medievallifeandthought

NOBILITY AND KINGSHIP IN MEDIEVAL ENGLAND

The Earls and Edward I, 1272–1307

ANDREW M. SPENCER

CAMBRIDGE
UNIVERSITY PRESS

CAMBRIDGE
UNIVERSITY PRESS

University Printing House, Cambridge CB2 8BS, United Kingdom

Published in the United States of America by Cambridge University Press, New York

Cambridge University Press is part of the University of Cambridge.

It furthers the University's mission by disseminating knowledge in the pursuit of education, learning and research at the highest international levels of excellence.

www.cambridge.org
Information on this title: www.cambridge.org/9781107026759

First published 2014

Printed in the United Kingdom by Clays, St Ives plc

A catalogue record for this publication is available from the British Library

Library of Congress Cataloguing in Publication data
Spencer, Andrew M.
Nobility and kingship in Medieval England : the earls and Edward I, 1272–1307 / Andrew M. Spencer.
pages cm. – (Cambridge studies in medieval life and thought: fourth series ; 91)
Includes bibliographical references and index.
ISBN 978-1-107-02675-9 (hardback)
1. Edward I, King of England, 1239–1307. 2. Great Britain–Politics and government–1272–1307. 3. Nobility–England–History–To 1500.
4. Patronage, Political–England–History–To 1500. I. Title.
DA229.S57 2013
942.03′5–dc23 2013018454

ISBN 978-1-107-02675-9 Hardback

For my father, John Spencer

CONTENTS

MAPS

TABLES

ACKNOWLEDGEMENTS

As a historian who is interested in relationships, the acknowledgments section has always been one of my favourite parts of any history book as it reveals modern connections between historians of the type that we ourselves often look for in our own work. More importantly, it is where we concede that our own work would not be possible without the generous help and patience of many other people. My first thanks, therefore, should go to the people and institutions whose financial investment has made this work possible. The AHRC funded my PhD, the research for which forms the basis of this book. I would also like to thank Bernard Jenkin MP and Cathy Perry for giving me a job as a parliamentary researcher which not only gave me three stimulating years in the Westminster Village but also enabled me to finish my doctorate. Finally, my thanks must go to the British Academy who gave me one of their post-doctoral research fellowships which has allowed me the time and space to do the extra thinking and research necessary to make this book a reality. To all of them I am forever indebted.

But while money may make the world go round, it is people who make it worth living in and I am most grateful for the people who have helped my intellectual development and without whom this would be a much poorer work. I would like to thank the Master and Fellows of Corpus Christi College, Cambridge, for the research fellowship they gave me and, more especially, the history fellows and students of Corpus with whom I have had numerous useful and stimulating conversations. Among my academic colleagues I would like to thank Dr Caroline Burt, Dr Carl Watkins, Dr Marc Morris, Dr Tony Moore, Dr David Simpkin, Dr Michael Ray, Richard Partington, Dr Lucy Rhymer, Dr Graham St John, Professor John Hatcher, Professor Christopher Andrew, Dr Pernille Røge, Dr Shruti Kapila, Dr Emma Spary, Dr Paul Dryburgh, Professor Rosamond McKitterick, Dr Adrian Jobson, Dr Huw Ridgeway,

Dr James Ross, Dr Andy King, Claire Fetherstonhaugh and Mark King. Professor Michael Prestwich and Dr Benjamin Thompson examined my PhD and I am most grateful for the useful and stimulating comments, suggestions and corrections that they offered. I would also like to thank Professor David Crouch for the generous use of his immensely valuable Comital Acta Project at Hull: three days spent there saved weeks elsewhere.

Two particular academic debts need to be singled out. The first is to Professor David Carpenter, my undergraduate tutor, who, with his boundless energy, enthusiasm and wisdom, ignited my interest in the middle ages and the thirteenth century. He also kindly read a draft of the book and his comments and suggestions have been illuminating and invaluable. The second is to my PhD supervisor, Christine Carpenter. A fount of knowledge and good counsel, hugely generous in her time and support long after her official position as supervisor ended, she has been a great friend and supporter as well as a great historian and teacher. My debt to her detailed attention to both the original thesis and this book will be obvious to any reader and much that is of worth in this comes from her counsel. Needless to say, after the help of all these people any mistakes that do remain are solely my responsibility.

I would also like to thank the staff of the National Archives, the British Library, the Institute of Historical Research and the University of Cambridge Library, all of whom have been most helpful, especially those at the National Archives who fetched and put back the hundreds of individual charters I needed to consult in the DL 25 and DL 27 classes!

My final thanks are for my family. My grandparents, for their support and faith in me, and especially my parents, who have given me the love and support of all kinds that I appreciate more than I can express. I must particularly thank my father for his tireless proof-reading of seemingly endless drafts and re-drafts and it is to him that I dedicate this book. My greatest gratitude, however, is reserved for my wife, Helen-Jane, whose love, friendship, support, advice and patience I could not do without.

ABBREVIATIONS

AM	*Annales Monastici*
App	*Appendix*
BIHR	*Bulletin of the Institute of Historical Research*
CAC	*Calendar of Ancient Correspondence Concerning Wales*
CChR	*Calendar of Charter Rolls*
CCR	*Calendar of Close Rolls*
CCRV	*Calendar of Chancery Rolls Various*
CFR	*Calendar of Fine Rolls*
CIM	*Calendar of Inquisitions Miscellaneous*
CIPM	*Calendar of Inquisitions Post Mortem*
CLR	*Calendar of Liberate Rolls*
CPR	*Calendar of Patent Rolls*
EHD	*English Historical Documents*
EHR	*English Historical Review*
GEC	*The Complete Peerage*
Gough	H. Gough (ed.), *Scotland in 1298: Documents Relating to the Campaign of Edward I in That Year and Especially to the Battle of Falkirk* (Paisley: A. Gardiner Press, 1888)
GTK	M. Morris, *A Great and Terrible King: Edward I and the Forging of Britain* (London: Hutchinson Press, 2008)
Guisborough	*The Chronicle of Walter of Guisborough*
Langtoft	*The Chronicle of Pierre de Langtoft*
ODNB	*Oxford Dictionary of National Biography*
Parl Writs	*Parliamentary Writs and Writs of Military Summons*
PROME	*The Parliament Rolls of Medieval England*
TCE	*Thirteenth Century England*

INTRODUCTION

A history of the politics of the reign of a medieval king that is told without the nobility at the heart would be, if not quite *Hamlet* without the prince, then the History Plays without the nobles. In some of these, it is not always easy to tell which character is which and what is the motivation of each. Without them, however, little would happen and less would make sense. A king's relations with his nobility, and particularly his earls, who were the greatest nobles in the kingdom, did more to shape his reign than perhaps anything else, as is clear from Shakespeare's dramas. As T.F. Tout put it, '[e]ven in the hands of a dull and commonplace person – provided that he were but brave and strenuous – the dignity of an earl was so great that it could not but exercise immense weight'.[1] Edward II's failure to meet the aspirations of his nobility fatally hampered his kingship. The clash between Richard II's view of kingship and that of his nobles blighted his reign and eventually brought him down. Henry III's personality never inspired confidence among his nobles and eventually convinced them that the kingdom would be better off under their stewardship. It was the breakdown in relations between King John and his nobles that led to Magna Carta. Conversely, the military and domestic successes of Edward III and Henry V can be attributed in no small part to their ability to carry their nobles with them and to put them to work in the interests of the crown.

It was K.B. McFarlane who first recognised that in the relationship of nobles and crown, so central to medieval politics, the interests of the crown and the nobles were not naturally at odds with each other and that quarrels between kings and nobles were not the product of an unending struggle between natural enemies, but rather specific failures

[1] T.F. Tout, 'The Earldoms under Edward I', *Transactions of the Royal Historical Society*, 2nd Series 8 (1894), 131.

of kingship by monarchs such as Edward II, Richard II and Henry VI.[2] Since McFarlane, historians have produced a plethora of monographs on individual nobles and on the nobility more broadly, starting in the early 1970s with the political biographies of Thomas of Lancaster and Aymer de Valence, earl of Pembroke, by John Maddicott and Seymour Phillips respectively.[3]

Until very recently, however, the nobles of Edward I's reign have remained largely free of historical inquiry, in large part because of McFarlane's own brief treatment of the subject. The first professional work on Edward I's earls was done by Tout in 1894 in an article that was as much concerned with the location of the earls' estates as with their political relations with the crown.[4] It did, however, argue that Edward had a very definite policy towards the earldoms, which was 'wherever he could to absorb them gradually into the sphere of the royal influence'.[5] Tout saw this as a mistake and a failure. Indeed, he went so far as to state plainly that, '[t]he family settlement of Edward I explains the reign of Edward II'.[6]

The most influential work on Edward I's earls remains McFarlane's 1965 article, which tackled Tout's thesis that Edward had a clear political policy towards the earldoms.[7] McFarlane rejected this, arguing

[2] K.B. McFarlane, *The Nobility of Later Medieval England* (Oxford: Clarendon Press, 1973), 120–1.

[3] Monographs of individual noblemen or noble families include: J.R. Maddicott, *Thomas of Lancaster, 1307–1322: a Study in the Reign of Edward II* (Oxford University Press, 1970); J.R.S. Phillips, *Aymer de Valence, Earl of Pembroke, 1307–1324: Baronial Politics in the Reign of Edward II* (Oxford University Press, 1972); C. Rawcliffe, *The Staffords, Earls of Stafford and Dukes of Buckingham, 1394–1521* (Cambridge University Press, 1978); D. Crouch, *The Beaumont Twins: the Roots and Branches of Power in the Twelfth Century* (Cambridge University Press, 1986); R. Horrox, *Richard III: a Study in Service* (Cambridge University Press, 1989), chapter 1; D. Crouch, *William Marshal: Court, Career and Chivalry in the Angevin Empire, c.1147–1219* (Harlow: Longfield Press, 1990); S.K. Walker, *The Lancastrian Affinity, 1361–1399* (Oxford University Press, 1990); J.R. Maddicott, *Simon de Montfort* (Cambridge University Press, 1994); M. Morris, *The Bigod Earls of Norfolk in the Thirteenth Century* (Woodbridge: Boydell and Brewer Press, 2005); J. Ross, *John de Vere, Thirteenth Earl of Oxford (1442–1513): 'The Foremost Man of the Kingdom'* (Woodbridge: Boydell and Brewer Press, 2011). More general books on the nobility include G.A. Holmes, *The Estates of the Higher Nobility in Fourteenth-Century England* (Cambridge University Press, 1957); A. Tuck, *Crown and Nobility, 1272–1461: Political Conflict in Late Medieval England* (Totowa, NJ: Barnes and Noble Press, 1985); C. Given-Wilson, *The English Nobility in the Late Middle Ages: the Fourteenth-Century Political Community* (London and New York: Routledge & Kegan Paul, 1987); J.S. Bothwell, *Edward III and the English Peerage: Royal Patronage, Social Mobility and Political Control in Fourteenth-Century England* (Woodbridge: Boydell and Brewer Press, 2004); D. Crouch, *The Birth of Nobility: Constructing Aristocracy in England and France, 900–1300* (Harlow: Longfield Press, 2005); R.R. Davies, *Lords and Lordship in the British Isles in the Late Middle Ages*, ed. B. Smith (Oxford University Press, 2009); D. Crouch, *The English Aristocracy, 1070–1272: a Social Transformation* (New Haven, CT and London: Yale University Press, 2011).

[4] Tout, 'Earldoms'.

[5] Ibid., 140.

[6] Ibid., 154–5.

[7] McFarlane, *Nobility*, 248–67.

that, although the aggrandisement of his kin was a conscious policy on Edward's part, it was not a political policy.

However, Edward's pursuit of such a policy resulted in behaviour that did not accord with McFarlane's understanding that the essence of successful late medieval kingship was 'unite and rule', of co-operation between crown and nobles.[8] He confessed that he 'found it difficult to account for what happened to a number of comital families during his reign on the assumption that the king's intentions were honourable'.[9] In his Ford Lectures of 1953 McFarlane had placed Edward I with Edward III and Henry V as the most authentic examples of co-operation between the king and his greatest subjects, but a dozen years later he summed up Edward's dealings with his earls in unflattering terms: the king, he wrote, 'preferred masterfulness to the arts of political management. In that sense he belonged less to the future than to the past'.[10] Closer examination of his behaviour convinced McFarlane that Edward was not behaving like a late medieval monarch ought to and he therefore pushed Edward out of the late middle ages.

While McFarlane damned Edward I for his domination of his magnates, it was this very quality that had earned him the praise of earlier historians. From Fabian Phillips in the seventeenth century, through David Hume in the eighteenth and culminating with Bishop Stubbs at the end of the nineteenth century, Edward I was, in Stubbs' words, 'the necessary check on … an aggressive baronage, the hope and support of a rising people'.[11] The last major treatment of Edward I before McFarlane was Sir Maurice Powicke's and he, unlike his Whiggish predecessors or his McFarlaneite successors, presented a generally positive view of Edward I's relations with his earls.[12] He saw them essentially as 'one large family', held together by a common interest and a common outlook.[13] It is McFarlane's interpretation rather than Powicke's that has gained most traction in the last fifty years of scholarship on the reign, and his view of the relations between king and earls has helped to shape perceptions of Edward's kingship more generally: McFarlane's acerbity has clouded the king's historical reputation.

[8] Ibid., 121.

[9] Ibid., 249.

[10] Ibid., 267.

[11] W. Stubbs, *The Constitutional History of England*, 4th edn, 3 vols. (Oxford University Press, 1906), II, 306; G. Templeman, 'Edward I and the Historians', *Cambridge Historical Journal* 10 (1950), 16–35.

[12] F.M. Powicke, *King Henry III and the Lord Edward: the Community of the Realm in the Thirteenth Century*, 2 vols. (Oxford: Clarendon Press, 1947).

[13] Ibid., II, 711.

In Rees Davies' work on the Welsh March, McFarlane's Edward I is on display in full Technicolor, imposing his will upon the Marcher lords in such a way as to build up dangerous resentment.[14] E.B. Fryde also saw Edward's relations with his magnates in terms of confrontation and domination.[15] Michael Prestwich, the leading historian of Edward I of the past forty years, has no doubt that Edward was a 'formidable king' and his reign 'a great one', and yet he too sees defects in Edward's relations with his greatest subjects.[16] Again, the picture is one of confrontation. Some of Edward's policies were 'designed more with the intention of asserting his authority over the magnates than of winning their co-operation'; his attitude was 'one of aggressiveness which might be modified if he needed support for his wars'.[17] Prestwich sums up Edward I's relations with his magnates in McFarlaneite terms, stating that the king 'did not possess the sympathy with his aristocracy that was to be displayed by his grandson, Edward III'.[18]

Given this historiographic consensus, based as it is on the work of the man who founded the modern study of crown–noble relations in the English middle ages, it may be asked why a new book on the earls under Edward I is needed. The answer is that relatively little is known about them, their individual relations with each other and with the king, and therefore a full understanding of the politics of Edward I's reign is impossible. The earls occupy only walk-on parts in the two major biographies of Edward in the past twenty years, those by Michael Prestwich and Marc Morris.[19] Morris' earlier book on the earls of Norfolk does provide a vivid picture of the career of a single earl in Edward I's reign, but only one, while Caroline Burt's article on the earls of Warwick focuses on their local networks of power rather than on national politics.[20] A full-scale treatment of Edward I's relations with his earls will help to provide a proper picture of politics in his reign. A thorough engagement with McFarlane's vision of Edward will thus be necessary for a clearer picture to emerge.

[14] R.R. Davies, *Lordship and Society in the March of Wales, 1282–1400* (Oxford University Press, 1978), 254–67.

[15] E.B. Fryde, 'Magnate Debts to Edward I and Edward III: a Study of Common Problems and Contrasting Royal Reactions to Them', *The National Library of Wales Journal* 27 (1992), 249–88.

[16] M.C. Prestwich, *Edward I*, 2nd edn (New Haven, CT and London: Yale University Press, 1997), 567.

[17] M.C. Prestwich, *War, Politics and Finance under Edward I* (London: Rowman & Littlefield Press, 1972), 225, 235.

[18] Ibid., 245.

[19] Prestwich, *Edward I*; Morris, *GTK*.

[20] Morris, *Bigod Earls*; C. Burt, 'A "Bastard Feudal" Affinity in the Making? The Followings of William and Guy de Beauchamp, Earls of Warwick, 1268–1315', *Midlands History* 34 (2009), 156–80.

A comprehensive understanding of Edward's kingship, which can only be achieved once his relationship with the nobility is fully chronicled, will provide historians with a better idea of the place of the reign of Edward I in English history and historiography, and in particular the question of whether Edward was the last of the Angevins or the first late medieval king. Historians have been rightly cautious about giving a simplistic answer to this question since Tout muddied the clear water of Stubbs who had regarded Edward, in Tout's words, as laying 'the foundations of the English constitution and of the English nation, such as we have known them in subsequent ages … and saved us from the danger both of a small aristocratic oligarchy and of the infinitely extended privileged noblesse of most continental countries'. Tout happily accepted this but suggested that 'it is quite as true to regard the work of the most conservative of our great reforming kings as summing up the tendencies of preceding generations'. To contemporaries, he argued, 'ignorant of the future, his reign seemed rather the end of the old than the beginning of the new'.[21] As has been noted, McFarlane's Ford Lectures on the English Nobility began their subject in 1290, and in them Edward I was very much part of late medieval kingship but subsequently very definitely cast out from the late middle ages.[22]

Late medievalists since McFarlane have remained uncertain about the proper place of Edward I's reign in their work. Textbooks on the late middle ages variously begin in 1272, 1290 and 1307.[23] Nor is this uncertainty restricted to late medievalists. Michael Clanchy's textbook on England after the Conquest has gone through three editions.[24] In the first edition, Edward I is excluded; the book finishes in 1272. In the second, an epilogue on Edward I is included. The most recent edition, however, incorporates Edward into the main body of the book, ending firmly in 1307. David Carpenter, on the other hand, in his chapter on the thirteenth-century kings of England in the *New Cambridge Medieval History*, has restated a more traditional picture of Edward's achievements in 'laying the foundations for late-medieval monarchy', in particular through the development of parliament.[25] By illuminating not only Edward I's kingship, but also the political lives of his earls, it is hoped that this book will

[21] Tout, 'Earldoms', 130.

[22] See above, 3.

[23] See, for instance, M.H. Keen, *England in the Later Middle Ages: a Political History* (London: Methuen Press, 1973); Tuck, *Crown and Nobility*.

[24] M.T. Clanchy, *England and Its Rulers, 1066–1272: Foreign Lordship and National Identity* (Oxford University Press, 1983); *England and Its Rulers, 1066–1272*, 2nd edn (Oxford University Press, 1998); *England and Its Rulers, 1066–1307*, 3rd edn (Oxford University Press, 2006).

[25] D.A. Carpenter, 'The Plantagenet Kings', in D. Abulafia (ed.), *New Cambridge Medieval History, c.1198–1300*, vol. v (Cambridge University Press, 1999), 343.

bring some clarity to a question that goes beyond attributing simple and artificial labels to certain periods, to the heart of understanding how the English constitution developed in the two centuries after Magna Carta.

This uncertainty about Edward I's position poses problems for the historian who approaches his reign, but it also offers an opportunity to engage with the history of the thirteenth century from the perspective of the detailed and sophisticated historiography of the late middle ages that has been produced since McFarlane. Although some thirteenth-century historians, as will be discussed in detail, have engaged with late medieval historiographical ideas such as 'bastard feudalism', this has not always been done with any great familiarity with more recent developments in late medieval historiography. In part this is because, with a few notable exceptions such as Michael Prestwich and Peter Coss, few thirteenth-century historians venture into the fourteenth century in their own research and thus something of a barrier has arisen between work on the thirteenth century and that focusing on the subsequent two centuries. The aim of this book is to help break down that barrier and to examine Edward with a full knowledge of the historiography of what came later as well as looking backwards to the reign of Henry III. Edward I's reign thus offers the opportunity to act as a bridge between the historiography of both the high and the late middle ages and, hopefully, has something to offer students of both periods.

At the start of this book, then, it is worth considering where English kingship stood at the opening of Edward I's reign and the challenges that he faced. In older European historiography the thirteenth century was seen as the culmination of the middle ages, the high point of medieval culture, from which it slowly decayed into the corruption, violence and stagnation of the fourteenth and fifteenth centuries before rising again to something even greater with the Renaissance and Reformation.[26] Such a view is no longer current among most historians, who recognise both the vitality and creativity of the later middle ages and the incompleteness and inconsistencies of thirteenth-century achievements. The thirteenth century was a transitional and transformative period in the history of English kingship, falling as it did between the sprawling, restless rule of the Angevins and the national monarchy of Edward III.[27] It took the kings of England a long time to accept the reality of the end of the Angevin empire. The legacy of Henry II's accumulation of French titles continued

[26] See J.L. Watts, *The Making of Polities: Europe, 1300–1500* (Cambridge University Press, 2009), 43–8, for a discussion of historiographical trends in the history of thirteenth-century Europe.

[27] R. Bartlett, *England under the Norman and Angevin Kings: 1075–1225* (Oxford: Clarendon Press, 2000); M.C. Prestwich, *Plantagenet England, 1225–1360* (Oxford University Press, 2005).

to affect the history of England and its monarchy fundamentally for the remainder of the middle ages and beyond. In Henry III's reign, moreover, English kingship was still reeling from the twin shocks at the beginning of the century of military disaster in France and humiliation in England. The effects of Magna Carta profoundly hampered the kingship of Henry III throughout his long reign. Royal government and law continued to grow, for the charter was never aimed at restricting them, only controlling their abuse by the king, and the crown was doing considerably more by 1272 than it had been doing in 1216. It is important, however, not to mistake governmental aspirations and mechanisms for power, and there can be no doubt that Henry III was a much weaker king than any of his Angevin predecessors. This was as much to do with the structural position of the monarchy as with the obvious personal inadequacies of Henry himself. Magna Carta had severely curtailed two highly profitable financial tools available to the Angevins: the manipulation of royal feudal rights and the selling of justice. William Ralegh's financial reforms between 1236 and 1239 stabilised the crown's finances after the largely hand-to-mouth experience of the minority but these finances could not survive Henry's determination to recover Poitou, let alone the rest of the Angevin possessions.[28] In other words, the English crown under Henry III was solvent only if it decided to keep out of European politics, an idea wholly alien to his dynasty. Henry's madcap plans in the 1250s for challenging the dominance of the Capetians forced him back on increasingly intense exploitation of his inadequate resources, which culminated in financial and political collapse in 1258. The power, authority and prestige of the monarchy was further debased during the years of Reform and Rebellion, reaching their nadir between the battles of Lewes and Evesham, when the king's heir was imprisoned and denuded of his inheritance and Henry himself was dragged around the country as little more than a miserable cipher, rubber-stamping the decisions of his bitterest enemy.[29]

Simon de Montfort's defeat and death at Evesham, while it solved Henry and Lord Edward's immediate problem, could not by itself solve the endemic problems that had afflicted the monarchy during Henry's reign nor fully eradicate the stain of the humiliations of 1258–65. Some progress was made between Evesham and Henry III's death but the principal challenges facing Edward when he returned from crusade as king in 1274 were the restoration of royal authority and to find a way to make

[28] R.C. Stacey, *Politics, Policy, and Royal Finance under Henry III, 1216–1245* (Oxford: Clarendon Press, 1987).

[29] See Maddicott, *Simon de Montfort*, chapter 8.

Magna Carta work politically and financially for the king and for the community of the realm. For too long under his father the interests of the king and the community of the realm had seemed to be in conflict; it was Edward's task to bring them into harmony.

Illuminating the nature of Edward I's kingship and the way he rose to these challenges thus forms one part of this book and its title, and Part I deals largely with this, but the other part of the book concerns the earls themselves and the key questions of nobility and noble power in the late thirteenth century, and this forms the focus of Part II. For the nobility, too, the thirteenth century was one of transition and they too faced significant challenges at the opening of Edward I's reign. They had begun the century under the tyranny of King John and had risen up in 1215 to force the king to abide by his own law.[30] Following Richard Marshal's rebellion and the Upavon judgment of 1234, the author of *Bracton* penned these famous words:

> No one may pass upon the king's act (or his charter) so as to nullify it, but one must say that the king had committed an *injuria*, and thus charge him with amending it, lest he (and the justices) fall into the judgment of the living God because of it. The king has a superior, namely, God. Also the law by which he is made king. Also his *curia*, namely, the earls and barons, because if he is without a bridle, that is without the law, they ought to put the bridle on him (that is why the earls are called 'partners', so to speak of the king; he who has a partner has a master).[31]

In this most establishment of texts, the earls specifically, and the nobility in general, were given an injunction to restrain the king, were he to act beyond the law. This was something they were very willing to do at various points in Henry III's reign and most obviously, of course, in 1258, when, in response to Henry's denial of justice to one of their number, a group of nobles took *Bracton*'s words to heart and resolved to bridle the king on an enduring basis.[32] In their hubris, they believed that, with the adequate safeguard of a broad-based council, they could order England better than the king: the terrible violence of 1263–5, the worst England had seen since Stephen's reign, proved their safeguards worthless and shattered the nobility's mid-century confidence. They had seemingly forgotten that *Bracton*'s famous passage continued: 'When even they [the

[30] J.C. Holt, *Magna Carta,* 2nd edn (Cambridge University Press, 1992).

[31] *Bracton De Legibus Et Consuetudinibus Angliæ*, ed. and trans. S.E. Thorne, 2 vols. (Cambridge, MA: Harvard University Press, 1968), II, 110; D.A. Carpenter, *The Reign of Henry III* (London: Hambledon Press, 1996), 40–1.

[32] Carpenter, *Reign of Henry III,* 192–3.

earls and barons], like the king, are without bridle, then will the subjects cry out and say "Lord Jesus, bind fast their jaws in rein and bridle.'"[33]

The years of Reform and Rebellion also demonstrated to the nobility the rising power and influence of the gentry, whose grievances were directed as much at the abuses of the nobility as at those of the crown.[34] Thus for the nobility the final third of the thirteenth century threatened the possibility that their power would be squeezed by the combination of the rising ambition of the gentry and the determination of the crown to reassert its authority. How they handled these challenges will be an important theme of this book.

Again, as with kingship, the influence of McFarlane on the history of the nobility is inescapable, as he did so much to establish the thriving historiography of the nobility and gentry of late medieval England. There is no consensus among late medievalists about McFarlane's legacy, but it has produced a rich and sophisticated corpus of writings.[35] By contrast, work on the thirteenth-century nobility is less abundant and much of it has been of a general nature rather than the detailed investigation of individual nobles, families or regions that characterises so much of the work on the fifteenth century.[36] That is neither to underestimate the value that these broad studies of the nobility possess, nor to forget that some important detailed work has been done by Michael Altschul, Peter Coss, Marc Morris, David Crouch and John Maddicott among others, but work on the thirteenth-century nobility thus far lacks the depth and range of that on their fifteenth-century counterparts.[37]

A compromise has been chosen between range and depth. Studies of individual nobles offer unparalleled depth and give the historian a firmer grasp of the individual motivations, interests and situation of his

[33] *Bracton*, II, 110.

[34] See, for instance, D.A. Carpenter, 'The Second Century of English Feudalism', *Past and Present* 168 (2000), 41–3, for gentry grievances against magnates over suit of court.

[35] For evidence of McFarlane's disputed legacy, see, for instance, R.H. Britnell and A.J. Pollard (eds.), *The McFarlane Legacy: Studies in Late Medieval Politics and Society* (Stroud and New York: Sutton and St Martin's Press, 1995). For the corpus of literature influenced by McFarlane, see note 3 above.

[36] See, for instance, P.R. Coss, 'Bastard Feudalism Revised', *Past and Present* 125 (1989), 27–64; P.R. Coss, D. Crouch and D.A. Carpenter, 'Debate: Bastard Feudalism Revised', *Past and Present* 131 (1991), 165–203; Crouch, *Birth of Nobility*; Crouch, *English Aristocracy*.

[37] M. Altschul, *A Baronial Family in Medieval England: the Clares, 1217–1314* (Baltimore, MD: Johns Hopkins University Press, 1965); G.G. Simpson, 'The *Familia* of Roger de Quincy, Earl of Winchester and Constable of Scotland', in K.J. Stringer (ed.), *Essays on the Nobility of Medieval Scotland* (Edinburgh: John Donald Publishers, 1985); P.R. Coss, *Lordship, Knighthood and Locality: a Study in England Society, c. 1180–c. 1280* (Cambridge University Press, 1991); H.W. Ridgeway, 'William de Valence and His *Familiares*, 1247–1272', *Historical Research* 65 (1992), 239–57; Maddicott, *Simon de Montfort*; D. Crouch, 'The Local Influence of the Earls of Warwick, 1088–1241: a Study in Decline and Resourcefulness', *Midland History* 21 (1996), 1–22; Morris, *Bigod Earls*; Burt, 'A "Bastard Feudal" Affinity in the Making?'.

or her chosen noble than is possible in a more general work, but there are obvious dangers. As Christine Carpenter has put it: 'If all politics is seen in terms of individual protagonists, each driven by his own inner daemon, we can come to no other conclusion than that politics were exclusively personal and, regardless of what ideological front might be put up to justify political action, each was out for what he could get.'[38] This is not always the case; John Maddicott has skilfully described Simon de Montfort's peculiar blend of high idealism and low self-interest.[39] A delicate balance, therefore, needs to be struck to ensure that enough is known about individual noblemen to understand their unique circumstances, while acknowledging that each nobleman was part of a broader group of people who shared common assumptions, activities and interests, politically, socially and economically.

With this in mind, a small group of nobles has been chosen for this book. Choosing the earls as a distinct group to study is certainly unrepresentative of the nobility as a whole. The earls were much richer, more prestigious and fundamentally more powerful people than the average nobleman. Sidney Painter calculated the median baronial income in the late thirteenth century of twenty-seven barons (including six earls) as £339. In comparison, most earls had incomes in excess of £2,000 a year.[40] They were the billionaires compared to the mere millionaires of the rest of the nobility. Today it is fruitless to learn about the ways of the rich by looking at the lives of the super-rich, but this is not so in the middle ages. This was a much smaller and more tightly knit society and, though they were richer and more influential than the majority of the nobility, the earls shared the common heritage and outlook of the nobility as a whole.

That said, one also has to acknowledge that there were great differences in wealth and influence among the earls themselves and it could be questioned whether it is helpful to treat the earls corporately, if indeed there was such a thing as a shared comital experience. Such questions are valid and important but there is enough evidence to suggest that earls were a definable grouping within the nobility and were recognised as such by themselves and others. They were addressed separately by the royal government, thought of separately by lawyers and thinkers and regarded themselves as something special within English society. It is,

[38] M.C. Carpenter, *Locality and Polity: a Study of Warwickshire Landed Society, 1401–1499* (Cambridge University Press, 1992), 6.

[39] Maddicott, *Simon de Montfort*. By contrast, see J.L. Watts, *Henry VI and the Politics of Kingship* (Cambridge University Press, 1996), for what a group approach towards the nobility can achieve.

[40] S. Painter, *Studies in the History of the English Feudal Barony* (Baltimore, MD: Johns Hopkins University Press, 1943), 173.

therefore, legitimate to treat them and their experiences together, while remaining aware that the experiences of individual earls were sometimes shared by their fellow earls and sometimes not.

This is particularly the case when looking at the role of the earls in local society, where the nature of their individual landholding had a profound influence on consequent power and influence. The book investigates the vehicles of comital power in the localities during Edward I's reign, and looks in detail at how the earls constructed their followings and how they used them. Of particular interest will be the extent to which they relied upon their knightly tenants to provide them service and the methods they used to attract, retain and reward service. Another focus of Part II will be on how far the earls sought to control the apparatus of royal law and administration in the localities, especially given recent historiography that has suggested important similarities between the thirteenth century and the fourteenth and fifteenth centuries.[41] This work on Edward I's earls will help to place them within the broader picture of noble power in medieval England. The place of the thirteenth century within this story is of particular interest, given the trend in the historiography of the fifteenth century and, more recently, the eleventh, which has tended to emphasise the role of the nobility in the shires as supporters, promoters and vehicles of royal authority and power as well as their own.[42] Recent thirteenth-century historians, on the other hand, while now taking an interest in 'bastard feudalism' in their period, have largely come to see noble power as a corrupting force, acting to frustrate, even subvert royal authority.[43] Reconciling these positions within the three periods would do much to enhance our understanding of the place of the nobility in the history of the English middle ages.

The third part of the book, Part III, will bring together the themes of the first two parts to help provide an integrated political history of the reign from the perspective of the earls. Given the space available in a monograph of this nature, a comprehensive political narrative of every aspect of the reign is impossible, and this book looks at political events from the earls' point of view alone. There will be much, consequently, that will be omitted, such as discussions of Edward's relations with the church, or the intimate details of the Edwardian statutes. Such

41 See, in particular, Coss, 'Bastard Feudalism Revised'; Coss *et al.*, 'Debate'.

42 See, for instance, Carpenter, *Locality and Polity*; M.C. Carpenter, 'Who Ruled the Midlands in the Later Middle Ages?', *Midland History* 19 (1994), 1–20; S. Baxter, *The Earls of Mercia: Lordship and Power in Late Anglo-Saxon England* (Oxford University Press, 2007); Ross, *John de Vere*.

43 See especially Coss, 'Bastard Feudalism Revised'; Coss *et al.*, 'Debate'; P.R. Coss, 'From Feudalism to Bastard Feudalism', in N. Fryde, P. Monnet and O.G. Oexle (eds.), *Die Gegenwart des Feudalismus* (Göttingen: Vandehoeck and Ruprecht Press, 2002), 79–107.

an approach will, however, help to shed new light on well-known events and themes in Edward's reign and offer a corrective to traditional narratives of the reign that have naturally been written largely from the king's perspective – part of the general trend for historians to be 'king's friends'.[44] The earls emerge from this study not as the crown's 'hereditary foes', as Stubbs and Tout would have it, nor as the rather anaemic, helpless group of men whom McFarlane believed Edward 'slimmed down', but as fully rounded and fleshed-out nobles with their own collective and individual traits and interests.

[44] Powicke, *Henry III*; McFarlane, *Nobility*, 2; Prestwich, *Edward I*; Morris, *GTK*.

Chapter 1

THE EARLS AND THEIR LANDS

Who, then, were the earls of Edward I? Twelve families held comital titles in England and the March of Wales during Edward I's reign, and the remainder of this introduction will focus upon explaining briefly who these families were and where their lands lay, as well as upon their relative positions within the comital hierarchy, before offering a few short observations on them collectively. The basic framework for this is provided by Tout's century-old article on the earldoms, on to which can be grafted more recent research, from which new conclusions can be drawn.[1]

Three comital families, Lancaster, Cornwall and Pembroke, were offshoots of the royal family itself and it seems appropriate to begin with these. Edmund of Lancaster was Edward I's younger brother and was born to Henry III and Eleanor of Provence on 16 January 1245. Like his elder brother, the boy was given the name of an Anglo-Saxon king-saint, this time the martyred Edmund of East Anglia.[2] If Henry III had had his way, Edmund would have been a far more important personage than an English earl, but the failure of his project to place Edmund on the throne of Sicily in the 1250s forced Henry to look closer to home in the next decade to provide a suitable inheritance for his second son.[3] The aftermath of the Barons' Wars gave Henry the perfect opportunity to endow Edmund, and the foundations of much of the Lancastrian inheritance were built upon the ruins of families who had opposed the crown. Edmund's first grant was of Simon de Montfort's lands, together with his earldom of Leicester and office of Steward of England.[4] Then there were

[1] Tout, 'Earldoms'.

[2] Matthew Paris, *Chronica Majora*, ed. H.R. Luard, 7 vols., Rolls Series (1872–83), IV, 406; W.E. Rhodes, 'Edmund, Earl of Lancaster', *EHR* 10 (1895), 19.

[3] For the most recent scholarship on the Sicilian project, see B.K. Weiler, 'Henry III and the Sicilian Business: a Reinterpretation', *Historical Research* 74 (2001), 127–50; D.A. Carpenter, 'Henry III and the Sicilian Affair', *Fine of the Month*, www.finerollshenry3.org.uk (2012).

[4] *CPR 1258–1266*, 470.

the lands of Robert de Ferrers, earl of Derby. Edmund acquired Ferrers' lands through a combination of royal grant and extremely sharp practice, and with the connivance of Lord Edward and others, the details of which are described below.[5]

Edmund's third earldom, that of Lancaster itself, was not a confiscated one, but a new creation in August 1267.[6] It was probably because this earldom had no competing claims upon it, unlike those of Leicester and Derby, that Lancaster became the title synonymous with the family. Henry III went through the full suit of patronage in creating his son's inheritance and, having already used forfeiture and new creation, fell back on the old favourite of marriage to provide Lancaster, temporarily at least, with a fourth earldom and the promise of a fifth. On 9 April 1269 Lancaster married Aveline de Forz, the ten-year-old daughter and heiress of William de Forz, count of Aumale, and Isabella de Redvers, countess of Devon.[7] Aveline died childless in 1274, however, aged only fifteen, and the prospect of her twin inheritances of Aumale and Devon slipped from her husband's grasp.[8] Lancaster turned to France for his second bride. In August 1275 he sailed to France, where a few months later he was married in Paris to Blanche, dowager queen of Navarre and countess of Champagne.[9] For eight years Lancaster enjoyed the considerable revenues of the county of Champagne and this marriage, together with other lands he held in France, gave him a truly cross-channel status.[10] The couple's first son, Thomas, was born around 1278, and two other sons and a daughter followed. Earl Edmund died on campaign in Gascony on 5 June 1296. His body was returned to England the following year and he was buried in Westminster Abbey near the shrine of St Edward the Confessor. Thomas of Lancaster duly succeeded his father as earl of Lancaster, Leicester and Derby.[11] By that time he was already married to Alice de Lacy, heiress to the earldoms of Lincoln and Salisbury. They were married in 1294 and the earldoms of Lincoln and Salisbury were entailed on Edmund and Thomas of Lancaster.[12] On the death of his wife's parents in 1311, Earl Thomas was to add the huge Lacy inheritance to his own, making him by far the wealthiest earl under Edward II.[13]

Edmund of Lancaster's inquisition post-mortem (IPM) reveals just how extensive the Lancastrian inheritance was, even before the addition

[5] See below, 182–4. [6] *CPR 1266–1272*, 100.

[7] *CPR 1266–1272*, 303; Rhodes, 'Edmund, Earl of Lancaster', 210.

[8] Many of Aveline's lands eventually ended up in Edward's hands after two of his more dubious land transactions. McFarlane, *Nobility*, 256–9.

[9] *CPR 1272–1281*, 101; Rhodes, 'Edmund, Earl of Lancaster', 214.

[10] Rhodes, 'Edmund, Earl of Lancaster', 214–17.

[11] *CPR 1292–1301*, 291. [12] *CChR 1257–1300*, 427, 455–6; McFarlane, *Nobility*, 263.

[13] Maddicott, *Thomas of Lancaster*.

of the Lacy lands.[14] Earl Edmund possessed forty-nine manors in fourteen English counties and his three earldoms each provided him with different centres of power. The former Montfort estates were focused on Leicester.[15] Montfort's half of the honour of Leicester also included manors in Wiltshire, Dorset and Berkshire.[16] Montfort's remaining lands were the barony of Embleton in Northumberland and a life grant of the castle of Kenilworth in Warwickshire.[17] Maddicott has estimated that, under Montfort, the honour of Leicester was worth about £500 p.a. and the barony of Embleton around £300 p.a., while Edmund's IPM rates Kenilworth as worth £20.[18]

The earldom of Derby consisted of the honour of Tutbury in Staffordshire and Derbyshire, together with part of the Chester inheritance, bringing lands in south Lancashire between the Rivers Ribble and Mersey. The Chester lands were worth £257 10*s* in 1257 and included the boroughs of Liverpool and Salford and the manor and forest of West Derby, together with the outlying manor of Bugbrook in Northamptonshire.[19] The honour of Tutbury centred on Tutbury Castle and the five Staffordshire demesne manors around the nearby forest of Needwood. The Derbyshire lands of the honour were clustered around the manor of Duffield and the forest of Duffield Frith. The Tutbury lands brought in £660 in 1257, forming the basis of Lancastrian influence in the north midlands.[20] The remaining Ferrers lands brought the total to about £1,500 p.a.[21]

The Lancastrian position in the midlands was further enhanced by the possession of the Staffordshire honour of Newcastle-under-Lyme, granted as part of the earldom of Lancaster in 1267 and worth around £100 a year.[22] Elsewhere in the earldom, the *caput* of the honour of Lancaster was the eponymous town and castle but the honour also encompassed the forests of Wyresdale and Lonsdale.[23] Edmund's IPM gives the value of the honour as £140, though this seems a little low. The remainder of the earldom was made up of the twin Huntingdonshire towns of Godmanchester and Huntingdon and the honour of Pickering in north Yorkshire.[24] The IPM values Pickering at £53 14*s* 11½*d*, though this does not include the value of the castle and manor of Pickering itself,

[14] *CIPM*, III, no. 423; Rhodes, 'Edmund, Earl of Lancaster', 30. [15] *CIPM*, III, no. 423, p. 289.
[16] Ibid., p. 288. [17] Ibid., pp. 304–5, 288–9.
[18] Ibid., pp. 288–9; Maddicott, *Simon de Montfort*, 49, 142.
[19] P.E. Golob, 'The Ferrers Earls of Derby: a Study in the Honour of Tutbury, 1066–1279', unpublished PhD thesis, University of Cambridge (1984), 302.
[20] Ibid., 295. [21] Ibid., 309.
[22] *CChR 1257–1300*, 78; Maddicott, *Simon de Montfort*, 321.
[23] *CIPM*, III, no. 423, pp. 292–5. [24] *CChR 1257–1300*, 78.

nor the value of the wapentake court which was in Lancaster's hands, the later being worth 30 marks a year in 1275.[25] Lancaster used the borough of Godmanchester to buy off the dower claims of Eleanor de Ferrers in 1281 with a life interest in the town but kept Huntingdon in his own hands and it brought in an annual income of £64.[26]

Edmund of Lancaster's interests were not confined to England. As well as the French lands of his wife, he was also an important lord of the Welsh March. He had succeeded to his brother's Welsh lands in the aftermath of the Barons' Wars and these consisted, in the first instance, of the counties of Cardigan and Carmarthen in west Wales and the honours of Monmouth and the Three Castles (Skenfrith, Grosmont and White Castle) in south-east Wales.[27] In 1280 Edmund exchanged Cardigan and Carmarthen for the wapentakes of Ashbourne and Wirksworth in Derbyshire.[28] The honours of Monmouth and the Three Castles were amalgamated under Edmund. Rees Davies gives a valuation of the lordship in the fourteenth century as £527.[29]

A rough estimate of Edmund of Lancaster's English and Welsh lands can now be attempted but it must be borne in mind that the nature of the sources makes any estimation of noble income in this period very tentative. The Montfort lands were worth around £820 p.a. and the earldom of Derby about £1,500. The earldom of Lancaster was worth at least £380 p.a., and very probably considerably more, while his Welsh lordships probably brought in about £500 a year. This gives a total income of at least £3,200 but it was almost certainly a good deal more. A royal valuation of Lancaster's estate, dated from negotiations in 1290 between Edward I and Philip IV over the proposed marriage of Thomas of Lancaster to Beatrice of Burgundy, stated its value as £4,500 a year, but royal valuations could be on the generous side, especially when negotiating marriages.[30] Lancaster's true wealth in 1290 was probably around £4,000 a year, making him one of the richest of Edward I's earls.

The richest earldom of all was undoubtedly that of Cornwall, held by Edmund of Lancaster's namesake and first cousin twice over, Edmund of Cornwall. Born on 26 December 1249, Edmund, named after St Edmund of Abingdon, should never have been earl of Cornwall.[31] He only became heir to the earldom after the notorious murder of his elder

[25] *CIPM*, III, no. 423, pp. 291–2; *Yorkshire Hundred and Quo Warranto Rolls 1274–1294*, ed. and trans. B. English, Yorkshire Archaeological Society 151 (1994), 38.

[26] *CPR 1266–1272*, 358; *CPR 1272–1281*, 440.

[27] *CChR 1257–1300*, 78. [28] *CChR 1257–1300*, 215.

[29] R.R. Davies, *The Age of Conquest: Wales, 1063–1415* (Oxford University Press, 1987), 417.

[30] *Foedera Conventiones, Litterae, et Cujuscunque Generis Acta Publica*, eds. T. Rymer and R. Sanderson, 16 vols. (London: Record Commission, 1816), I, ii, 738.

[31] N. Vincent, 'Edmund of Almain, Second Earl of Cornwall (1249–1300)', in *ODNB*.

half-brother Henry of Almain at Viterbo in 1271 at the hands of Guy and Simon de Montfort.[32] Tout was clearly impressed at the scale of the inheritance Edmund entered the following year, on the death of his father, Richard of Cornwall.[33] In Cornwall, he was the only man of baronial status, and his holdings included the castles of Tintagel, Lostwithiel, Trematon and Restormel, together with the castle and borough of Launceston and many additional manors. In Devon, he held the rent of the city of Exeter with its castle, the whole of Dartmoor and the huge manor of Lidford, together with extensive juridical and financial rights across the south-west. He had lands all along the Thames Valley, including extensive estates in Oxfordshire, Berkshire and Middlesex, which were administered from Wallingford. Berkhamsted Castle formed the centre of another tract of territory north of London, in Buckinghamshire and Hertfordshire. A group of manors in Gloucestershire, Wiltshire and Dorset linked his Thames Valley holdings with those in the far south-west. Cornwall was also a major lord in the east midlands, especially in eastern Lincolnshire, Rutland, where he was hereditary sheriff, and Northamptonshire, where his lands were centred on the great castle of Rockingham. Like many other earls, Cornwall also had an estate in East Anglia, the Suffolk honour of Eye. In the North Riding of Yorkshire, he had a further estate based on the castle of Knaresborough.

Noel Denholm-Young reckoned the income of Edmund's father, Richard, to have been between £5,000 and £6,000 and Nicholas Vincent has recently placed Edmund's income at as much as £8,000.[34] However, an account for 1296–7 gives a figure of £6,355 1*s* 10¼*d*, of which £4,602 12*s* 1*d* was clear profit.[35] His marriage to Margaret de Clare, sister of the earl of Gloucester, was unhappy and resulted in an acrimonious separation in 1294. On this separation, Cornwall assigned her £800 of land, making his pre-1294 gross income £7,155.[36] His vast income allowed him to lend very large sums of money, not only to the king, but also to other earls and prelates as well.[37] His marriage produced no issue, meaning that his great wealth passed to his cousin, the king, when he died in September 1300 aged fifty-one.[38]

32 Powicke, *Henry III*, II, 609. 33 For the following paragraph, see Tout, 'Earldoms', 142–4.

34 Painter, *Studies*, 174; N. Denholm-Young, *Richard of Cornwall* (Oxford: Blackwell, 1947), 163; Vincent, 'Edmund of Almain'.

35 Taken from my examination of the figures in *Ministers' Accounts of the Earldom of Cornwall*, ed. L.M. Midgley, Camden Society, 3rd Series 66, 68 (1942–5).

36 Ibid., I, xvi, n. 4.

37 Ibid., II, 248–52; *CCR 1272–1279*, 238–9; *CCR 1296–1302*, 376; *CPR 1266–1272*, 683; *CPR 1292–1301*, 145, 188; S.L. Waugh, 'The Fiscal Uses of Royal Wardships in the Reign of Edward I', *TCE* I (1986), 59.

38 Vincent, 'Edmund of Almain'.

The king's half-uncle, William de Valence, was the third and final royal earl in Edward I's reign. Valence was the uterine brother of Henry III and arrived in England in 1247. He was married to Joan de Munchesney, one of the Marshal co-heiresses and, later, countess of Pembroke.[39] William was well-favoured by his brother, but he found permanent estates hard to come by, so that, although his income has been estimated as *c.*£2,500 by 1272, only about half of this actually came from land, the rest being made up mainly from royal wardships.[40] In Wales he held the small lordship of Goodrich in the south-east, together with the much larger lordship of Pembroke and half the lordship of Haverford in west Wales. In England, he had some lands in Norfolk, Kent and Berkshire but his only consolidated holdings were in Hertfordshire, where he held the town and castle of Hertford; in Suffolk, where he held a number of manors; and the barony of Mitford in Northumberland. Valence died in 1296 and, as his wife was still living, his son Aymer did not inherit most of these lands nor the title until 1307, surviving in the meantime on his father's French lands and £200 of land that his mother granted to him in 1297 for his maintenance.[41]

Like William de Valence, the earls of Richmond were foreigners but, unlike Valence, did not make their permanent home in England for most of Edward I's reign. This was because the earl for most of the reign was also the duke of Brittany.[42] Duke John had married Henry III's daughter in 1260 and had eventually been granted the earldom of Richmond, but naturally remained resident in Brittany, exercising power in England through local agents. In 1306 he was succeeded in the earldom by his younger son, John, who had been brought up in England and served Edward I during the French and Scottish wars after 1294. This John did settle in England but never married and, on his death in 1333, his earldom, worth an estimated £1,800, reverted to the dukes of Brittany.[43] The Richmond lands lay in the vicinity of Richmond itself in north Yorkshire and the rape of Hastings in eastern Sussex, and also included assorted manors in south-east Lincolnshire, Norfolk and Cambridgeshire.

Other earls married into the royal family in the course of the reign. The most prominent was Gilbert de Clare, earl of Gloucester, who married the king's daughter, Joan of Acre, in 1290.[44] Gilbert was born on 2

[39] Paris, *Chronica Majora*, IV, 629. For references to Joan as 'countess of Pembroke', see, for instance, *CPR 1301–1307*, 91. For the following paragraph, see Ridgeway, 'William de Valence'; also Phillips, *Aymer de Valence*, 241–2.

[40] Phillips, *Aymer de Valence*, 242.

[41] *CPR 1292–1301*, 289; Phillips, *Aymer de Valence*, 22.

[42] Tout, 'Earldoms', 154.

[43] M. Jones, 'Brittany, John of, Earl of Richmond (1266?–1334)', in *ODNB*.

[44] McFarlane, *Nobility*, 259–61; see below, 41–2.

September 1243, eldest son of Richard de Clare, earl of Gloucester and Hertford, and Maud de Lacy, daughter of John, earl of Lincoln.[45] When aged only nine Gilbert married Alice de Lusignan, Henry III's niece. The marriage was not a happy one and, although they had two daughters, they were separated by 1267 and divorced in 1285.[46] His subsequent marriage to Joan of Acre lasted only five years before Gilbert's death in December 1295, but it was fruitful, producing a son and three daughters. Just over a year later, and to the frustration of her father's plans, Joan married her household knight, Ralph de Monthermer, whom Edward grudgingly recognised as earl of Gloucester in right of his wife.[47]

Earl Gilbert's full possession of his estates was delayed by the survival of his mother until 1289.[48] Michael Altschul's study of the Clare family makes clear just how extensive these lands were.[49] The Clares had three great English honours, Gloucester, Clare and Tonbridge, which gave them lands in almost every county in southern England. The Gloucester honour was based mainly in Gloucestershire, Dorset and Devon but had outlying castles, towns and manors in seven other counties.[50] The centre of the honour of Clare was the town and castle of that name in Suffolk and they also held fourteen other manors in Norfolk, Suffolk and Essex, as well as outlying manors in Hertfordshire and Northamptonshire. The honour of Tonbridge in Kent was held not in chief of the king but from the archbishop of Canterbury. It consisted of the borough and castle of Tonbridge and the surrounding lowy and stretched over the Kentish border into Surrey and Sussex.

These English lands alone, estimated at over £2,200 at Gloucester's death in 1295, made the Clares one of the richest comital families, but their status as the greatest of the Marcher lords raised them to the top branches of the comital tree.[51] They held the lordship of Glamorgan in south Wales, whose focal points were the town of Cardiff and the huge new castle of Caerphilly, together with the lordships of Usk and Caerleon.[52] As befitted a relative of Strongbow, the first great Anglo-Irish magnate, Gloucester was also lord of Kilkenny in Ireland. Gloucester's father, Richard, probably had an income of around £3,700 at his death in 1262 and Altschul has estimated Gilbert's gross income at £4,500–£5,000.[53]

45 C.H. Knowles, 'Clare, Gilbert de, Seventh Earl of Gloucester and Sixth Earl of Hertford (1243–1295)', in *ODNB*.

46 Altschul, *Baronial Family*, 209. 47 Ibid., 261. 48 Ibid., 209.

49 For the following paragraph see ibid., 201–13; *CIPM*, III, no. 371.

50 Buckinghamshire, Berkshire, Hampshire, Oxfordshire, Somerset, Surrey and Worcestershire.

51 Altschul, *Baronial Family*, 204. 52 Davies, *Conquest*, 467.

53 Altschul, *Baronial Family*, 203, 205.

Gloucester's near neighbours, and future opponents, on the Welsh March were the Bohun earls of Hereford and Essex and they too married into the royal family during Edward's reign. This was the culmination of a remarkable series of successful marriage alliances that had accompanied and propelled the Bohuns' rise to prominence in the twelfth and thirteenth centuries and that, in succession, brought them the earldoms of Hereford and Essex and the great Marcher lordship of Brecon.[54] Earl Humphrey II was born *c.*1249, grandson of Earl Humphrey I and son and heir of Humphrey de Bohun the younger and Eleanor de Braose, lady of Brecon.[55] His father had been an enthusiastic Montfortian and was wounded and captured at the Battle of Evesham in August 1265, dying shortly after from his wounds.[56] Humphrey *minimus* was at this stage still a minor and his mother's inheritance and his marriage were entrusted to the wardship of the earl of Gloucester.[57] Much of their future enmity stemmed from this, particularly from the fact that Gloucester seems to have done little to safeguard the future interests of his ward in Brecon against the incursions of the ascendant Llywelyn ap Gruffydd.[58] Bohun was to spend much of the early years of his majority striving to win control of Brecon from Llywelyn.[59] By the summer of 1275, he felt secure enough in his Welsh inheritance to wed, and his bride was Maud de Fiennes, a French cousin of Edward I's mother.[60] Not long after, Bohun's grandfather died and this brought him the earldoms of Hereford and Essex as well as the hereditary constableship of England.[61] His heir, predictably enough another Humphrey, was born a short time after his marriage, in or around 1276. Earl Humphrey II died on 31 December 1298, aged forty-nine, and was buried at Waltham Abbey, near one of his chief manors.[62] His heir was then of age and was granted seisin of his father's lands and titles on 16 February 1299.[63] In 1302 he achieved his family's most brilliant marriage yet when he married Elizabeth, dowager countess of Holland and daughter of King Edward himself, at Caversham on 25 November.[64] He and Elizabeth had ten children in fourteen years of

[54] G. Jones, 'The Bohun Earls of Hereford and Essex, c.1270–1322', unpublished MLitt thesis, University of Oxford (1984), 6–8.

[55] S.L. Waugh, 'Bohun, Humphrey (VI) de, Third Earl of Hereford and Eighth Earl of Essex (*c.*1249–1298)', in *ODNB*.

[56] F.M. Powicke, *The Thirteenth Century, 1216–1307*, 2nd edn (Oxford University Press, 1962), 182, 185, 192, 202.

[57] TNA KB 27/5, m. 11.

[58] See below, 186–7; Jones, 'Bohun Earls', 87.

[59] See below, 81, 186–7.

[60] *CChR 1257–1300*, 191–2.

[61] *CFR 1272–1307*, 52, 53.

[62] *AM*, IV, 540; *CFR 1272–1307*, 408–9.

[63] *CFR 1272–1307*, 409.

[64] H. Johnstone, *Edward of Carnarvon, 1284–1307* (Manchester University Press, 1946), 24. For the negotiations surrounding the marriage, see *CChR 1300–1326*, 33; *CFR 1272–1307*, 458–9; *CPR 1301–1307*, 96; McFarlane, *Nobility*, 261; and below, 42, 251.

marriage, before Elizabeth's death in 1316.[65] Hereford himself was killed at the Battle of Boroughbridge in 1322 fighting against Edward II.[66]

Despite Hereford's brilliant marriage, the Bohuns were, at this stage, very much among the second tier of English earls. An extent of Earl Humphrey III's lands, drawn up in 1302 at the time of his marriage to Elizabeth, provides valuable information about the Bohun inheritance.[67] The family's English lands had two main centres, one from each earldom. In the east they had seven manors in north-west Essex around their *caput* and chief residence of Pleshey. In addition they had two Hertfordshire manors and one each in Buckinghamshire and Middlesex, together with the castle and manor of Kimbolton in Huntingdonshire. In the west, the Bohuns held the manor of Oaksey in Wiltshire and two manors in Gloucestershire. These lands in western England were but an adjunct to their extensive properties in the Welsh March. The great lordship of Brecon with its castle was supplemented further north on the March by the castles of Huntingdon, Hay and Caldicot and the manor of Newton. Using the IPMs of Earls Humphrey I and II and the inquisition of 1302, Gwenllian Jones has estimated that the Bohun lands were worth around £1,500 p.a. gross under Earl Humphrey III, yet admits this figure is likely to be too low.[68] Jones estimates that the Marcher lordships were probably not worth more than £1,000, although in 1302 a royal commissioner reckoned that, properly managed, Brecon alone could produce 2,000 marks a year, an estimate given credence by Rees Davies' figures for Brecon's fourteenth-century yield.[69] Given this evidence, the value of the Welsh lordships may be pushed up to around £1,200 when Huntingdon, Hay and Caldicot are added to Brecon. Earl Humphrey III's IPM of 1322 gives a valuation of between £780 and £900 for his English estates, which again seems too low, and it might more probably have been in the region of £1,000, a sum considered the minimum income for an earl.[70] A very rough estimate of the earls of Hereford's gross income, therefore, would be in the region of £2,000–£2,200.

The Bohuns had built up their landed inheritance and political influence by a series of judicious marriages, and the marriage into the royal family was but the culmination of this. For Henry de Lacy, earl of Lincoln, however, the marriage of his daughter, Alice, into the royal family in 1294 was a sign that his earldom was coming to an end in the male line. The

[65] McFarlane, *Nobility*, 261.

[66] M. McKisack, *The Fourteenth Century, 1307–1399* (Oxford University Press, 1959), 66.

[67] *CIM*, I, no. 1870. [68] Jones, 'Bohun Earls', 19–26.

[69] Ibid., 26; *CIM*, I, no. 1870, p. 509; Davies, *Conquest*, 467. Davies gives Brecon's fourteenth-century value as £1,547 p.a.

[70] Jones, 'Bohun Earls', 23.

Lacy earldom was not an old one; Henry's grandfather, John de Lacy, had only been granted the earldom in 1232, and his father, Edmund, had died young.[71] Henry himself was born in 1250, the product of one of those marriages between English nobles and Henry III's foreign relatives of which Matthew Paris so disapproved.[72] Lacy's mother was Alice, daughter of the marquis of Saluzzo, a relative of Eleanor of Provence, Henry III's queen. Lacy's father died in 1256 and Henry was brought up at court during the turbulent politics of the 1260s.[73] In 1268 he married Margaret Longsword, countess of Salisbury in her own right. The couple had two sons and a daughter but both sons died prematurely, leaving their daughter Alice as heiress to both her parents' earldoms and, as already observed, in 1294 she was married to Thomas of Lancaster.[74] As Tout commented, the properties that Alice inherited in 1311 were 'admirably qualified to round off the inheritance of Edmund of Lancaster'.[75] In many places Lacy lands lay cheek-by-jowl with those of Lancaster.[76]

In Lancashire, for instance, Clitheroe Castle and extensive properties elsewhere in the county, including Burnley, Darwin, Widnes, Rochdale and Bury, were all close to Lancaster's boroughs of Liverpool and Salford. Linked geographically to Lincoln's Lancashire lands were the Lacy holdings in Cheshire, where he had Halton Castle and was hereditary constable of Chester. From 1282, Lincoln was also lord of Denbigh in north Wales. In Lincolnshire, Lacy's castle of Bolingbroke was near Lancaster's lands in Lindsey, while he also held the town and castle of Lincoln itself. Lincoln's estates in the west and south-west were also not far from the Lancastrian lordships in south Wales and Lancaster manors in Dorset and Wiltshire. Even in London, the respective Lincoln and Lancaster properties of Holborn and the Savoy Palace were less than a mile apart. Lacy's estate administration was formed around seven receiverships, each under the supervision of a steward and a receiver, at Halton, Clitheroe, Denbigh, Pontefract, Bolingbroke, Lincoln and Holborn.[77]

The income Lincoln enjoyed was clearly very considerable and the effectiveness of his administration, which has been described as a 'model of economy and practical efficiency', helped it reach this high level.[78] Maddicott gave Thomas of Lancaster's income from his combined inheritance as £11,000 p.a. and in doing so he assigned a value to the Lacy

[71] N. Vincent, 'Lacy, John de, Third Earl of Lincoln (*c.*1192–1240)', in *ODNB*.

[72] Paris, *Chronica Majora*, IV, 628–9. [73] *CLR 1251–60*, 184.

[74] J.S. Hamilton, 'Lacy, Henry de, Fifth Earl of Lincoln (1249–1311)', in *ODNB*.

[75] Tout, 'Earldoms', 146.

[76] For the next paragraph see ibid., 146–8; *CIPM*, V, no. 279.

[77] J.F. Baldwin, 'The Household Administration of Henry Lacy and Thomas of Lancaster', *EHR* 42 (1927), 183–4.

[78] Ibid., 189.

estates of 10,000 marks.[79] He found no reason to doubt this valuation, believing it to be a 'fair enough estimate', but admitted that it ultimately has no source.[80] Such an income seems excessive, as it would have made Lincoln considerably richer than every other earl with the exception of Cornwall.[81] Somewhere around £3,500 gross seems a more realistic figure.

By the end of his career Lincoln had become the grand old man of English politics, the last earl at the beginning of Edward II's reign who could remember the circumstances of the civil war of the 1260s. Before 1304 this role was filled by John de Warenne, who could not only remember the quarrels of the 1250s and 1260s but had played an important supporting role in them. Though the earl drew his third penny, the distinguishing mark of an earl, from the county of Surrey and was usually referred to in government records by that title, the earls seem to have preferred the simple familial title Warenne, and it is by this name that they will be referred to henceforth. John de Warenne was born in 1231 and had the longest active career of any of Edward I's earls.[82] He married Alice de Lusignan, uterine sister of Henry III, in 1247 and remained an important figure in English politics for the next fifty-seven years, until his death at Michaelmas 1304.[83] Warenne's wife bore him two daughters, before dying shortly after giving birth to a son in January 1256.[84] Unusually, Warenne never remarried, though he did have at least two bastard sons, both of whom went into the church.[85] Warenne's heir, William, was married in 1285 to Joan de Vere, daughter of the earl of Oxford but, barely eighteen months later, he was killed at a tournament at Croydon.[86] He left behind an infant daughter and a pregnant widow who gave birth a few months later to a son, named John after his paternal grandfather. This John was still a minor when his grandfather died. He

79 Maddicott, *Thomas of Lancaster*, 22–3.

80 Ibid., 22n. Maddicott states that his ultimate source for this valuation is T.D. Whitaker, *An History of the Original Parish of Whalley and the Honour of Clitheroe*, 4 vols. (London: George Routledge and Sons, 1872), I, 249, but admits that Whitaker gives no source.

81 The Clare earldom is estimated above as having an income of between £4,500 and £5,000. There is no hint from contemporary sources that Lincoln was considered to be around £2,000 p.a. richer than Gilbert de Clare. See above, 19.

82 Gervase of Canterbury, *The Historical Works of Gervase of Canterbury*, ed. W. Stubbs, 2 vols., Rolls Series (1880), II, 219.

83 *CFR 1272–1307*, 498; Paris, *Chronica Majora*, IV, 629.

84 W.H. Blaauw, 'On the Early History of Lewes Priory and Its Seals, with Extracts from an MS Chronicle', *Sussex Archaeological Collections* 2 (1849), 27; Paris, *Chronica Majora*, V, 551.

85 A.B. Emden (ed.), *Biographical Register of the University of Oxford to AD 1500*, 3 vols. (Oxford University Press, 1957–9), III, 1987.

86 *CPR 1281–1292*, 173; *The Chronicle of Bury St Edmunds, 1212–1301*, ed. and trans. A. Gransden (London: Thomas Nelson and Sons, 1964), 87.

entered his inheritance in 1307, a year after his marriage to Edward I's granddaughter, Joan of Bar.[87]

The younger John died without legitimate direct heirs in 1347. His IPM is, unfortunately, the only surviving Warenne one, and his estate at his death bears only a limited resemblance to that held by his grandfather, thanks to the various personal and political disasters he suffered during his long career.[88] However, it is possible to piece together a picture of the lands of John I de Warenne, although an accurate estimate of his wealth is more difficult.[89] The Warenne lands at the outset of Edward I's reign lay almost entirely in the eastern half of England, essentially in three major clusters, with the usual outlying manors that one finds in almost all earldoms. In the south, their chief seat was Lewes Castle, *caput* of the rape of Lewes in Sussex, which had been in the family since the Norman Conquest and in which they possessed fourteen demesne manors and four boroughs. Warenne's lands in Surrey, the castle and town of Reigate, together with the manors of Dorking and Betchworth and some property in Southwark, formed an appendage to his much more extensive Sussex lands. In Norfolk, Warenne's castle and Cluniac priory at Castle Acre mirrored his property at Lewes. On the Great North Road lay the twin Lincolnshire towns of Stamford and Grantham, which had been granted to Earl William IV de Warenne by King John, as *Terrae Normannorum*, in compensation for the earl's lost lands in Normandy. On William's death, the towns had reverted to the crown and had formed part of Lord Edward's appanage in 1254 before Edward re-granted them to Warenne in 1263.[90] These wealthy towns served as a link between Warenne's southern properties and his lands in south Yorkshire. The twin castles of Sandal and Conisbrough, with thirteen appended manors, served to make Warenne one of the greatest lords of the West Riding. Warenne was also a major beneficiary of Edward I's patronage in Wales and, in October 1282, had the new Marcher lordship of Bromfield and Yale created for him in north-east Wales.[91]

The lack of an IPM for John I or his father hampers attempts to put a value on the earldom. Accounting for six months' revenue from Warenne's lands north of the Trent in 1305, the escheator recorded gross

[87] S.L. Waugh, 'Warenne, John de, Seventh Earl of Surrey (1286–1347)', in *ODNB*.

[88] *CIPM*, IX, no. 54.

[89] *Feudal Aids*, 6 vols. (London: HMSO, 1899–1920); *The Book of Fees*, 3 vols. (London: HMSO, 1920–31); W. Farrer, *Honors and Knights' Fees*, 3 vols. (Manchester University Press, 1923), III; *Victoria County History for Sussex*, VII.

[90] *Stamford in the Thirteenth Century: Two Inquisitions from the Reign of Edward I*, ed. D. Roffe (Stamford: Paul Wilkins, 1994), 10.

[91] *CCRV*, 240; M. Rogers, 'The Welsh Marcher Lordship of Bromfield and Yale, 1282–1485', unpublished PhD thesis, University of Aberystwyth (1992), 3, 58.

income of £321 4*s* 9¼*d*, giving an approximate annual value for these of £650.[92] Stamford was valued by the jurors of the Hundred Rolls Inquiry in 1274–5 as worth £220, while Grantham brought in £148 to Lord Edward in 1256–7.[93] The first valuation of Bromfield and Yale in 1287 gave the value of the lordship as 400 marks but by the time of a seigniorial survey in 1315 this had increased to £459, suggesting an income of *c.*£400 at the turn of the century.[94] This totals around £1,400 but excludes figures from his most valuable English estates, in Norfolk, Surrey and Sussex, for which no valuation survives. Were these to be included, the earl's annual income around 1300 would probably be at or above £3,000.

Warenne's near neighbour in East Anglia was Roger Bigod, earl of Norfolk, who was also, incidentally, Warenne's half-nephew. Bigod's life and estates have recently been studied by Marc Morris, who has used extensive surviving private records to create a clearer and more accurate picture of his lands and wealth than is possible for any of his contemporaries.[95] Born *c.*1245, Roger was the son of the baronial justiciar of 1258, Hugh Bigod, and the nephew of Roger III Bigod, earl of Norfolk.[96] He succeeded his uncle as earl of Norfolk and hereditary marshal of England in 1270, having inherited his father's lands four years previously.[97] Bigod was married twice, first in 1271 to Aline Basset, widow of the Montfortian Hugh le Despenser, heiress of the royalist Philip Basset. The marriage was childless and she died a decade later, leaving Norfolk still without a direct heir.[98] He looked abroad for his second wife, marrying, in 1290, Alice, daughter of the count of Hainault.[99] This marriage proved no more fruitful than his first and by 1302, for reasons discussed below, Norfolk decided to cut his losses and make a deal with the king.[100] In exchange for a life-grant of lands worth £1,000 p.a., Bigod agreed to disinherit his brother and collateral heirs and to promise the reversion of his inheritance to the crown. The bulk of his lands were eventually granted to Thomas of Brotherton, Edward I's son by his second marriage to Margaret of France.[101]

92 TNA E 372/150, m. 33.

93 *Stamford in the Thirteenth Century*, 58; Prestwich, *Edward I*, 19.

94 Rogers, 'Marcher Lordship of Bromfield and Yale', 167.

95 Morris, *Bigod Earls*, especially chapters 2 and 4.

96 M.C. Prestwich, 'Bigod, Roger (IV), Fifth Earl of Norfolk (*c.*1245–1306)', in *ODNB*.

97 Morris, *Bigod Earls*, 98–9.

98 Prestwich, 'Bigod, Roger (IV)'.

99 Morris, *Bigod Earls*, 138.

100 *CFR 1272–1307*, 452, 452–3; *CPR 1301–1307*, 29–30; McFarlane, *Nobility*, 262; M. Morris, 'The "Murder" of an English Earldom? Roger Bigod IV and Edward I', *TCE* 9 (2003), 89–99; see below, 249–52.

101 S.L. Waugh, 'Thomas, First Earl of Norfolk (1300–1338)', in *ODNB*.

This inheritance was reckoned by the crown in 1304 to be worth £4,000 annually, but Morris believes that this estimate was too high and has placed Roger III's gross income at around £2,500.[102] The addition of Roger IV's own patrimony from his parents boosted his income further, as did his temporary enjoyment of his first wife's estates and dower during her lifetime. Its value before the agreement of 1302 was probably between £3,000 and £3,500, and between £3,500 and £4,000 during his first marriage. The bulk of Bigod's lands, of course, came from his uncle's earldom of Norfolk. This consisted of the original patrimonial lands and the newly acquired Marshal estates, which came to Roger III from his mother, Maud, on her death in 1248. The Bigods had long been one of the greatest of East Anglian lords, with twenty-three manors in the region, centred on Framlingham and Bungay Castles in Suffolk.[103] The great Marshal inheritance brought outlying manors in the Home Counties and, more importantly, made Norfolk a lord of the Welsh March at Chepstow and a major landholder in Ireland, encompassing the county of Carlow and lands and towns in Counties Kildare and Wexford.[104] From his father, Norfolk also inherited the valuable Marshal manor of Bosham in Sussex, together with other properties that Hugh Bigod had purchased there, as well as two further Norfolk manors, Kennet in Cambridgeshire, three Yorkshire manors and riverside property in London.[105] Upon his first marriage to Aline Basset, Norfolk acquired four midland manors held in dower by Aline from the estate of her first husband, Hugh le Despenser, and upon the death of Aline's father in 1271 a further fifteen manors came into his hands, mostly in Essex, Wiltshire and the home counties.[106] These additions were only of a temporary nature, however, and upon Aline's death in 1281 they passed out of Norfolk's hands.

The Bigod earldom had been a fixture of twelfth- and thirteenth-century politics but was extinguished in Edward I's reign. The Beauchamp earldom of Warwick, on the other hand, which was to be such an important part of fourteenth- and fifteenth-century politics, was only just beginning under Edward I. Born around 1238 into a Worcestershire baronial family that held the hereditary shrievalty of that shire, William Beauchamp had inherited the earldom of Warwick from his uncle, William Mauduit, in 1268.[107] He was married during the 1260s to Maud, daughter of John Fitz Geoffrey. They had seven children, the eldest of whom, Guy, was born *c.*1272 and became earl on William's

[102] Morris, *Bigod Earls*, 41. [103] Ibid., 32. [104] Ibid., 37–8.
[105] Ibid., 102–3. [106] Ibid., 105.
[107] P.R. Coss, 'Beauchamp, William (IV) de, Ninth Earl of Warwick (*c.*1238–1298)', in *ODNB*.

death in 1298. From his father, Beauchamp inherited the Worcestershire barony of Elmley, including Worcester, Droitwich and Elmley Castle. As earl of Warwick, he sought to restore the position of the earldom in Warwickshire itself, which had been eroded by a series of dowagers.[108] He held the town and castle of Warwick and in the 1270s he increased the family's long-term territorial strength in Warwickshire by purchasing the reversion of three manors.[109] By the time Guy Beauchamp died in 1315, he held eleven Warwickshire manors.[110] The Beauchamps' financial position was also improved in 1297 when Maud Beauchamp became one of four co-heiresses of the Fitz John estates.[111] The west midlands was the core of Beauchamp influence and it was from here that later Beauchamp power was to grow.[112]

Another earldom that, from a low base in Edward I's reign, was to grow to great proportions in later centuries was the Fitz Alan earldom of Arundel. For much of Edward I's reign the two Fitz Alans, Richard and Edmund, were minors and so they had little impact on politics. Richard was born in 1267 to John Fitz Alan and Isabel Mortimer, daughter of Roger Mortimer of Wigmore.[113] Richard's father died in 1272 and Richard's lands passed through a number of hands until he came of age in 1288.[114] In 1291 Richard was accepted as the first Fitz Alan earl of Arundel but died barely ten years later, in January 1302.[115] His son, Edmund, born to him and his wife Alice, daughter of the marquess of Saluzzo, around 1285, came of age in 1306 and, after some initial reluctance, married Alice de Warenne, granddaughter of John I de Warenne.[116] This Warenne marriage was eventually exponentially to increase the Fitz Alan resources following the death, in 1347, of Alice's brother, John II de Warenne. The Fitz Alans had long been lords of the Welsh March on the borders of Shropshire, with their two castles of Clun and Oswestry, but their inheritance of the d'Aubigny lordship of Arundel in 1243 widened their interests. The honour of Arundel in west Sussex, together with their

[108] Tout, 'Earldoms', 153.

[109] C. Burt, 'The Governance of Edward I, 1272–1307, with Special Reference to Shropshire, Warwickshire and Kent', unpublished PhD thesis, University of Cambridge (2004), 28. Dr Burt's book on Edward I's governance was not published at the time of writing so all references are to her PhD thesis. Readers should be directed to her book.

[110] Ibid., 29. The resources of the earldom suffered during the thirteenth century by the long survival of three dowager countesses, the last of whom did not die until Earl Guy's time. E. Mason, 'The Resources of the Earldom of Warwick in the Thirteenth Century', *Midland History* 3 (1975), 67–75.

[111] *CCR 1296–1302*, 137.

[112] *CIPM*, III, no. 477.

[113] T.F. Tout, 'Fitzalan, Richard (I), First Earl of Arundel (1267–1302)', rev. Nigel Saul, in *ODNB*.

[114] For the descent of Fitz Alan lands during Richard's minority, see *CFR 1272–1307*, 2, 33, 74, 77, 163, 171.

[115] *CPR 1301–1307*, 11.

[116] *CPR 1301–1307*, 308; *GEC*, I, 241.

ancestral Marcher lands, brought them an income of around £1,600 at the time of Richard's death.[117]

The least wealthy earldom in the thirteenth century was that of Oxford, held by the de Vere family. Their chief estate was in northern Essex, at Castle Hedingham, together with some outlying manors near Harwich.[118] These lands could barely support the comital dignity and were worth, perhaps, £1,000 p.a. Robert de Vere had been a Montfortian during the Barons' War and, under Edward I, made little impact on national politics. He was married to Alice de Sandford, heiress of the queen's hereditary chamberlain, and died in 1296 when he was succeeded by his son, also called Robert.[119]

These then were the twelve earldoms of Edward I's reign and the men who filled them, but there were two other people of comital status during the king's reign, Isabella de Forz, née Redvers, and her daughter Aveline de Forz. Aveline, as has already been noted, was the heiress to her father William's earldom of Aumale and was married, in 1269, to Edmund of Lancaster. She died childless in 1274 and her inheritance fell into the king's own hands, following some sharp practice on Edward's part.[120] Aveline's mother, however, outlived her daughter by nearly two decades, dying in November 1293.[121] By virtue of her own inheritance and her possession of her husband's dower lands, Isabella was a very wealthy woman. Her father, Baldwin de Redvers, had been earl of Devon and possessor of the twin honours of Plympton in Devon, from which came the earldom, and Carisbrooke on the Isle of Wight, which had provided the earl not only with the island itself, but with important manors on the mainland as well. Denholm-Young calculated her clear profit to be *c.*£2,500 a year, estimating that her gross annual income was between £3,000 and £4,000.[122]

What conclusions is it possible to draw from this survey of the earldoms under Edward I? An examination of the nature of landholding among the earls may yield some instructive patterns. With regard to wealth, the earls fall into three ranks. In the top tier of 'super earls', those with annual gross incomes all well over £3,500, can be placed the earls of Cornwall, Lancaster and Gloucester. The second rank of earls, those with incomes of £2,000–£3,500, is populated at the top end by the earls of Lincoln, Norfolk and Warenne, and towards the bottom by the earls of Hereford

[117] C. Given-Wilson, 'Wealth and Credit, Public and Private: the Earls of Arundel, 1306–97', *EHR* 106 (1991), 2.

[118] Tout, 'Earldoms', 154. [119] *GEC*, X, 217–18. [120] See above, 14.

[121] B. English, 'Forz, Isabella de, Suo Jure Countess of Devon, and Countess of Aumale (1237–1293)', in *ODNB*.

[122] N. Denholm-Young, *Seignorial Administration in England* (Oxford University Press, 1937), 22–3.

and Pembroke. In the bottom tier of earls, those with an income of less than £2,000, can be found the earls of Warwick, Richmond, Arundel and Oxford. This is, however, all relative: the incomes of all the earls placed them above, in some cases far above, their baronial contemporaries.

While money enabled the earls to live at a suitably grand level, their real power came from the land they held across England and in Wales.[123] Power in the middle ages came from lordship over men, and the more manors a magnate held the more men he had lordship over and the more physical force he could call upon.[124] Part II will explore in more detail how important the earls were in the rule of the localities but it is certainly true that the more consolidated a lord's holdings were, the more likely he was to be the dominant figure in the region.[125] Moreover, concentrated lands gave them the local power that enabled them more easily to raise men. As this survey has shown, nearly all the earls had lands in many different counties but their main power came from those areas where they had many manors close together. It was rare for a single earl to be the only great landholder of note in a county. In East Anglia, for example, the earl of Norfolk held the most land but other earls were also major landholders in the region, including Warenne, Gloucester, Pembroke, Arundel and Richmond. In addition to competition from other national figures, an earl might also face stiff local competition from the lesser local nobility, who had the advantage of being permanently resident in the county and might be able to call on historic links with other prominent local families. The church too was a major landholder in every region, and monastic houses, bishops and cathedral chapters would be important and powerful figures in local society.

Nowhere was the local nobility more prominent than in the far north, and it is notable how few comital estates there were in the most northerly shires. In the counties of Northumberland, Cumberland, Westmoreland and Durham, only Lancaster at Embleton and William de Valence at Mitford, both in Northumberland, and, from the very end of the reign, Guy Beauchamp, earl of Warwick, at Barnard Castle (Co. Durham) represented the comital interest. The great border earldoms of the later middle ages had yet to appear and, until the disputed Scottish succession, Edward I's earls had little reason to give much thought to events north of Yorkshire.

The Welsh Marches were different from the more scattered nature of landholding in England. In 1200 the interests of the Marcher lords were

[123] In terms of London properties, Lincoln, for example, held the manor of Holborn, Lancaster the Savoy Palace, Cornwall the manor of Twickenham, Warenne had a town house in Southwark and Hereford possessed the manor of Enfield.

[124] Carpenter, *Locality and Polity*, 283.

[125] See Part II.

largely confined to the Marches themselves. By 1284 the situation on the March had altered dramatically, with only eight of the twenty-four major Marcher barons having a history on the March stretching back to 1200.[126] Many incomers were earls. In 1200 only one earl, William Marshal of Pembroke, held substantial Marcher estates, but by 1300 eight comital families possessed Marcher lordships.[127] As Rees Davies argued, this radically changed the nature of the March: 'as a group the Marchers in 1284 were a less cohesive community than they were in 1250. The new blood, whose experience and fortunes were forged in England, had greatly reduced their Marcher outlook.'[128] This is undoubtedly true, but the influx of some of England's most powerful lords to the March, with its ancient liberties and independence, is also likely to have changed the crown's view of the March. Davies believed that 'the March of 1300 was very different from the March of 1275; it bore heavily the mark of Edward I's personality and politics'.[129] The more aggressive attitude of the crown towards Marcher liberties in Edward's reign, which Davies so vividly illustrates, was not solely the result of Edward's dominant personality but was also a reaction by the crown to the changes on the March in the thirteenth century.[130] The March bore the imprint not just of Edward's personality but also that of the earls who now had huge potential manpower available to them from their new lordships and the unusually concentrated landed and judicial power that came with them.

These, then, are some of the broad conclusions that can be drawn from patterns of comital landholding in the late thirteenth century. But what about the earls themselves, what can be said of them? There are two things that immediately strike one when looking at them corporately. The first, which Tout noted, was their remarkable personal robustness.[131] For twenty years, from 1275 until 1295, not one earl died, an unmatched degree of continuity at the very top of English society. The king himself was thirty-five in 1274. He and his earls were largely of the same generation and were, at the beginning of the reign, either in, or entering, the prime of life. Only Hereford failed to pass fifty, dying aged forty-nine in 1298, while John de Warenne was still active in Scotland at the age of seventy-three. The earls grew old together in Edward's service and,

[126] Davies, *Lordship and Society*, 37.

[127] Ibid., 39. Davies states that by the end of the reign seven of the ten earls were Marcher lords but eight comital families held lordships during the reign. They were Norfolk (Chepstow), Hereford (Brecon, Huntingdon and Hay), Gloucester (Glamorgan, Netherwent, Caerleon and Usk), Lincoln (Denbigh), Arundel (Clun and Oswestry), Lancaster (Monmouth and the Three Castles), Pembroke (Pembroke) and Warenne (Bromfield and Yale).

[128] Ibid., 38–9. [129] Ibid., 32.

[130] Ibid., 258–67. For a detailed discussion of Edward I's attitude towards the March, see below, 68–70.

[131] Tout, 'Earldoms', 135.

despite the occasional quarrel among themselves or with the king, it will be argued that they stand out as an example of the kind of co-operation between king and magnate that was the essence of successful late medieval politics.[132]

The second striking feature of Edward I's earls is the extent to which they were interrelated and related to the king himself. Many of the earls were direct descendants of the two dominant figures in English politics at the beginning of the thirteenth century, King John and William Marshal. One can find familial and marital links between the earls almost wherever one looks. Edmund of Cornwall, for example, was first cousin to the king and Edmund of Lancaster, and half-nephew of William de Valence. Valence's sister had married John de Warenne, which made Warenne Cornwall's uncle by marriage and Warenne's son, William, his first cousin of the half blood. Cornwall was married to Margaret de Clare, who was sister of the earl of Gloucester and first cousin of the earl of Lincoln. This is one connecting thread of many but it illustrates the intimacy between the earls. A successful marriage alliance, such as that between Valence and Warenne, could lead to a life-long friendship, while the failure of Edmund of Cornwall's marriage led him into serious dispute with his brother-in-law, the earl of Gloucester. How these alliances and quarrels affected English politics is one of the themes of this book. The most important political relationship of all for an earl, however, was undoubtedly with the king, and it is analysing this with which the next part will deal.

[132] McFarlane, *Nobility*, 121.

PART I

The king and the earls

Chapter 2

CONSORTS, COMPANIONS AND COUNSELLORS

The historiography of Edward I's kingship has been dominated by McFarlane's quotation that the king 'preferred masterfulness to the arts of political management'.[1] It is surprising, perhaps even a little alarming, to know that a short article written nearly fifty years ago still dictates the historiography not only of Edward I's relationship with his earls but also that of his kingship as a whole. As noted earlier, it is Edward's masterfulness that has been to the fore in writings on his dealings with Wales and Scotland, his attitude towards the law, the politics of the last decade of the reign and, above all, his relations with his nobility.[2] The conclusion to Prestwich's biography of the king sums up the received wisdom of Edward as a monarch 'ready to threaten men into obedience'. Despite this, Prestwich acknowledges that 'it would be quite wrong to see the king and the lay nobles as being constantly at loggerheads … [his] management of the lay magnates was not subtle, but for the most part it proved very effective'.[3] Edward's success, thus, was due to his masterfulness: the force of his personality was usually enough to cow any opposition and ensure that he got his own way. This was, Christine Carpenter suggests, one of two methods of successful kingship in the late middle ages. There were disciplinarians like Edward I and enablers such as Edward III.[4]

What this part aims to do is to challenge both these assumptions. Given the overwhelming dominance of the 'masterfulness' trope within the historiography, it is necessary to engage it head-on. It will be argued

[1] McFarlane, *Nobility*, 267.

[2] For a brief assessment of the historiographical position when he first wrote his biography of Edward I, see Prestwich, *Edward I*, xi. See above, 2–4.

[3] Ibid., 562.

[4] M.C. Carpenter, *Wars of the Roses: Politics and the Constitution in England, c.1437–1509* (Cambridge University Press, 1997), 65. Carpenter acknowledges that Edward I 'mostly got on well with his nobles' and that Edward III was 'by no means pliable', but still sees a difference in emphasis in the kingships of the two men.

that, while masterfulness was certainly part of Edward's style of kingship, he was no stranger to the arts of political management and that his political skills were considerably more subtle than has been appreciated. Moreover, it will be suggested that successful kingship required a blend of the authoritarian and the enabler and that Edward I, like all other successful medieval English kings, possessed both, qualities that were the essence of strong kingship. To demonstrate this, the relationship between the king and his earls will be looked at from several different angles in an effort to provide as broad a perspective as possible. This chapter will focus on those aspects of the relationship that, if well managed, acted to strengthen it: the ideal of the earls as natural companions, advisers and governmental aides of the king, and it will be argued that Edward's marriage policy regarding the earls should also be seen in this light. The following chapter will look at potentially more divisive issues of war, patronage and justice together with a reassessment of the *quo warranto* campaign. In each of these areas it is possible to see Edward's masterfulness but, on close examination, one can appreciate that masterfulness was blended with political management in an attempt to reach his strategic end. McFarlane agreed with Powicke that Edward had no strategic vision in his relationship with his baronage, but this is to underestimate the king.[5] Edward's policy towards the earldoms was the same as his overall strategic vision of kingship: to rescue the authority of the crown from the morass into which it had sunk at times during his father's reign and that he had witnessed first hand. Edward I was a practical man, not a deep thinker, but this was his big idea. He pursued it with a characteristic ruthless single-mindedness but also with a good deal more subtlety than has usually been appreciated.

THE KING'S COMPANIONS

Various persons are established under the king, namely, earls, who take the name 'comites' from 'comitatus', or from 'societas', a partnership [who may also be called consuls from counselling].[6]

Bracton, *De Legibus Et Consuetudinibus Angliæ*

The sentiment expressed in *Bracton* that the earls were, by their very names, the king's natural companions was a commonplace in thirteenth- and fourteenth-century political discourse. The author of the *Vita Edwardi Secundi* described the nobility as 'the king's chief member, without which

[5] McFarlane, *Nobility*, 266. [6] *Bracton*, II, 32.

the king cannot attempt or accomplish anything of importance'.[7] The *Mirror of Justices*, dated to Edward I's reign, further elaborated on the meaning of *comes* as 'companion': 'it was agreed as law that the king should have companions ... these companions are now called counts, from the Latin *comites*'.[8]

It was considered seemly for a king to wish to spend his time with those who came from the highest ranks of the nobility, and a king who did not, as the response to Edward II's association with rustic pursuits and peoples shows, came in for bewildered and stinging criticism.[9] The need for Edward I to establish a good rapport with his earls was particularly acute following a period of civil war and the reign of a king who, with his ineptitude in war and dislike of the aristocratic pursuit of tourneying, had little in common with his nobility.[10] Grand set-piece occasions offered a king the chance to broadcast his companionship with his earls by involving them in the ceremony.

The grandest formal occasion of all was, of course, the coronation itself and this offered Edward the opportunity to send a message to his people through the gathered crowds that this was a new start, a clean break from the civil war period under a new king freshly burnished with the laurels of a crusader and surrounded by a group of earls from the same generation, most of whom had come to maturity after the Battle of Evesham.[11] Political society, from the prelates of the church to the nobles, knights and the citizens of London, would come together for the coronation and then go home with tales of the king and his greatest subjects. According to custom, several of the earls had important symbolic roles to perform during the ceremony: Norfolk acted in his role as Earl Marshal, Oxford may have performed his hereditary office of chamberlain, while Warenne probably filled the role of butler.[12] The earls of Lincoln and Warwick probably carried two of the swords, while the earl of Gloucester bore the blunted sword of mercy, *Curtana*.[13] Cracks in the happy façade Edward was trying to present appeared over this very issue, for his own brother, Edmund of Lancaster, refused to attend the ceremony after his claims to carry *Curtana* were overlooked.[14] Lancaster's unseemly and unusual act of pique illustrates how sensitive and important such matters could be,

7 *Vita Edwardi Secundi: the Life of Edward the Second*, ed. and trans. W.A. Childs (Oxford University Press, 2005), 48.

8 *The Mirror of Justices*, ed. and trans. W.J. Whitaker and F.W. Maitland, Selden Society 7 (1893), xxiii–xxv, 7.

9 J.R.S. Phillips, *Edward II* (New Haven, CT and London: Yale University Press, 2010), 72.

10 See below, 47, for how little time Henry spent in the company of his major magnates.

11 See above, 30–1.

12 H.G. Richardson, 'The Coronation of Edward I', *BIHR* 15 (1937), 98.

13 Ibid., 98. 14 Ibid., 97.

especially as there were, as yet, no gradations in the titled nobility. A more heartening story comes from the coronation banquet. The king of Scots and the earls of Lancaster, Cornwall, Gloucester, Pembroke and Warenne, each with a company of 100 men-at-arms, came before King Edward and released 600 horses to be taken by any who could catch them.[15] Such a story well encapsulates the camaraderie and sense of new beginning that a coronation would naturally engender and for which Edward must fervently have wished.

At the other end of the reign, the knighting of Prince Edward in 1306 was a public event on a similar scale to the coronation and offered Edward I the opportunity to bind himself and his son to both the surviving members of his own generation and the new generation of political society who would be his son's companions. Unsurprisingly, the earls played prominent parts in the festivities. Naturally, it was the king himself who girded his son with the sword of knighthood but the prince's spurs were fastened by the earls of Lincoln and Hereford. The entrusting of this duty to the senior surviving earl (Lincoln) and the constable (Hereford) vividly illustrated Edward I's recognition of the idea of companionship between a king and his earls and his sure sense of the proprieties of such an occasion. After his knighting in the chapel of St Stephen, the newly dubbed princely knight made his way to Westminster Abbey and began to knight the 300 young men who were waiting there to receive the honour from their future king. First to be dubbed were the young earls of Arundel and Warenne, a further demonstration that earls were intended to be prominent companions of the next king as they had been for his father.[16]

The Feast of the Swans, as the elaborate celebratory meal held afterwards in Westminster Hall became known, was informed by Arthurian imagery.[17] Other types of public acts of unity also infused with Arthurian pageantry were the various tournaments and 'Round Tables' that Edward engaged in both before and during his reign. As a young man, Edward was an enthusiastic participant on the continental tournament circuit, and on his first tour in 1260–1 his companions included no fewer than six members of comital families, strong evidence of the type of company the young Edward liked to keep.[18] He was a prince used to

[15] Ibid., 98.

[16] *Chronicles of the Reigns of Edward I and Edward II*, ed. W. Stubbs, 2 vols., Rolls Series (1882), I, 146; *Flores Historiarum*, ed. H.E. Luard, 3 vols., Rolls Series (1890), III, 132; Johnstone, *Edward of Carnarvon*, 108; Phillips, *Edward II*, 110–11.

[17] R.S. Loomis, 'Edward I: Arthurian Enthusiast', *Speculum* 28 (1953), 122–4; Phillips, *Edward II*, 111.

[18] These were John de Warenne, Henry of Almain (son of Richard of Cornwall), Henry and Simon de Montfort, John of Brittany (later earl of Richmond) and William de Valence. H.A. Wait, 'The Household and Resources of the Lord Edward, 1239–1272', unpublished DPhil thesis, University of Oxford (1988), 258–9.

surrounding himself with the men who, as king, were to become his natural companions. Following the Barons' Wars, tournaments were reintroduced into England and Edward very probably took a leading part in such events in the late 1260s, along with his contemporaries among the comital families.[19] Once Edward became king, the opportunities for his own participation became fewer but the important part earls played in the propagation and administration of tournaments in Edward's reign can be seen from the *Statuta Armorum* of 1292, which established a committee, headed by four earls, charged with the administration of the ordinance.[20] One tournament in which the king did take part was the Round Table of 1279, arranged by Roger Mortimer to celebrate his retirement from tourneying.[21] The event was planned with the co-operation of Edmund and Blanche of Lancaster, for it was held at their castle of Kenilworth and they seem also to have made a considerable contribution towards Mortimer's expenses.[22] Another Round Table was held at Nefyn in July 1284, following the conquest of Wales, and a further one in 1302 at Falkirk, probably to commemorate Edward's victory over William Wallace there in 1298.[23] Later literature employed the Round Table to signify the body politic and the use of the image was clearly a symbolic statement of the unity of purpose and community of interests between the king and those who participated.[24]

The marriages of the king's daughters provided another occasion when Edward was able to call together people from across his realm to a formal occasion where he could project an image of political unity at a time of celebration for him and the realm. The most lavish occasion was the marriage in London in July 1290 between Edward's daughter Margaret and John, heir to the duke of Brabant. Bartholomew Cotton, the Norwich chronicler, described in detail the number of followers each earl brought to the wedding, from the earl of Gloucester with 163 high-status companions down to Oxford with just 12 knights. In addition, he says that 709 lords and knights attended, along with 915 citizens of London.[25]

19 J.R.V. Barker, *The Tournament in England, 1100–1400* (Woodbridge: Boydell and Brewer Press, 1986), 56; Prestwich, *Edward I*, 60.

20 M.H. Keen, *Nobles, Knights and Men-at-Arms in the Middle Ages* (London: Hambledon Press, 1996), 87–8. The four earls were Lancaster, Gloucester, Lincoln and Pembroke.

21 Nicholas Trivet, *Annales Sex Regum Angliae*, ed. T. Hogg (London: English Historical Society, 1845), 300; *AM*, IV, 281; Loomis, 'Arthurian Enthusiast', 116.

22 Blanche made a gift to Mortimer of a number of barrels purporting to contain wine that, when opened, were found to contain gold. Loomis, 'Arthurian Enthusiast', 116–17.

23 Ibid., 117, 122.

24 For the use of the metaphor of the Round Table for the body politic in the *Morte d'Arthur*, see Watts, *Henry VI*, 34–5.

25 Bartholomew Cotton, *Historia Anglicana*, ed. H.R. Luard, Rolls Series (1859), 177.

This is an appropriate point to discuss Edward's marriage policy since it impacts heavily on the issue of the earls as natural companions of the king and, since McFarlane, has been the cornerstone of the negative historiographic interpretation of the relationship between the king and his leading subjects. First, it needs to be seen in the round, not just as part of a supposed policy of property acquisition. Earls like Lancaster, Cornwall, William de Valence and John de Warenne were already related to Edward I but further ties of marriage were created between the crown and a number of comital families in a series of remarkable weddings that took place after 1290. They had not escaped the attentions of historians before McFarlane: indeed his article was shaped by his response to their interpretations. For Tout, Edward's policy towards the earldoms had 'a very definite shape'. The king sought, 'wherever he could, to absorb them gradually into the sphere of the royal influence. He strove to acquire for the royal family as many of the earldoms as he could, and thus to turn to the service of the crown resources which, for many previous generations, had been employed in keeping the crown in check'.[26] This was thus, in Tout's view, a firmly anti-comital policy and one that backfired spectacularly under his son. McFarlane, on the other hand, rejected the idea that this was a political policy on the part of the king aimed at creating a group of earls closely related to the royal family. Rather, he argued, any policy Edward might have had was concerned only with the 'aggrandisement of his kin'.[27] As to whether Edward was interested in creating family ties with comital houses, McFarlane concluded that it was 'more likely that he did not care; and I should be prepared to argue that he was right not to care'.[28] While the king's policy, according to McFarlane, was not consciously anti-comital, his desire to enrich himself and his family nevertheless had a negative effect on the material prospects of those comital families involved and was conducted with the masterfulness and unscrupulousness that McFarlane had come to believe was Edward's style.

Neither interpretation gives either the king or the earls much credit. In one, Edward was consciously pursuing a policy designed to harm the interests of his leading subjects, while, in the other, he seems callously indifferent to the collateral damage the 'aggrandisement of his kin' caused, and in both interpretations the earls themselves are hapless objects on whose inheritances damage is wreaked without so much as a whimper of protest. Such a picture underestimates the men involved. The key marriages involved were deliberate acts of policy on Edward's part, designed to serve particular political circumstances, and were not

[26] Tout, 'Earldoms', 140. [27] McFarlane, *Nobility*, 265. [28] Ibid., 266.

imposed upon helpless members of the nobility but were actually marks of great favour.

There are three marriages in particular that must be considered: Gilbert de Clare, earl of Gloucester, to Joan of Acre in 1290; Humphrey de Bohun, earl of Hereford (d. 1322), to Elizabeth, dowager countess of Holland, in 1302; and Alice de Lacy, heiress of the earldoms of Lincoln and Salisbury, to Thomas of Lancaster in 1294. The fact that the settlements for these marriages were all heavily weighted towards the royal partner, should the marriages prove fruitless, has led to them being interpreted as aggressive moves by the king against the earldoms, which, in turn, feeds into the general historiographical tendency to view Edward as confrontational towards the nobility.[29]

Taking the marriage of Alice de Lacy and Thomas of Lancaster first, the marriage settlement involved the surrender of the combined Lacy and Longsword inheritances to the crown and their subsequent re-grant to the earl and countess of Lincoln for life, with the remainder to Thomas and Alice and, failing heirs of their bodies, to the heirs of Thomas.[30] McFarlane found it hard to explain the Lacys' willingness to be a party to such an arrangement. He surely answered his own question though, when he mused that 'perhaps it was not too high a price to pay for so advantageous a match for their only child'.[31] In 1294 Alice was the only surviving child of the earl of Lincoln and it was unlikely that his countess would bear him any more children. Aside from the king's own son, what greater marital prize might there be for Lincoln's daughter than Thomas of Lancaster? Lincoln had no reason to doubt that they would have children, and in the meantime the marriage cemented his life-long friendships with Edmund of Lancaster and Edward I. It also meant that he would be father-in-law to Thomas, a man seemingly destined to be the vital prop of Edward II's regime.[32]

The earl of Gloucester's unhappy marriage to Alice de Lusignan had produced two daughters but no son, meaning that the earl faced the distressing prospect of the vast Clare inheritance being broken up at his death.[33] This is crucial for understanding Gloucester's motives. McFarlane

[29] The views of Tout and McFarlane have already been discussed. A more recent interpretation, by Alan Harding, sees Edward sustaining the royal family 'by the plundering of the earldoms'. A. Harding, *England in the Thirteenth Century* (Cambridge University Press, 1993), 257.

[30] *CChR 1257–1300*, 455–6.

[31] McFarlane, *Nobility*, 263

[32] For the friendship between Lincoln and Edmund of Lancaster, see, for example, *CPR 1281–1292*, 53; *CPR 1292–1301*, 15, 102, 144; TNA DL 42/1, ff. 130v–131; *The Coucher Book of Whalley Abbey*, ed. W.A. Hulton, 4 vols. Chetham Society, Original Series (1847–9), III, 884–5; *The Coucher Book of Furness Abbey*, ed. J. Brownbill, Chetham Society, New Series 74 (1915), 186.

[33] Altschul, *Baronial Family*, 50–1. See above, 19.

believed that it was Edward I's settlement of the kingdom upon his own daughters, should he die without a son, ahead of Edmund of Lancaster that persuaded Gloucester to marry the 'apparently portionless' Joan of Acre.[34] The negotiations for the marriage, however, had been continuing since 1283, even before the earl's divorce, and had been delayed only by the king's absence abroad and by the need for a papal dispensation for the couple, which duly arrived in November 1289, six months before the wedding took place and before Edward's settlement of the kingdom.[35] Gloucester was not railroaded into a marriage that jeopardised part of his inheritance: his inheritance was already due for partition. Rather, it was a calculated risk to secure a male heir with a lady who, if she brought no significant dowry, brought him the status of the king's son-in-law: something surely to be coveted.[36] This union ought to be seen in a positive light, as the culmination of a long, occasionally bumpy, period of reconciliation between Edward and Gloucester, a story that is explored in more depth below.[37]

A similar motive lay behind the marriage of the earl of Hereford and Princess Elizabeth in 1302. McFarlane was at a loss to find the earl's reason for entering into a marriage that could possibly have cost his brother half the family's lands.[38] But, again, there is no evidence of compulsion on the king's part and, rather than being seen as a sinister attempt by the king to get his hands on the Bohun patrimony, this marriage also should be viewed in conciliatory terms: as an attempt by the king to reconcile the earl after the opposition of his father in 1297–8.[39] It certainly seems to have worked, for Hereford was one of the king's most constant companions in the remaining years of the reign, witnessing 236 (68 per cent of the total) charters in the last five years of the reign.[40]

The insurance clauses the king imposed in each of these settlements were, of course, highly advantageous to the crown and that should not be

[34] McFarlane, *Nobility*, 260. [35] Altschul, *Baronial Family*, 148–9.

[36] The terms of the marriage stated that any children of the union were to have precedence over those of his first marriage, and that should the marriage prove barren twenty-five manors were to be detached from the Clare inheritance and to pass to Joan's heirs by any subsequent marriage; *CChR 1257–1300*, 350–1.

[37] Gloucester's sometimes difficult relationship with Edward I is examined by Altschul, *Baronial Family*, 110–56. For their relationship in the build-up to Edward's crusade, see S.D. Lloyd, 'Gilbert de Clare, Richard of Cornwall and the Lord Edward's Crusade', *Nottingham Medieval Studies* 30 (1986), 46–66. For a more positive view, see below, 200–1, 220–2.

[38] *CChR 1300–1326*, 33; McFarlane, *Nobility*, 261. Under the terms of the agreement, were Hereford to die without producing an heir, then half his estate would be settled on his wife and any subsequent children of hers, to the exclusion of the Bohun heirs in fee.

[39] See below, 251–2.

[40] Taken from this author's study of comital witness in *The Royal Charter Witness Lists of Edward I (1272–1307) from the Charter Rolls in the Public Record Office*, ed. R. Huscroft, List and Index Society 279 (2000).

ignored, but it must be concluded that, in the eyes of the earls involved, these were prices well worth paying to secure a royal bride. It is important not to underestimate how attractive such a prospect could be, as Gloucester's lavish celebrations of his marriage make clear.[41]

The effect of these marriages was profound. In 1215 there were fifteen earls, of whom only two were close blood relations of King John.[42] A century later, six of the nine earls were closely related to Edward II by blood or marriage.[43] To these six should be added Edmund of Woodstock, Edward II's half-brother, who was created earl of Kent in 1321 and also Gilbert de Clare, earl of Gloucester, the king's first cousin, who had been killed at Bannockburn in 1314. Edward I's family settlement, subsequently reinforced by Edward III's family settlement, played a key part in the creation of the late medieval polity, one in which most of the titled nobility were closely related to the crown by blood and which, for good or ill, had a major effect on the nature of English politics for the next two centuries.[44]

Acknowledging this, however, begs further questions about the extent to which this was part of a deliberate policy, whether it was an inevitable consequence of the more insular nature of the English monarchy after the loss of the Angevin empire, or whether it was merely the accidental by-product of a series of unrelated political decisions and biological situations that left Edward I, and later Edward III, with a large number of children for whom to provide. It seems unlikely that Edward I did not appreciate that he was creating a situation whereby most of the earls were, or would be in the future, related to the royal family. Given the events of Edward II's reign and, indeed, the internecine struggles of the Angevins in the later twelfth century and Edward's own experience of Simon de Montfort, one might question the wisdom of a policy

41 Davies, *Lords and Lordship*, 70.

42 The earls were William Marshal, earl of Pembroke; Ranulph de Blundeville, earl of Chester; William, Earl Warenne; William Longsword, earl of Salisbury; David of Scotland, earl of Huntingdon; Roger Bigod, earl of Norfolk; Geoffrey de Mandeville, earl of Essex and Gloucester; Henry de Bohun, earl of Hereford; Henry de Beaumont, earl of Warwick; William de Fors, earl of Aumale; William de Ferrers, earl of Derby; William de Redvers, earl of Devon; Saer de Quincy, earl of Winchester; William d'Aubigny, earl of Arundel; and Aubrey de Vere, earl of Oxford. Longsword was an illegitimate son of Henry II making him John's half-brother, while Warenne was the son of Hamelin de Warenne, Henry II's illegitimate brother, and therefore John's first cousin of the half blood.

43 Thomas, earl of Lancaster; Thomas of Brotherton, earl of Norfolk; Humphrey de Bohun, earl of Hereford and Essex; John, Earl Warenne; John of Brittany, earl of Richmond; Aymer de Valence, earl of Pembroke; Guy Beauchamp, earl of Warwick; Edmund Fitz Alan, earl of Arundel; and Robert de Vere, earl of Oxford. Norfolk was Edward II's half-brother, Lancaster and Richmond were his first cousins, Pembroke was a first cousin once removed of the half blood, Hereford Edward's brother-in-law and Warenne his nephew by marriage.

44 Tout, 'Earldoms', 155.

designed to increase the size and wealth of collateral members of the royal family, but it is important to remember Edward I's own immediate circumstances and experiences. Richard of Cornwall had given Henry III powerful political and military support during the years of crisis (if not always before) and suffered imprisonment for his loyalty. During Edward's own reign he had received unstinting support from the royal earls, Lancaster, Cornwall and William de Valence, and he went to considerable lengths to ensure that the earls of Lancaster, Lincoln and Hereford, involved in the royal marriages of 1294 and 1302, were close companions of the future Edward II during his upbringing.[45] The marriage of Earl John II de Warenne to the king's granddaughter, Joan of Bar, in 1306 further reinforced the old king's desire to bind the earls to the royal family. This was a repeated pattern that, although each occurrence had its own particular circumstances, seems to have had a broader purpose behind it beyond simply the need to provide for his growing family without reducing the crown's own landed stock.

The policy had distinctly mixed results in the short and medium term, as the remainder of Edward's own reign and those of his son and grandson demonstrate, but it is more important to try to discern what he was trying to do at the time and whether it was part of a definite policy. The evidence suggests that it was and that he believed that it was to the crown's advantage to have more members of the titled nobility connected by blood to the royal family. He was not forced into doing so by the increased insularity of the English monarchy in the thirteenth century. Edward, like his father before him, was still prepared to look beyond the Channel in seeking bridegrooms for his daughters and he still regarded himself as a continental rather than simply an insular powerbroker. The naming of his heir Alfonso, his shuttle diplomacy over the Pyrenees in the late 1280s, the marriages of his daughters to the duke of Brabant and the counts of Bar and Holland in the 1290s and, above all, his unceasing desire to lead another crusade to the Holy Land, all show a king determined not to be hemmed in by the bounds of his island kingdom. That, despite all this, Edward was prepared to marry two of his daughters to his English vassals and to sanction the marriage of Thomas of Lancaster to the daughter of another, having first negotiated for a continental marriage, suggests that these marriages were part of an important domestic policy that aimed at binding important noble families closer to the crown. The example of Simon de Montfort, married to Henry III's sister, seems not to have put him off. For those noblemen involved there is no

[45] Maddicott, *Thomas of Lancaster*, 6. See Phillips, *Edward II*, 88, for presence of mentoring earls on Prince Edward's early Scottish campaigns.

hint that this was a policy to which they objected: indeed, the security clauses notwithstanding, becoming the king's son-in-law was, it seems, an outcome devoutly to be wished. Freed from preconceptions that there were suspicion and hostility among the main actors, it is possible to see the marriages, and consequently the whole relationship between Edward and his earls, in a much more constructive and realistic light: as one in which both the king and the nobility saw mutual benefit in strengthening the ties between them.

The marriages, together with the other grand occasions discussed, provided the king with opportunities to stage-manage public demonstrations of political unity and companionship with his greatest subjects. However, such events would only have a practical symbolic value if they were reinforced by companionship between the king and the earls at a more prosaic level, the day-to-day life of the king when the eyes of his people were not trained upon him. Here the huge corpus of evidence provided by the witness lists of royal charters comes to the fore. In the later fourteenth century and afterwards, as royal charters themselves became rarer and the seals multiplied, the reliability of the witness lists as a guide to who was actually present with the king at the granting of an individual charter becomes suspect, but in the thirteenth century the witness lists have been regarded as reliable.[46] There are 1,597 royal charters with appended witness lists surviving from Edward I's reign, and of these 1,382 (86.54 per cent) were witnessed by at least one earl.[47] Almost three-quarters of the charters were witnessed by more than one earl and, on average, there were 2.67 comital witnesses to each royal charter, which suggest that some at least of the earls were habitual companions of the king.

If the figures from Edward I's reign are considered alongside those from the reigns of Henry III, Edward II and Edward III, then interesting comparisons are possible, especially with the reigns of Edward I's immediate predecessor and successor. The results for these other kings are not particularly surprising but they are instructive nonetheless, especially when one takes into account historians' ingrained assumptions that there was mistrust in the relationship between Edward I and his earls.

Perhaps the most striking thing about the witness lists is that they clearly reflect the political harmony with the earls achieved by Edward I. This emerges especially clearly when compared to the situation under his son. Under Edward II, some earls, like Pembroke and Gloucester, were hugged close, demonstrating the king's reliance upon their support

46 For a discussion of this by Richard Huscroft, see *Royal Charter Witness Lists of Edward I*, xi–xvi.

47 The following section and paragraph is based largely on my own study of the witness lists. Any unsubstantiated statements regarding charters are based on this study.

Table 2.1 *Comital witnesses to royal charters, 1274–1307*

Earl	Year of death	Number of charters witnessed	Average number of charters witnessed per annum[a]	Percentage of royal charters witnessed[b]
Henry de Lacy, earl of Lincoln	1311	735	22.97	46.02
John, Earl Warenne	1304	496	17.10	35.20
William de Valence	1296	394	18.76	38.51
Edmund, earl of Lancaster	1296	385	18.33	37.16
Gilbert de Clare, earl of Gloucester	1295	348	16.57	33.59
Roger Bigod, earl of Norfolk	1306	268	8.66	17.56
Humphrey III de Bohun, earl of Hereford	1322	252	28	47.81
Thomas, earl of Lancaster	1322	235	23.5	43.52
Edmund, earl of Cornwall	1300	226	9.04	19.72
Guy Beauchamp, earl of Warwick	1315	225	22.5	42.69
Aymer de Valence	1324	194	17.64	33.80
Humphrey II de Bohun, earl of Hereford	1298	176	7.65	15.92
Ralph de Monthermer, earl of Gloucester	1324	169	16.9	31.30
William Beauchamp, earl of Warwick	1298	129	5.61	12.06
Robert de Vere, earl of Oxford	1296	16	0.76	01.54
Richard Fitz Alan, earl of Arundel	1302	11	0.92	02.29

[a] There are thirty-two regnal years in which royal charters were enrolled on the Charter Roll (there are no lists for the regnal years 1, 15 and 16 Edward I) and these are the ones used to calculate the average. Therefore the average is taken from the number of years from a given earl's accession to his title or the start of the reign (whichever is the later) up to and including the year of his death or the end of the reign (whichever is the sooner).

[b] This percentage is based on the total number of charter years from a given earl's accession to his title or the start of the reign (whichever is the later) up to and including the year of his death or the end of the reign (whichever is the sooner).

Table 2.2 *Comital witnesses to royal charters, 1234–58*[a]

Earl	Number of charters witnessed	Percentage of charters witnessed
Richard, earl of Cornwall	253	15.82
Simon de Montfort, earl of Leicester	213	13.32
Richard de Clare, earl of Gloucester	210	13.13
Roger Bigod, earl of Norfolk	189	11.82
Humphrey I de Bohun, earl of Hereford	133	08.31

[a] Taken from a study of *The Royal Charter Witness Lists of Henry III.*

and advice, while others, notably Lancaster and Warwick, were largely excluded, except during the periods of their political ascendancy. Others still, such as Arundel and Warenne, seem to have witnessed extensively only when their enemies were excluded or dead. The political quarrels of Edward II are thus writ large in the witness lists: Earl Warenne and the earl of Lancaster stopped witnessing charters together after the abduction of Lancaster's wife by one of Warenne's knights in 1317; Lancaster and Hereford did not witness with the Despensers.[48] Under Edward I, on the other hand, such mutual avoidance is almost entirely absent. Despite their violent quarrel with each other in the late 1280s and early 1290s and their animosity stretching back to the early 1270s, the earls of Hereford and Gloucester continued to witness royal charters together until the autumn of 1290.[49] After that they witnessed together on only two occasions: either they avoided each other or Edward decided to keep them apart. This, however, is the only clear example where disputes between Edward I's earls manifest themselves on the charter witness lists. Edward's ability to keep his nobility in the same room as each other is another reason for the political successes he enjoyed in his reign.

A further contrast between the witness lists of Edward I and Edward II can be drawn from the fact that the most frequent witnesses to the former's charters were generally the wealthiest and most powerful earls. Of the eight wealthiest earldoms, only the earls of Hereford (d. 1298), Norfolk, and Cornwall witnessed less than a third of royal charters during their active years. Two of these, of course, went on to lead the opposition to the king in 1297. Their opposition will be discussed in detail in Chapter 8, but their relative isolation from the king may have been a factor and certainly

[48] Similarly, in the late 1460s, political tensions between the Nevilles and the Woodvilles were evident in the charter witness lists. T. Westervelt, 'Royal Charter Witness Lists and the Politics of the Reign of Edward IV', *Historical Research* 81 (2008), 218–19.

[49] For their animosity and quarrel, see below, 81, 186–8, 199, 214–15, 217–19.

Table 2.3 *Comital witnesses to royal charters, 1307–26*[a]

Earl	Year of death	Number of charters witnessed	Percentage of charters witnessed[b]
Gilbert de Clare, earl of Gloucester	1314	222	61.5
Aymer de Valence, earl of Pembroke	1324	449	49.8
Humphrey, earl of Hereford	1322	348	43.7
Henry, earl of Lincoln	1311	79	40.3
John of Brittany, earl of Richmond	1334	252	26.6
Hugh le Despenser, earl of Winchester[c]	1326	32	21.1
John, Earl Warenne	1347	183	19.2
Edmund Fitz Alan, earl of Arundel	1326	170	17.9
Thomas of Brotherton, earl of Norfolk	1338	77	17.9
Thomas, earl of Lancaster	1322	102	12.8
Guy Beauchamp, earl of Warwick	1315	50	12
Edmund of Woodstock, earl of Kent	1330	18	9.7

[a] Taken from a study of *The Royal Charter Witness Lists of Edward II (1307–1326) from the Charter Rolls in the Public Record Office*, ed. J.S. Hamilton, List and Index Society 288 (2001).

[b] This percentage is based on the total number of charter years from a given earl's accession to his title or the start of the reign (whichever is the later) up to and including the year of his death or the end of the reign (whichever is the sooner).

[c] Hugh le Despenser the elder's witnessing is only counted from his creation as earl of Winchester in 1322.

would have made opposition easier, though this should not be overstated.[50] Cornwall's surprisingly modest witnessing is more difficult to explain, since he seems to have been on good terms with his cousin the king and was twice appointed as regent when Edward visited France in 1279 and 1286–9, but perhaps his extensive interest in money-lending and the managing of his own vast estates kept him away from court.[51] The other major earls,

[50] See below, 235–45.

[51] *CPR 1272–1281*, 309–10; *CPR 1281–1292*, 248. For information on Cornwall's estates and business interests, see the introduction to *Ministers' Accounts*.

Table 2.4 *Comital witnesses to royal charters, 1331–48*[a]

Earl	Numbers of charters witnessed	Percentage of charters witnessed
John, Earl Warenne	292	39.83[b]
William de Montacute, earl of Salisbury	283	36.28
Richard Fitz Alan, earl of Arundel	199	25.51
Thomas Beauchamp, earl of Warwick	198	25.38
William de Clinton, earl of Huntingdon	190	24.36
Henry of Grosmont, earl of Derby	182	23.33
Robert de Ufford, earl of Suffolk	130	16.67

[a] Compiled from appendix to C. Given-Wilson, 'Royal Charter Witness Lists, 1327–1399', *Medieval Prosopography* 12 (1991), 63–5.
[b] Warenne's percentage is calculated to the end of 1347, the year in which he died.

however, all witnessed over a third of Edward's charters, a very high proportion given the fact that any earl had, as a matter of course, many varied interests of his own to attend to that would inevitably keep him away from court for long periods. Under Edward I, only the relatively minor earls of Arundel and Oxford were very infrequent witnesses to royal charters. By contrast, various political and personal reasons kept rich and powerful earls such as Lancaster, Norfolk, Kent, Warwick and Warenne from witnessing more than a fifth of Edward II's charters. That they were so infrequently in the king's company, in stark contrast to the situation under Edward I, was both a symptom and a cause of Edward II's failure to create a unity of purpose in his political community, for, without the support of his most powerful subjects, any king would find life difficult.

The comparisons with Henry III and Edward III are more straightforward but the results remain interesting. It is striking just how low the comital witnessing rate was during Henry III's personal rule, and the contrast with Edward I could not be clearer: for all his efforts to be accommodating to the nobility from the mid-1240s, Henry's court was simply not a place where his greatest native subjects appear to have wished to spend much time.[52] As for Edward III, it is interesting to note that a king so lauded for his ability to create a sense of comradeship with his nobility appears to

[52] For Henry's laxity towards the nobility, see D.A. Carpenter, 'King, Magnates and Society: the Personal Rule of King Henry III, 1234–1258', *Speculum* 40 (1985), 39–70.

have had them in his company for considerably less time than his grandfather, a king notorious for his domineering relationship with his nobles. While no earl under Edward III witnessed as many as 40 per cent of that king's charters, four of Edward I's surpassed this figure.[53] The explanation for this may well lie largely in the absence of Edward III's earls on military duties in the 1330s and 1340s. Despite this, it is an interesting straw in the wind that suggests that historians may have been too hasty, both in ascribing mutual suspicion to Edward I's relations with his nobility and in contrasting Edward I's kingship so starkly with that of Edward III.

A few more observations may be made about charter-witnessing under Edward I before leaving the subject. The first is that it is important to recognise that very many royal charters were witnessed during sessions of parliament or on military campaign, times when it was expected that most earls would be present.[54] To try to offset this bias in the evidence, one can look at other times to obtain a better picture of the king's chosen associates. There are, for instance, twenty Christmas periods (25 December–5 January) covered by the charter record and the results are similar to the overall picture revealed in Table 2.1. There were on average three earls with the king each Yuletide, of whom Lincoln was the most regular, being at court for twelve Christmases, while the younger earl of Hereford, the earls of Lancaster, William de Valence and Earl Warenne were also regular guests at royal Christmases.[55]

The witness lists also provide a fascinating insight into the internal hierarchy of the group of earls from the perspective of the royal government. As with the distinction of wealth made in the Introduction, it is possible to discern three distinct groupings within the class; although, interestingly, they are subtly different from those arrived at through the consideration of wealth.[56] Listed immediately after the bishops were members of the royal family: William de Valence, Edmund of Lancaster and Edmund of Cornwall. The second group of earls, the internal ordering of whom was not consistent, included the earls of Gloucester, Warenne, Norfolk, Hereford and Lincoln, while the final grouping consisted of Warwick, Oxford and, after his accession to the earldom in 1291, Arundel.[57] Towards the end of the reign, as the generations changed, there was a shift in

[53] Hereford (d. 1322), Lincoln, Lancaster (d. 1322) and Warwick (d. 1315).

[54] By way of example, the earls of Hereford witnessed 106 and 45 charters respectively during parliaments, the earls of Gloucester 207 and 27, the earls of Lancaster 208 and 36, Earl Warenne 216, and the earl of Lincoln 330.

[55] The younger Hereford attended 5 out of the 7 Christmases after his accession to the earldom, Edmund of Lancaster and William de Valence 6 out of 12, Thomas of Lancaster 4 out of 8, and John de Warenne 8 out of 17.

[56] See above, 28–9.

[57] See, for example, *Royal Charter Witness Lists of Edward I*, nos. 3.4, 8.85, 11.8–7, 13.146.

the hierarchy, with the older earls, Warenne and Lincoln, usually heading the list, followed among the regular comital witnesses by Thomas of Lancaster, and then the earls of Hereford and Warwick.[58] When he was present, Aymer de Valence always headed the baronial witnesses, almost certainly because he was considered of comital status while he waited to inherit the earldom of Pembroke from his mother.[59] It is interesting to note this change in the ordering of these lists, with age and experience coming to mean more at the end of the reign than the familial relationships and wealth that had been to the fore in the first part of the reign, perhaps because Edward increasingly valued those whom he had known the longest as his own generation began to die off.

Finally, the witness lists offer important evidence concerning Edward I's success in developing links with the generation of earls that succeeded his own; far more successfully, it may be added, than his son ever did. It is noticeable that the earls of Lancaster, Hereford and Warwick, who became three of Edward II's bitterest opponents, each witnessed more than 40 per cent of royal charters in the last decade of Edward I's reign. In each case, moreover, these new earls witnessed a higher proportion of royal charters than their fathers managed. Edward I's achievement here was remarkable and exceedingly rare. Even successful kings, such as William the Conqueror, Henry II and Edward III, found it hard to develop the kind of links with the younger generation of the nobility that the witness lists and other evidence suggests that Edward I was able to do.[60]

This is an intriguing and suggestive note on which to leave this discussion of companionship. From the varying and extensive evidence presented above, it would seem that the author of *Bracton* would have found little in Edward I's behaviour out of place with his comment that the title of earl was derived from their companionship or association with kings.[61] Both Edward I and his earls appear to have regarded this as entirely natural, and to have gone to considerable lengths to strengthen that companionship both symbolically and practically as the reign went on.

COUNSEL AND ADMINISTRATION

> Despite the statement that the will of the prince has the force of law … [it is not] anything rashly put forward of his own will, but what has been rightly decided with the counsel of his magnates, deliberation and consultation having been had thereon, the king giving it *auctoritas*.[62]
>
> Bracton, *De Legibus Et Consuetudinibus Angliæ*

[58] See, for example, ibid., nos. 27.21–20, 28.26–5, 31.47–44, 32.109–84.
[59] See, for example, ibid., nos.30.9–1, 31.48–37.
[60] For a further discussion of this, see below, 257. [61] See above, 36. [62] *Bracton*, II, 305.

Bracton and other theorists knew that, as well as being the king's natural companions, the nobility also performed a vital role as his natural counsellors. Bracton concludes his remarks on the name *comes* by saying that earls 'may also be called consuls from counselling, for kings associate such persons with themselves in governing the people of God'.[63] Edward I's contemporary and the author of the most famous and influential 'mirror' of the middle ages, Giles of Rome, concurred that the nobility would be foremost among those from whom a king should seek counsel.[64] As great landholders, with large numbers of men of all social ranks under their lordship and influence, the nobility in general, and earls in particular, could claim to represent a considerable body of interest by their counsel. Although their claims to represent the community of the realm comprehensively, very evident at the time of Magna Carta, diminished as the thirteenth century progressed and the gentry came specifically to be represented in the community of the realm, the residual baronial authority in this respect remained very strong, and the authority of the earls most potent of all.[65]

It is important to distinguish between 'counsel', the noun meaning advice and the verb of giving advice, and 'council', a formal body that provided the king with advice. Royal counsel, as John Watts has observed, could mean three distinct things in the middle ages: first, distinct bodies with binding and extensive powers imposed at times of crisis, either because of a minority, as in 1377 or 1422, or, more controversially, because of a king's incompetence, as happened in 1258, 1311 and 1388; second, a formal constituted council of a grouping of administrative officials along with a greater or lesser number of nobles, i.e. what most historians have recognised as the king's council; and third, the informal dialogue between the king and his leading subjects that would usually be categorised as 'counsel'.[66] Watts, in an important and controversial article on the counsels of Henry VI, argued that in medieval government under normal circumstances 'no part was played by a permanent advisory council' and that the council was normally bureaucratic rather than political, hence the survival of several of its members after the depositions of 1399, 1461 and 1485.[67] Watts has since resiled a little from this position and recognises the existence of what he calls an 'administrative' council in one form

[63] Ibid., II, 32.

[64] Giles of Rome, *De Regimine Principum* (Rome, 1556), 1.4.5, 2.3.18, 3.2.4, 3.2.17–19. Edward may have come across Giles and/or his work during his extended stay in France, part of which was spent in Paris, from 1286 to 1289. The earl of Lincoln almost certainly met Giles when he led an embassy to Rome in 1300 at a time when Giles stood high in the papal curia.

[65] See G.L. Harriss, *King, Parliament, and Public Finance in Medieval England to 1369* (Oxford: Clarendon Press, 1975), for a general overview of these events.

[66] J.L. Watts, 'The Counsels of Henry VI', *EHR* 106 (1991), 282. [67] Ibid., 284, 282.

or another, and, though the records for such a council are maddeningly elusive, there is plenty of incidental evidence to support the idea of the existence of a formal body of this kind from the thirteenth century as well as in later centuries.[68]

One of the most important pieces of evidence is the existence of a councillor's oath: the first reference to which comes from the rebellion of Richard Marshal in 1233 and the first surviving example of which dates from 1257.[69] The 1257 oath was in use during Edward I's reign, but was modified in 1294 at the very end of Edward's reign in 1307 and again in 1308 under his son.[70] The existence of a councillor's oath provides evidence of a king's council of some sort but not of its membership. Baldwin believed that, for the most part, the nucleus of the council at this time consisted not of a group of nobles but of a hard core of officials in the royal household, headed by the chancellor and treasurer, but also including the steward and the keeper and controller of the wardrobe.[71] Thus far, therefore, the composition of the council seems to be bureaucratic rather than political in nature, a point underlined by the general absence under Edward I and Edward II of the 'knights of the council', several of whom, during Edward III's reign, were on the council for their political rather than bureaucratic talents.[72] There is indisputable evidence, however, to show that some magnates were on the king's council. At the close of parliament in 1305, the king dismissed all the ranks of those assembled in parliament, but required the bishops, earls, barons, justices and others of his council to remain.[73] This not only reveals that there were some great magnates, including earls, on the council, but also suggests that it had a political and advisory role, in this instance in what was probably a plenary session after parliament, as well as a bureaucratic one. A separate piece of evidence, also dating from 1305, suggests that the earls involved were Lincoln and Warwick.[74] For the most part, however, it would seem that counsel from the magnates was sought and given not through their membership of the king's council, to which most of them did not belong, but through other channels, either formally at times of parliament or informally when they attended on the king's person.

Edward I well understood the importance of being seen to act through wise counsel, and charter-witnessing was perhaps the most

[68] Watts, *Henry VI*, 82–6.

[69] J.F. Baldwin, *The King's Council during the Middle Ages* (Oxford: Clarendon Press, 1913), 346.

[70] Ibid., 347–9. [71] Ibid., 73. [72] Ibid., 87–90. [73] Ibid., 91.

[74] *CCR 1302–1307*, 334. In the close rolls' record of the trial of Nicholas de Segrave members of the King's Council witness the mainpernors' promise to produce Segrave before them and the king to stand trial. The witnesses were the bishops of Durham, Coventry and Carlisle, the earls of Lincoln and Warwick and the justices Roger Brabazon and Ralph de Hengham.

basic example of this.[75] At their most fundamental level, royal charters were evidence of the king's will in action. The witnesses, as well as being there to validate a charter in the case of a dispute, were also public evidence of the king having taken counsel. The more eminent the witnesses, the wiser it was assumed the counsel had been. Thus, the issues of companionship and counsel, always interlinked, come together most obviously. Typically, however, what Edward I regarded as wise was what would strengthen and defend the power and rights of the crown. In 1275 he wrote to Pope Gregory X on the matter of England's feudal tribute to Rome, a legacy of King John's surrender of the realm to Innocent III in 1213, stating that he could not send money to Rome without first consulting his prelates and magnates. He was bound by his coronation oath, he wrote, 'to do nothing which touched the crown without the consent of the prelates and magnates'.[76] Edward here prayed in aid the counsel of his magnates, ecclesiastical and lay, to excuse himself from something he had no wish to do. Similarly, in 1294 Edward was able to refuse the clergy's petition for the repeal of the Statute of Mortmain by reminding them that the statute had been enacted with the consent of the magnates and could not be undone without the same.[77] As John Maddicott has remarked, 'the need to consult might liberate a king as well as constrain him'.[78]

Edward went further in using the obligation of counsel to bolster the power of the crown. The councillors' oath of 1294, sworn by members of the king's council, placed a formal obligation on councillors to protect the rights of the crown. They were to swear that, 'to the best of your ability, you will give and devote your care, aid and counsel to keep and maintain, to safeguard and restore, the rights of the king and of the crown'. More simply, but even more bindingly, they had to swear that, 'to the best of your ability and in loyal fashion, you will support the crown'.[79] The oath of 1294 was far more explicit, detailed and constraining in the obligations it placed on councillors to protect the rights of the crown than the oath of 1257, where their only obligation to the crown specifically, rather than the individual king, was not to consent to alienations

[75] It was Maitland who first suggested that 'in the absence of official lists of the king's councillors', the witnesses to royal charters might suffice as an alternative. F.W. Maitland, 'History from the Charter Roll', *EHR* 8 (1893), 726.

[76] *Parl Writs*, I, 381–2.

[77] *Guisborough*, 250; J.R. Maddicott, *The Origins of the English Parliament, 924–1327* (Oxford University Press, 2010), 281.

[78] *Ibid.*, 281.

[79] *Statutes of the Realm*, 10 vols. (London: Record Commission, 1810–28), I, 248. Baldwin, *King's Council*, 347–8. Baldwin gives the oath in the 1307 version but the same oath dates from 1294, the only difference being the order of the clauses. Prestwich, *Edward I*, 438n.; TNA E 159/68, m. 64.

of the royal demesne.[80] It was possible, of course, for those who opposed a king's policy to interpret the oath of 1294 as providing them with an obligation to defend the rights of the crown against the harmful policies of an individual king, as happened under Edward II, but this was not Edward I's intention. In his reign 'the rights of the crown' was a slogan used to advance rather than constrain royal power.

Undoubtedly Edward I was single-minded in his pursuit of his aims and there were clearly occasions when this lapsed into narrow-mindedness and an inability to accept anyone's point of view other than his own. Such occasions were, however, relatively rare and an inevitable consequence of the fundamental ambiguity and contradiction at the heart of medieval conceptions of counsel. On the one hand, kings regarded it as their prerogative to seek counsel, while on the other hand the magnates saw giving counsel to the king as their right and duty. Normally these contradictory positions did not come into conflict, as the right of the magnates to proffer counsel was usually freely given by the king. It was only, as Watts has put it, 'when military failure or royal overmightiness or paranoia broke the spell, [that] king and nobility resorted to theoretical positions which were mutually irreconcilable'.[81] That this happened so infrequently under Edward I is testament to his political skill and a reflection of that fact that, more often than not, his point of view was similar to, or at least not in conflict with, those who might claim the right to counsel him. That his 'natural companions' were also his 'natural counsellors' generally suited Edward's purposes very well.

The most formal method by which the king could receive counsel was at meetings of parliament.[82] Parliaments were very frequent under Edward I. For much of the reign, he held two each year and even when, from 1294, this was no longer possible, thanks to the demands of war, it was rare for there not to be a parliament at least once a year. Most of Edward's parliaments did not involve the summoning of knights of the shire and burgesses, generally only required when matters of taxation

[80] Baldwin, *King's Council*, 346.

[81] Watts, 'Counsels', 281.

[82] For the development of parliament in the thirteenth and early fourteenth centuries, see Stubbs, *Constitutional History*, II, 134, 267; J.E. Powell and K. Wallis, *The House of Lords in the Middle Ages: a History of the English House of Lords to 1540* (London: Weidenfeld and Nicolson, 1968); E.B. Fryde and E. Miller (eds.), *Historical Studies of the English Parliament* (Cambridge University Press, 1970); Harriss, *King, Parliament, and Public Finance*; G.O. Sayles, *The King's Parliament of England* (London: Edward Arnold, 1975); R.G. Davies and J.H. Denton (eds.), *The English Parliament in the Middle Ages* (Manchester University Press, 1981); H.G. Richardson and G.O. Sayles (eds.), *The English Parliament in the Middle Ages* (London: Hambledon Press, 1981); Maddicott, *Origins*. For the operation and function of Edward I's parliament, see Prestwich, *Edward I*, 451–62 and Maddicott, *Origins*, chapter 6.

were to be discussed, and for the most part those summoned were the lay and ecclesiastical magnates together with the king's principal officials and justices.[83] The frequency of parliaments shows how much Edward valued them as a means of publicly expressing good kingship, through the redress of petitions, the passing of good laws, obtaining of supply where necessary and, importantly for the purposes of this section, the taking of counsel. It provided him with 'a public stage for consensus politics'.[84] The personal writs of summons for the parliament of 1295 express Edward's formal recognition of the importance of parliament for the latter. The writs stressed that there were serious matters touching the king and realm needing action but which 'without your presence and theirs [the other 'chief men and magnates'] we do not wish to be dispatched'. The writs commanded those given a personal summons 'to treat with us on the said matters and to give us your counsel'.[85] The king did not always listen to the advice given to him in parliament, as his stormy confrontation with the earl of Norfolk at Salisbury in February 1297 and his continual prevarications over the perambulation of the royal forest between 1297 and 1301 demonstrate, but he obviously valued the opportunity to receive the counsel of his greatest subjects.[86]

Edward was careful to use parliament to bolster his diplomatic and military efforts, most obviously in the grants of taxation he obtained, but also in other ways. The declaration of war on Llywelyn ap Gruffydd following Llywelyn's failure to do homage was made at parliament in November 1276; the declaration is very clear that the decision was taken in the presence of, and with counsel from, the bishops, earls and barons who were present at parliament.[87] Similarly, in 1301 at the Lincoln parliament seven earls and sixty-four barons put their seals to a declaration to the pope in support of Edward I's claims to Scotland, which went as far as stating that they would continue to defend the crown's rights there, even were Edward to accept the pope's mandate that Scotland belonged to the papacy and not to the king of England.[88] It is not clear whether the letter was ever sent to the pope but, to judge by its inclusion in a number of chronicles, it was certainly circulated widely domestically.[89] This shows how keen Edward was to stress to the community of the realm the support his Scottish venture still commanded among the nobility at a time

[83] Maddicott, *Origins*, 287–92.

[84] Ibid., 279. [85] Cited by Powell and Wallis, *House of Lords*, 222.

[86] *Guisborough*, 289–90; Prestwich, *Edward I*, 518–19, 524–7.

[87] *CCR 1272–1279*, 359–61. [88] *Foedera*, I, ii, 926–7.

[89] William Rishanger, *Chronica et Annales*, ed. H.T. Riley, Rolls Series (1865), 208–10; *Guisborough*, 344–5; Prestwich, *Edward I*, 492.

when he was still finding parliament difficult to handle.[90] Nor was this the only occasion on which the earls and barons wrote to the pope in support of the king. In 1290, seven earls and seven barons wrote to Pope Nicholas IV, further to Edward's own letter, asking the pope to cease the practice of appropriating English cathedral prebendaries for the use of Roman cardinals.[91] In the Easter parliament of 1299, when the papal proposals for peace between England and France had been read out, Edward asked his magnates assembled in parliament for their advice as to what to do. That this was no mere formality is shown by their response. A chronicler reports that they debated apart for a while and then returned to advise the king 'with one voice' that he should accept the pope's proposals, which he duly did.[92] Such examples show Edward in a more subtle light than the authoritarian sledgehammer depicted in some of the historiography. This was a king able to rally his nobles in support of his objectives, who could, for the most part, use parliament to unite the nobility behind him.

But, if the king found parliaments a useful tool for obtaining counsel, how did the earls regard them? It was rare for attendance to be obligatory.[93] In general, Edward I's earls had a good attendance rate at parliaments, being on average individually present for at least 60 per cent of parliaments.[94] Such a record is impressive, considering that there were several parliaments during which a number of earls were abroad or engaged elsewhere on the king's business.[95] It should not be surprising that earls were relatively assiduous in their attendance: parliaments were times when they could make and renew political, social and business contacts.

Kings could thus seek counsel from their magnates in a number of different ways, through the king's council, through parliaments and, more informally, from those who were in his company, a window on to which is provided by the charter witness lists. But, as has been suggested above,

[90] See Prestwich, *Edward I*, 525–8, for circumstances of this parliament.

[91] *CCR 1288–1296*, 135. [92] Rishanger, *Chronica*, 389–90; Maddicott, *Origins*, 281.

[93] Prestwich, *Edward I*, 447.

[94] The best evidence for attendance comes, once again, from the witness lists to royal charters and the figures below should be regarded as a bare minimum representing only those occasions where the evidence definitively proves a particular earl was present. From my analysis of the witness lists it can be seen that, for example, the earl of Lincoln was present at at least 34 of the 46 parliaments held during Edward I's reign, while Thomas of Lancaster and Humphrey III de Bohun, earl of Hereford, attended 10 of 11 and 7 of 10 parliaments, respectively, in the years after they became earls (1298 and 1299). The earl of Gloucester was at at least 20 of the 32 parliaments before his death, John de Warenne at 26 of 42, Humphrey II de Bohun, earl of Hereford, at 21 of 36 and Edmund of Lancaster at 18 of 32.

[95] For the generally unsatisfactory nature of magnate attendance at parliaments during the middle ages, see J.S. Roskell, 'The Problem of the Attendance of the Lords in Medieval Parliaments', *BIHR* 29 (1956), 153–204.

magnates had a strong sense of their own rights and duties to provide counsel to the king even, perhaps especially, at times when he did not wish to hear it. To a man with the strength of mind and purpose of Edward I, this sort of advice was much less welcome than the kind that has been discussed so far. This duty was made explicit in the councillor's oath of 1257, where the councillors swore 'to provide faithful counsel to the lord king *as often as they perceive it to be useful*'.[96] This was an invitation, even an obligation, to speak one's mind, even if the king did not wish to hear the contents. In a development revealing of Edward I's attitude, this sentiment finds no place in the oath of 1294. That such ideas did not disappear in Edward I's reign, however, can be seen, to take one example, from the *Mirror of Justices*. In its spurious history of early England, it claims that the role of the earls was 'to hear and determine in the parliaments all the writs and plaints concerning wrongs done by the king, the queen, their children, and their special ministers, for which wrongs one could not otherwise have obtained common right'.[97] Such a role, of course, had it existed, would have gone beyond mere counselling and involved correction of the king. The history of the thirteenth century, of 1215, 1258 and 1297, suggests that such a view of the role of the nobility was current among the earls themselves and in the wider political community. Wider political grievances against royal policy usually only coalesced into practical solutions in the middle ages when they were given voice by prominent members of the titled nobility.

The holders of the three great hereditary offices (steward, marshal and constable) were in the strongest position among the earls to offer unbidden advice to the king on behalf of the community of the realm. They had fallen, largely by collateral inheritance, into the hands of great earls, and were held respectively by the earls of Lancaster, Norfolk and Hereford in Edward I's reign. The potential threat these offices could pose to the king's freedom of action was revealed by Simon de Montfort's use of the hereditary stewardship in the 1260s. From 1260 Montfort began to turn the office from a largely honorific one into a position with real power, allowing him to appoint a deputy steward of the royal household.[98] Following Montfort's death, his lands and the earldom of Leicester were granted to Henry III's son, Edmund, but the office of steward was not yet revived.[99] Henry and Lord Edward, conscious of how the office had been used by Montfort, seem not to have been willing to risk the possibility of a revival of such claims of appointment, even by the king's younger son, while royal authority remained uncertain. Perhaps Henry remembered

[96] Baldwin, *King's Council*, 346 (italics added). [97] *Mirror of Justices*, 7.
[98] Maddicott, *Simon de Montfort*, 239–40. [99] *CChR 1257–1300*, 58.

the destabilising effect his own brother, Richard of Cornwall, had had on his entry into politics in the 1220s, when he felt the rights inherent in his lands and status were not being respected.[100] Whatever the motive may have been, it was not until May 1269 that Edmund was granted the stewardship, though for life only, an award confirmed by Edward I in February 1275, a few months after their spat over the role of the steward at the coronation.[101] Aside from that affair, however, the stewardship was never an issue of political controversy in Edward I's reign and the steward's claims to appoint a deputy in the household were not revived. The main reason for this, of course, was that, as the king's trusted brother, Edmund of Lancaster had no need to use the office aggressively. On Edmund's death in 1296 the office lapsed and neither Edward I nor Thomas of Lancaster seems to have made any move to revive it while the old king lived.[102] Lancaster's use of the stewardship, obtained in fee from Edward II in May 1308, as a political weapon between 1317 and 1321 demonstrates the potential threat such offices posed to the crown if their holders felt their counsel was being marginalised.[103]

The use by the marshal and constable of their hereditary offices to justify their opposition to the king in 1297 could hardly have induced Edward to look favourably on granting out another such office, even to his own nephew. Norfolk and Hereford used their offices as a platform from which they could thrust their counsel on an unwilling king.[104] The military nature both of their offices and of one of the principal grievances against Edward I in that year coincided to dramatic effect when they refused to draw up the muster list, on the basis that the king's summons was both novel and insufficient. Their objections, the chronicler Bartholomew Cotton makes clear, were made 'on behalf of the community of the kingdom' and in their capacity as hereditary military officials.[105] The immediate dismissal of Norfolk and Hereford from their offices by Edward was the result of a clash of wills between a king determined to ignore individual rights in pursuit of what he regarded as the common interest and two earls using their hereditary offices to press their counsel on the king on behalf, as they saw it, of the community of the realm. Edward wanted things on his own terms and he was quite prepared to play dirty to achieve this.[106]

100 Powicke, *Henry III*, I, 71–2.

101 *CPR 1266–1272*, 339; *CPR 1272–1281*, 81. See above, 36.

102 Maddicott, *Thomas of Lancaster*, 76. 103 Ibid., 76–7, 87, 208, 233, 241–3, 289–91, 321–2.

104 A.M. Spencer, 'The Lay Opposition to Edward I in 1297: Its Composition and Character', *TCE* 12 (2009), 97–9.

105 *EHD 1198–1327*, 215; Prestwich, *Edward I*, 420; Spencer, 'Lay Opposition', 99.

106 For an example of Edward's low tactics, see Morris, *Bigod Earls*, 157.

The crisis of 1297 and the king's subsequent domestic difficulties were caused in large part by this tendency on Edward's part not to listen to counsel with which he did not agree. When comparing Edward I to King Arthur, the chronicler Peter Langtoft noted that one of the areas in which Edward did not match up was that he acted according to will without taking sufficient counsel.[107] Langtoft may have been thinking specifically of the controversial grant of a tax of an eighth in July 1297, said to have been granted merely by 'people standing round in his chamber', rather than in full parliament, or he may have been thinking more generally of Edward's stubbornness in the years of opposition to him.[108] Edward I was hardly the first king, nor would he be the last, to fall prey to this particular vice, and the troubles of 1297–1301 were not representative of the reign as a whole and should not be taken as such. Edward recognised the importance and necessity of counsel and the right of earls to give it. If his views on counsel emphasised royal prerogative over magnate rights, this was a general trait of kings and not one peculiar to this individual monarch.

There was another side to counsel beyond the mere proffering of advice. Nobles in the late middle ages could expect to find themselves employed directly in royal administration, in stark contrast to the prevailing situation since the Norman Conquest. While, under the late Anglo-Saxons, the earls had, as a legacy from their origins as ealdormen, an important supervisory role to play in local administration, as royal government grew in scope and size at the centre and in the localities from the early twelfth century onwards the nobility did less, as the crown relied more upon clerics and other professional bureaucrats, curial sheriffs and, eventually, local knights to undertake routine royal administration at the centre and in the localities.[109] Long before Henry III's personal rule (1234–58), the earls were playing little if any part in directing royal administration at either a national or local level except at times of crisis. Of the three earls of Henry III whose lives have been studied in detail, Simon de Montfort, earl of Leicester, Richard de Clare, earl of Gloucester, and Roger III de Bigod, earl of Norfolk, only Montfort was directly employed by Henry in an administrative role, and that was in distant Gascony between 1248 and 1252 and was, in any case, as much a military as an administrative appointment.[110] Gloucester spent much of

[107] *Langtoft*, II, 326.

[108] *Flores Historiarum*, III, 296; *Documents Illustrating the Crisis of 1297–8 in England*, ed. M.C. Prestwich, Camden Society, 4th Series 24 (1980), 110.

[109] For the powers of late Anglo-Saxon earls, see Baxter, *Earls*, chapter 3. For a general overview of Anglo-Norman and Angevin government, see W.L. Warren, *The Governance of Norman and Angevin England, 1086–1272* (Stanford University Press, 1987).

[110] Altschul, *Baronial Family*; Maddicott, *Simon de Montfort*, 106–24; Morris, *Bigod Earls*.

his early career from 1243 establishing his lordship over Glamorgan but, when this was largely complete by 1247, he did not turn his hand to royal administration but spent his time engaged in 'pilgrimages, tournaments and other festivities' and adding further to the Clare estate.[111] Although he was cultivated by Henry III, going on the evidence of royal charter witness lists his attendance at court was only intermittent at best. Between his first appearance as a witness, in the regnal year 29 Henry III (1244–5), and the end of regnal year 41 Henry III (1256–7), Gloucester witnessed 173 royal charters out of a total of 1,096 enrolled on the charter rolls, just 15.78 per cent, a figure well below those for most of Edward I's earls including his son Gilbert.[112] By contrast, the minor baron and royal steward Robert Walerand, one of Henry III's closest councillors, witnessed 446 charters (40.69 per cent) in the same period.

In the late middle ages, an earl as important as Gloucester would rarely have had such time to indulge himself. In the fourteenth and fifteenth centuries, with the partially linked phenomena of near-permanent war with France, Scotland or both and still further expansion of government and law in the localities, the role of the nobility in government of almost all kinds was to grow considerably. This was a very different world from that of the twelfth and thirteenth centuries. There are many and varied structural reasons behind these changes, principally to do with the consequences of war and of the inexorable growth of royal government, and it is possible to see some of these at work under Edward I. This makes it worthwhile to consider the extent to which the earls in his reign were involved in royal administration.

The most important administrative role a king could give to one of his subjects was the regency when he was out of the kingdom. In 1279, when Edward went to France to negotiate the Treaty of Amiens, he appointed the earls of Cornwall and Lincoln, together with the bishop of Hereford, to the custody of the realm in his absence.[113] During his more prolonged absence in Gascony from 1286 to 1289, Cornwall, the senior male member of the royal family remaining in England, was again appointed regent by his cousin.[114] During other royal absences, however, a regent was not appointed and at these times a regency council was established instead. The first time this occurred in Edward I's reign was at the very beginning when Edward was still on crusade at the moment of his father's

111 Altschul, *Baronial Family*, 66–77 (quotation is from 74–5).

112 Taken from my own study of Henry III's charters from *Royal Charter Witness Lists of Henry III (1226–1272) from the Charter Rolls in the Public Record Office*, ed. M. Morris, 2 vols., List and Index Society 291–2 (2001).

113 *CPR 1272–1281*, 309–10. This was, of course, not a new phenomenon.

114 *CPR 1281–1292*, 248.

death in November 1272.[115] Independently of Edward's instructions, a standing executive council was established, headed by two royal clerks, Robert Burnell and Walter Merton, bishop of Rochester, and including the Marcher baron and executor of Lord Edward, Roger Mortimer of Wigmore.[116] Beyond this, four guardians of the realm were appointed by the 'assent of all the magnates', including the earls of Cornwall, Gloucester and Warenne.[117] These guardians demonstrate that, in the king's absence, the earls, as the leading men in the land, expected, and were expected, to take a major role in the maintenance of the king's peace. In 1297, when Edward appointed a regency council under the nominal leadership of his eldest son, he expected its noble participants to take a more active and less decorative role. The council was broad-based, as was necessary at a time of political crisis, and included four bishops, three earls (Cornwall, Warenne and Warwick) and three barons.[118] The royalist earls would provide the political and military muscle to counter the potential efforts of the two opposition earls, Hereford and Norfolk.

The earls' political and military skills were also called upon when Edward appointed them to positions in his dominions outside England. Earl Warenne and the earl of Richmond as guardians of Scotland, and the earls of Lancaster and Lincoln as lieutenants of Gascony were, like Montfort under Henry III, expected to take personal charge of military and administrative affairs on the king's behalf.[119] Edward appreciated that in circumstances of war and crisis, the only men with the necessary political, military and financial weight to undertake offices that entailed not just military but also vice-regal powers were the great earls.

Within England, as shown above, it was rare, though far from unknown, for earls to serve on the king's council and the only earl who seems to have become actively involved in routine administration was Lincoln, one of Edward's oldest and most trusted friends.[120] Towards the end of the reign in particular, Lincoln was involved in such diverse matters of administration as the hearing of special judicial cases, the bailing of prisoners, dividing inheritances between co-heiresses, the opening of parliament in the king's absence and the handling of royal petitions.[121] Lincoln's activities,

115 For a more detailed discussion of this, see below, 189–92.

116 *AM*, I, 374, II, 113, IV, 462; R. Huscroft, 'Robert Burnell and the Governance of England, 1270–74', *TCE* 8 (2001), 64.

117 Blaauw, 'Early History of Lewes Priory', 30.

118 Johnstone, *Edward of Carnarvon*, 36.

119 *Guisborough*, 262; *CPR 1292–1301*, 196; Prestwich, *Edward I*, 384; F.J. Watson, *Under the Hammer: Edward I and Scotland, 1286–1306* (East Linton: Tuckwell Press, 1998), 217.

120 See above, 53.

121 *CCR 1296–1302*, 344; *CCR 1302–1307*, 362; *CPR 1292–1301*, 459; TNA C/153/1, item 28; *Select Cases in the Court of King's Bench*, ed. G.O. Sayles, 7 vols., Selden Society (1936–71), III, 175–8.

more often performed by royal clerks or professional lay administrators, demonstrate just how highly Edward valued not just his counsel but also his industry. His position was to be mirrored by Aymer de Valence during the more unusual circumstances of the reign of Edward II, but it was very rare for a thirteenth-century earl to be so deeply involved in day-to-day matters of administration.[122]

Much more common was the employment of earls on extraordinary royal business, where their status and influence would help to expedite the matter in hand and would add lustre, and perhaps force, to the work of the professionals. Their employment on this sort of work went well beyond anything seen during the personal rule of Henry III. Wide-ranging judicial commissions were the most common form of this type of employment. On Edward's return from Gascony in 1289, Lincoln and Warenne formed part of a commission to hear complaints by the Scots against extortions by the northern sheriffs, while Lincoln headed the commission of general inquiry into depredations committed by royal ministers and judges.[123] A similar commission was set up in November 1298, in which Warenne and Lincoln were joined by two bishops and two barons to deal with complaints arising from the crisis of 1297.[124] Much earlier in the reign, the earl of Warwick headed a commission to try to establish peace between Llywelyn ap Gruffydd and the Marcher lords.[125] Commissions could usually be entrusted to royal justices, sheriffs or county knights, but, on extraordinary occasions, the king obviously felt that the added status that an earl would bring could be of use, and it shows how the king worked in partnership with his earls to strengthen his kingship. Thus, gradually, after a long period when the earls had been largely absent from detailed involvement in government, except in emergencies, Edward was using the prestige and authority they possessed, and demonstrating that they, like everyone else, were expected to start shouldering their share of the burden for maintaining the king's governance where necessary.

In a number of different ways Edward had sought to strengthen the relationship between the crown and the earls and to use them as part of his overall strategy of restoring royal authority in the wake of the humiliations it had suffered under Henry III. For most of this chapter, it has been Edward the enabler on view rather than the disciplinarian with which historians are most familiar. That is not to say, of course, that authoritarianism was entirely absent. Like nearly all kings, he reacted with

122 For Valence, see, for example, Phillips, *Aymer de Valence*, 51–3, 106–7, 274–5.

123 *CPR 1281–1292*, 365, 408.

124 *CPR 1292–1301*, 373–4.

125 *CPR 1272–1281*, 48–9.

hostility to those who opposed his will and sought to thrust unbidden counsel upon him, while he used his authority to squeeze the best deal possible for himself and his relatives in their marriages into the nobility. These were flashes of masterfulness, however, that intruded starkly upon long periods of careful political management. The marriages were deliberately planned and in each case were designed to strengthen royal authority by binding the earldoms involved more closely to the crown. At every opportunity, on grand public occasions and more routine ones, he sought to emphasise the affinity between king and earls and their role in supporting and promoting royal authority. He was also careful to seek and obtain counsel from his earls at every convenient opportunity and to employ them in administrative roles where they could be useful for expediting royal policy. In the next chapter of this section other aspects of Edward's kingship, including justice, the *quo warranto* campaign, war and patronage will be similarly tested to determine the overall nature of Edward's style of kingship.

Chapter 3

JUSTICE, FRANCHISES, WAR AND REWARD

The previous chapter looked at the ways in which Edward I acted as an enabler for his nobility, how he enhanced the bond between the crown and the earls in symbolic and practical ways in order to strengthen the authority of the crown and of his kingship. This chapter will focus more on those areas of his kingship where there could be potential tension between a king and his nobility: the handling of justice, the position of noble franchises, the military demands of the crown and, finally, the distribution of patronage. In each of these areas it will be argued that although Edward did often employ the authoritarian style for which he is best known, this was by no means the only, or indeed the primary, weapon in his arsenal and that his skills of political management have been sorely underrated. Edward was a king who blended both approaches in pursuit of his strategy of reinvigorated royal power.

JUSTICE

Truly, justice pertains to the greatest extent to the king: through it quarrels are ended, discord is settled, malefactors are restrained, and right judgments among litigants are given in the royal court.[1]

Walter of Milemete, *On the Nobility, Wisdom and Prudence of Kings*

Justice was one of the four cardinal virtues, 'the stuff of the common weal' that produced both peace and harmony.[2] More than that, it was the very stuff of good kingship, the duty to do justice being included in the coronation oath.[3] It was justice that stood between kingship and tyranny. As Aquinas made clear, it was when a king fell away from justice that he

[1] Walter of Milemete, 'On the Nobility, Wisdom and Prudence of Kings', in C.J. Nederman (ed. and trans.), *Political Thought in Early Fourteenth-Century England: Treatises by Walter of Milemete, William of Pagula and William of Ockham* (Temple, AZ: Arizona Center for Medieval Studies, 2002), 38.

[2] Watts, *Henry VI*, 24. [3] *Statutes of the Realm*, I, 168.

became a tyrant.[4] In *Bracton*'s thought the king was placed above the law precisely so he could arbitrate fairly between those who were bound by it, although the king too, as an act of will, placed himself under the law.[5]

The king's general duty to do justice was thus well-established but his position above the fray, where he could adjudicate and arbitrate fairly, was of particular practical importance when it came to the disputes of his greatest subjects. Walter of Milemete, writing in the aftermath of the deadly quarrels among the nobility that had destroyed Edward II's kingship, was acutely conscious of this. The experience of that reign led him to conclude that 'the peace and tranquillity of the kingdom proceeds from the harmony of the great men'.[6] The way to achieve this, he believed, was 'to bind them together in the love of peace and judge justly among them in accordance with equity', for 'it is not fitting for the king to take part of one great man against another, since from this enmity increases among his subjects'.[7] Edward II's failure as king had come from his creation and nourishment of favourites and Milemete's advice would have been as relevant at the beginning of Edward I's reign as it was when it was written at the beginning of Edward III's half a century later, for the crisis of 1258 had been caused in part by Henry's refusal to do justice equitably among his great subjects.[8] The countess of Arundel's bitter outburst at Henry III that '[o]ne cannot now obtain what is just at your court' reflected the attitude of those Marcher lords who, two generations later, suffered depredations at the hands of the younger Despenser and illustrates the danger to a king who obtained a reputation for injustice.[9]

It was not merely just for a king to be impartial, it was also good politics. For example, Helen Castor has shown the disastrous consequences of Richard II's Cheshire affinity in undermining the perception of the king as a national, impartial symbol of authority.[10] During his reign, Edward I was able to show that he understood this principle better than his father, and better than either Edward II or Richard II ever would. Edward demonstrated that he was willing to punish those close to him if they transgressed; indeed he often dealt most harshly with those who he felt had betrayed his trust.[11] Edward had illustrated this point vividly

[4] St Thomas Aquinas, *De Regno: On Kingship to the King of Cyprus*, ed. and trans. G.B. Phelan and revised I.T. Eschmann (Toronto: Pontifical Institute of Medieval Studies, 1949), paragraphs 11, 24–6, 75–6, 84, 86, 90, 95.

[5] *Bracton*, II, 33. [6] Milemete, 'Nobility', 34. [7] Ibid., 35.

[8] Carpenter, 'King, Magnates and Society', 44–9; Carpenter, *Reign of Henry III*, 191–3.

[9] Paris, *Chronica Majora*, V, 336–7; N.M. Fryde, *The Tyranny and Fall of Edward II, 1321–1326* (Cambridge University Press, 1979), chapter 3.

[10] H. Castor, *The King, the Crown and the Duchy of Lancaster: Public Authority and Private Power, 1399–1461* (Oxford University Press, 2000), 11–18.

[11] See, for instance, his treatment of corrupt judges in 1289; Prestwich, *Edward I*, 339–41.

even before he had become king. Earl Warenne's murderous assault on the midlands baron, Sir Alan la Zouche, in 1270 provoked a furious reaction from Lord Edward.[12] Edward took the initiative in chasing down Warenne, who had been one of his closest associates, and in negotiating the terms of the earl's surrender.[13] Edward's anger was accentuated by the offence to royal dignity caused by the perpetration of the act in full court in Westminster Hall in front of the king's own justices. Warenne's punishment was severe, a fine of 10,000 marks and a barefoot penance; evidence that, now Edward was helping to run the kingdom with his father, the blatant favouritism and denial of justice that characterised the years of Henry III's personal rule were to be a thing of the past. The earl was not broken, however, much to one chronicler's disappointment, and, once Edward became king, he relaxed the terms of Warenne's payment, reduced the amount and, eventually, gave up on it altogether.[14] This was an acute blend of carrot and stick to ensure that a powerful supporter was punished but not unnecessarily alienated.

Thus, though a transgressing earl or major baron might be treated more leniently than, say, a judge found guilty of excessive corruption, Edward demonstrated throughout his reign that those close to him could not infringe the crown's rights with impunity, as had occurred so often under his father. Earl Warenne and the earl of Gloucester were targeted during the *quo warranto* campaign as notorious usurpers of royal rights and examples were made of both men.[15] Even Lincoln was not exempt from the king's anger when he transgressed. In 1277, the earl had to bail his officials from Windsor Castle, where they had been imprisoned for an unspecified 'contempt and enormous trespass committed by them upon the king and his men'.[16] Edward was not prepared to allow even his most trusted earl to get away with acts of contempt against the crown and made a public example of the earl's men. Important bannerets of the household were also, on occasion, denied preferential treatment. William Latimer the elder (d. 1304), one of Edward's most distinguished household knights, was refused a writ to replevy several liberties in Northamptonshire that had been seized to the crown under *quo warranto*.[17] In 1303, Henry Percy, Earl Warenne's grandson and one of Edward's most important and dedicated military commanders in the war against Scotland, was almost outlawed

[12] *Chronicle of Bury St Edmunds*, 47. See below, 180–1, for more details.

[13] *Flores Historiarum*, III, 18.

[14] See below, 181.

[15] Lists of their usurpations were drawn up by the king's officials: TNA E 163/2/30; TNA JUST 1/1340. For a more detailed discussion of their treatment, see below, 74–5.

[16] *CCR 1272–1279*, 373.

[17] *CCR 1288–1296*, 150. For Latimer's career as a household knight, see Prestwich, *Edward I*, 149–50.

for a trespass in the king's warrens and parks, and only escaped by having to report with mainpernors to York prison and stand trial.[18] In all of this a message was being sent out to the men involved that such behaviour was not acceptable, while ensuring that the punishment was not severe enough to alienate them permanently. At the same time, the king was broadcasting to others that he would not overlook the transgressions of those who had royal favour: a powerful demonstration of his determination to uphold good kingship.

A king was thus to be a judge and to punish those who transgressed royal law and the king's peace, no matter what their status, but he was also supposed to be the ultimate arbiter in his kingdom. The nobility needed the king to be impartial so that he could intervene and mediate fairly in their inevitable disputes with each other. Without him and his justice, such disputes tended to descend into violence. The danger of this was vividly illustrated when the king was abroad, as three such cases involving earls make clear. The dispute between Robert de Ferrers, the dispossessed earl of Derby, and Edmund of Lancaster boiled over into violence and the siege of Chartley Castle by Lancaster during Edward's absence on crusade.[19] The dispute divided political opinion among the earls, with Lincoln joining the siege on Lancaster's side and Gloucester and Warenne lobbying the regency council on Ferrers' behalf. A case that similarly threatened to drag in seemingly unconnected magnates occurred between Earl Warenne and Reginald de Grey, Marcher neighbours and two of Edward I's closest associates, during the king's three-year absence in Gascony.[20] The threat of general violence in the March was so serious that the regent, Edmund of Cornwall, had to issue a specific prohibition against armed activity, not just to the antagonists themselves, but also to the earls of Norfolk, Gloucester and Warwick, along with several other barons.[21] Most notorious was the dispute between the earls of Gloucester and Hereford, which also erupted during Edward's long stay in Gascony. Attempts by Edmund of Cornwall as regent to stop Gloucester's activities in Hereford's lordship of Brecon failed and it took the king's personal and sustained intervention finally to bring a halt to the conflict three years later.[22]

Two of these three cases involved the special circumstances of the March of Wales, a region that, thanks to its tradition of private war, had long been a source of political violence and that had stood outside the

[18] *CCR 1302–1307*, 27. Unfortunately, the outcome is unknown, but Percy was soon back in royal favour.

[19] For a more detailed discussion of this dispute, see below, 192–3.

[20] This case is discussed in more detail below, 213–14.

[21] *CCR 1288–1296*, 547.

[22] *CCR 1288–1296*, 47; *CFR 1272–1307*, 305–6. See below, 214–15, 217–19, for a full description of this case.

crown's normal judicial activities. The justification for the special status of the Marcher lordships lay in their role as England's bulwark against the native Welsh but, following the conquest of Gwynedd in 1283, this justification disappeared. Rees Davies wrote in detail about Edward I's haphazard and incomplete attempts to bring the Marcher lordships more in line with England but, as he recognised, the situation was more complicated than a simple listing of the king's interventions in the March in the 1290s and early 1300s might suggest.[23] Edward was not an enemy of the March: he had relied on Marcher support to defeat Montfort in 1265 and had created new Marcher lordships in 1282–3.[24] He did not wish to see an end to Marcher privilege, recognising that any attempt would be doomed to failure, but what he wanted was definition of their status vis-à-vis the crown and to uphold and extend royal rights in the March. As Davies wrote, Edward 'approved of franchises so long as their title was clearly founded on royal charter and thereby subject to his control'.[25] The new lordships were held directly of the crown (later the principality of Wales) and, through his marriage deals with the earls of Gloucester and Hereford, he was able to transform the legal and tenurial position of two of the oldest and largest Marcher lordships in the south by ensuring that they were held explicitly from the crown like any English fief.[26]

Two further points need to be made relating to Edward's dealings with the March. First, Caroline Burt has recently shown how several Marcher lords had taken advantage of Edward's absence in Gascony between 1286 and 1289 to assert their lordship aggressively, and she argues that Edward's actions on the March in the 1290s should be seen not as a premeditated attack on Marcher privilege, but as a response to Marcher misbehaviour.[27] Second, the Marchers' own complicity in the undermining of their sovereignty must be acknowledged. Marcher lords were not above calling on the king's justice against another Marcher lord if they felt it would help them in a specific case. Collectively such behaviour fatally undermined the principle of Marcher autonomy.

There are numerous examples of this, but three, involving the earls of Norfolk and Hereford, will suffice to make the point. Hereford and Norfolk, when opposing Edward in 1297, used the complaint that lords were being 'arbitrarily put out of' their ancient liberties by the king, a rallying cry particularly appealing to Marcher sentiment.[28] Yet both earls were guilty of inviting the crown into ancient liberties. At Easter 1290 Norfolk brought a case in King's Bench against the earl of Gloucester,

[23] Davies, *Lordship and Society*, 249–67. [24] Prestwich, *Edward I*, 46–52.
[25] Davies, *Lordship and Society*, 267. [26] *CChR 1257–1300*, 350; *CChR 1300–1326*, 33.
[27] Burt, 'Governance', 107–8. [28] *EHD 1189–1327*, 472.

accusing him of raiding his Marcher lordship of Chepstow.[29] Abandoning the principle that Marcher lords resolved their own disputes, Norfolk stressed that he held Chepstow of the king in chief and effectively called upon Edward as his superior lord to aid him.[30] When he too was attacked by Gloucester, the earl of Hereford called in the king, thereby bringing Edward into the dispute with disastrous consequences for both earls.[31] A few years later in 1293, however, Hereford tried hard to prevent a case of park-breaking brought against him by Roger Mortimer of Chirk, part of a long-running dispute between the two men, from being transferred from his own court at Brecon to King's Bench. The plea, he argued, belonged to him as pertaining to Marcher custom.[32]

In each case the weaker party had sought the protection of the king and the king's law, thereby undermining the principle of Marcher autonomy and admitting the Trojan Horse of royal jurisdiction. It could indeed be said that the Marchers found it impossible to maintain the integrity of Marcher privilege because they themselves were so inconsistent in its application. In this the changing makeup of the March must have had a large part to play.[33] The earls, used to invoking the king's justice when it suited them elsewhere on their estates, were prepared to do so in the March when the king's law might protect or advantage them, but failed to see what this meant for Marcher privileges. A combination of Edward's determination to establish royal authority over all of Wales, and the Marchers' own complicity in this, altered the nature of the March fundamentally and permanently and led to the establishment of the late medieval March, which was a very different, though still undomesticated, beast from what came before. Such cases emphasise again the need great lords had for the king to intervene in their disputes, for only the king could save them from their own worst nature, a point reinforced by what had happened to law and order during the king's absence.[34]

Several earls found themselves bruised at the hands of the king's justice but Edward's justice offered more benefits than harm, for while it protected them from predatory competitors, they themselves were able to use it to their advantage to bolster their own lordship at a local level, as will be demonstrated in the next section. Edward certainly displayed masterfulness in his exercise of justice and it was sometimes needed to restore peace between quarrelsome nobles. Though on occasion, as with

[29] KB 27/123, m. 1. [30] KB 27/124, m. 10d. [31] KB 27/123, m. 1.

[32] KB 27/138, m. 32d; KB 27/139, m. 6d. For evidence of earlier dispute between them, see *CPR 1281–1292*, 515.

[33] See above, 29–30.

[34] Burt, 'Governance', 49–50, 56, 63, 111–14, 121–2, 126. See below, 163–4, for breakdown of order in Sussex during Edward's absence on crusade.

the earl of Gloucester in 1292, he went too far and created political problems for himself, he usually blended it with skilful political management that ensured that internal peace was one of Edward I's greatest achievements.

FRANCHISES

As prelates, earls, barons and others of the kingdom claim to have various liberties, for the examination and judgment of which the king gave these same prelates, earls, barons and others shall have the use of such liberties, provided that nothing accrues to them by usurpation or occupation and that they occupy nothing at the expense of the king, until the king's next coming through the county or the next coming of itinerant justices for common pleas into the same county or until the king orders otherwise, saving the king's right when he wishes to take proceedings thereon, as is contained in the king's writ.[35]

The Statute of Gloucester, 7 August 1278

The Marcher lordships discussed above were, in one sense, simply the greatest franchises in the dominions of the king of England. Within England itself, outside the palatinates, franchises were much less extensive in their powers but numerically much greater than they were on the March, for thousands of individual landholders throughout England exercised one or more of the numerous franchises available. These ranged from, for example, the assize of bread and ale, which gave the holder the power to check the quality of these products within his liberty, up to the return of writs, which gave the holder the authority to carry out royal writs within their lands and thus prevent the sheriff from entering them on official business.[36]

As the thirteenth century progressed it became obvious that a yawning gap was developing between royal rhetoric and reality on the issue of franchises. Increasingly, royal lawyers were emphasising the inalienability of franchises, arguing that all liberties flowed directly from the crown, something that would give the king the supreme judicial authority he needed to exercise effectively his power as ultimate judge and arbiter within his realm. Such arguments were presented in late-thirteenth-century legal tracts like *Fleta* and *Britton* to an even greater extent than they had been in the earlier *Bracton*.[37] Under Henry III,

35 *EHD 1189–1327*, 414.

36 For full descriptions of the various different types of franchises in thirteenth-century England, see H.M. Cam, *The Hundred and the Hundred Rolls: an Outline of Local Government in Medieval England* (London: Methuen Press, 1930), 202–20.

37 D.W. Sutherland, *Quo Warranto Proceedings in the Reign of Edward I* (Oxford: Clarendon Press, 1963), 13; Harriss, *King, Parliament, and Public Finance*, 135.

however, and particularly after 1258, ambitious magnates, partly from a desire to increase their local power, partly out of a need to protect their interests at a time when the crown was not strong enough to do so and partly to shore up the loss of their feudal authority, seized new rights and liberties for themselves at the expense of the crown and local societies.[38] Edward expressed this sense of loss at his coronation in the additional oath he swore to recover what had been lost under his father.[39] The Hundred Rolls Inquiry of 1274–5 confirmed that the king's suspicions had been true: the scale of alleged usurpations contained in them is staggering.[40]

The language of the Hundred Rolls Inquiry and the *quo warranto* campaign that followed was of recovery, of a wholesale resumption by the crown of the liberties that had been lost. Judged against this authoritarian rhetoric, the *quo warranto* campaign was undoubtedly a failure, an 'almost ludicrous failure' at times, both in its prosecution and in its ultimate conclusion in the Statute of *Quo Warranto* of 1290.[41] Sutherland, the principal historian of *quo warranto*, memorably summed up the proceedings as 'always slow, usually incomplete, and often futile'.[42] It would be a mistake, however, to judge *quo warranto* by its inflated rhetoric. As Paul Brand has noted, there 'seems to have been no general consensus among the judiciary as to the main principles of "quo warranto" law'.[43] That this is so suggests that Edward never provided them with firm instructions about how they should proceed and, at the outset of the campaign, long tenure was generally seen as acceptable. It was only as time progressed that the king's lawyers began to press the argument that franchises could not be claimed in this way.[44] In 1285, however, Chief Justice Hengham recognised that such arguments were impracticable and that 'the combined evidence of long tenure and tenure by a large number of people is, in itself, sufficient to create a general "custom" in favour of such franchise-holders'.[45]

Edward seems to have been happy, for the most part, to let the lawyers argue and to wait and see where they ended up. The compromise hammered out in the Statute of *Quo Warranto* was engendered by the brinkmanship in the spring of 1290 of Chief Justice Thornton, one of the king's chief pleaders in the 1280s, when he briefly clarified the arguments over the legitimacy of long tenure firmly in the crown's favour

38 Carpenter, 'Second Century'. 39 Prestwich, *Edward I*, 90–1.

40 *Rotuli Hundredorum*, 2 vols. (London: Record Commission, 1812–18).

41 Sutherland, *Quo Warranto*, 145–61 (quotation is from 161). 42 Ibid., 188.

43 P.A. Brand, '"Quo Warranto" Law in the Reign of Edward I', in Brand, *The Making of the Common Law* (London: Hambledon Press, 1992), 399.

44 Ibid., 427–8. 45 Ibid., 432.

and it suited Edward well.[46] The statute determined that long usage since at least 1189 was permitted as a justification for possessing a franchise but that usage had now to be explicitly confirmed by the crown.[47] This was a practical victory for franchise-holders, as it allowed them to keep their franchises, but it was an important theoretical victory for the crown. The campaign 'had served to make it clear that the exercise of local rights of jurisdiction was a delegation of royal authority'.[48] The importance of this victory and its implications for the future were profound. The Statute of *Quo Warranto* stopped dead in its tracks an alternative theory about the nature of power and authority within England.

Claims of prescription (long tenure), which were the usual defence against a plea of *quo warranto*, could have been made on the basis that time had run against the crown: that long inactivity and tolerance on the part of the crown had rendered usage of a franchise legitimate.[49] Effectively this claim was recognised as legitimate in the statute of 1290. Far more inimical to royal authority, however, were claims of prescription on the basis of 'conquest theory', which effectively denied that liberties were regalia at all. Instead, they were claimed as the spoils of conquest.[50] This seems to have been developed as an idea during the thirteenth century and found its clearest expression in Earl Warenne's brandishing of his rusty sword before the king's justices: 'Here my lords, here is my warrant! My ancestors came with William the Bastard and conquered their lands with the sword, and I shall defend them with the sword against anyone who tries to usurp them.'[51]

A more subtle, and perhaps more invidious, threat to royal authority was the idea of its ultimate source, expressed in the *Mirror of Justices*. This stated that the English earldoms had originally been kingdoms and that they had elected a king from among their number to maintain the peace between them and that, as earls, they retained the right and duty to judge the king's wrongs.[52] Conquest theory was this idea made manifest and it clashed with that of regalian right being promoted by the king and his lawyers. Conquest theory would never, of course, gain legal recognition but, while it persisted as a living concept, it was dangerous to any attempt to re-establish royal authority in the wake of the shocks it had received during the thirteenth century.

[46] Sutherland, *Quo Warranto*, 94–6; Prestwich, *Edward I*, 264, 346–7.

[47] *EHD 1189–1327*, 464–6. [48] Prestwich, *Edward I*, 264.

[49] Sutherland, *Quo Warranto*, 81–2. [50] Ibid., 82.

[51] *Guisborough*, 216n. For uses of conquest theory in the thirteenth century, see Powicke, *The Thirteenth Century*, 521.

[52] *Mirror of Justices*, 6–7.

Edward and his lawyers recognised the threat that conquest theory posed and were determined to quash it. Gilbert de Thornton, that most royalist of lawyers, argued against the earl of Hereford in 1286 that 'at the Conquest of England all these franchises, jurisdictions, and other things which concern the protection of the people were attached to the king's crown'.[53] The clash between the conquest theory of the earls and magnates and the regalian right of the king and his lawyers was a clash of wills between a nobility for whom the thirteenth century had been, in David Crouch's words, 'a time of aristocratic self-confidence and strength' and a newly resurgent crown worn by a king as clever as he was determined.[54] It was Edward who won and, in the Statute of *Quo Warranto*, obtained the magnates' acceptance once and for all that their authority came not from themselves but from the crown. A nobility that accepted this was, over time, likely to become more closely integrated into the apparatus of royal government and the Statute of *Quo Warranto* was an important moment in the process of the development of the late medieval polity and of the service nobility who were integral to it.

The means Edward I used to obtain this victory demonstrate clearly his skills as a politician. He and his officials targeted the two men, both earls, who were seen as the most notorious usurpers of franchises during the reign of Henry III, the earls of Gloucester and Warenne. For both, special lists of their usurpations were drawn up and both suffered high-profile losses of franchises.[55] Gloucester lost a number of liberties in Kent and Dorset, while Warenne had the valuable franchise of return of writs in his towns of Stamford and Grantham confiscated.[56] Warenne's claim to the franchises had almost led to a military confrontation with the sheriff of Lincolnshire and the king's justification for recovering the franchise involved one of the neatest and most duplicitous pieces of legal footwork in the middle ages.[57] The king's prosecutor, the ubiquitous Thornton, successfully claimed that Edward himself had usurped the franchise from his father 'through the evil prompting of his bailiffs and the sheriff' before he had granted the towns to Warenne in 1263. Because he was now 'of a higher condition than he was before and is as if a different person', the king intended to regain the 'wrongfully alienated regalia

[53] *Placita de Quo Warranto*, ed. W. Illingworth (London: Record Commission, 1818), 303; Sutherland, *Quo Warranto*, 83.

[54] Crouch, *English Aristocracy*, 83.

[55] TNA E 163/2/30; JUST 1/1340.

[56] *Placita de Quo Warranto*, 183, 184–5, 337–41, 348–50, 739–40. A full list of Gloucester's losses is provided by Sutherland, *Quo Warranto*, 147n. Warenne's case is in *Placita de Quo Warranto*, 429–30.

[57] R.C. Palmer, *The County Courts of Medieval England, 1150–1350* (Princeton University Press, 1982), 265.

which belonged wholly to the crown'.[58] Warenne, then, had reason to feel aggrieved in this case, but this was the only major reverse he suffered during the proceedings; in dozens of other cases his claims were upheld, even when he justified them only by prescriptive right, and the same was true of Gloucester.[59] Set against the vast number of liberties these two earls held, their losses were very small beer indeed. Gloucester may have felt that he was being persecuted unduly, as he complained to parliament, but his losses were no more than a warning shot aimed not just at him but at the whole of political society.[60] Usurpations of royal liberties were no longer acceptable and even the highest in the land were not exempt. Such high-profile casualties undoubtedly deterred others from seeking any fresh usurpations and this was the greatest practical benefit that accrued to the crown from the campaign.[61] As a song popular among the magnates at the time put it, 'the writ of *quo warranto* / will give us all enough to do!'[62]

Edward recognised, however, that a policy that was too aggressive towards the earls would be likely to provide leadership from the very top of political society against a royal policy that was controversial and unpopular, particularly among magnates. If a great earl took up the banner of opposition, it would be much harder for the king to achieve his ends. Thus, the earls were, in general, treated with much greater leniency by the *quo warranto* pleaders and judges than were their non-titled neighbours. The large numbers of liberties claimed by the earls of Lancaster and Lincoln in Lancashire all seem to have been upheld; Lancaster's franchises were even increased as a result of the 1292 eyre.[63] In the Gloucestershire eyre of 1287, the earls of Gloucester and Warwick were largely excluded from the customary plea of the king's pleader, that franchises could not be claimed by prescriptive right. Similarly in Norfolk, the previous year, William of Gislingham regularly objected to all prescriptive claims except those of the earls of Norfolk and Warenne.[64] In general it seems as if the earls were given a great deal more slack than others when they claimed by prescriptive right, a fact illustrating the awareness on the part of the king's pleaders that they should not antagonise unduly their master's leading subjects. Edward's handling of this issue demonstrates his subtleness and skill as a politician. He killed conquest theory with kindness,

[58] Translation from *Stamford in the Thirteenth Century*, 76, 77.

[59] *Placita de Quo Warranto*, 191, 421, 429–30, 485, 498, 751.

[60] 'Edward I: Petition 1, Text and Translation', in *PROME*, item i–8.

[61] Prestwich, *Edward I*, 264. [62] *Guisborough*, 216.

[63] Prestwich, *Edward I*, 262; *The Pleas of Quo Warranto for the County of Lancashire*, ed. A. Cantle, Chetham Society 98 (1937), 121.

[64] Sutherland, *Quo Warranto*, 83.

but, as Gloucester and Warenne discovered, there was a mailed fist lurking beneath the velvet glove.

WAR

For kings associate such persons [earls] with themselves in governing the people of God, investing them with great honour, power and name when they gird them with swords … for the sword signifies the defence of the realm and the country.[65]

Bracton, *De Legibus Et Consuetudinibus Angliæ*

In a warlike society, the most natural companionship the earls could offer the king was on military campaign. Nobles were trained for war from the moment they could first sit on a horse and it was, above all else, prowess in warfare that defined them as a class.[66] Their very purpose was as '*bellatores*', those who fought, and the tripartite division was a very powerful idea of how society was constituted throughout the middle ages and beyond.[67]

Earls in particular had long been associated with the defence of the realm, as *Bracton* makes clear in the quotation above. The Norman kings had created earls sparingly and had positioned them in frontier areas like Kent, Cornwall, the far north and the Welsh Marches, where they took a prime role in the defence and expansion of the newly won kingdom.[68] Earls, barons and knights all held their land in chief by knight service and, though the practical implications of this had waned since the Conquest, the theory persisted, and ideas of military obligations to the crown by the nobility helped to create and sustain ideas of their function in society. The story of the earls and warfare in Edward I's reign is a curious one, marked as it was by great success on the king's part but also by significant failures in two important areas: paid service and overseas service.[69] It should be recognised, of course, that war offered all sorts of desirable things to the nobility, including companionship with the king, the chance to prove their valour on campaign and the prospect of booty and rewards from a grateful king. Indeed, one can probably say that what the nobility wanted most of all was a warrior king under whom they could fight.

65 *Bracton*, II, 32.

66 N. Orme, *Medieval Children* (New Haven, CT and London: Yale University Press, 2001), 181–2.

67 G. Duby, *The Chivalrous Society*, trans. C. Postan (London: Edward Arnold, 1977), 88–93; Adalbéron de Laon, *Poème au Roi Robert*, ed. C. Carozzi (Paris: Les Belle Lettres, 1979).

68 J.A. Green, *The Aristocracy of Anglo-Norman England* (Cambridge University Press, 1997), 268.

69 For detailed studies of the war service of the earls and of the political community more broadly, see A.M. Spencer, 'The Comital Military Retinue in the Reign of Edward I', *Historical Research*

Given all this, the extent of Edward I's success in obtaining military service from his earls, as revealed by Table 3.1, is not surprising. The earls were conspicuous in their support for his military designs, far more so than those further down the social scale, and the earls and their retinues formed the backbone of most royal armies of this period.[70] In the best-documented campaign of the reign, that of Falkirk in 1298, the names of 1,600 men-at-arms survive from a total contingent of around 2,400. Of these, 313, or just under one-fifth, appeared in comital retinues.[71] The earls and those they brought to the muster were thus important cogs in the Edwardian military machine but, more than this, the shared experience of campaigning undoubtedly served to foster ties of friendship and companionship both between the king and his earls and among the earls themselves. The contrast between Edward I's success in obtaining military service from his earls and Edward II's repeated failures to muster a full contingent of earls for his campaigns in Scotland in 1310 and 1314 is striking.[72]

A major part of the dignity of the earls lay in their right to command. They were not merely recruiters for the king, they were also his lieutenants in the field, with a right and duty to subordinate or separate command that others of less exalted title and status could not claim. Michael Prestwich suggests that Edward I may have preferred not to appoint earls to lead armies but the evidence does not seem to bear this out.[73] Edward did not exclude the earls from leadership positions; indeed earls were given military commands throughout the reign.[74] The earls of Lincoln, Warwick and Lancaster, for instance, all led independent detachments of royal forces in the First Welsh War of 1277, while in 1282–3 separate forces were headed by the earls of Lincoln, Warenne, Gloucester and

83 (2010), 45–59; A.M. Spencer, 'A Warlike People? Gentry Enthusiasm for Edward I's Scottish Campaigns, 1296–1307', in A. Bell and A. Curry (eds.), *England's Wars, 1272–1399: The Soldier Experience* (Woodbridge: Boydell and Brewer Press, 2011), 95–108.

[70] For the increasing reluctance of the gentry to serve in Scotland, see Spencer, 'Warlike People?'.

[71] J.E. Morris, *The Welsh Wars of Edward I* (Oxford: Clarendon Press, 1901), 288–92. Morris gives the number of comital lances as 221, but my own calculations give a somewhat higher figure, including as they do the retinue of Aymer de Valence, who, though he had not yet inherited the title of earl of Pembroke from his mother, was certainly of comital rank. Were the rolls complete, the number of men in comital retinues would undoubtedly be higher as there are several retinues, Lincoln's and Warwick's particularly, that appear from the records to be considerably under the strength that might be expected.

[72] Phillips, *Edward II*, 168–9, 227.

[73] M.C. Prestwich, *Armies and Warfare in the Middle Ages: the English Experience* (New Haven, CT and London: Yale University Press, 1996), 164–5.

[74] For a full survey of the command roles Edward I gave to his earls and full references to the following paragraph, see A.M. Spencer, 'The Earls in the Reign of Edward I, 1272–1307', unpublished PhD thesis, University of Cambridge (2009), 137–45.

Table 3.1 *Comital participation in Edward I's wars*

Earls	Death	No. of campaigns	Campaigns
Humphrey II de Bohun, earl of Hereford	1298	7	W 1277, W 1282–3, W 1287, W 1294–5, S 1296, S 1297–8, S 1298[a]
Humphrey III de Bohun, earl of Hereford	1322	4	S 1300, S 1301, S 1303–4, S 1306[b]
Gilbert de Clare, earl of Gloucester	1295	4	W 1277, W 1282–3, W 1287, W 1294–5[c]
Edmund, earl of Lancaster	1296	4	W 1277, W 1282–3, W 1294–5, G 1296[d]
Thomas, earl of Lancaster	1322	6	F 1297, S 1298, S 1300, S 1301, S 1303–4, S 1306[e]
Henry de Lacy, earl of Lincoln	1311	9	W 1277, W 1282–3, W 1294–5, G 1296–8, S 1298, S 1300, S 1301, S 1306, S 1307[f]
Earl John I de Warenne	1304	11	W 1277, W 1282–3, W 1287, W 1294–5, S 1296, S 1297, S 1297–8, S 1298, S 1300, S 1301, S 1303–4[g]
Earl John II de Warenne	1346	2	S 1306, S 1307[h]
Ralph de Monthermer, earl of Gloucester	1324	6	S 1297–8, S 1298, S 1300, S 1301, S 1303–4, S 1306[i]
Edmund, earl of Cornwall	1300	3	W 1277, W 1287, W 1294–5[j]
Roger Bigod, earl of Norfolk	1306	7	W 1277, W 1282–3, W 1287, W 1294–5, S 1296, S 1297–8, S 1298[k]
William Beauchamp, earl of Warwick	1298	6	W 1277, W 1282–3, W 1287, W 1294–5, S 1296, S 1297–8[l]
Guy Beauchamp, earl of Warwick	1315	8	W 1294–5, S 1296, F 1297, S 1298, S 1300, S 1301, S 1303–4, S 1306[m]
Richard Fitz Alan, earl of Arundel	1302	4	W 1294–5, S 1296, S 1297–8, S 1298[n]
William de Valence, earl of Pembroke	1296	3	W 1277, W 1282–3, W 1294–5[o]
Aymer de Valence, heir to the earldom of Pembroke	1324	7	F 1297, S 1298, S 1300, S 1301, S 1303–4, S 1306, S 1307[p]

Key: W – Wales; S – Scotland; F – Flanders; G – Gascony.

[a] Wales 1277, *CPR 1272–1281*, 179, 190; Wales 1282–3, Morris, *Welsh Wars*, 170–1; Wales 1287, *CPR 1281–1292*, 262, 271, 289; Wales 1294–5, *CAC*, 149; Scotland 1296, C 67/11, m. 1; Scotland 1297–8, *Gough*, 17, 18, 21, 22; Scotland 1298, *Gough*, 33, 34, 44, 46, 47, 49.

[b] Scotland 1300, TNA C 67/14, m. 8; Scotland 1301, C 67/14, m. 1; Scotland 1303–4, C 67/15, m. 13d; Scotland 1306, C 67/16, m. 6.

[c] Wales 1277, *CPR 1272–1281*, 208; Wales 1282–3, *CPR 1281–1292*, 15; Wales 1287, *CPR 1281–1292*, 271; Wales 1294–5, *CAC*, 150.

[d] Wales 1277, *CPR 1272–1281*, 199, 200; Wales 1282–3, *CAC*, 56; Wales 1294–5, *Calendar of Chancery Warrants 1244–1326* (London: HMSO, 1927), 57; Gascony 1296, *Rôles Gascons*, ed. C. Bémont, 3 vols. (Paris: Imprimerie Nationale, 1896–1906), III, no. 3912.

[e] Flanders 1297, TNA E 101/6/37, m. 8; Scotland 1298, *Gough*, 179–81; Scotland 1300, C 67/14, m. 15; Scotland 1301, C 67/14, m. 4; Scotland 1303–4, C 67/15, m. 11; Scotland 1306, C 67/16, m. 4.

[f] Wales 1277, *CPR 1272–1281*, 189, 190; Wales 1282–3, *CPR 1282–1292*, 13; Wales 1294–5, C 67/10, m. 1; Gascony 1296, *Rôles Gascons*, III, no. 3893; Scotland 1298, *Gough*, 33; Scotland 1300, C 67/14, m. 9; Scotland 1301, C 67/14, m. 2; Scotland 1306, C 67/16, m. 5; Scotland 1307, C 67/16, m. 1.

[g] Wales 1277, *CPR 1272–1281*, 222; Wales 1282–3, C 67/8, m. 3; Wales 1287, *CPR 1281–1292*, 272; Wales 1294–5, C 67/10, m. 1; Scotland 1296, C 67/11, m. 1; Scotland 1297, *Rotuli Scotiae, 1291–1377* (London: Record Commission, 1814), 47b; Scotland 1297–8; *Gough*, 12; Scotland 1298, *Gough*, 26; Scotland 1300, C 67/14, m. 8; Scotland 1301, C67/14, m. 1; Scotland 1303–4, C 67/15, m. 4.

[h] Scotland 1306, C 67/16, m. 5; Scotland 1307, C 67/16, m. 3.

[i] Scotland 1297–8, *Gough*, 17; Scotland 1298, *Gough*, 20; Scotland 1300, C 67/14, m. 10; Scotland 1301, C 67/14, m. 2; Scotland 1303–4, C 67/15, m. 6; Scotland 1306, C 67/16, m. 5.

[j] Wales 1277, *CPR 1272–1281*, 211; Wales 1287, *CPR 1281–1292*, 272–3; Wales 1294–5, Morris, *Welsh Wars*, 248.

[k] Wales 1277, *CPR 1272–1281*, 209; Wales 1282–3, C 67/8, m. 7; Wales 1287, *CPR 1281–1292*, 272; Wales 1294–5, C 67/10, m. 1; Scotland 1296, C 67/11, m. 1; Scotland 1297–8, *Gough*, 16; Scotland 1298, *Gough*, 25.

[l] Wales 1277, *CPR 1272–1281*, 189–92; Wales 1282–3, C 67/8, m. 7; Wales 1287, Morris, *Welsh Wars*, 210; Wales 1294–5, *CAC*, 142; Scotland 1296, C 67/11, m. 5; Scotland 1297–8, *Gough*, 17.

[m] Wales 1294–5, C 67/10, m. 5; Scotland 1296, C 67/11, m. 6; Flanders 1297, E 101/6/37, m. 7; Scotland 1298, *Gough*, 38, 41; Scotland 1300, C 67/14, m. 9; Scotland 1301, C 67/14, m. 2; Scotland 1303–4, C 67/15, m. 11; Scotland 1306, C 67/16, m. 4.

[n] Wales 1294–5, C 67/10, m. 1; Scotland 1296, *Royal Charter Witness Lists of Edward I*, nos. 24.13–10, 24.8; Scotland 1297–8, *Gough*, 17; Scotland 1298, *Gough*, 26.

[o] Wales 1277, Morris, *Welsh Wars*, 126; Wales 1282–3, ibid., 156, 167–9; Wales 1294–5, C 67/10, m. 1.

[p] Flanders 1297, E 101/6/28, m. 2; Scotland 1298, *Gough*, 216; Scotland 1300; C 67/14, m. 9; Scotland 1301, C 67/14, m. 2; Scotland 1303–4, C 67/15, m. 4; Scotland 1306, C 67/16, m. 4; Scotland 1307, C 67/16, m. 2.

William de Valence. In the 1290s and early 1300s, royal armies in Gascony were led by the earls of Lancaster and Lincoln, while in Scotland Earl Warenne, Aymer de Valence and the earl of Richmond all commanded royal armies in the king's absence.

Edward I clearly had no qualms in appointing earls to positions of military leadership. This is hardly surprising: the earls were the king's greatest subjects and his closest companions among the noble military elite; they brought with them the greatest number of troops to the muster and therefore had strong claims to positions of responsibility. It was expected that they should fill such positions. When offered the office of guardian of Scotland in August 1297 to replace Earl Warenne, Brian Fitz Alan of Bedale wrote to the king to say that 'I do not think that I in my poverty can be able either well or honourably to keep the land in peace to your profit and honour, when such a nobleman as the earl cannot well keep it in peace for what he receives from you'.[75] Fitz Alan presumed that such an office would be held by an earl, if only because no one other than an earl had the financial resources to take on such a responsibility.

Edward I's use of earls as military commanders, therefore, was entirely conventional and little different from their employment in the Hundred Years War. What was different was the quality of comital generalship available to Edward I, compared to that under Edward III and Henry V. There was no outstanding general among Edward I's earls, no Henry of Grosmont or Edmund Mortimer, no John, duke of Bedford or Richard Beauchamp. Although earls won several important victories in Edward I's reign, notably Maes Moydog, Dunbar and Methven, their record of generalship as a group was mixed. Gloucester was heavily defeated in 1282 when commanding in south Wales and was unable to put down Morgan ap Maredudd's revolt in 1294–5. Lincoln suffered defeats in Wales and Gascony in 1294 and 1297 respectively. Though the situation was undoubtedly difficult in Gascony, Lincoln only began to make any headway there once the main French army had departed.[76] Warenne's defeat at Stirling Bridge in 1297 was crushing, while his victory at Dunbar the year before was as much the result of Scottish ill-discipline as of good generalship.[77] Edmund of Lancaster, unlike his grandson Henry of Grosmont, was nothing more than competent, while Aymer de Valence failed to follow up his victory over Bruce at Methven in 1306 and Edward

[75] *Documents Illustrative of the History of Scotland*, ed. J. Stevenson, 2 vols. (Edinburgh: General Register Office, 1870), II, 223–4.

[76] Prestwich, *Edward I*, 385.

[77] For a detailed discussion of Warenne's generalship, see A.M. Spencer, 'John de Warenne, Guardian of Scotland, and the Battle of Stirling Bridge', in A. King and D. Simpkin (eds.), *England and Scotland at War, c.1296–c.1513* (Leiden and Boston: Brill, 2012).

clearly believed that Valence was being too cautious in his prosecution of the war.[78] The king's fears were realised when, in May 1307, Bruce routed Valence at Loudoun Hill.[79]

Two earls who may, perhaps, be considered as more than merely competent were William Beauchamp, earl of Warwick, and Humphrey de Bohun, earl of Hereford (d. 1298). In November 1276 Warwick was appointed captain of the Chester army, the most difficult command in the run-up to the first Welsh war because of its proximity to Gwynedd.[80] He was able to clear the Welsh from the western bank of the Dee, allowing Edward I a clear march on Flint with the main royal host in the summer.[81] Almost twenty years later, in the war of 1294–5, commanding a large force in mid-Wales, Warwick achieved a considerable victory over the rebel leader, Madog ap Llywelyn, at the Battle of Maes Moydog.[82] These achievements suggest that Warwick was a cut above the other earls in the conduct of war. Edward appears to have recognised this by appointing him to these two difficult and important commands in 1276 and 1294 and the value he placed on the earl's abilities can be inferred from the efforts he employed to detach Warwick from the opposition in 1297 and to get him to serve in Flanders.[83]

But while the king seems to have valued highly Warwick's abilities, the same cannot be said for his view of the undoubted military skills of Hereford. His abilities were evident from an early age. At the death of his father after Evesham, Bohun was only sixteen, and his lordship of Brecon was under threat from three powerful rivals, Llywelyn ap Gruffydd, Roger Mortimer and the earl of Gloucester. They fought over Brecon, Llywelyn having much the best of it.[84] Bohun came of age in 1270 and, with the outbreak of renewed fighting between Llywelyn and Gloucester in 1271, he saw his chance to regain his inheritance and began to chip away at Llywelyn's position in Brecon.[85] Combining with Roger Mortimer, Bohun seems to have prevented further encroachment by Llywelyn, and he seized the opportunity of the war of 1277, by which time he had succeeded his grandfather as earl of Hereford, to complete his re-conquest of Brecon.[86] In 1282, he dealt quickly with the rebellion in Brecon before extending his activities into Cantref Bychan, conquering the commote of Iscennen, which later, much to Hereford's chagrin, Edward granted to

78 *Calendar of Documents Relating to Scotland*, ed. J. Bain, 4 vols. (Edinburgh: General Register Office, 1881–5), II, nos. 1895–6.

79 Prestwich, *Edward I*, 510.

80 *CPR 1272–1281*, 171.

81 Morris, *Welsh Wars*, 119.

82 Prestwich, *Edward I*, 221, 223.

83 J.H. Denton, 'The Crisis of 1297 from the Evesham Chronicle', *EHR* 93 (1978), 576.

84 Jones, 'Bohun Earls', 86–7.

85 Ibid., 88.

86 *CAC*, 10–11, 57–8, 109–10; Jones, 'Bohun Earls', 89, 94.

John Giffard.[87] In 1287 he defended the lands in his custody without the need for reinforcements from paid troops, while in 1294–5 he achieved 'striking victories in the south-east', acting under his own auspices rather than holding any royal command.[88] Through long experience Hereford had become an expert in the type of warfare needed in Wales but he does not seem to have been given major responsibilities by the king. Perhaps this was because his position as constable meant that, if possible, he wished to serve with the king in person, or perhaps it was because the situation in Brecon so often needed his personal attention. Whatever the reason may have been, Edward appears to have under-used one of his most militarily talented earls.

This was a minor failure on Edward's part; more significant was his failure to obtain the wholehearted support of the earls for two important aspects of his military policies. In both these areas, paid service and service overseas, Edward glimpsed the future but was unable to persuade his earls, and others, to go there. His defeat over paid service was more comprehensive but, as shall be seen, less important than that over service abroad. Edward tried to change the nature of the nobility's obligation to provide military service to the crown, and to place it on terms more convenient to the crown. In doing so, he met stubborn resistance, a resistance only finally overcome in the two decades after his death. That Edward was treading on sensitive toes in attempting to change the terms of military obligation to the crown is illustrated by the famous 'rusty sword' story of Earl Warenne. As Warenne was reputed to have told the *quo warranto* justices in the outburst referred to already in a different context, Duke William had not 'conquer[ed] and subject[ed] this land by himself, but our ancestors were with him as partners and co-workers'.[89] The nobility had been the Conqueror's partners in warfare and their status and position in society flowed from their participation in that joint venture. They were very conscious of their dignity and would prove suspicious of any attempt to change or undermine their status. Dignity was leavened with an eye for profit, however, because unpaid feudal service allowed tenants-in-chief to collect scutage payments of their own, which could prove very lucrative. The earl of Lincoln, for example, collected over £125 in scutage from the honour of Pontefract alone following the Caerlaverock campaign of 1300.[90]

Their attitude, dignity and profit conflicted with the needs of Edward I and was the latest manifestation of an old problem of how kings recruited

[87] Jones, 'Bohun Earls', 97–8. [88] Ibid., 100; Davies, *Conquest*, 383.
[89] *Guisborough*, 216n. See above, 73. [90] Prestwich, *War, Politics and Finance*, 82.

and financed armies.[91] The Anglo-Norman and Angevin kings had long depended on paid knights and mercenaries but the forces of the earls and barons, vital to any royal army, remained outside this arrangement.[92] The advantages of a fully contracted force over a hybrid one, part in royal pay and part raised by a traditional feudal levy, are obvious. An army whose size, structure and length of service could be predicted and regulated offered strategic and logistical advantages over a mixed army.[93] Edward sought to create just such a force at the opening of the Second Welsh War and the first clash of his reign over pay erupted at a military council at Devizes in April 1282. During the campaign of 1277 in Wales, two earls, Lincoln and Warwick, had taken royal pay as commanders of detachments independent from the main royal army, but those earls who had been with Edward personally had not taken pay.[94] The campaign in 1277 had been essentially a large-scale punitive expedition designed to bring Llywelyn to heel, force him to pay homage and to undo the Treaty of Montgomery, which had been negotiated a decade before from a position of Welsh strength and English weakness. In the war of 1282–3 Edward's plans were very different. A campaign of conquest was what he had in mind and to effect this he wished to raise an army that would be entirely in his pay.

For the earls, however, things were not so simple. They saw military service *with* the king, rather than simply *for* the king, as their right as well as their duty. To take pay would have been to reduce their status: they were the king's 'partners', to use Warenne's reputed word, not his hired muscle. Edward underestimated the strength of their objections and found himself forced to back down to secure their continued support. The following month he issued a traditional summons that made no mention of pay.[95] There the matter rested for the remainder of Edward I's reign. Henceforth the earls took pay under exceptional circumstances only, and no earl took pay for a summer campaign in Britain.[96] Edward I's attempts to introduce novel recruiting techniques in both 1297 and 1300 met stern resistance and he fell back on older methods in the final years of his

91 For an overview of this problem, see M. Powicke, *Military Obligation in Medieval England: a Study in Liberty and Duty* (Oxford: Clarendon Press, 1962).

92 M. Chibnall, 'Mercenaries and the *Familia Regis* under Henry I', *History* 62 (1977), 15–23; J.O. Prestwich, 'The Military Household of the Norman Kings', *EHR* 96 (1981), 1–35; Crouch, *English Aristocracy*, 27.

93 A. Ayton, *Knights and Warhorses: Military Service and the English Aristocracy under Edward III* (Woodbridge: Boydell and Brewer Press, 1994), 89.

94 Prestwich, *War, Politics and Finance*, 71–2.

95 Morris, *Welsh Wars*, 75; Prestwich, *War, Politics and Finance*, 72.

96 The exceptional occasions include fighting in Gascony and the winter campaign in 1297–8 after the disaster of Stirling Bridge. Prestwich, *War, Politics and Finance*, 73; Prestwich, *Armies*, 91, 98.

reign.[97] Where the earls led, the baronage largely followed: at Falkirk, 62 out of 110 bannerets were not paid, while in 1300, 64 out of 87 served at their own expense.[98]

But, while the earls and most of the barons refused to take royal pay, these figures show that Edward had managed to persuade a portion of his tenants-in-chief to accept royal pay, and his idea of a fully paid and contracted royal army was eventually to come to fruition under Edward III with profound consequences for English military power. Some earls held out against accepting royal pay during Edward II's reign, including the last Clare earl of Gloucester, Thomas of Lancaster and, surprisingly, Piers Gaveston, but they were a dwindling band and, thanks to the scale of their wealth, an unrepresentative one. The other earls all took royal pay at some point during Edward II's reign. The catalyst for change is likely to have been the shift in the nature of the Scottish war, from an offensive war, with the opportunity for plunder, ransoms and new lands, to a defensive one that involved little profit and glory and even the prospect of capture. Unpaid service was expensive, even supremely wealthy earls like Gloucester and Lancaster under Edward II found it necessary to look beyond their own resources to finance unpaid service, and it must have seemed counter-productive to hold out against royal pay unless, like Lancaster, taking the king's shilling was a political impossibility.[99] The political circumstances of Edward II's reign also led to the use, by the king, of contracts to bind the nobility to the crown. Contracts had been used by Edward I's regency council in the winter of 1297 as an emergency measure to raise troops to defend the north from a Scottish invasion in the wake of Stirling Bridge and there are similar isolated examples from early in Edward II's reign. In 1316, however, in response to the permanent military might of Thomas of Lancaster's affinity, the king adopted an indenture policy of his own, contracting with several key magnates in a way similar to the one by which they recruited their own followers.[100] Edward III adopted this method and in 1337 it was applied for the first time to the recruitment of an entire army.[101] Even before then, by the Weardale campaign of 1327, 'virtually the whole cavalry force, save for the feudal contingents who were making their last appearance in an English army, were paid. The situation had been transformed since

[97] M.C. Prestwich, 'Cavalry Service in Early Fourteenth Century England', in J. Gillingham and J.C. Holt (eds.), *War and Government in the Middle Ages: Essays in Honour of J. O. Prestwich* (Woodbridge: Boydell and Brewer Press, 1984), 151–2.

[98] Prestwich, *Armies*, 98. [99] Prestwich, 'Cavalry Service', 152–3.

[100] Ibid., 156–7; Phillips, *Aymer de Valence*, 148–50, 312–15.

[101] N.B. Lewis, 'The Recruitment and Organisation of a Contract Army, May to November 1337', *BIHR* 37 (1964), 1–19; Prestwich, 'Cavalry Service', 157.

1300'.[102] Edward I may have been unable to solve the age-old problem of the English crown in recruiting its armies but he had at least seen the solution and made some progress towards achieving it. He failed, however, to realise or overcome the resistance such a solution would face from his nobility. This represented a marked change in the philosophical position of the nobility vis-à-vis the crown. The children and grandchildren of those at Devizes in 1282 accepted what they could not: that they would serve the king in war at his terms and for his money. This subtly changed the nature of the relationship between crown and nobility, drawing them closer to each other and integrating the nobility more closely into the military apparatus of the crown.

Edward I's failure to persuade his earls and the rest of the military elite to accept royal pay caused him political and military problems as he tried to find other means of recruiting armies but, with the exception of the period of political crisis between 1299 and 1301, it did not hamper unduly his ability to wage war within Britain.[103] Of greater significance to the overall conduct of the war in the mid-to-late 1290s was his failure to gain widespread commitment from his earls and others to the war against France. The reluctance of English landholders to serve overseas was long-standing and had only intensified following the separation of England and Normandy in 1204, which broke the landed link that many of the most important landholders in England had retained during the twelfth century. While the kings of England still had extensive lands in France, these were no longer in areas where English lords also had lands, and Henry III found it difficult after 1230 to persuade his English subjects of the merits of trying to defend the remaining lands, let alone win back those lost under John.[104]

On the outbreak of war with France, Edward was not without some success in persuading the earls of the merits of serving overseas. Many were considerably more enthusiastic about such service than those further down the social scale and, had Edward been able to launch a full-scale invasion of Gascony in 1294, as was his intention, there seems little doubt that most of the earls would have been with him.[105] Poor weather in the summer of 1294 and news of the Welsh rebellion in early autumn 1294 put paid to that plan, however, and by the autumn of 1295 Edward had to resort to one of his most naked displays of power to persuade the earl of Arundel and several minor barons to reinforce the small English

[102] Prestwich, 'Cavalry Service', 157. [103] See below, 246–7.

[104] Powicke, *Military Obligation*, chapters 4 and 5. For the difficulties Henry had in 1242, see Stacey, *Politics, Policy and Royal Finance*, 170, 185–6, 190–3.

[105] See below, 228–9; Morris, *GTK*, 270–1.

army in Gascony by threatening to foreclose on their debts.[106] Two earls, Lancaster and Lincoln, did lead the main English relief force to Gascony at the beginning of 1296. However, Edward's reliance on compulsion at the Salisbury parliament of February 1297 failed to persuade the earl of Norfolk or the other nobles gathered there of his plans for them to form a relief force for the embattled Anglo-Gascon forces in the duchy, while he himself led another force to Flanders to pressurise Philip IV on his vulnerable north-eastern border.[107] The king had some success in recruiting comital and Marcher support for the Flanders campaign but, by the summer of 1297, the earls of Norfolk and Hereford were in open opposition both to the king's strategy and to his attempts to force overseas service where no obligation existed.[108]

Thus, though Edward was able to obtain some comital support for overseas service, it was only achieved with the greatest difficulty and through authoritarian techniques that ultimately proved as much trouble as they were worth. In this, at least, Edward's methods of man management failed him and it was not until Edward III asserted his claim to the French throne in 1340 that it became easier for the king of England to persuade both his high nobility and the political community more broadly of the necessity of overseas service.[109] In Edward I's reign the attitude of the nobility towards the king's foreign war was summed up in the chronicle of Pierre Langtoft when he records their response to the news of Philip's confiscation of Gascony. Langtoft puts a fine bellicose speech into the mouth of Bishop Bek of Durham: 'If thou [Edward] wilt recover thy land of Gascony … bestir yourself, sleep not like a monk; put on the hauberks, trample down the carrion, mount the steeds, and take spear in fist.'[110] In addition to this, Bek urged the king to seek support from European allies against the French. The barons, Langtoft says, wholeheartedly agreed with this last sentiment.

> Send messengers to the king of Germany, and write by letter to the king of the Aragonese, and to all the others who are before named; bind yourself to live and to die together. If thou wilt succeed, spare no money. So great force and power has the king of France, that thou hast no other way of recovering thy fees.[111]

In sum, the attitude of the late-thirteenth-century English political community to war in France could easily have been that of the stereotypical British parliamentarians in the eighteenth and early nineteenth centuries: pay the Germans to fight the French for us!

[106] Fryde, 'Magnate Debts', 262–6. [107] See below, 235; *Guisborough*, 289–90.
[108] See below, 241. [109] Harriss, *King, Parliament, and Public Finance*, 318–19.
[110] *Langtoft*, II, 203. [111] Ibid., 205.

REWARD

And when [the king's subjects] are assembled together, they will say to one another: 'Behold, this noble lord, to whom we have offered our service, has conferred gifts upon us from his largesse and has shown courteous regard for our labours; for he has liberally given his gifts to us according to what we deserve.'[112]

Walter of Milemete, *On the Nobility, Wisdom and Prudence of Kings*, *c.*1327

Participation in the king's wars offered the earls the prospect of gain. Such gain could come in the form of plunder or ransoms but it was also expected that a wise king would reward the good service of his lords. Such service need not have been performed only in war and patronage was often bestowed as a sign of the king's favour and friendship. The study of patronage from this latter perspective has become a central preoccupation for many late medievalists.[113] It has indeed often been assumed by some historians that loyalty was up for sale to the highest bidder. Such a view is best summed up by J.R. Lander, who wrote that 'strengthening the peerage with loyal adherents had become a major means of buying support in periods of tension and crisis'.[114] It has begun to be applied to the thirteenth century as well, and many of Henry III's difficulties have been seen as stemming from the failure of his patronage policies.[115]

The need for a monarch to exercise patronage was well established among medieval political theorists. John of Salisbury, in the middle of the twelfth century, wrote that a ruler should 'provide for his advisors in order that they do not need', and that all office holders should 'be recompensed to a sufficient extent'.[116] Walter of Milemete, quoted above, writing almost two centuries later, claimed that 'it is extremely necessary for the king to be liberal; for royal liberality is the preparatory cause of a good regime and triumphant success'.[117] Milemete, however, made it plain that 'liberality' was a middle course that a successful king needed to steer between the two vices of prodigality and avarice. Moreover, it was essential that patronage was given to the right sort of person; a 'lord

[112] Milemete, 'Nobility', 38.

[113] Much of this section is reproduced in a fuller form in A.M. Spencer, 'Royal Patronage and the Earls in the Reign of Edward I', *History* 93 (2008), 20–46.

[114] J.R. Lander, *Government and Community: England 1450–1509* (London: Edward Arnold Press, 1980), 43.

[115] H.W. Ridgeway, 'Foreign Favourites and Henry III's Problems of Patronage, 1247–1258', *EHR* 104 (1989), 590–610.

[116] John of Salisbury, *Policraticus: of the Frivolities of Courtiers and the Footprints of Philosophers*, ed. and trans. C.J. Nederman (Cambridge University Press, 1990), 84.

[117] Milemete, 'Nobility', 53.

of illustrious liberty ... rewards the well-deserving; it assists the worthy and the needy'.[118] For Milemete, patronage was something merited; in other words, it was purchased by loyal service rather than being used to obtain service.

In recent years the idea that liberal use of royal patronage was essential to make government work has come under fire from some historians, led by Christine Carpenter and Edward Powell, who have sought to promote the contemporary idea that patronage was used as a reward for good service.[119] Under such an interpretation, Henry III's 'cheque-book kingship' was always bound to fail.[120] Conflict was inevitable when a king who survived by making lavish grants to his supporters and relatives eventually ran out of money. Moreover, kings did not need to buy a loyalty that they already had. Despite this reinterpretation of how patronage ought to work, Edward I retains a reputation for meanness. As with seemingly so much else, it was the judgement of McFarlane that has been most influential in sealing Edward's parsimonious reputation. In McFarlane's eyes, Edward committed the cardinal error in not even rewarding service: 'lifelong and devoted service was too often inadequately rewarded.' His lordship was exacting rather than 'good', showing that he had 'no great belief in the virtues of largesse'.[121] Michael Prestwich, believing patronage to be a necessary part of good governance, has since argued that Edward did grease the wheels of government with patronage but that his use of it was essentially 'limited'.[122] Elsewhere in his writings, Prestwich characterises Edward as 'ungenerous', stating that he 'did not use the techniques of persuasion and patronage with any real ease: his preferred style was one of confrontation and compulsion'.[123] Other historians have taken this up with gusto, and parsimony is one of the defining historiographical characteristics of Edward I.[124] Individual acts of generosity by the king are met with surprise by historians.[125] The evidence available, however, suggests that Edward was more generous than his reputation allows but, more importantly, that he handled patronage in a way that was very

[118] Ibid., 54.

[119] E. Powell, 'After "After McFarlane": the Poverty of Patronage and the Case for Constitutional History', in D.J. Clayton, R.G. Davies and P. McNiven (eds.), *Trade, Devotion, and Governance: Papers in Later Medieval History* (Stroud: Sutton Press, 1994); Carpenter, *Wars of the Roses*, 43–4.

[120] A phrase used by Professor Christine Carpenter in her undergraduate lectures at the University of Cambridge.

[121] McFarlane, *Nobility*, 267.

[122] M.C. Prestwich, 'Royal Patronage under Edward I', *TCE* 1 (1986), 42, 43, 50, 52.

[123] M.C. Prestwich, *The Three Edwards: War and State in England, 1272–1377* (London: Methuen Press, 1980), 146; Prestwich, *Edward I*, 562.

[124] See, for example, Tuck, *Crown and Nobility*, 48; D.A. Carpenter, *The Struggle for Mastery: Britain, 1066–1284* (London: Penguin, 2003), 476.

[125] Given-Wilson, 'Wealth and Credit', 2.

much in line with contemporary expectations in that patronage was a reward not an inducement for good service.

Edward was able to use the techniques of minor patronage with skill.[126] He was generous with grants of deer from the royal forest and particularly so with paid-for privileges such as charters of free warren, for which his annual number of grants outstripped both Henry III and Edward II. Thus, he was able to reward good service while keeping the cost to the crown at a minimum. Minor patronage was all very well, of course, but what about the greatest prize of royal patronage, permanent grants of land? In emphasising what he sees as the limited nature of Edward I's generosity, Prestwich has pointed to the king's failure to make substantial grants of land in England outside the royal family.[127] Such a view, however, has two important flaws. First, the relative tranquillity of Edward I's reign meant that there simply was not the same volume of confiscated rebel lands that there was in most medieval reigns. Second, the lack of readily available lands through confiscation meant that the only other source of land available to the king was the royal demesne, and the permanent alienation of this was out of the question. Indeed, Edward spent much of his reign trying to build up royal estates rather than give them away. At his coronation, Edward swore, as well as the traditional oath, an additional oath to preserve the rights of the crown. More than this, though, the Hagnaby Chronicle reported that when Archbishop Kilwardby placed the crown on his head, Edward immediately removed it, saying that he would not wear it again until he had recovered all the lands his father had granted away.[128] In this atmosphere, it was clearly not in Edward's mind to make widespread grants from the royal demesne. Edward went further, adding considerably to the crown's resources.[129] The growing royal family in the last years of the reign made a pressing need to provide a patrimony for them, something he had explicitly promised King Philip of France when marrying his sister.[130]

Prestwich acknowledges these constraints on the king and yet he sees this 'policy' of retaining lands in crown hands as 'a severe restraint upon his exercise of patronage'.[131] It can be argued, however, that, as the new work on late medieval patronage implies, Edward's magnates did not in the normal course of events expect or even want him to make extensive grants of land in England. The baronial case presented to Louis IX in 1264 complained that Henry III had 'almost completely exhausted' the

[126] For this paragraph, see Spencer, 'Royal Patronage', 26–31.

[127] Prestwich, 'Royal Patronage', 42–4.

[128] Prestwich, *Edward I*, 91.

[129] McFarlane, *Nobility*, 257–8, 262, 265; for the acquisition of the earldom of Norfolk, see also Morris, 'Murder'.

[130] McFarlane, *Nobility*, 264. See above, 43.

[131] Prestwich, 'Royal Patronage', 46.

royal demesne through his prodigality, while the Ordinances of 1311 forbade the king to make any grants involving land without the permission of the Ordainers.[132] Given these circumstances, it would hardly have been politic for Edward I to make widespread permanent grants of royal lands in England, even had he wanted to do so, especially when, as his reign progressed, he was increasingly calling upon the financial resources of his subjects through taxation to pay for his wars.

Fortunately for Edward, his military successes in Wales and Scotland brought many new lands into his hands and the earls benefited considerably from Edward's patronage in both Wales and Scotland. Two of the biggest winners from the Welsh wars were the earl of Lincoln and Earl Warenne, for whom Edward created valuable new Marcher lordships in the north-east of the country. On the other hand, Prestwich has suggested that the earls of Gloucester, Hereford and Pembroke 'may well have felt that [they] deserved more from Edward' in return for their war service in Wales.[133] Gloucester's service, however, was hardly of the highest quality, while Hereford spent most of the wars of 1277 and 1282–3 securing control over his own lordship of Brecon and played little part in the wider royal campaign.[134] Hereford, however, does appear to have had a legitimate grievance concerning his conquest of Iscennen.[135] Edward I granted the territory to John Giffard, who was the commander of the English forces at Irfon Bridge where Llywelyn was killed, and this illustrates his attitude towards grants of land in Wales. Men like Warenne, Lincoln, Giffard and the Mortimers, who had served the king to great effect, were rewarded in like manner, while others who had, for the most part, done only their duty were not given permanent rewards of land. Edward did spread his generosity wider in Scotland than he had in Wales. Just over forty barons, including five earls, obtained grants of land there, though most of these proved difficult to realise or hold on to.[136]

As a group, then, the earls did rather better out of Edward's major patronage than has been suggested. While McFarlane demonstrated how eight comital families underwent or were threatened with a 'course of slimming' in Edward I's reign, only four of those families can actually be said to have suffered material loss at Edward's hands.[137] Seven comital

[132] *EHD 1189–1327*, 527–8; *Documents of the Baronial Movement of Reform and Rebellion, 1258–1267*, eds. and trans. R.F. Treharne and I.J. Sanders (Oxford University Press, 1972), 277.

[133] Prestwich, *Edward I*, 204.

[134] See above, 80–2. Morris, *Welsh Wars*, 166–7; Altschul, *Baronial Family*, 139–40; Jones, 'Bohun Earls', 94, 97.

[135] Morris, *Welsh Wars*, 222–3.

[136] D.A. Barrie, 'The *Maiores Barones* in the Second Half of the Reign of Edward I, 1290–1307', unpublished PhD thesis, University of St Andrews (1991), 298.

[137] McFarlane, *Nobility*, 253. Those earldoms were Ferrers, Bigod, Fors and Redvers.

families, on the other hand, benefited directly from land grants by the king. Lincoln was granted extensive lands in both Wales and Scotland, although in the latter case they were exchanged for wardships;[138] Warenne got Bromfield and Yale in north-east Wales; John of Brittany, earl of Richmond, was given £1,000-worth of lands in England;[139] Aymer de Valence was granted the barony of Bothwell in Scotland;[140] Guy Beauchamp, earl of Warwick, gained the valuable lordship of Barnard Castle in Co. Durham;[141] the king's son-in-law, the younger earl of Hereford, was given Robert Bruce's chief lordship of Annandale following Bruce's rebellion in 1306, a lordship that he was able to gain possession of for a while at least.[142] In addition to these grants it should also be added that Edmund of Lancaster benefited from Edward's benevolent indulgence of the fraud perpetrated on Robert de Ferrers. Most of the English earldoms, then, had profited materially from Edward; not a bad return for a king whose patronage has been seen as 'limited'. While grants in Scotland proved not to be lasting, the majority of these comital families were permanently enriched by these royal grants. This was not the behaviour of a king who, in McFarlane's words, 'showed no great belief in the virtues of largesse'.[143] Crucially, however, Edward I's largesse had to be earned through good service, in contrast to what happened under both Henry III and Edward II when, too often, the recipients of lavish royal patronage were, in the eyes of the political community, unworthy of the honours bestowed upon them.

The third and final area of patronage is 'negative' patronage: alleviating difficulties rather than adding to resources. The principal method for this was the remission of debts owed to the crown. Manipulation of magnate debts to the crown had a long history and had reached a peak under King John but, as his reign showed, such manipulation could become very dangerous if mishandled.[144] Edward I was clearly well aware of the potential hold over noble families that debts gave him and he was not afraid, on occasion, to tighten that hold to obtain what he wanted.[145] His policy towards the debts of his magnates has been contrasted unfavourably with that of Edward III, who cancelled many debts during the Scottish wars of the 1330s.[146] But this focuses too narrowly on specific incidents in Edward I's reign and ignores both Edward I's general policy towards debts and a series of cancellations of comital debts from 1294 onwards. Strict levels of repayment were sometimes applied, such as the £100 a

138 Davies, *Conquest*, 363; *CCR 1302–1307*, 481.
139 Prestwich, 'Royal Patronage', 43–4.
140 *Calendar of Documents Relating to Scotland*, II, 308.
141 *CChR*, III, 79.
142 Ibid., 66; TNA DL 25/92, 1451, 1994; TNA DL 27/42.
143 McFarlane, *Nobility*, 267.
144 Holt, *Magna Carta*, 109–10, 190–2.
145 Prestwich, *Edward I*, 384.
146 Fryde, 'Magnate Debts'.

year demanded from the earl of Norfolk in 1276, but there are far more numerous instances of lower levels of repayment being set, such as the £10 a year, also in 1276, expected from the earl of Warwick to settle his debts.[147] With respect to comital debts, historians have preferred to highlight the tensions evident between the king and the earls of Arundel and Norfolk over their debts, rather than such calculated acts of generosity towards the debts of his earls.[148] Between 1294 and the end of the reign, moreover, six earls received full remission of all their debts, a remarkable series of grants that has gone almost completely unnoticed. In 1294, Edward pardoned all the debts of the earl of Lincoln, perhaps as part of the marriage settlement of his daughter and Edward's nephew, Thomas of Lancaster.[149] Thomas himself was the beneficiary of a similar full pardon in 1306 and a third earl, John II de Warenne, also obtained total remission of his family's debts the following year.[150] Warenne's brother-in-law, Edmund Fitz Alan, the new earl of Arundel, also had all his debts cancelled in April 1307.[151] Between them, the debts of these two earls totalled an impressive £9,937 10*s* 3¼*d*, and their cancellation amounts to a significant act of generosity by an elderly king towards two young earls entering into inheritances long encumbered by debts to the crown. In 1305, three years after their initial deal, Edward pardoned the earl of Norfolk all his remaining debts, while the Anglo-Irish earl, Richard de Burgh of Ulster, who acted as one of the king's chief negotiators for the settlement of Scotland in 1304, was another who was given full remission of all his debts, totalling over £11,600, a staggering sum.[152]

It might be argued that all these remissions are a sign that Edward was on the defensive from 1294 but all were undertaken at times of royal strength with regard to the individual men concerned. It is significant that two of the six earls granted full debt relief, Arundel and Norfolk, have been regarded as targets of Edward's authoritarianism in the context of the issue of debt management.[153] In their different ways, Edward's handling of these two debts displays a political subtlety at odds with this commonplace image. Norfolk had been involved in a long-running dispute with the exchequer over the magnitude of his debts and in early 1305 the exchequer officials had once again raised his liability, from £710 to £1,812.[154] At this point, Edward intervened and pardoned all Norfolk's remaining debts, in return for his 'laudable

[147] *CFR 1272–1307*, 75; *CPR 1272–1281*, 176.
[148] Fryde, 'Magnate Debts', 264–5; Prestwich, *Edward I*, 413–14.
[149] *CPR 1292–1301*, 72. [150] *CPR 1301–1307*, 468, 492. [151] Ibid., 521.
[152] *CPR 1301–1307*, 317, 256; J.S. Hamilton, *Piers Gaveston, Earl of Cornwall, 1307–1312: Politics and Patronage in the Reign of Edward II* (Detroit, MI: Wayne State University Press, 1988), 56.
[153] Fryde, 'Magnate Debts', 258–60, 263–5. [154] Morris, *Bigod Earls*, 181.

service … up to this point'.[155] Edward, aware that Norfolk's debt had long been an issue of friction between the two of them, anxious not to re-open old wounds between himself and the earl and aware that following Norfolk's death and the reversion of his estates to the crown the debt would disappear anyway, dealt with the issue once and for all to the satisfaction of everyone, except perhaps the exchequer officials. In the case of young Edmund Fitz Alan, Edward had been well aware of his father's financial difficulties and may have decided that, in order better to facilitate service from the new earl, it would be best to remove the encumbrance of debt.[156]

Edward I's use of patronage in relation to his earls, then, should be seen in an altogether different light from before. It was not limited but judicious and targeted; based above all on the contemporary principle of service. Edward, like medieval writers on the subject, saw patronage as a reward for service or as a means of better enabling future service, rather than as a means to buy the support of his magnates. Aside from a political complaint by the earls of Norfolk and Hereford about distribution of the spoils after the Battle of Falkirk in 1298, there is no other contemporary evidence that the earls and greater magnates themselves felt that they had received a poor deal from the king.[157] Many earldoms, in fact, came out of the reign significantly better off than at the start, thanks to Edward's patronage. It might properly be suggested that Edward I, unlike his father and son, had succeeded in steering the middle course between prodigality and avarice that Walter of Milemete believed was the hallmark of true 'liberality'.

CONCLUSION

It is all too easy to be persuaded by the great set-pieces of Edwardian masterfulness that this was a king who knew only one method of kingship. Such episodes hint at a king who was the apotheosis of Angevin authoritarianism and who, to quote McFarlane's words again, 'belonged less to the future than to the past'.[158] What this part has attempted to do is to show that such a picture of Edward is crudely unrealistic. No successful king could rely so heavily upon compulsion and confrontation to achieve his aims. Edward had other, more subtle, weapons in his armoury. Masterfulness was certainly one of the political tactics he employed but this was blended with other, less eye-catching, but equally effective methods, through which he was able, for the most part, to obtain the political

[155] TNA E 159/78, m. 14d. [156] *Documents Illustrating the Crisis of 1297–8*, 6, 30, 141–2.

[157] Prestwich, *Edward I*, 482–3.

[158] McFarlane, *Nobility*, 267. See above for first use of this quotation, 3.

support of his earls. A king who was able to avoid armed rebellion from his English subjects for his entire reign did not confuse the tactic of being overbearing, one used on occasion by almost all kings, for a strategy of kingship. It may be hoped that the word 'masterfulness' is used less often in future discussions of Edward's kingship.

There is a danger, of course, of going too far the other way, of glossing over Edward's mistakes and presenting too rosy a picture of his kingship with regard to his earls. Edward's political management was far from flawless: he overplayed his hand on occasions, which alienated individual earls like Gloucester in 1292 and Norfolk in 1297. Too often he was unable to appreciate any point of view but his own, particularly from 1294 onwards. He disliked counsel with which he did not agree and he proved incapable of solving the ancient problems of recruiting armies and getting them to serve overseas. Edward's particular blend of masterfulness and political management did not always taste sweet to his greatest subjects. Even so, most of the time they had few complaints to make.

Edward's success came in large measure from being so conventional. Unlike Henry III, with his unusually ostentatious piety, or Edward II and his rustic country pursuits, Edward I was an uncomplicated man whose pleasures fitted well with those of his nobility: war and the pastimes used in its imitation, hunting, falconry and tourneying, were precisely the sort of things his earls liked to do.[159] But, while he shared their interests and was able to understand their concerns, he also recognised that a king was a man apart from his nobles. As Edward's lawyer, Gilbert de Thornton, put it during a *quo warranto* case, upon acceding to the throne the king became 'of a higher condition than he was before and is as if a different person'.[160] Edward's conviction of this truth enabled him to rise above his nobles, to adjudicate between them and to keep his court free of the partisan infighting that crippled the kingships of both Henry III and Edward II.

In his conventionality and in his recognition of the importance of relative impartiality, Edward I resembled strongly the man, and king, his grandson Edward III would become. In his recent biography of Edward III, Mark Ormrod, acknowledging the impact of recent scholarship on that king's relations with his nobility, writes that 'the king's fabled indulgence of the nobility was in fact highly conditional in nature, imposing a heavy moral obligation on the elite to give unstinting respect, loyalty and service to the crown'.[161] Such a view of the nobility's relationship with the crown in the reign of Edward III can be said even

[159] Prestwich, *Edward I*, 115–17. [160] *Stamford in the Thirteenth Century*, 76.

[161] W.M. Ormrod, *Edward III* (New Haven, CT and London: Yale University Press, 2011), 597–8.

more strongly of Edward I's attitude towards his nobles. Nor should this be surprising. Edward III had a special reverence for his grandfather's memory and achievements and, in many ways, modelled his kingship upon him. Edward I was 'the focus of Edward III's family piety'.[162] At Edward III's coronation, Edward I's tomb was covered with cloth of gold, something repeated in 1353 when the king and his sons held a special mass in Westminster Abbey. Throughout his reign, Edward III observed Edward I's obit, 7 July, at his court, even when he was fighting in Scotland and France. In 1359 the king gave up his intention to be buried in Cologne, preferring, according to John of Reading, to be laid to rest near Edward I, 'that most illustrious and courageous soldier, and the most prudent statesman'.[163] By such actions Edward III was deliberately associating himself with his predecessor. His style of kingship was not new. Rather, it called vividly upon the memory of an earlier time. Both Edwards were able to use the characteristics of the 'disciplinarian' and the 'enabler' to create their blend of strong and successful kingship.[164] Edward I was thus, in many ways, the model on which McFarlane's vision of the 'future' was based.

[162] For this and much of the following paragraph, see W.M. Ormrod, 'The Personal Religion of Edward III', *Speculum* 64 (1989), 871–2.

[163] *Chronicon Johannis de Reading et Anonymi Cantuariensis*, ed. J. Tait (Manchester University Press, 1914), 132–3.

[164] See above, 35.

PART II

The earls in local society

Chapter 4

INTRODUCTION TO EARLS IN LOCAL SOCIETY

If an earl's prestige came from his title and his relationship with the king, his power began in the vast estates he had acquired through inheritance, marriage or royal grant. A king's favour could, of course, augment an earl's power and influence, either through direct intervention and patronage or by turning a blind eye to dubious practice, but it was his local power and wealth that gave an earl a national platform of power and influence. Any study of medieval nobility must have as its cornerstone an understanding of how nobles obtained and exercised power at a local level, for without this it is impossible to grasp how and why the king's relationship with his nobles mattered so much and why the nobility are central to the political story of medieval England.

Fortunately, the local power of the English nobility in the late middle ages has been the focus of much important research over the past seventy years that will allow the findings for Edward I's reign to be placed within a lively and unfinished historiographical debate. This introductory chapter of this part on the earls in local society will set out the historiographical and historical context for such an investigation by discussing, first, the historiographical debate concerning 'bastard feudalism' and the local power of magnates and, second, the legal and governmental structure of Edward I's England within which noble local power operated. The next chapter will look at how earls put together their knightly followings, with particular focus on the earls of Lancaster, Lincoln and Cornwall. The following chapter will then proceed to a general discussion of how earls used their followings and how they exercised local power, before moving back from the general to the particular to look in detail at two local case studies of comital power: the earl of Lincoln's lordship of Pontefract in Yorkshire and Earl Warenne's power in Sussex. By focusing on both the macro and micro pictures this part will shed light upon both the particular circumstances of Edward I's reign and the wider debate about noble power in the middle ages.

NOBLE POWER AND THE 'BASTARD FEUDALISM' DEBATE

Many historians shy away from using either 'feudalism' or 'bastard feudalism' in their work, believing them both to be redundant concepts that serve to bring more confusion than clarity, largely because no two historians can agree about what is meant by either term. Writing twenty years ago, Professor Colin Richmond stated that recent work had 'tackled that old senile adversary Bastard Feudalism. It is dealt a knock-out blow; it may hereafter only be resurrected as an Aunt Sally … we are left in no doubt: Bastard Feudalism is dead: I do not think I ever believed that it was alive'.[1] Aunt Sally has not rested quietly in her grave, however, and the issue of 'bastard feudalism' and the nature of noble power in the late middle ages are still very much live ones. One of the aims of this book is to perform a little historical necromancy, to raise her up once more, not to knock her down again, but to explain something of how and why she came into existence. To discuss 'bastard feudalism' in the thirteenth century, it is essential to acknowledge that one is dealing with a late-medieval concept, to appreciate how understanding of that concept had developed and to engage with the current late-medieval paradigm. The phrase itself has a long historical pedigree, being first coined by Charles Plummer in 1885 in the introduction to his edition of the famous fifteenth-century political tract by Sir John Fortescue, *The Governance of England*. Writing with the moral certainty that could only come from the pen of a late Victorian, Plummer memorably described 'bastard feudalism' as a debased form of feudalism, an 'evil' that, 'in place of the primitive relation of a lord to his tenants, surrounded the great man with a horde of retainers, who wore his livery and fought his battles … while he in turn maintained their quarrels and shielded them from punishment'.[2] Thus, Plummer introduced 'bastard feudalism' as a twofold concept. First, there is a narrow, technical one describing the changing means by which a lord obtained service, from the land grants of feudalism that created a supposedly stable bond involving respectable, landed people, to the cash

[1] C. Richmond, 'An English Mafia?', *Nottingham Medieval Studies* 36 (1992), 240.

[2] John Fortescue, *The Governance of England: Otherwise Called the Difference Between a Limited and an Absolute Monarchy*, ed. C. Plummer (Oxford: Clarendon Press, 1885), 15–16. The following summary of 'bastard feudalism' draws heavily upon earlier summaries, particularly G.L. Harriss' introduction to K.B. McFarlane, *England in the Fifteenth Century: Collected Essays* (London: Hambledon Press, 1981) and Carpenter, *Wars of the Roses*, 1–66.

grants of 'bastard feudalism', which were given to people recruited in the first place for war and whom Plummer regarded as inherently violent and destabilising. Second, it is also a way of life, an epithet for society and politics as a whole, and not an approving one. This was a society in which the nobility dominated the localities by corrupting and intimidating the legitimate agents of royal law and administration. This competition for local power led to conflict between rival noble dynasties for control over particular localities and a race to the bottom in methods as each side reached for more frequent and deadly violence. These local disputes, it was suggested, destabilised national politics and sapped the withering authority of the crown inadequately worn by Henry VI, leading, inevitably, to the Wars of the Roses in which the old nobility destroyed itself and its power, allowing the Tudors to establish the 'new monarchy' of the sixteenth century.

This was the accepted view until the middle of the twentieth century and the phrase 'bastard feudalism' lingered over the fifteenth century like an unsavoury odour clouding the reputation of both the nobility and the period as a whole. Both were rescued and partially cleansed from opprobrium by McFarlane.[3] Rather than seeking to blame the nobility, the nature of late-medieval kingship or society for the instability of the fifteenth century, he placed the responsibility firmly on 'the personal inadequacies of the kings themselves': no monarchical society, however ordered, he argued, could have survived peacefully the reign of Henry VI.[4] McFarlane and the scholars that followed him dragged the 'bastard feudal' affinity out of the lord's household, where Plummer thought it belonged, and placed it instead in the localities. The members of noble 'affinities', those with a close association to a particular lord, were not Plummer's lawless thugs, but the gentry who formed the backbone of late-medieval England's local society, law and government. 'Bastard feudal' affinities were, in George Holmes' words, 'part of the normal fabric of society'.[5] 'Bastard feudalism' was not the disease that sapped royal authority under Henry VI, it was an accepted part of the way England was governed in the late fourteenth and fifteenth centuries, at times of royal strength as well as weakness.

McFarlane's legacy has influenced three generations of scholars on the fourteenth and fifteenth centuries and their work has provided a detailed and sophisticated framework on which to base the understanding of law,

[3] McFarlane, *Fifteenth Century*, 23–43; M.C. Carpenter, 'Political and Constitutional History: Before and After McFarlane', in Britnell and Pollard (eds.), *McFarlane Legacy*, 175–206.

[4] McFarlane, *Fifteenth Century*, 42.

[5] G.A. Holmes, *The Later Middle Ages, 1272–1485* (Edinburgh: Thomas Nelson and Sons, 1962), 167.

government and society in late-medieval England.[6] Their work has made the later middles ages one of the most vibrant and fertile areas of English historical research in the past half-century but there remains considerable dispute among scholars over McFarlane's legacy, particularly over the question of 'bastard feudalism' and the extent to which the nobility controlled the localities and the nature of that control.[7] What has emerged from the wealth of detailed research into the English localities and noble dynasties in the late middle ages is a kaleidoscopic picture. In some places noble affinities exercised almost blanket control over local society and crown offices, whereas in other places and times noble control was less clear-cut, possibly virtually absent. But, while it is important to acknowledge that the power and authority of the nobility was not the same everywhere and at all times, and to accept that all generalities are subject to caveats, there does seem to have been a presumption among contemporaries that noble rule of the localities was the expected norm even if there were places and times when it did not apply. This was most plainly stated by Bishop Russell in his draft sermon for the opening of parliament in 1483, when he wrote that 'the polityk rule of every region wele ordeigned stondithe in the nobles'.[8]

Russell's sentiment was repeated explicitly and implicitly on many occasions in the late middle ages. The earl of Oxford wrote to the citizens of Norwich and Ipswich in 1497 reminding them that they were of 'the counties whereof his highness ... hath given me the rule and governance'.[9] In the early 1450s, the duke of Norfolk told the Pastons that 'next the king our sovereign lord ... we will have the principal rule and

[6] Among the many works influenced by McFarlane's work on 'bastard feudalism' include the following: Maddicott, *Thomas of Lancaster*; Phillips, *Aymer de Valence*; Rawcliffe, *Staffords*; M. Cherry, 'The Courtenay Earls of Devon: the Formation and Disintegration of a Late Medieval Aristocratic Affinity', *Southern History* 1 (1979), 71–97; M.C. Carpenter, 'The Beauchamp Affinity: a Study of Bastard Feudalism at Work', *EHR* 131 (1980), 514–33; N.E. Saul, *Knights and Esquires: the Gloucestershire Gentry in the Fourteenth Century* (Oxford: Clarendon Press, 1981); M.J. Bennett, *Community, Class and Careerism: Cheshire and Lancashire in the Age of* Sir Gawain and the Green Knight (Cambridge University Press, 1983); S.Wright, *The Derbyshire Gentry in the Fifteenth Century*, Derbyshire Record Society (1983); N.E. Saul, *Scenes from Provincial Life: Knightly Families in Sussex, 1280–1400* (Oxford: Clarendon Press, 1986); Horrox, *Richard III*; E. Powell, *Kingship, Law and Society: Criminal Justice in the Reign of Henry V* (Oxford: Clarendon Press, 1989); Walker, *Lancastrian Affinity*; S. Payling, *Political Society in Lancastrian England: the Greater Gentry of Nottinghamshire* (Oxford: Clarendon Press, 1991); Carpenter, *Locality and Polity*; Carpenter, 'Midlands'; Castor, *King, Crown and Duchy*; A. Gundy, 'The Earl of Warwick and the Royal Affinity', *The Fifteenth Century* 2 (2001), 57–70. There is, of course, by no means a homogeneous view among these historians about how exactly 'bastard feudalism' worked, but the sheer volume of work produced is testimony to McFarlane's legacy.

[7] See, for instance, Britnell and Pollard (eds.), *McFarlane Legacy*.

[8] S.B. Chrimes, *English Constitutional Ideas in the Fifteenth Century* (Cambridge University Press, 1936), 172.

[9] Ross, *John de Vere*, 150.

governance through all this shire'.[10] Norfolk's pretensions to governance in East Anglia came, of course, to nothing, but they foundered not in the face of the independent 'county community', but of other noble leadership: that of Suffolk in the 1440s and Lord Scales in the 1450s.[11] James Ross has very recently described Oxford's 'satrapy' over East Anglia in the reign of Henry VII, and the earl's position of dominance had parallels elsewhere and earlier in the century: the Nevilles and Gloucester in the north, both created to a greater or lesser extent by Edward IV; the Stanleys in Lancashire and Cheshire; and the Beauchamps in Warwickshire under Henry V and VI.[12]

Russell's speech laid out the template for the 'bastard feudal' society: the nobility acting as the bridge between centre and locality, controlling to a greater or lesser extent communication between the two. To be effective in such a role, a 'bastard feudal' magnate needed actively or passively to control the key local legal and administrative positions such as sheriff and justices of the peace in order to help his followers and secure their support, though the actual number of men he retained need not be that large. The routine appointment of local noblemen and their connections to the peace commission suggests that central government was quite prepared to recognise the role of the nobility in keeping the king's peace in the localities. These appointments, and that of members of the affinity to the shrievalty, or their election as MPs, not only gave the lord practical power but also recognised and emphasised his pre-eminence in local society. This is a crucial thing to understand about bastard feudal affinities, indeed about any relationship between patron and patronised: lordship, at its heart, is about mutual support. A magnate's retainers supported him and increased his worship locally and nationally and he, in turn, supported and maintained his retainers. Lordship was natural for medieval man: he sought it out and, when it did not exist, he often tried to create it.[13]

It was this mutual support that made joining a late medieval magnate affinity so attractive to a lesser landholder. Any society based on landholding is intrinsically competitive and potentially violent. As there was usually only a finite amount of land to go around, landholders were for the most part involved in a zero-sum game, whereby the increase of one man's estate came by definition at the expense of another's. Although not every landholder was drawn into large-scale disputes, each had to be

[10] *Paston Letters and Papers of the Fifteenth Century*, ed. N. Davis, 2 vols. (Oxford University Press, 1971–6), II, 259.

[11] Watts, *Henry VI*, 64–6.

[12] Carpenter, 'Beauchamp Affinity'; Horrox, *Richard III*, chapter 1; Ross, *John de Vere*, chapter 5.

[13] Carpenter, 'Beauchamp Affinity', 517.

prepared *in extremis* to fight to maintain what he had especially in the face of the upwardly mobile, and it was rare for any estate to be entirely free of legal claims upon it. Beyond this, there remained the day-to-day friction between landholders over boundaries, hunting rights and the other complexities of medieval land law. The first instinct of any landholder, therefore, before he thought about adding to his estate through marriage or purchase, was to hold onto what he already had.[14] If a landholder were to protect his estate from predators, he needed allies: allies in the law court and, if necessary, allies in arms, and membership of an affinity offered this. The lord would guarantee his man's land transactions and inheritance arrangements, would arbitrate for him in disputes and would protect his interests with all the instruments available to him, including, if necessary and usually only as a last resort, force. The members of the affinity would likewise guarantee each other's transactions, and such horizontal links were often strengthened by more permanent bonds such as marriage alliances. The plethora of horizontal ties that each member of the affinity had, both within and beyond the affinity itself, meant that a magnate need only ever directly retain a relatively small proportion of the gentry within his 'country', the region where his influence was at its most powerful, for, if there was general acceptance of his authority, then nearly all transactions could eventually be traced backed to him and his guarantee would ensure them.[15] Given the extent of some magnates' networks, it is not for nothing that historians sometimes talk of a 'web of control' when discussing 'bastard feudalism'.[16] A noble's lordship and rule was not disinterested, he gained control over his 'country' and recognition that he was the key local agent of the king, but then one should not imagine or expect it to have been so. In most circumstances, however, it was enough to keep the peace most of the time, which, in a society with no means of public law enforcement, was the best that could be managed. Like all methods of governing and keeping the peace, it was an imperfect system and could at times be a dangerously unstable society, but it was one in which all elements of landholding society at least had a stake.

Although the threat of overwhelming violence lay ultimately at the heart of an affinity's power, it was a foolish magnate who resorted to violence too quickly or too often, for frequent bouts of violent disorder in a region were likely to attract the complaints of the gentry and thus unwanted attention from the king, who might begin to ask whether the rule of the magnate in question was causing more problems than it was solving.[17] Consequently, a lord needed to be more subtle in his exercise

[14] Carpenter, *Wars of the Roses*, 63. [15] Ibid., 59. [16] Coss *et al.*, 'Debate', 178.

[17] Carpenter, *Locality and Polity*, 622; Carpenter, *Wars of the Roses*, 60.

of authority. It was the legal system that lay at the heart of the stability of local society. It was so important because it was the king's law that was the ultimate guarantor of landholding. As Edward Powell makes clear, it was 'through the legal system that royal power was formally conveyed to the localities', and any understanding of how local society worked has to incorporate how men saw and used the king's law.[18] A successful 'bastard feudal' magnate had to be able to have his voice heard in the public arena of the law as well as being able to exercise private influence through friendship, negotiation or violence.

Since by the fifteenth century the lord and a number of his followers would expect to sit on the commissions of the peace, this gave him the opportunity to guarantee, and even direct, the king's peace. Justices of the peace could initiate criminal cases, and their powers of detention could be used to arrest or harass tenants of their opponents, which could be an important weapon for protecting and furthering the interests of affinity members.[19] As Simon Walker puts it when discussing justices of the peace in Yorkshire in the late fourteenth century, 'any magnate with substantial estates in the county might include a number of justices of the peace among his servants'.[20] Such control was frequently exercised by magnates elsewhere in England during the later middle ages.[21]

Controlling the sheriff, however, could provide a magnate with an even more effective means of exercising influence over the law. The sheriff was vital at all stages of the legal process. As the returner of writs in the shire, he was responsible for attaching the defendant and bringing him to court, summoning the jury, taking them to Westminster and executing any verdict. The office's power, then, made it natural for magnates to wish to have one of their men exercise it and any magnate with pretentions to influence had 'to control as much of the county as possible, for it was only by dominating the local administration that he could really help his men and secure their support'.[22] This was, in many parts of England in the later middle ages, absolutely essential for the continuation of the king's government. A successful 'bastard feudal' magnate acted not in conflict with the king or his government but as part of it, with a strong and developing sense of public duty for their mutual benefit.[23]

18 Powell, *Kingship, Law and Society*, 6.

19 Ibid., 14–17, for the development and role of justices of the peace.

20 S.K. Walker, 'Yorkshire Justices of the Peace', *EHR* 108 (1993), 287.

21 Cherry, 'Courtenay', 75; Walker, *Lancastrian Affinity*, 243–6; Carpenter, *Locality and Polity*, 374; Gundy, 'Warwick', 63.

22 Carpenter, 'Beauchamp Affinity', 517.

23 Watts, *Henry VI*, chapter 2; M.C. Carpenter, 'England: the Nobility and the Gentry', in S. Rigby (ed.), *A Companion to Britain in the Later Middle Ages* (Oxford: Blackwell, 2003), 275–7.

This, then, in broad outline is the template for the broader definition of 'bastard feudalism' in the late middle ages and it has been essential to gain a proper understanding of what historians of the late middle ages have taken 'bastard feudalism' to be, before now turning to discuss the way in which thirteenth-century historians have tackled the subject. These two historiographies thus provide the full context for the evidence that will be presented in this part from Edward I's reign. If one accepts that the evidence is strong enough for the late fourteenth and fifteenth centuries to be described in 'bastard feudal' terms, then it begs the question of how this society developed. The key causes for both 'feudal' and 'bastard feudal' models of society are the magnate's need for service and the protection he could offer to those in his service; the context is the nature of the politico-social ties between lord and man, the continuing utility of the feudal bond as opposed to the contractual one and the extent to which royal power had been devolved to the localities.

McFarlane himself initially believed that 'bastard feudalism' developed out of Edward I's military recruiting techniques but his and subsequent work on late medieval affinities showed that their primary focus was domestic rather than military. Thus a 'bastard feudal' model of society developed because the feudal tie was no longer effective and it occurred within the context of, and as a result of, the more devolved system of law and government that developed as the middle ages wore on.[24] Historians of the thirteenth century, who have relatively recently begun to discuss whether 'bastard feudalism' existed before the late middle ages, have now adopted the maxim that everything is older than it looks and have sought to push back the onset of 'bastard feudalism' well into the thirteenth century and even beyond.

This work was begun by Peter Coss in his article in *Past & Present* in 1989, 'Bastard Feudalism Revised'.[25] Here, Coss identifies the origins of 'bastard feudalism' as being in the aftermath of the legal reforms of Henry II.[26] Drawing on work by Bean, Maddicott, Waugh and David Carpenter, which all appear to show different elements of what we understand as 'bastard feudalism', Coss believes that McFarlane's view of the origins of 'bastard feudalism' is untenable.[27] Instead, Coss sees 'bastard feudalism' as a

[24] Carpenter, 'Beauchamp Affinity', 519–20; McFarlane, *Fifteenth Century*, 23–4; Harriss in McFarlane, *Fifteenth Century*, x–xi.

[25] Coss, 'Bastard Feudalism Revised'.

[26] Ibid., 30–1.

[27] Ibid., 33–8; J.M.W. Bean, *The Decline of English Feudalism, 1215–1540* (Manchester University Press, 1968), 306–9; J.M.W. Bean, '"Bachelor" and Retainer', *Medievalia et Humanistica*, New Series 3 (1972), 126–7; J.R. Maddicott, 'Law and Lordship: Royal Justices as Retainers in Thirteenth- and Fourteenth-Century England', *Past and Present* supplementary 4 (1978); Carpenter, 'King,

magnate reaction to the Angevin legal reforms that threatened to undermine magnate authority by establishing a direct relationship between the crown and lesser landholders. He sees honorial influence waning between 1180 and 1230, and that this period was therefore 'transitional', as magnates adapted new forms of exerting their authority at a local level to counteract this latent threat.[28] They responded to this threat, Coss believes, 'increasingly by penetrating this new type of public authority and by binding to them the lesser landowners, and indeed all those who were likely to benefit from the development of this direct, public relationship to the crown'.[29] As is clear from the type of language used here, 'bastard feudalism' for Coss is much more the negative beast described by Plummer, distorting the relationship between the crown and gentry, than the neutral animal of McFarlane and his successors. Indeed, Coss doubts the 'somewhat roseate picture' that late medievalists have painted of fifteenth-century society 'and of its aristocracy in particular'.[30]

Two fellow central medievalists, David Crouch and David Carpenter, have each sought to modify Coss' thesis, one more radically than the other. Crouch, coming at the debate from the perspective of the twelfth century, takes issue with Coss' idea that the twelfth century had been 'highly feudalised', and argues that changes between 1100 and 1300 were 'matters of degree and cosmetic'.[31] Crouch believes that magnates had never solely relied on the honour as an instrument for exercising authority in the localities. Lords since the Conquest had used a variety of methods to reward their followers and permanent grants of land had held only a temporary edge over other forms of reward.[32] He also finds evidence of 'bastard feudal' affinities with little or no basis in tenurial grants in the mid-to-late twelfth century; 'uncomfortably early' for Coss' theory of a period of fracture between 1180 and 1230.[33] Crouch's subsequent work, particularly on the earls of Warwick in the early thirteenth century, has continued to unearth examples of what might be considered 'bastard feudal' affinities, though he rejects the term, and believes that what late medievalists would call affinities existed in the twelfth century alongside the classic honorial structure.[34]

Magnates and Society', 40, 45; S.L. Waugh, 'From Tenure to Contract: Lordship and Clientage in Thirteenth-Century England', *EHR* 101 (1986), 811–39.

[28] Coss, 'Bastard Feudalism Revised', 40–3.

[29] Ibid., 50–1. [30] Ibid., 28.

[31] Coss *et al.*, 'Debate', 166, 168. By focusing on the nature of the relationship between lord and man, Crouch largely ignores the legal and governmental contexts, both of which changed dramatically between 1100 and 1300 and changed again in the two centuries following 1300, which are regarded as the classically 'bastard feudal' centuries.

[32] Ibid., 172. [33] Ibid., 172–5.

[34] Crouch, 'Local Influence', 9, 13; Crouch, *Birth of Nobility*, 185.

Carpenter, on the other hand, although in broad agreement with Coss about the content and chronology of the development of 'bastard feudalism', has seen the Angevin reforms not as a threat to magnate power, as Coss does, but 'rather the means of their salvation', giving them, through the 'employment of gentry as sheriffs, judges and so forth … the opportunity to pervert the whole system'. [35] Carpenter sees the decline of the curial sheriff as an important marker on the way towards magnate domination of local administration.[36] More recently, while acknowledging other developments in magnate power, he has warned against being too quick to discard feudalism as a useful concept in the thirteenth century and demonstrated that it retained political and social importance in certain situations right through the reign of Henry III.[37]

Carpenter's rear-guard action on behalf of feudalism runs counter to much of the current historiography of twelfth- and thirteenth-century magnate followings. The work of Paul Dalton and Hugh Thomas on Norman and Angevin Yorkshire, for example, has described the swift disintegration of honorial communities as both lords and vassals sought to break free of the 'honorial strait-jacket'.[38] This does not make these two strands of argument incompatible, however. Carpenter himself highlights the desire of lords and tenants to seek service and lordship from the best possible sources and not to restrict themselves to the structures of their own honour or honours.[39] At the same time as magnates were looking beyond traditional methods of obtaining service, however, they had no desire to see their traditional feudal power over their knightly tenants eroded and fought to maintain them long into the thirteenth century; hence the very feudal issue of suit of court becoming a political battleground in 1258–9.[40] As Crouch puts it, 'we should think of medieval aristocratic society in the twelfth century as an overlapping network of diverse communities – local, tenurial and informal'.[41] The same holds true for the thirteenth century.

It is here that the distinctions between the two different definitions of 'bastard feudalism', technical and societal, come to the fore. Much of the work of twelfth- and thirteenth-century historians has illustrated how many of the 'bastard feudal' techniques to obtain service were already, to a greater or lesser extent, being employed in this period, but this does not mean that the way magnates used their followings in this period was the same as in the later fourteenth and fifteenth centuries. Coss argues forcefully that in the thirteenth century, as in the fifteenth century, there

[35] Coss *et al.*, 'Debate', 180, 181. [36] Ibid., 181–2. [37] Carpenter, 'Second Century'.

[38] H.M. Thomas, *Vassals, Heiresses, Crusaders and Thugs: the Gentry of Angevin Yorkshire, 1154–1216* (Philadelphia: University of Pennsylvania Press, 1993), 47; P. Dalton, *Conquest, Anarchy and Lordship: Yorkshire, 1066–1154* (Cambridge University Press, 1994), 249–72.

[39] Coss *et al.*, 'Debate', 185–6. [40] Carpenter, 'Second Century', 41–3. [41] Ibid., 186.

was 'the same concern for control over the localities and their courts, the same tendency to recruit and sway officials, the same interconnection here between power at the centre and power in the provinces, the same rivalry among aristocrats and aristocratic factions'.[42] The conceptual work of Coss, Crouch, Carpenter and Waugh on 'bastard feudalism' in the thirteenth century, however, has not for the most part been followed up by the kind of detailed local studies that have been done for the late middle ages, so the case of whether the thirteenth century was truly a 'bastard feudal' society in the broadest sense, rather than simply one in which lords used 'bastard feudal' techniques to recruit and retain their followers, has not yet been proven.[43] It is not enough simply to know *how* magnate followings were created in the thirteenth century, their purpose must be divined also. This study of local comital power and followings, therefore, must be divided into two parts covering their structure and function.[44] Before that is done, however, it is essential to describe the structures of local administration and the law in thirteenth-century England.

LOCAL ADMINISTRATION AND THE LAW IN THE THIRTEENTH CENTURY: AN OVERVIEW

A description of the administrative and legal structures of Edward I's England is necessary, not only to provide the context for understanding the findings of the main body of this part, but also because a comparison between the thirteenth and fifteenth centuries will help to make it clear whether the conditions for 'bastard feudalism' in the broadest sense are likely to have existed in the thirteenth century. As noted above, one of the principal factors that made 'bastard feudalism' possible was the devolved system of government and law that operated in the fifteenth century. If 'bastard feudalism' was indeed the negative phenomenon damaging to the interests of the crown that Plummer and Coss believed it to be, it would be much harder for nobles to control the operation of government and law at a local level if these were still controlled from the centre. Equally, the more neutral view of 'bastard feudalism' needs devolved

[42] Coss, 'Bastard Feudalism Revised', 39.

[43] S.L. Waugh, 'The Third Century of English Feudalism', *TCE* 7 (1999), 47–59. There have, of course, been several studies of thirteenth- and early-fourteenth-century noblemen, and these will be listed and their findings discussed throughout this part but, with a few notable exceptions, they have not engaged with the conceptual work on 'bastard feudalism' in the thirteenth century.

[44] The word 'following' is used here to describe those in association with magnates in the thirteenth century. 'Affinity' has late medieval overtones that it would be premature to use at this point before it has been ascertained whether something akin to late medieval affinities did actually exist in the thirteenth century.

administrative and legal structures that allow for the nobility to control the shires for the king as well as in their own interests.

By the opening of Edward I's reign, the effects of Henry II's legal reforms a century earlier were still working their way through. The writ of right and the writs of *mort d'ancestor* and *novel disseisin* had gravely undermined the authority of seigniorial courts and transferred the balance of power in land law away from private and local courts to royal and central courts.[45] However, the county court, to which writs of right removed cases in private courts, still retained some importance. It was the premier local court and was held every twenty-eight days and, in most counties, at a fixed venue.[46] The court was presided over by the sheriff, who was also charged with executing its judgments, and was attended by those who owed suit to the county court: between 60 and 200 people, mostly of knightly status.[47] Below the county court were the hundred courts of each county, again presided over in theory by the sheriff, although this duty was often performed by the hundred bailiffs.[48] Gradually, as the thirteenth century unfolded, the authority of the county court was reduced by local resistance to its authority and the growing power and usefulness of the central courts based at Westminster and of the eyre. From the beginning of Henry III's reign, it became cheaper and easier to obtain the writs of *praecipe* and *pone*, which transferred cases from local to central courts, and, as Tony Moore has shown in an unpublished PhD thesis, the trickle of cases before 1217 had become a flood by 1250, when thousands of such writs were being issued every year.[49] The county court was also losing the attendance of large numbers of those who owed it suit.[50] Of course, suit at the county court was an arduous duty for many knights, especially if they lived a long way from the regular venue or owed suit in several counties, but it was not just idleness that created this trend: magnates sought to restrict attendance by their tenants at the county court during Henry III's reign. Some paid for the privilege, as in the case of the barony of Pevensey in Sussex, but, elsewhere, withdrawal from suit of court was unilateral.[51]

[45] S.F.C. Milsom, *Historical Foundations of the Common Law*, 2nd edn (Oxford University Press, 1981), 125–30, 134–41, 150–1; J. Hudson, *Land, Law and Lordship in Anglo-Norman England* (Oxford University Press, 1994), 262–5.

[46] Palmer, *County Courts*, 4, 7. [47] Ibid., 28, 80. [48] Cam, *Hundred Rolls*, 167.

[49] T.K. Moore, 'Government and Locality in Essex in the Reign of Henry III', unpublished PhD thesis, University of Cambridge (2006), 99.

[50] By 1279, up to 60 of the 162 suitors to the Cambridgeshire county court were no longer attending and it is estimated that by the end of the century county courts had lost as many as half of their suitors. Palmer, *County Courts*, 80.

[51] 'The Hundred Roll for Sussex Part Two', ed. and trans. L.F. Salzman, *Sussex Archaeological Collections* 83 (1944), 37. For unilateral withdrawals of suit of court, see ibid., 44. *Yorkshire Hundred and Quo Warranto Rolls*, 61, 140.

By the end of Henry III's reign, one of the most obvious effects of Henry II's legal reforms had been vastly to increase the number of cases held in the central courts of King's Bench, Common Pleas and Exchequer.[52] But, although royal justice was increasingly being dispensed at Westminster rather than in the shires, every seven years all cases in the royal courts involving a given county were suspended while the justices in eyre descended on the shire to hear all existing pleas and any new ones people cared to bring.[53] The key result of Henry II's reforms, then, was the centralising of royal justice. The central courts grew in power and usefulness, while the eyre should not be mistaken for devolved justice but was rather a majestic carrying of central justice and supervision into the localities.

The eyre was eventually suspended all but permanently in 1294, but even before then there were a number of other ways in which royal justice was brought directly to the shires. The *oyer* and *terminer* commission, developed during Henry III's reign, expanded rapidly under Edward I.[54] These were staffed by a combination of royal justices and local figures but were initiated centrally rather than locally. They were a targeted device and used frequently by earls, 155 being issued to earls during Edward I's reign, accounting for nearly 8 per cent of all commissions.[55] Commissions of gaol delivery were appointed on a frequent basis to empty, or 'deliver', the county gaols of prisoners held there on remand and were staffed either by royal justices or, frequently until 1292, by local knights.[56] Again, as with *oyer* and *terminer* commissions, although these commissions were administered locally, they were appointed and directed centrally. Royal justice was thus dispensed in various ways under Edward I and lords were keen to use the central courts but also to obtain powerful royal commissions that could bypass the often interminable progress of cases through the central courts. The centralised nature of the law in Edward I's reign is in stark contrast to the situation a century later when the final emergence of the justices of the peace marked a significant devolution of justice.[57]

52 See P.A. Brand, 'The Origins of the English Legal Profession', in Brand, *The Making of the Common Law*, 19–20, especially nn. 61 and 62.

53 A.L. Brown, *The Governance of Late Medieval England, 1272–1461* (London: Hodder Arnold, 1989), 116–17. See A. Harding, *The Law Courts of Medieval England* (London: George Allen & Unwin Ltd, 1973), chapter 2, for a longer discussion of the eyre and its place in English justice before 1300.

54 R.W. Kaeuper, 'Law and Order in Fourteenth-Century England: the Evidence of Special Commissions of Oyer and Terminer', *Speculum* 54 (1979), 734–84.

55 This figure is taken from my own examination of *oyer* and *terminer* commissions from the patent rolls.

56 Burt, 'Governance', 102.

57 See Powell, *Kingship, Law and Society*, 14–17. See also Carpenter, 'War, Government and Governance', 20–1 (especially nn. 83–4), for an idea that this occurred later than Powell (and Putnam) suggest.

As with the legal system, so also with the administration of local government. The central government offices of the chancery and exchequer had much greater oversight of local administration in the thirteenth century than they had by the end of the fourteenth century. The thirteenth-century sheriff may no longer have been the 'dread agent of Norman monarchy', and the powerful curial sheriff of the twelfth and early thirteenth centuries may have been disappearing, but the crown maintained a keen interest in the appointment of the man who was unquestionably still the fount of royal government in each shire and by no means yet a universally local man.[58] As well as his duties at the county court, the sheriff's responsibilities were numerous, including the arrest and custody of criminals, execution of royal writs, empanelling juries of all kinds, distraining the king's debtors, summoning the *posse comitatus*, undertaking the sheriff's tourn and overseeing the election of the shire's coroners.[59]

The sheriff had a large number of officials working under him, either at the county castle or within the shire. The former were the under-sheriff, sheriff's clerk and receiver, while principal among the latter were the hundred bailiffs. Beyond the sheriff's staff, the only other permanent local crown office was that of coroner. The coroners, of whom there were two to four in each shire, were able to act in the sheriff's place in an emergency and also had duties of their own.[60] Unlike the sheriff, who was appointed by the exchequer, coroners were elected in the shire court. They kept a record of all crime and of other occurrences involving crown rights. When the justices in eyre visited the shire, they acted upon the coroners' rolls. This gave coroners influence over the direction of the administration of royal justice in the county, which might be useful to a magnate who did not wish the justices to pry too closely into his activities. In addition to the sheriff and the coroners, other permanent local officials were those of the royal forests to be found in almost every county. These men administered the royal forests, which were extensive, stretching well beyond purely wooded areas, and exercised considerable powers within their jurisdiction under the oversight of the two justiciars of the royal forest, one north of the Trent and the other south.

While all these local officers were permanent officials of the crown, the thirteenth century, and particularly Edward I's reign, saw a significant increase in the number, scope and frequency of temporary or extraordinary local commissions. The most important of these were commissioners

[58] The quotation is from W.A. Morris, *The Medieval English Sheriff to 1300* (Manchester University Press, 1927), 73; D.A. Carpenter, 'The Decline of the Curial Sheriff in England, 1194–1258', *EHR* 91 (1976), 1–32; Burt, 'Governance', 73–4, 80–1, 88–9.

[59] For the best summary of the sheriff's duties *c.*1275, see Cam, *Hundred Rolls*, 67–128.

[60] Ibid., 128–31, for a summary of the coroners' duties.

of array, who raised infantry for military campaigns and conducted them to the muster; knights of the shire who were summoned to parliament and were elected in the county court; commissioners of prise, who collected foodstuffs to be sent to the royal army; and tax commissioners, who assessed and collected taxation on moveable goods. These four offices were particularly vital for the war effort and their emergence demonstrates the increasingly intrusive nature of royal government, since most of these were tasks that might previously have been carried out by the sheriff alone. His duties had thus expanded to such an extent that they needed to be shared among other officials, as did the new local burdens. The material, financial and manpower needs of Edward I and his fourteenth-century successors forced a deepening and a widening of royal government that made it impossible for the centre to maintain effective oversight of the localities. The pressure for the expansion of royal law and government came not just from on high, however, but also from below.[61] The result was eventually to be the development of the gentry as a magistracy and expansion of the reach of royal government, but of a royal government that was now, at its best, a partnership between crown, nobility and gentry. The expansion of royal government made engagement with it a necessity rather than an optional extra, which for the very powerful it had threatened to become at times earlier in the thirteenth century. This process was only just beginning in earnest in Edward I's reign and, as will be argued in the following chapters, until it was complete, and crown, nobles and gentry had time to adapt to the changing circumstances it brought about, then it is difficult to believe that this was a 'bastard feudal' society.

[61] G.L. Harriss, 'Political Society and the Growth of Government in Late Medieval England', *Past and Present* 138 (1993), 28–57.

Chapter 5

THE CREATION OF COMITAL FOLLOWINGS

In its crudest form, power consists of the amount of physical violence that can be brought to bear on a given situation.[1] In the twenty-first century state violence can be delivered remotely by machines controlled by the press of a button thousands of miles away. In the middle ages, however, violence was always personal, face-to-face or not more than the distance an arrow or cannonball could fly. In other words, it relied upon the number and quality of men that a man of power could call upon to inflict violence on his enemies. Lordship meant control over territory but at its heart it meant power to direct men and, if necessary, to direct them to violence. Great nobles were powerful men because they could call upon the service of great numbers of people of many different ranks to perform many different types of service, from peasant tenants who provided them not just with rents and services but with instant, locally available manpower, to clerks, administrators and those of gentle birth. This chapter will focus mainly on the last of these for two reasons. First, they are the easiest to identify. They were lords themselves, though on a lesser scale, and therefore appear more often in surviving records and their independent interests make it possible partially to reconstruct their lives. Second, these men were the most prestigious and most useful of a nobleman's associates, as they too had command over men, their own and, if they held local office, others, making them integral to a lord's power. Moreover, the details of their service with him can tell a great deal about the type of lord any particular nobleman was. Much can be known about a man from the type of company he likes to keep.

[1] For much of what follows and an overview of the development of central and local power in medieval England, see M.C. Carpenter, 'Political and Geographic Space: the Geopolitics of Medieval England', in B. Kümin (ed.), *Political Space in Pre-industrial Europe* (Farnham: Ashgate Publishing, 2009), 119–33.

Identifying such company, therefore, is a prime task for any historian wishing to understand the power of the medieval nobility in the localities. The methodology for doing so is similar for the thirteenth century as for later centuries, but there are significant differences. These can largely be explained by the lack of the range and wealth of sources in the thirteenth century that are available to historians of the fourteenth and fifteenth centuries. To identify the membership of a magnate affinity, later historians can call upon sources such as livery rolls, which list the number and amount of fees paid in a given year to a magnate's retainers; household or estate accounts, which would identify his officials and, sometimes, payments to retainers and annuitants; manorial court rolls, which often give the name of the lord's steward and may offer incidental information about those close to him; property deeds, which list his feoffees, witnesses and other associates; wills, which enumerate a magnate's bequests and also his executors; indentures of retainer, which were formal documents laying out the specific terms of service and reward between a lord and his retainer. A few of these do exist in the thirteenth century but they are exceedingly rare compared to their later survival rate, which even then is frustratingly patchy.[2]

The relative paucity of surviving private records for thirteenth-century nobles forces a greater reliance upon the records of royal government than is desirable but these records are very helpful, if somewhat haphazard, in providing copious evidence of men connected to the earls of Edward I's reign. Some of the secrets they occasionally divulge are the names of executors;[3] letters of protection listing those accompanying a

[2] Household accounts survive, for instance, for Eleanor de Montfort, countess of Leicester, for Bogo de Clare, the clerical brother of the earl of Gloucester, and for Earl Warenne: *Manners and Household Expenses of England in the Thirteenth and Fifteenth Centuries*, ed. T.H. Turner (London: William Nicol Press, 1841); E 101/91/1–7; E 101/505/17. A list of the members of Roger IV Bigod, earl of Norfolk, from *c.*1297 exists: *Documents Illustrating the Crisis of 1297–8*, no. 154. Estate accounts exist for the earl of Cornwall, the earl of Norfolk and the earl of Lincoln in Edward I's reign: *Ministers' Accounts*; Norfolk's scattered accounts can be found in TNA SC 6; *Two Compoti of the Lancashire and Cheshire Manors of Henry de Lacy, Earl of Lincoln, 24 and 33 Edward I*, ed. and trans. P.A. Lyons, Chetham Society, Old Series 112 (1884). Relatively few manorial court rolls exist for the thirteenth century, of those a single roll exists for Earl Warenne's estates in Lewes and a much fuller series of rolls for his estates in Wakefield: *Records of the Barony and Honour of the Rape of Lewes*, ed. A.J. Taylor, Sussex Records Society 44 (1939); *Court Rolls of the Manor of Wakefield, vol. 1: 1274–1297*, ed. and trans. W.P. Baildon, Yorkshire Archaeological Record Society 29 (1901). Only thirteen indentures of retainer survive before 1307, and just five of these refer to retaining by earls: 'Private Indentures for Life Service in Peace and War, 1278–1476', eds. M. Jones and S.K. Walker, *Camden Miscellany*, Camden Society, Fifth Series 3 (1994), nos. 1–12, 14. The only comital wills to survive from the thirteenth century are Simon de Montfort's, written in 1259, and Roger III Bigod's, drawn up in 1258: C. Bémont, *Simon de Montfort*, trans. E.F. Jacob, 2nd edn (Oxford: Clarendon Press, 1930), 276–7; Morris, *Bigod Earls*, 218–19. The earliest surviving comital livery roll, or approximation to it, is one for Thomas of Lancaster, drawn up some time before 1316: Holmes, *Estates*, app. 2.

[3] *CCR 1296–1302*, 387.

magnate on military service or abroad on diplomatic or private business;[4] letters of attorney where a nobleman placed his affairs in the hands of a trusted administrator or lawyer;[5] the occasional order sent to a named official of a magnate;[6] favours from the king granted or requested by a nobleman for an associate of his;[7] and those linked with him when he was accused of some nefarious activity.[8] All such instances need to be used carefully. Multiple appearances of a man in connection with a nobleman obviously allows for surer categorisation of him as a close associate. Also, it is essential to bear in mind when using government sources that they by no means give a complete or balanced picture of a nobleman's following. The government records were not created for the purpose of allowing historians to put together accurate lists of noble followings and, by their nature, certain types of people are more likely to appear in these records than others, with a particular bias in Edward I's reign towards those appearing in a military context.[9] Moreover, certain noblemen are more likely to appear more frequently in these records than others, given the nature of their political and military careers. Nevertheless, with these caveats in mind, the voluminous legal and central government records provide the historian with an imperfect skeletal outline of those known to be close to thirteenth-century noblemen.

It is fortunate, however, that for many thirteenth-century nobles significant additional evidence does survive in the form of charters. For those where a considerable corpus of charter evidence exists, it becomes possible to put a little flesh on the bones of their following. Charter evidence has been the basis of most of the studies of thirteenth-century noble followings that have thus far been undertaken and it is the best route available given the evidence available. Charters offer several different angles of evidence, all of which are useful in piecing together noble followings. First, and most obviously, they provide evidence of a lord's grants. Often these are routine pieces of petty patronage or land transactions but they also include significant grants of land, annual rents or fees to those who can be identified as annuitants. Second, charters were witnessed by a range of people, something that shows who were around the grantor at a given moment. If a large number of charters survive, then men providing multiple attestations might be identified as being close associates of the

[4] *CPR 1272–1281*, 157, 220–1; *CPR 1292–1301*, 538.

[5] *CPR 1272–1281*, 101. [6] Ibid., 189.

[7] *CPR 1301–1307*, 378. [8] *CCRV*, 334.

[9] By the late middle ages it is problematic to use retinue evidence to establish links between lords and men. See Carpenter, 'Beauchamp Affinity', 519–20. In the thirteenth century there appears to be a clearer link between domestic and military service, and those who appear most frequently in domestic settings also appear most often in military retinues. Spencer, 'Earls', apps. C and D.

grantor. Third, if a witness was an official of the grantor, such as his steward, bailiff or castellan, then this was often made explicit in the witness list, thereby providing firm further evidence of a lord's administrative circle. Members of this administrative circle varied from clerks (mostly less significant for the purposes of this discussion) through lay officers with no independent means beyond those provided by their lord to members of the local gentry, those most relevant to this discussion.

But, as with other types of records, there are important caveats when dealing with what is inevitably incomplete and skewed evidence. The numbers of charters for several earls who have been studied, like Roger III Bigod, earl of Norfolk, and Simon de Montfort are very small, making it hard to draw firm conclusions.[10] The available charter evidence also often falls in clumps, with several charters bunched together chronologically and then long gaps stretching over several years when no charters survive, analysis being further complicated by the survival of many charters that are undated and for which dating from internal evidence can be at best approximate.[11] Another danger is that the charter evidence for some earls is restricted to particular places and this may skew analysis if care is not taken. Caroline Burt, having laid out her admirable methodology for her study of the first Beauchamp earls of Warwick, excludes from close study those 'who only witnessed charters relating to one manor or small area'.[12] To be confident that a charter witness really was someone who was close to the grantor, it is necessary to have evidence of his witnessing charters across a significant geographical area and, preferably, across a span of years.[13]

Two earldoms from Edward I's reign have already received detailed attention from scholars, the Bigod earldom of Norfolk and the Beauchamp earldom of Warwick.[14] For most of the remaining earldoms the corpus of surviving charter evidence is too small for firm and detailed conclusions to be drawn but, for three earldoms at least, Lancaster, Lincoln and Cornwall, it is possible to rely on large numbers of surviving charters. Their survival is made possible thanks to the records of these earldoms falling into royal hands through the duchies of Lancaster and Cornwall.

10 Montfort appears as grantor in just twenty-four charters from an English career spanning thirty-four years: Maddicott, *Simon de Montfort*, 60. Only thirteen Bigod charters survive from 1228 to 1270, the time that Roger III Bigod held the earldom of Norfolk; Morris, *Bigod Earls*, 60.

11 For some of these problems, see, for instance, Morris, *Bigod Earls*, 60.

12 Burt, '"Bastard Feudal" Affinity', 166.

13 A focus on geographical spread to identify close associates does, of course, exclude those who may have acted as their lord's agent in a specific geographical area. At this stage, however, one can only ensure that one remains aware of this possibility.

14 Morris, *Bigod Earls*; Burt, '"Bastard Feudal" Affinity'. Ridgeway, 'William de Valence', examines Valence's followers before the accession of Edward I but contains useful information for the latter's reign.

For Edmund of Lancaster, fifty *acta* survive, along with a further 120 charters in which he was the grantee.[15] It is those in which the lord was the grantor that are most useful since it is possible to be fairly certain that he was actually present when the charter was sealed, whereas the business in charters in which he was the grantee often seems to have been conducted by his officials. Thirty-nine of Lancaster's charters have a dating clause and a further seven were inspected and confirmed by royal charter, which provide a definite *terminus ante quem* for the grant. They span the earl's entire career from 1267 to 1295, the year before his death.[16] Of the charters with a date clause the vast majority fall in the middle two decades of his active career: two come from the 1260s, twenty-seven from the 1270s, fourteen from the 1280s and three from the 1290s. Fortunately there is also a very good spread with regard to both where the charters were granted and the places mentioned in them. Lancaster granted charters in no fewer than eighteen different locations stretching from Finkhale in County Durham to Monmouth in Wales and London and Westminster.

Although more of the earl of Lincoln's charters survive than of Lancaster's, fewer have a dating clause or come from an *inspeximus*: 35 of 53, along with a further 124 in which he was grantee.[17] His own *acta* fall between 1278 and 1308, leaving a short hiatus at the end of his life and a somewhat longer one at the start of his career.[18] Just a single charter survives from the 1270s, along with sixteen from the 1280s, eleven from the 1290s and seven from the 1300s, providing a reasonably balanced spread of charters from across the earl's career. As with Lancaster, there is a pleasing diversity to the places where the earl made his charters and the places to which they refer. He granted charters in twenty different locations including London, Pontefract, Cowick near Exeter, Rhuddlan and Paris.

Of the three earls under consideration, the smallest number of surviving and dateable *acta* belongs to Edmund of Cornwall. Thirty-six Cornwall *acta* survive, along with forty-five where he was the grantee.[19] Of the thirty-six, just nineteen have a dating clause, though a further eleven are royal confirmations that provide a final date for the charter. The date range for Cornwall's dateable charters is 1276 to 1300, leaving a four-year gap at the start of his career.[20] Two charters date from the 1270s (with a further three royal confirmations dating from this decade), eleven from the 1280s (with four additional royal confirmations), six from the

[15] See Appendix A. [16] Appendix A, nos. 1–46.
[17] See Appendix B. [18] Appendix B, nos. 1–35.
[19] See Appendix C. [20] Appendix C, nos. 1, 31.

1290s (with four more confirmations) and there is a single charter in 1300, the year he died. Again, it is fortunate that the surviving corpus both deals with a large number of different places and was drawn up in ten separate locations, ranging from Knaresborough in Yorkshire, through Berkhamsted, the earl's chief residence, to Restormel in Cornwall. Using the extensive charter evidence available for these three earls, in conjunction with the considerable amount of government records referring to them and their followers, it is possible to reconstruct their gentry followings with reasonable confidence, while acknowledging that a complete picture is lost in the mists of history. How the three earls constructed their followings is a key starting point for considering the questions of noble power and 'bastard feudalism' in the thirteenth century.

A crucial question is the 'feudal' one: to what extent they still surrounded themselves with and called upon their knightly tenants. Given the differing nature of the three earldoms under consideration, it is reasonable to expect different results. The Lacy earldom of Lincoln may only have been in its third generation with Earl Henry but he was the head of an ancient baronial family whose tenure of their greatest lordship, Pontefract, went back to the time of *Domesday*.[21] If feudal ties really did continue to matter in the thirteenth century, then the Lacys would be obvious candidates to provide proof. The earldom of Cornwall was much newer, having been created for Earl Edmund's father, Richard, in 1225 by his brother King Henry III.[22] Finally, Edmund of Lancaster was a very recently manufactured magnate. Although some of his new lands, especially those from the Ferrers inheritance, were compact, it would be harder for him to rely on tenants who had no history of serving his family (other than in the general sense of serving the crown), and indeed in many cases had seen their lord supplanted by Lancaster.

Such assumptions are borne out by the evidence. Of Lancaster's close followers only Sir Ranulph Dacre and Sir Gilbert Talbot had an existing tenurial relationship before entering his service.[23] Being a manufactured magnate undoubtedly explains much of this but there were other reasons too. Most importantly, as the king's brother, he transcended the normal rules and would never lack for potential clients for his lordship. Also, Lancaster spent time abroad attending to his French interests, which reduced his opportunities to foster relationships with his tenants. But, although it seems that Lancaster did not succeed in turning tenurial relationships into personal ones, or perhaps did not try to do so, it would be wrong to assume that he had abandoned feudal techniques altogether.

[21] See above, 21–2. [22] See above, 16–17.
[23] DL 42/1, f. 109; Wait, 'Household and Resources', 364.

In many ways, he retained a very traditional mindset in recruiting and rewarding followers, for, although very few of his followers had a prior tenurial relationship, Lancaster often lost little time in creating one. His method for rewarding his followers combined feudal and 'bastard feudal' techniques by making grants worth precise sums of money but tied to specific pieces of land, either as rent or, more often, as a grant of a manor. Lancaster's great resources and his clean start meant he could afford to be generous. For instance, although a common yearly grant for service to a knight around this time was £20, Lancaster granted Sir Gilbert Talbot the manor of Rodley in Gloucestershire, which was worth £43 5*s* 9*d* p.a.[24] Lancaster's most generous grants were to Sir Laurence de St Maur, who received £78 p.a. of land and rents in Northumberland and Sussex, as well as a marriage to a wealthy Northumbrian heiress that was probably arranged with Lancaster's aid.[25] The earl's patronage helped to promote the St Maurs from county knights with connections to the royal household to parliamentary peers in a single generation, a scale of transformatory largesse usually only in the king's gift.[26]

Lancaster seems to have set aside certain manors specifically to reward his followers. Rodley, for instance, was granted successively to Sir Gilbert Talbot, Sir Walter de Helyun and Sir William de Grandisson, before eventually becoming part of the appanage granted to the earl's second son, Henry.[27] The nearby manor of Minsterworth fell into the same category. Worth £20 p.a., it was granted first to Sir Robert de Turberville in 1271 for three years, then in 1281 to Sir William de Grandisson (terminated in 1284), before, like Rodley, descending to Henry of Lancaster.[28] Subsequently, Henry, like his father, continued to use these manors to reward his followers.[29] The manor of Kingshagh in Nottinghamshire was another manor Edmund of Lancaster made use of in this way.[30] Although such grants were not permanent alienations, it seems to have been important to Lancaster, and perhaps also to the beneficiaries, that they involved specific pieces of land. It was

[24] *CChR 1257–1300*, 162; *CIPM*, II, no. 80; DL 27/190; *Rotuli Hundredorum*, I, 180. For £20 being the standard grant, see, for instance, Appendix A, no. 15, Appendix B, nos. 33, 44.

[25] *CCR 1288–1296*, 12, 488; *CIPM*, I, no. 2030; *CIPM*, II, nos. 524, 723; *Three Early Assize Rolls for the County of Northumberland*, ed. W. Page, Surtees Society 88 (1891), 327; *The Northumberland Lay Subsidy Roll of 1296*, ed. C.M. Fraser, Society of Antiquaries of Newcastle-upon-Tyne 1 (1968), nos. 213, 262, 264, 410.

[26] Laurence St Maur's father, Nicholas, was a household knight of Henry III: *CPR 1247–1258*, 496.

[27] Appendix A, nos. 18, 36; DL 42/2, ff. 193–193r; DL 36/2/190.

[28] *CChR 1257–1300*, 161; DL 42/2, f. 194; Appendix A, no. 36; DL 42/2, f. 193r.

[29] *CPR 1307–1313*, 339; *CPR 1313–1317*, 620; *CPR 1317–1321*, 505; *CPR 1330–1334*, 321.

[30] *CChR 1257–1300*, 162; *CPR 1292–1301*, 105. It was granted successively to Sir Geoffrey de Langley the younger and Master William de Gloucester.

rare for Lancaster to make grants of rent only, as he did to Sir Henry de Glastonbury.[31] His traditional frame of mind is also demonstrated by the number of permanent feudal alienations he made to his followers: to Sir Laurence de St Maur in Northumberland, for instance; three knights' fees to Sir Roger Brabazon in Derbyshire; the manor of West Ildsley to Sir Richard Fukeram; and a third of a knight's fee in Northamptonshire to Sir Thomas de Bray.[32]

The earl of Lincoln's following provides an interesting contrast, for the feudal aspect of it is much clearer than in the case of Lancaster. There was a core of tenants at the heart of Lincoln's following. In Yorkshire, Sir William de Stopham, Sir William Vavasour and Sir Miles de Stapleton were all tenants of the earl.[33] Vavasour was also a tenant in Lincolnshire, as was Sir Robert Shireland and Sir John Newmarch, while, in Lancashire, Sir Adam de Huddleston held the manor of Clayton from the earl.[34] All of these men were frequent witnesses to the earl's charters and served him in numerous other ways too.[35]

Importantly, however, while a tenurial connection seems to have been an important entry point into Lincoln's service, it was not enough in itself to keep followers there. Lincoln reinforced an existing tenurial relationship with a further grant on five occasions: to Huddleston,[36] Newmarch,[37] Stapleton,[38] Stopham[39] and Vavasour.[40] As with Edmund of Lancaster, there is a strong link to specified pieces of land, even when the grant took the form of rents, revealing a firmly traditional mindset behind more 'modern' methods. This is also reflected in Lincoln's rewards to those without a pre-existing tenurial connection, such as Sir Robert Fitz Roger,[41] Sir Baldwin Manners[42] and the Leyburn brothers, Sir Robert and Sir Nicholas.[43]

Edmund of Cornwall, too, attracted several followers from among his existing tenants. Among them were the knights William de Bereford, Thomas le Archdeacon, Robert Malet, Theobald de Neville, Richard

[31] DL 42/2, f. 62r. This was £10 rent from the provostship of Leicester.

[32] *CIPM*, III, no. 423; *Three Early Assize Rolls*, 327; Appendix A, no. 14.

[33] For Stopham: 'Towton: the Battlefield Village (1461)', www.oldtykes.co.uk/towton.htm (last accessed 29 August 2008). The manor was granted to his father, Robert. For Vavasour: *CIPM*, III, no. 265; *CIPM*, V, no. 395. For Stapleton: *CIPM*, V, no. 498.

[34] For Shireland: *CCR 1279–1288*, 97. For Newmarch: Appendix B, no. 42. Granted to his father, Adam, by Lincoln. For Huddleston: *CIPM*, V, no. 279.

[35] See Appendix B, Table B.1. For detailed evidence of their other services to Lincoln, which were extensive, see Spencer, 'Earls', app. D.

[36] *Coucher Book of Whalley*, IV, 944–5.

[37] DL 25/265. Sir John's father, Adam, was granted lands and rents in tail in Saltfleetby, Lincolnshire, which he duly inherited.

[38] *CIPM*, V, no. 279. [39] DL 25/3249. [40] DL 25/2174; DL 36/1/119.

[41] DL 25/73. [42] DL 25/3421. [43] *Two Compoti*, 149.

de Seyton and the earl's nephew, Edmund de Cornubia.[44] Most of Cornwall's surviving charters are related to religious benefaction, but those of a secular nature also indicate a desire to create feudal bonds, even on a small scale, with his followers and a tendency to link reward to specific pieces of land.[45] Lincoln and Cornwall, then, like Lancaster, mixed 'feudal' reward (permanent grants of land) with 'bastard feudal' rewards (cash payments) but the traditional pull of a landed connection between lord and follower remained very strong. This suggests that the enduring nature of the feudal bond was an important factor well into the third century of English feudalism.[46] There are three important caveats, however. The first is that, for newer magnate dynasties, the feudal bond was quite weak and that, even for an established family like the Lacys, tenants made up only a minority of Lincoln's following. The second is that, as Lincoln's behaviour shows, an existing tenurial relationship often needed to be reinforced to ensure service from a new generation. This was not new, indeed it had been happening since the second generation after the Conquest, but it suggests that, while the tenurial bond still had a hold over men's imagination, it did not override more practical concerns when recruiting and retaining followers.[47] Finally, the sources very rarely indicate why a man might choose to enter a lord's service, and there is no way of knowing, when a pre-existing tenurial bond did exist, whether it was this that was the prime catalyst for bringing a man into a lord's service. Sometimes, as in the case of Sir Edmund de Cornubia, it is possible to speculate that it was the fact that he was the son of Cornwall's illegitimate half-brother that prompted his service with his uncle rather than that he was his feudal tenant.

It is not possible to be certain, therefore, about what the feudal bond really meant to lords and gentry in the late thirteenth century, but this has not stopped historians from speculating that by this time it was almost entirely fiscal in nature and had been stripped of any political meaning that it might once have possessed.[48] The two concepts are not necessarily antithetical: financial reward for the lord does not negate an action's political importance, indeed it might increase it. Suit of court became a major political issue during the reform period of 1258–9 and it remained important

[44] For Bereford: *CIPM*, III, no. 604, p. 480. For Archdeacon: *CIPM*, III, no. 604, pp. 476, 489. For Malet: *CIPM*, III, no. 276. For Neville: *CCR 1296–1302*, 437. For Seyton: *CIPM*, III, no. 604, p. 468. For Edmund de Cornubia: *CIPM*, III, no. 604, p. 479.

[45] Appendix C, nos. 29, 34.

[46] See Carpenter, 'Second Century', 47–59, 65–9, for the importance of the tenurial bond in the period 1166–1266.

[47] For an example of this, see Crouch, *Beaumont Twins*, 109–11, 113–14.

[48] Thomas, *Vassals*, 42–3; Carpenter, 'Second Century', 44.

under Edward I.[49] Lords fought so hard to retain suit of court from their feudal tenants because of the financial benefits that knightly attendance at their court brought, but there were political and social implications as well.[50] Several grants of small pieces of land by Edmund of Lancaster made it expressly clear that the grantee still owed him suit and it was only to chosen *familiares* that suit was remitted, while in 1285 Sir Robert Tiptoft made a grant to Lancaster solely for the purposes of confirming that he owed suit at the earl's court of Tutbury.[51] That Lancaster was willing to use remission of suit as a kind of patronage suggests that he regarded it in political terms, as a particular favour to be bestowed only on his most valued followers. Earl Warenne, in his typically robust fashion, had his stewards at Wakefield make strenuous efforts to ensure suit was paid to the court by knightly tenants, ordering regular distraints upon those who defaulted.[52] These knights at Tutbury and Wakefield were not close associates of either earl and the issue at stake here, besides the obvious financial one, was not in the first instance lordship over men. Rather, by enforcing suit of court, nobles were exercising and broadcasting their rights over the land that their tenants held and then, by extension, over the landholder himself and his tenants. Thus, even in the later thirteenth century, lords were marking out their territory, their fee and their lordship and ensuring that everyone knew it. The prolonged importance of the traditional idea of the fee, and its combination of political and financial elements, can be seen in other ways. The continued use of the feudal levy, at the earls' insistence, meant that scutage could continue to be taken by tenants-in-chief from their tenants. As has been seen, this provided a welcome source of revenue for tenants-in-chief but it also served to reinforce the sense of their fee.[53] A financial measure it may have been but, like suit of court, it maintained the principle of lordship over pieces of land. Thus, financial exactions remained socially and politically important and bore heavily upon the issue of lordship.

If traditional methods of lordship did indeed remain a powerful tool for Edward I's earls, it is clear that this was far from the only string to their bow. In the way that the earls mixed traditional and newer methods, it is possible to reconcile David Crouch's 'overlapping network of diverse communities – local, tenurial and informal', with David Carpenter's emphasis on the continuing importance of the feudal bond.[54] Thirteenth-century followings were clearly not classically 'feudal' but it remains to

[49] Ibid., 41–2. [50] Ibid., 43. [51] Appendix A, nos. 8, 54; DL 25/1665.

[52] *Court Rolls of the Manor of Wakefield, vol. I: 1274–1297*, 101, 109, 125, 135, 136.

[53] See above, 82.

[54] Carpenter, 'Second Century'; Crouch, *Birth of Nobility*, 186.

be seen whether they can be regarded as recognisably 'bastard feudal'. If these earls were not recruiting exclusively or even predominantly from their knightly tenants, were they bringing their gentry neighbours into their service?

This sort of regional recruiting was de rigueur in the affinities of the late middle ages as it allowed lords to mark out and dominate their 'countries'.[55] It also seems to have been common among thirteenth- and early fourteenth-century earls, though the scale of their recruitment was not on that of the late middle ages. Earl Henry II of Warwick in the 1220s had several prominent members of the Warwickshire county court in his following, while Simon de Montfort had several influential Leicestershire landholders among his adherents and Roger III Bigod's following was full of middling East Anglian knights.[56] Two generations later, Thomas of Lancaster drew most of his retainers from among his gentry neighbours, and these included several very important local figures.[57] Lancaster's friend, Guy Beauchamp, earl of Warwick, and Beauchamp's father, Earl William, had followings drawn almost exclusively from near their west midlands estates.[58] There is also some evidence to suggest that Thomas of Brotherton drew many of his adherents from the eastern counties where the bulk of his estates lay.[59] Of those nobles studied by others, only William de Valence, the alien courtier par excellence at the court of his brother, Henry III, seems to have made no significant attempt to recruit men in the counties where he had lands.[60]

Edmund of Lancaster's following seems to have followed Valence's pattern. It was dispersed, and it was his men's links to the king's household and their military prowess that he seems to have valued more than their local influence.[61] Crucially, although Lancaster had few strong personal ties with his feudal tenants, he was not extending local ties through those who were not his tenants. He recruited widely but not deeply and, even in areas where he was the dominant landholder, there was not the web of connections with the local gentry that one would expect to find in the classic 'bastard feudal' affinity. No more than a handful of Lancaster's followers came from counties such as Lancashire, Yorkshire, Derbyshire, Leicestershire and Staffordshire where he held extensive lands. William

[55] Rawcliffe, *Staffords*, chapter 4; Cherry, 'Courtenay'; Saul, *Knights and Esquires*, chapter 3; Carpenter, *Locality and Polity*, chapter 10.

[56] Maddicott, *Simon de Montfort*, 61–2; Crouch, 'Local Influence', 13; Morris, *Bigod Earls*, 71–2.

[57] Maddicott, *Thomas of Lancaster*, 54–6.

[58] Burt, '"Bastard Feudal" Affinity', 169, 175.

[59] A. Marshall, 'An Early Fourteenth-Century Affinity: the Earl of Norfolk and His Followers', *Fourteenth Century England* 5 (2008), 5–6.

[60] Ridgeway, 'William de Valence', 255–6.

[61] Maddicott, *Thomas of Lancaster*, 54.

Wyther was a Staffordshire knight involved in county administration, as was Ranulph Dacre in Lancashire and Yorkshire.[62] Sir Alan de Waldeshef had lands in Mugginton in Derbyshire, near Lancaster's hunting grounds of Duffield Chase, and in 1280 the earl purchased lands there that backed on to Waldeshef's.[63] Sir Roger Brabazon was born at Mowsley in Leicestershire, just eleven miles from the earl's town of Leicester.[64] These are mean pickings indeed from the heart of the Lancastrian lands.

In Warwickshire, where Lancaster held Kenilworth Castle, four of his knightly followers, Roger Somery, Richard Fukeram, Geoffrey de Langley and William Bagot, had lands, though, interestingly, none were his tenants. Fukeram's main interests were in Berkshire, Somery's *caput* of Dudley is thirty-five miles from Kenilworth and, while Langley's three manors near Coventry were much closer to Kenilworth, it was Langley's prior relationship with Lord Edward that brought him into association with Lancaster.[65] The St Maur family and Sir Reginald de St Martin held lands in Wiltshire, where Lancaster also had three manors, but was not one of the county's major landholders.[66] Sir William Kugeho's chief manor of Cogenhoe in Northamptonshire lay just twelve miles from Higham Ferrers, Lancaster's chief manor in the county, and it is likely that it was this link of neighbourhood that brought him into the earl's service.[67] Several of Lancaster's close knightly associates, however, were from counties where he had no interests: Henry de Glastonbury and John Meriet, for example, from Somerset and Thomas de Bray from Bedfordshire, and it is hard to know how they came into Lancaster's service.[68]

None of this means, of course, that Lancaster had no dealings with his neighbours. On the contrary, on the rare occasions when the earl came to Lancashire, to take one instance, he drew a crowd from among both his neighbours and his knightly tenants, men such as Adam Hoghton and Adam Holland in 1278, or William le Botiller, Robert Banaster, Robert Holland and Robert de Lathum in 1286.[69] It was natural for these men to wish to attend the earl and witness his charters on his infrequent

[62] For Wyther: C. Moor, *The Knights of Edward I*, 5 vols. (Leeds: Harleian Society, 1929–32), V, 206; Spencer, 'Earls', app. C, no. 14. For Dacre: Spencer, 'Earls', app. C, no. 3.

[63] DL 25/1842.

[64] P.A. Brand, 'Brabazon, Sir Roger (*b.* in or before 1247?–*d.* 1317)', in *ODNB*; Spencer, 'Earls', app. C, no. 1.

[65] *CIPM*, II, nos. 198, 813; *CPR 1272–1281*, 433; Wait, 'Household and Resources', 30.

[66] *CIPM*, III, no. 386; *CIPM*, III, no. 423, p. 288; *CPR 1292–1301*, 83, 87, 426; Spencer, 'Earls', app. C, nos. 8–10.

[67] Moor, *Knights of Edward I*, II, 296.

[68] For their links with Lancaster and their estates, see Glastonbury: *CPR 1281–1292*, 239; *CPR 1292–1301*, 62; DL 42/2m f. 62v; *Parl Writs*, I, 366. Meriet: *CPR 1281–1292*, 239; *CPR 1292–1301*, 169; TNA C 67/10, mm. 4, 5d; *Rôles Gascons*, III, nos. 3822, 4043. Bray: Spencer, 'Earls', app. C, no. 2.

[69] Appendix A, no. 43; DL 42/1, f. 135; DL 25/1213.

arrivals in their neighbourhood, but he seems to have formed no lasting connection with them. They did not witness any of his charters outside Lancashire and none of the other important Lancashire families, such as Grelley, Trafford, Molyneux or Hulton, appear in connection with the earl in the surviving records. The contrast with later lords of Lancaster is striking, even when one takes into account the increased hold those later lords had over the county and the better survival of records. John of Gaunt retained around a third of the Lancashire gentry, while his son, King Henry IV, had retained at least twenty-one of the most important gentry in the county by 1405.[70] The same picture emerges from the earl of Lincoln's Lancashire charters. He too, when visiting the county, was attended by knights such as Adam Hoghton and Adam Holland, and when he was in Dorset by local knights there, but none of these men appear to have had any other contact with him.[71] The extent to which such people could be considered part of an earl's wider circle of influence is open to question: in the later middle ages, they might be considered as among a magnate's 'well-willers', but there can be little doubt that such men were not among these thirteenth-century earls' intimates: not the core of their power and influence in the localities.

Thus, although most of Lancaster's followers had lands near the earl, and this may have been the stimulus for service in the cases of some of them, their local links do not appear to have been the earl's primary motive for recruiting them. Had it been, one would expect to find a more systematic attempt on his part to recruit gentry followers within particular districts where he was a major landholder. His following was not one of the soil, but, as stated above, his position as the king's brother meant that he exercised power and influence in a way different from other lords.[72] He sought and attracted men from beyond the narrow confines of neighbourhood, something that suited his purposes, given the courtly and chivalric nature of his life.[73]

If Lancaster was exceptional thanks to his royal status and newly created earldom, then Lincoln was much more likely to have been 'typical', if such a thing can be said of any earl's following. The earl clearly exercised a powerful lordship in south Yorkshire, centred on his castle of Pontefract, and a number of his knightly followers had lands in Yorkshire,

[70] Bennett, *Community, Class and Careerism*, 38–9; Walker, *Lancastrian Affinity*, 147.

[71] DL 25/2369, 2337, 2338; DL 36/1/108; Appendix B, nos. 19–20.

[72] See above, 119.

[73] A similar point is made in relation to John of Gaunt's affinity, where his courtly and chivalric ambitions led him to recruit men with little weight in local society, in A. Goodman, 'John of Gaunt: Paradigm of the Late Fourteenth-Century Crisis', *Transactions of the Royal Historical Society*, 5th Series 37 (1987), 146–8.

including William Vavasour, William de Stopham, Robert de Hertford, John Newmarch, Miles de Stapleton, John de Stapleton, John Spring and Robert de Roos, of whom several were his tenants.[74] In Lincolnshire, the earl could call upon Vavasour (again), Sir John Bek, Sir Robert Shireland, and Roos (again).[75] Given Lincoln's extensive estates in both these counties, such links with important local gentry are similar to those one would expect to find in a classic late medieval regionally based 'bastard feudal' affinity. There are, however, some important caveats. First, as has been seen already, many of these links came through an existing tenurial link and are therefore more traditional than 'bastard feudal'.[76] Second, not all of these men were in Lincoln's following at any one time, making his penetration of local society rather less extensive than it seems at first sight. Finally, and perhaps most importantly, both Yorkshire and Lincolnshire are very large counties, and some of the earl's followers held lands considerable distances from where he did. For instance, Sir John de Stapleton's Yorkshire lands at Dalton and Melsonby were over sixty miles from Pontefract.[77] Lincoln's recruitment did not penetrate very deeply into the great pool of gentry families in either of these counties.

Elsewhere across Lincoln's estates, there were a number of men linked to the earl by neighbourhood but there is no sense that he was trying to establish any sort of lordship over these areas by recruiting significant numbers of local knights. Indeed, knights found in connection with Lincoln in his lands outside Yorkshire, and to a lesser extent Lincolnshire, tend to be isolated examples. Sir Maurice le Brun, who appears in Lincoln's service around 1300, held lands in Kent and Hampshire but also the manor of Ranston in Dorset, just twelve miles from Kingston Lacy, Lincoln's chief manor in the south-west.[78] Roger de Trumpington and, following his death in 1289, his son Giles held the manor of Trumpington near Cambridge, very near Lincoln's manor of Grantchester.[79] Lincoln and Trumpington both held these lands from the Mortimers of Wigmore and it is interesting that the Trumpingtons sought service with the earl rather than with their feudal lord. While neighbourhood was an obvious

[74] For Vavasour, Stopham and Miles de Stapleton: see above, 121. For Hertford: *CPR 1292–1301*, 71. For Newmarch: *CIPM*, IV, no. 236. For John de Stapleton: *CIPM*, VI, no. 49. For Spring: *CCR 1288–1296*, 311. For Roos: *CIPM*, V, no. 252.

[75] For Vavasour: *CIPM*, III, no. 265. For Bek: *CPR 1272–1281*, 141. For Shireland: *CCR 1279–1288*, 97, where he is named erroneously as 'Roger'. For Roos: *CIPM*, V, no. 252.

[76] See above, 121. There were, of course, feudal tenants to be found in the affinities of late medieval magnates but the proportion is usually much lower than in thirteenth-century followings.

[77] *CCR 1302–1307*, 230; *CIPM*, VI, no. 49.

[78] TNA C 67/14, m. 11; *CIPM*, IV, no. 34; *CIPM*, V, nos. 63, 372; *CIPM*, VI, no. 585; *CCR 1296–1302*, 444; *CPR 1292–1301*, 538.

[79] *CIPM*, II, no. 711; *CIPM*, V, no. 279, p. 154.

means of enlisting members of a late medieval affinity, outside Yorkshire, Lincoln seems to have been happy to recruit very scantily among the local gentry, even in areas where he held extensive lands, such as Dorset and Wiltshire.

A similar pattern emerges with the earl of Cornwall: mostly small numbers of followers in the counties where the earl had significant lands, except perhaps along the Thames Valley, the heart of his estates and where he spent most of his time, where he had twelve associates across Berkshire and Oxfordshire.[80] Even here, though, the numbers involved are again quite small compared to later affinities and there seems to be no systematic recruitment of major figures in these counties.

The recruiting patterns of these three major earls owed much to both the feudal past and the 'bastard feudal' future. The hard core of tenants in the followings of both Lincoln and Cornwall, coupled with Lancaster's obvious attempts to create new feudal ties of his own, suggest that traditional attitudes remained but that the earls did not feel themselves constrained to act in feudal ways only. This does not mean, however, that they recruited in the same manner, for the same purposes or on the same scale as their descendants in the fourteenth and fifteenth centuries. Their purposes will be investigated more thoroughly in the next chapter but caution warns that, though these followings may look in some ways like late medieval affinities, when the veneer is scratched away there remain troubling differences that suggest that these earls may have been relying on very different methods from their late fourteenth- and fifteenth-century counterparts in creating and sustaining their power and influence.

One of those key and troubling differences is that of scale. All thirteenth-century comital followings that have been studied are considerably smaller than those of the late fourteenth and fifteenth centuries. It would be foolish, of course, to expect thirteenth-century earls to have been recruiting on the scale of John of Gaunt, but their local recruiting is, in many cases, not even on the scale of such a relative late-fourteenth-century comital small-fry as Edward Courtenay, earl of Devon. Courtenay liveried eight knights, forty-one esquires and fourteen lawyers in 1384–5 and he was one of the poorest earls in late-fourteenth-century England.[81] The contrast with the situation in the thirteenth century is clear. Edmund of Lancaster's following was large by thirteenth-century standards and numbered around fifteen knights around 1270, near the beginning of his

[80] William de Bereford, Richard de Cornubia, Thomas Danvers, Walter de Puylle, Henry de Shottesbroke, Robert Damory, Walter de Aylesbury, Thomas de Breaute, Robert de Malet, Thomas de Kancia, Adam le Despenser and Richard de Seyton.

[81] Cherry, 'Courtenay', 72.

career, at a time when the title of knight was more common than it had become a century later.[82] By 1295, the number of Lancastrian knights seems to have grown somewhat, perhaps as a result of the pressures of war. In April 1295, Lancaster submitted a list of twelve knights, described as 'his people', to the chancellor to obtain respites from taxation on the grounds of their military service in Wales.[83] To this list might be added Brabazon, Meriet, Helyun, Glastonbury, Richard Fukeram junior, Nicholas and Ralph de St Maur, Walter de Bath, Reginald de St Martin and Alan de Waldeshef, all in close association with the earl of Lancaster at the same time. This brings the number of knights with strong links to Lancaster in *c.*1295 to twenty-one. Given that only relatively few members of the gentry were knights by the late fourteenth century and that the 'esquires' of Devon's affinity would mostly have been knights in the thirteenth century, the gentry following of one of the richest earls of the late thirteenth century was smaller than that of one of the poorest earls a century later.[84]

Lincoln's following was smaller than Lancaster's but still large by the standards of the time. For instance, six to eight knights are known to have been in the service of Simon de Montfort at any one time, twelve with William de Valence, and a similar number in the followings of Rogers III and IV Bigod, earls of Norfolk, while the largest were the fifteen and eighteen knights connected respectively with Roger de Quincy, earl of Winchester, or William Marshal.[85] Around 1280, ten knights can be identified as Lincoln's regular associates, although three of these were lawyers.[86] By the turn of the fourteenth century, the number of knights had risen, largely as a result of the war, and stood at fifteen.[87]

It might be thought that these differences in size can be explained away simply by the quality of evidence available in the thirteenth century compared with the later period. The evidence for the most complete

[82] Sirs Hamo de Aungerville, William Bagot, Thomas de Bray, Roger de Clifford, Richard Fukeram, Walter de Helyun, Geoffrey de Langley, Alan Lascelles, John de Oketon, Walter de Percy, Laurence de St Maur, Roger Somery, Gilbert Talbot, Robert de Turberville, Richard de Wyk.

[83] *Calendar of Chancery Warrants, 1244–1326*, 57. Sirs William de Grandisson, Laurence St Maur, William le Long, Geoffrey de Langley, William Wyther, Robert Farnham, William Kugeho, Richard Talbot, John de Turbeville, Ralph le Botiller, Thomas de Bermingham, Thomas le Botiller.

[84] Saul, *Knights and Esquires*, 6–25, has a useful survey of this change.

[85] Simpson, '*Familia* of Roger de Quincy', 107; Crouch, *William Marshal*, 137–41; Ridgeway, 'William de Valence', 245; Maddicott, *Simon de Montfort*, 69; Morris, *Bigod Earls*, 68–70, 148–9.

[86] John Bek, Huw de Dutton, Robert Fitz Roger, Robert de Hertford, Peter Malore, James de Neville, William de Stopham, Ralph de Trehampton, Roger de Trumpington and William Vavasour. The three lawyers were Bek, Hertford and Malore.

[87] Robert de Hertford, Adam de Huddleston, John de Huddleston, Alexander de Ledes, Nicholas de Leyburn, James de Neville, John Newmarch, Robert Shireland, John Spring, John de Stapleton, Miles de Stapleton, William de Stopham, Richard de Sutton, Giles de Trumpington and William Vavasour.

followings of the early fourteenth century, however, does not allow for such confidence when comparisons are made with later in the century. Thomas of Lancaster had by far the largest comital following of the early fourteenth century; no one else even came close to matching the numbers of men in his service. During the delicate negotiations surrounding the Treaty of Leake in 1318, Earl Thomas could call directly upon perhaps fifty knights, who might themselves bring many more to his service, but most of the time his following was around half that number.[88] John of Gaunt, on the other hand, had 173 indentured retainers in 1382 – seven bannerets, seventy knights and ninety-six esquires – and three years later he had further increased the size of his affinity with a net addition of a further eight knights and twenty esquires.[89] Of course, both Earl Thomas and Duke John were, for different reasons, exceptional in the extent of their recruiting, but the differences in scale between them are reflected in other contemporary evidence. The survival of two Lancastrian *valors* from the early 1330s, during the time of Earl Thomas' younger brother, Henry, provide a rare survival from before the Hundred Years War of records of payments made to retainers.[90] In 1330–1 Lancaster made payments totalling £386 13*s* 3*d* to eight knights, three clerks, two women and fifteen other men who, though not designated as such, can be taken as esquires. The following year, Earl Henry paid £335 6*s* 2½*d* in life fees to six knights, three clerks, three women and seventeen other men.[91] Only four knights, two clerks, two women and nine esquires appear in both lists, meaning that Lancaster paid fees to ten knights, four clerks, three women and twenty-three esquires between 1330 and 1332.[92] Other evidence in the *valors*, such as gifts to various named knights and payments to his officials, most of whom are not named, together with evidence of grants of lands rather than money fees to retainers and charter-witnessing demonstrate that Lancaster's following was somewhat larger than that glimpsed in the *valors*: a further ten knights and sixteen esquires can be added.[93] Earl Henry's following in the late 1320s to the early 1330s, then,

88 Maddicott, *Thomas of Lancaster*, 45.

89 Walker, *Lancastrian Affinity*, 14.

90 TNA DL 41/1/11, ff. 45v, 51v–52.

91 When discussing an earl's power and influence, the fees paid to women and clerks are largely irrelevant as they possessed no independent power of their own.

92 Those knights receiving fees in both years were Henry de Ferrers (£100), John de Twyford, (£33 6*s* 8*d*), Roger de Quilly (£20) and William de Walkington (£10 and £7 10*s*). Those receiving fees only in 1330–1 were Henry de Glastonbury (£40), Philip Darcy (£26 13*s* 4*d*), John de Mygrave (£16 13*s* 4*d*) and John de Barkworth (£6 13*s* 4*d*). Those receiving fees in 1331–2 only were Sir Ralph de Hastings (£40) and John de Miners (£16 13*s* 4*d*).

93 Fees totalling £227 6*s* 8*d* were paid in 1330–1 to twenty-two sheriffs, stewards, constables, receivers and bailiffs of the Lancastrian estates and castles: DL 41/1/11, f. 45. Only four of these were named, Robert Foucher, John de Holt, Robert de Hungerford and John le Serjaunt, only the last

was around twenty knights and thirty-nine esquires. Lancaster was, of course, at the very top end of comital income (the *valor* for 1330–1 gives an income, after fees to retainers and officials, of £6,463 16*s* 3¼*d* and £5,370 9*s* 5*d* for 1331–2)[94] and was recruiting extensively for political purposes, but even so his following was not much larger than that of the much poorer Edward Courtenay, earl of Devon. John Holland, earl of Huntingdon, with an income of just over £1,000 was spending £170 12*s* retaining twenty-six annuitants in 1436, a much higher proportion of his income than Henry of Lancaster was spending.[95] In 1442 the duke of Buckingham, whose income was closer to Lancaster's bracket, was paying eighty-three annuitants, more than double the number to whom Lancaster was paying fees in the early 1330s and over a third more than the fuller numbers who can be shown to have been in Lancaster's service at the time.[96] In 1509, the will of the thirteenth earl of Oxford listed payments to thirteen knights and thirty-three esquires, a higher number than those paid fees by Henry of Lancaster, and, like Lancaster, a figure that could be significantly supplemented by other evidence.[97] Looking beyond simply lists of annuitants to a magnate's wider affinity, no fewer than eighty-eight members of Warwickshire landed society have been identified as linked in one way or another to Richard Beauchamp, earl of Warwick, during his long career in the early fifteenth century.[98] Henry of Lancaster's following, easily one of the largest of his day, was in scale a much closer fit to those of mid-ranking nobles of the later fourteenth and fifteenth centuries and never approached the size of the greatest late medieval affinities, such as Richard of Gloucester's or John of Gaunt's, and the same can be said of the greatest noble followings of his father's day.

Fees, whether directly linked to land or simply in the form of cash, were, of course, the most obvious, visible and regular means by which a lord could reward the service of one of his followers. It was not the only

of whom appears in the list of fees paid. The following year only Robert de Hungerford is named as one of the officials to whom payments were made: ibid., fol. 51. In 1331–2, three knights, John de Sapy, William Trussell and Ralph de Beeston, not named elsewhere in the *valor* received cash gifts from the earl: ibid., fols. 53, 53v, 54v. Holmes, *Estates*, 67–9, discusses the *valors* and also other grants by Earl Henry from around this time and earlier. To those mentioned above can be added Sirs William and Thomas le Blount, Sir Richard Rivers, Sir Thomas de Rosselin and Sir William Wyther (d. 1329), along with Bertram de Fanacourt and Simon de Kinardesey, Michael le Armerer and Thomas le Porter. From charter evidence of the early 1330s, it would also be prudent to add the names of Sir Henry de Hambury, Robert de Radcliffe and John de Freeland to those closely associated with Earl Henry: *CPR 1330–34*, 321; *CCR 1330–33*, 598; DL 42/1, fols. 24v, 66v, 67v, 67v–68, 68–68v, 68v–69, 69; DL 42/2, fols. 84, 101–101v, 104v, 104v–105, 120v–121, 121–121v.

94 DL 41/1/11, fols. 48r, 55.

95 M.M.N. Stansfield, 'The Holland Family, Dukes of Exeter, Earls of Kent and Huntingdon, 1352–1475', unpublished DPhil thesis, University of Oxford (1987), 271.

96 Rawcliffe, *Staffords*, 73. 97 Ross, *John de Vere*, 184.

98 Carpenter, *Locality and Polity*, 684–90.

way, however, and lords could, and did, intervene for their men in other ways, particularly with the royal government. There is some evidence of the earls under Edward I obtaining royal favour for their close associates. Sir Laurence de St Maur, for example, received permission from the king to hunt in Selwood Forest in Wiltshire in 1283 at the instance of Edmund of Lancaster.[99] Similarly, Lancaster wrote to the treasurer, John de Kirkby, requesting the latter's assistance for his knight, and Laurence's brother, Sir Ralph de St Maur.[100] Lincoln obtained a favourable marriage for John de Stapleton.[101] A large number of people were granted royal pardons having first sought the intervention of an earl, particularly from those earls such as Lincoln, Warenne and Edmund of Lancaster, who were close to the king.[102] Most of these came from the period after the Barons' Wars and after 1294, with the opening of a protracted period of war, and where it is possible to identify the origins of men requesting pardons, they often came from counties where their benefactor had no interests.[103] It is possible, therefore, that such people merely sought the intercession of someone they knew was close to the king, but with whom they had no prior or future connection. Earls might obtain grants for their towns, as Warenne did for Stamford, Lancaster for Cardigan and Leicester, and Cornwall for the citizens of Exeter.[104] There is little evidence of more than this, however. The problem with this type of evidence is that so often influence is an invisible agent. Having said that, the evidence for lords intervening for their followers in the thirteenth century is greater than for the fifteenth century, where the loss of privy seal and signet seals records makes lords' influence on the great seal much less visible.[105] There is in fact not a great deal of evidence that fifteenth-century magnates got much out of the king for their men. In a period that is rather better documented in this respect, there seems to be little, beyond the obtaining of pardons, that the thirteenth-century earls did for men beyond their immediate followings.[106]

[99] *CPR 1281–1292*, 59. [100] TNA SC 1/8/119. [101] *CPR 1301–1307*, 378.

[102] For Lancaster: *CPR 1266–1272*, 9, 13, 60, 63, 78, 185, 201, 202, 203, 317, 333, 359, 407, 409, 411–12, 444, 458, 460, 467, 501, 519; *CPR 1272–1281*, 38, 39–40, 53, 79, 220; *CPR 1292–1301*, 13. For Warenne: *CPR 1266–1272*, 200, 204, 227, 382, 516; *CPR 1292–1301*, 83, 483, 617; *CPR 1301–1307*, 4, 248. For Lincoln: *CPR 1272–1281*, 226; *CPR 1281–1292*, 444; *CPR 1292–1301*, 88, 129, 136, 138, 141, 158, 246, 347, 535, 606; *CPR 1301–1307*, 38, 229, 244, 246–7, 252, 314, 379, 389, 392, 423.

[103] For instance, John Buk of Norfolk obtained a royal pardon for murder at Lincoln's instance in 1298, but Norfolk was not a county where Lincoln had any interests. *CPR 1292–1301*, 347.

[104] *CPR 1266–1272*, 121, 333, 410; *CPR 1281–1292*, 149.

[105] See Brown, *Governance*, 52.

[106] See Carpenter, *Locality and Polity*, 630–1, for the argument that access to royal patronage was of little importance to the recruitment and functioning of fifteenth-century magnate affinities. Much the same could be said of the evidence presented here.

The final point to be considered in this chapter is the continuity of comital affinities. Four of the ten knights serving Lincoln around 1280 were still in his service two decades later, while another, Sir Roger de Trumpington, was the father of one of those serving Lincoln in 1300.[107] Of the twenty-one knights serving Edmund of Lancaster in 1295, three were among the fifteen serving him in 1270, while a further five were relatives of the 1270 knights.[108] The estates of both earls were, of course, eventually united in the person of Thomas of Lancaster and there is strong evidence of continuity from both parts of Earl Thomas' inheritance. Of a sample of thirty knights of Thomas of Lancaster's affinity picked out by John Maddicott, eight can be shown to have served Edmund of Lancaster or had a relative who did so.[109] A further five had either served the earl of Lincoln or had relatives who had served him.[110] To these should also be added the names of Nicholas de St Maur, Richard Fukeram junior, Peter de Grandisson and Richard Talbot, all of whom provided second-generation service to either Edmund or Thomas or both.[111] Such levels of continuity should not surprise but they help to demonstrate the inner workings of a thirteenth-century comital following. Furthermore, one of the reasons put forward for the decline of the feudal bond is that both lords and men were keen to escape from the 'honorial straitjacket' of service from or with one particular family.[112] The continuity demonstrated here, however, reminds one that the instinct of human beings to copy the life choices of their parents was not something created by feudalism, nor likely to be eradicated by the waning of feudal ties.

CONCLUSION

This chapter has used all the evidence available to piece together the followings of three of Edward I's earls. This allows conclusions to be

[107] The four were Hertford, Neville, Stopham and Vavasour.

[108] The three original knights were Sir Laurence de St Maur, Sir Walter de Helyun and Sir Geoffrey de Langley (himself the son of an earlier associate of Lancaster's). The five knights in 1295 who were relatives of knights serving Lancaster in 1270 were Sir Richard de Fukeram junior (Sir Richard de Fukeram senior), Sirs Ralph and Nicholas de St Maur (Sir Laurence de St Maur), Sir John de Turberville (Sir Robert de Turberville) and Sir Richard Talbot (Sir Gilbert Talbot).

[109] Maddicott, *Thomas of Lancaster*, 53–4. Hugh de Cuilly, Fulk Fitz Warin, William Latimer, Fulk Lestrange, Hugh de Meynill, Nicholas and Stephen de Segrave and Thomas Wyther.

[110] John Bek, John de Clavering, Adam de Huddleston, Edmund de Neville and William de Roos of Ingmanthorp.

[111] St Maur: *Gough*, 179; C 67/14, mm. 5, 11d; C 67/15, m. 12. Fukeram: C 67/10, m. 4; *CIM*, II, no. 817; *CPR 1292–1301*, 105, 353, 393; *CPR 1313–17*, 22, where a *Reynald* de Fukeram is mentioned as an adherent of Thomas of Lancaster, though this may be a clerical error for Richard; *Rôles Gascons*, III, no. 2830. Grandisson: *CPR 1327–1330*, 245; TNA LR 14/1083; DL 42/2, f. 66; *Gough*, 179. Talbot, the son of Gilbert de Talbot: *Calendar of Chancery Warrants 1244–1326*, 57; *CPR 1272–1281*, 156; *Rôles Gascons*, III, 338.

[112] Coss *et al.*, 'Debate', 185–6.

drawn about where these nobles looked for service and to compare the size and nature of these followings with the 'bastard feudal' affinities of the late middle ages. Acknowledging that the answer is not complete, it is possible to say at this stage that there are definite similarities in the way thirteenth-century comital followings were created to those of the late fourteenth and fifteenth centuries but significant differences as well.

The earls of Lancaster, Lincoln and Cornwall were all looking well beyond their feudal tenants for service, as did the nobles of the fifteenth century, and in many cases the rewards offered by the earls for service were not the permanent feudal alienations of the eleventh century but were temporary or life grants of land with a fixed and determinable value. The bias towards the temporary nature of reward is a hallmark of 'bastard feudalism'. Before claiming that this means that these earls were offering 'bastard feudal' rewards as a means of attracting service, there are two important caveats that must be made. The first is the continuing presence of a feudal mindset in the selection and reward of retainers. A hard core of the close associates of the earls of Lincoln and Cornwall were their feudal tenants, while Edmund of Lancaster made permanent grants of land by knight service to several of his closest followers. In addition to this there is a clear preference among these three earls for rewards to be linked to specific pieces of land rather than simple grants of fees, something that had become more common by the middle of the fourteenth century, as Henry of Lancaster's *valors* make clear.[113] Similar accounts from the estates of the earls of Cornwall, Lincoln and Norfolk in Edward I's reign provide little evidence to suggest that cash rewards were the normal way of remunerating service as they were to be in the fourteenth and fifteenth centuries.[114] The second caveat is that it would be wrong to assume that there was a linear progression from a feudal system, where permanent alienation was the means of rewarding service, to a 'bastard feudal' system in which every retainer simply received a cash fee from his lord. The reality, as historians have recognised, is more complex than this. There is much to be said for Crouch's view that little changed in the way that magnates recruited their followers between 1100 and 1300 and that the temporary ascendancy of grants by knight's service disappeared with the first generation after Hastings.[115] The evidence presented here,

[113] See above, 130.

[114] The only obvious example of cash payments to retainers who were not also officials is *Two Compoti*, 149.

[115] Coss *et al.*, 'Debate', 168, 172.

moreover, suggests that the feudal bond may well have been stronger in the thirteenth century than Crouch allows for, as Carpenter has also argued. The means by which the earls of Edward I's reign obtained service and rewarded their followers would not have been unfamiliar to William Marshal at the end of the twelfth century or Earl Roger of Hereford in the 1140s.[116] Twelfth- and thirteenth-century nobles had a variety of ways in which they could reward their followers, including both permanent and temporary grants, whereas in the later fourteenth and fifteenth centuries, while fees from his lord formed a small part of a retainer's overall income, the real inducement magnate service offered was usually the lord's control over the local legal process.[117]

The geographical distribution of these earls' followers offers a similar picture. There is evidence that Lincoln and Cornwall were recruiting close to their main centres of power, south Yorkshire and the Thames Valley, as might be expected of a 'bastard feudal' magnate, but one would expect a medieval lord from any century to look to his neighbours for service; that in itself is not 'bastard feudal'. It is here that the issue of size comes to the fore. A 'bastard feudal' magnate did not need to have complete penetration of the local gentry elite to exercise rule of his 'country', but he needed sufficient numbers of the greater gentry to gain general acceptance of his authority and to ensure that he could have a greater or lesser role in the validation of the transactions of many of the middling and greater gentry of his 'country'.[118] None of the three earls in this chapter came close to achieving this level of penetration of the local gentry in any of their areas of influence, nor is there any indication that they sought so to do. At this stage, however, the job of answering whether the thirteenth century was a 'bastard feudal' one is only half done. The purpose of comital followings and the nature of noble power are just as important components in coming to a full answer to the question of 'bastard feudalism' in the thirteenth century as the way these followings were created. This chapter has focused mainly on the first of the two definitions of 'bastard feudalism', that is, the narrow, technical means by which service was obtained; the next chapter will broaden out to look at whether the claims of Coss and others that the way society worked in the thirteenth century was the same as in the fifteenth century are sustainable.

[116] Crouch, *William Marshal*, 157–68; Coss *et al.*, 'Debate', 173.

[117] Carpenter, *Wars of the Roses*, 59–61. [118] Ibid., 59.

Chapter 6

THE EXERCISE OF COMITAL POWER

The previous chapter looked at the structure of comital followings in Edward I's reign and how they were created. It is necessary now to answer the wider questions of how earls used their followings and how they exercised power in the localities. As noted already, one of the key planks of Peter Coss' argument about the development of 'bastard feudalism' is that it was a response to the legal reforms of Henry II's reign.[1]

If Coss is correct and the thirteenth century was indeed a 'bastard feudal' one, then one would expect to find the kind of penetration of royal law and administration by magnates in the reign of Edward I that is found in later centuries. As Alan Harding has written, echoing historians of the fifteenth century, magnates' local influence in the thirteenth century 'depended on the number of county justices and officials they could attract into their retinues'.[2] In discovering how late-thirteenth-century magnates exercised their power, it is necessary, therefore, to put this idea to the test.

Edmund of Lancaster was hereditary sheriff of Lancashire but he appears to have shown relatively little concern about ensuring that his own man was serving as deputy sheriff. None of the three known deputy sheriffs of Lancashire in his lifetime were particularly close to him, as far as the incomplete evidence available suggests.[3] Those appointed must have been considered trustworthy by the earl, but Lancaster's apparent

[1] Coss, 'Bastard Feudalism Revised'; see above, 106–7.

[2] Harding, *England in the Thirteenth Century*, 263.

[3] *List of Sheriffs of England and Wales from the Earliest Times to A.D. 1831*, List and Index Society 9 (1963), 72. Gilbert de Clifton was an official of the earl of Lincoln, Henry de Lee may have been a relative of Edmund's receiver Nicholas de Lee, while Ralph de Mountjoy was a tenant of Edmund in Derbyshire and associated with him on one or two occasions, but was clearly not one of Edmund's intimates. *CIPM*, III, no. 423; *Rotuli Hundredorum*, I, 300; R. Somerville, *History of the Duchy of Lancaster* (London: Chancellor and Council of the Duchy of Lancaster, 1953), 347, 348; *Yorkshire Hundred and Quo Warranto Rolls*, 50; *The Rolls of the 1281 Derbyshire Eyre*, ed. A.M. Hopkinson, Derbyshire Record Society 28 (2000), no. 290; E 159/66, m. 6.

lack of close interest in the Lancashire shrievalty is reflected elsewhere. Outside Lancashire, the earl had just four associates who served as sheriffs at some point during their career. John de Oketon was sheriff of Yorkshire in 1260 and again in 1265;[4] Ranulph Dacre, Edmund's steward in Lancashire, was sheriff of Yorkshire between October 1278 and May 1280;[5] William Bagot sheriff of Shropshire–Staffordshire in 1258–9 and then of Warwickshire–Leicestershire in 1259–61, 1262–4 and 1265–71; and Thomas de Bray sheriff of Bedfordshire–Buckinghamshire between 1270 and 1274.[6] Only two of them served in the same county (Yorkshire), meaning that Lancaster was clearly making no attempt to achieve that hallmark of 'bastard feudalism', domination of local administration, in any particular county. Furthermore, their tenure of office often did not coincide with their service to Lancaster. John de Oketon, for example, was sheriff of Yorkshire long before he first appears in association with Lancaster some time around 1270.[7] William Bagot was already on his third tenure of the Warwickshire–Leicestershire shrievalty when he first appears in Lancaster's service in 1267.[8] It should also be noted in connection with Thomas de Bray that Lancaster had major estates in neither Bedfordshire nor Buckinghamshire. However, Bray did hold other local crown office – crown bailiff of the Peak in 1281 – where Lancaster did have estates, while William Wyther, one of Edmund's most important officials in Staffordshire, also acted as coroner there.[9] Besides Wyther, Geoffrey de Langley and Richard Talbot also acted as crown agents, but only in the temporary role of commissioner of array.[10] Lancaster, thus,

[4] *List of Sheriffs*, 161. [5] Ibid., 161.

[6] H.W. Ridgeway, 'Mid-Thirteenth Century Reformers and the Locality: the Sheriffs of the Baronial Regime, 1258–1261', in P. Fleming, A. Gross and J.R. Lander (eds.), *Regionalism and Revision: the Crown and Its Provinces in England, 1250–1650* (London: Hambledon Press, 1998), 66, 72, 81; *List of Sheriffs*, 144.

[7] He was sheriff of Yorkshire in 1260 and again in 1265; *List of Sheriffs*, 161. His first association with Lancaster comes from an undated charter, confirmed in February 1270; *CChR 1257–1300*, 135–6.

[8] *List of Sheriffs*, 144. He witnessed Edmund's first known charter, which dates from 29 May 1267; *CChR 1257–1300*, 150. The nature of the evidence, of course, makes it very difficult to say precisely when a man did enter the service of a magnate but in the cases of Oketon and Bagot it is certain that their terms as sheriff occurred before their association with Lancaster as the earl's landed career did not begin until 1265.

[9] For Bray, see *CPR 1281–1292*, 43. For Wyther as coroner, see Somerville, *Duchy of Lancaster*, 349. He is recorded as Lancaster's steward in Tutbury in 1285, 1286 and 1294, DL 25/1844, 1850, 2205. He was also justice of Lancaster's forests in the north in 1287 and 1288, *CPR 1281–1292*, 263, 292; as Lancaster's attorney at the Staffordshire eyre in 1293, 'Extracts from the Plea Rolls, 1272 to 1294', ed. and trans. G. Wrottesley, *W.M. Salt Archaeological Society* 6 (1885), 211; and as a commissioner of *oyer* and *terminer* into trespasses in Lancaster's midland parks, *CPR 1281–1292*, 279.

[10] For Wyther, see *Parl Writs*, I, 245. For Langley, see *CCRV*, 259. For Talbot, see *Parl Writs*, I, 358. Though Talbot was not commissioner in Gloucestershire until 1301, five years after Edmund's death, he was in the service of Earl Thomas by that time.

cannot be said to have attempted to dominate local administration in any meaningful way.

There is even less evidence of association between the earl of Lincoln and local royal officials. His only known associate among the sheriffs was Gilbert de Clifton, who served as Lancaster's deputy in Lancashire in 1284–5 and who had been Lincoln's steward at Pontefract in Yorkshire a decade previously.[11] A few of his followers, Robert Fitz Roger, John de Huddleston and William Vavasour, held military office from the crown, as commanders in the Scottish Marches or as commissioners of array, but this says more about the earls' roles as important and natural channels of recruitment for the king's armies than of any desire on their part to control the operation of royal government in peacetime.[12] Lincoln, as one of Edward I's closest friends and coming from a long-established and settled magnate family, is an ideal candidate to be a 'bastard feudal' magnate in the late medieval mould, yet there is no indication that he was acting as such. John de Warenne had links with two sheriffs of Sussex and Surrey, Roger de Loges and John de Wauton, but none in Yorkshire, Norfolk or Lincolnshire, other counties where he had important interests.[13] No sheriff during Edward I's reign is known to have been an associate of the Bohun earls of Hereford.

By way of comparison, Caroline Burt's work on the Beauchamp earls of Warwick reveals that Earl William (d. 1298) was not seeking to influence local government but that in the last years of Edward I's reign Earl Guy (d. 1315) exercised significant control over local government in Warwickshire.[14] The other earls mentioned so far follow more of the pattern of Earl William, with little indication that they were seeking to dominate local administration, but there are two earls who did have more significant links with local officers. The first, Gilbert de Clare, earl of Gloucester, had ties with several sheriffs but, as with Lancaster and unlike Guy Beauchamp, these were not in any way systematic. Roger de Loges, as well as serving as Warenne's steward at Lewes, had earlier been steward to Gloucester's father, Richard, and Hamo de Hautein, Gloucester's steward in 1268, had twice been sheriff of Lincolnshire and also sheriff of Norfolk and Suffolk, but this was before the Barons' Wars.[15]

[11] *List of Sheriffs*, 72; *Yorkshire Hundred and Quo Warranto Rolls*, 50.

[12] *CPR 1292–1301*, 312, 313, 438, 491, 512; *CPR 1301–1307*, 132, 133, 146; *CCR 1296–1302*, 77, 381.

[13] *Records of the Barony and Honour of the Rape of Lewes*, 34; *Cartulary of Lewes Priory: the Portion Relating to Counties Other Than Sussex: Surrey*, Sussex Record Society, Extra Vol. (1943), no. 62; *List of Sheriffs*, 135; *The 1263 Surrey Eyre*, ed. and trans. S. Stewart, Surrey Record Society 40 (2006), xxxii; The British Library, MS Additional 43972, f. 77r; *CChR 1257–1300*, 455.

[14] Burt, '"Bastard Feudal" Affinity', 173, 176–8.

[15] Altschul, *Baronial Family*, 228; *The 1263 Surrey Eyre*, xxxii.

Two other associates of Gloucester served as sheriff. John de Thedmersh was in the earl's service for more than thirty years but his native county of Berkshire, where he was sheriff between 1281 and 1285, was not one where Gloucester had important interests.[16] John de Crepping, on the other hand, although sheriff of Gloucester's county of Glamorgan during the earl's lifetime, did not become a sheriff in England – in Durham – until 1302, seven years after his lord's death.[17] Of the four men associated with Gloucester who were also sheriffs, only Hautein served in a county (Suffolk) where the earl had important interests and this was during the time of Gloucester's father. There is no indication that Gloucester sought to dominate any shrievalty and he had no connection with any sheriffs in counties such as Kent, Gloucestershire or Dorset, where it might have been expected if he was aiming at domination of local administration in the heart of his English estates.

The earl with the greatest number of associations with sheriffs was Edmund of Cornwall. Cornwall had considerable control over administration in the county from which he drew his title but this was not without controversy. The Cornish had paid both King John and Henry III for the right to elect their own sheriff but Henry had quickly reneged on the deal and given control of the shrievalty to his brother, Richard, when appointing him earl in 1227.[18] The offices of comital steward and sheriff were combined by Earl Richard after the Barons' Wars, and leading Cornish knights were excluded by both Richard and Edmund.[19] Several of the men appointed to the Cornish shrievalty were not only close associates of the earl but were also outsiders to the county.[20] It is clear, however, that this policy was very unpopular within Cornwall. The county unsuccessfully appealed to Edward I for the restoration of

[16] *CFR 1272–1307*, 146; *CIM*, I, nos. 390, 729; *CPR 1281–1292*, 183; *CPR 1292–1301*, 9, 39, 179.

[17] W. de Gray-Birch, *A History of Neath Abbey* (Neath: John E. Richards, 1902), 321–2; *List of Sheriffs*, 42A. He was later sheriff in Northumberland and Yorkshire; *List of Sheriffs*, 97, 161.

[18] M. Page, 'Cornwall, Earl Richard and the Barons' War', *EHR* 115 (2000), 27–8.

[19] Ibid., 31.

[20] For Cornish sheriffs, see *List of Sheriffs*, 21. Richard de Seyton, sheriff 1273–8, held most of his lands in the east midlands, particularly Rutland, but was a tenant of the earl in Oxfordshire: *CCR 1272–1279*, 350; *CCR 1279–1288*, 281; *CIPM*, III, no. 604, p. 468; *CPR 1266–1272*, 289. Thomas le Erckedene, sheriff 1279–80, was a Cornish knight and tenant of the earl, but in addition to acting as sheriff and steward in Cornwall, he was also the earl's steward at Berkhamsted, demonstrating a connection beyond the county of Cornwall: *CIPM*, III, no. 604, pp. 476, 489; TNA E 36/57, no. 116. Walter de Aylesbury, sheriff 1289–90, was from Oxfordshire and was one of Edmund's closest associates, eventually designated as one of his executors: *CIPM*, III, no. 604, pp. 476, 480, 485; *CPR 1292–1301*, 603. Thomas Danvers witnessed a number of charters relating to Edmund and was also sheriff in both Anglesey and Oxfordshire, indicating his status as an outsider: *The Cartulary of Launceston Priory*, ed. and trans. P.L. Hull, Devon and Exeter Record Society, New Series 30 (1987), no. 16; E 36/57, nos. 53, 158, 198, 237. Theobald de Neville, sheriff 1292–5, was a Rutland tenant of the earl who also held lands in Warwickshire: *CCR 1296–1302*, 437; *CIPM*, II, no. 116.

their right to appoint their own sheriff in 1276 and 1302, and they frequently complained about Earl Edmund's choices.[21] His control of the Cornish shrievalty has parallels with the 'curialist' model employed by monarchs until the middle of Henry III's reign, whereby a trusted outsider was used to dominate the locals.

Earl Edmund's control over the Rutland shrievalty seems to have been less complete than his dominance in Cornwall, despite the fact that he was hereditary sheriff in both counties. Of the known under-sheriffs in Rutland, only Sir Geoffrey de Russell, the earl's steward and one of his most frequent charter witnesses, was one of his intimates.[22] Outside Cornwall and Rutland, there were four associates of Earl Edmund who served as sheriff. Master Roger de Seyton, a member of a Rutland family with links to the earl, was sheriff of Northamptonshire between 1272 and 1274 and later served on two commissions of *oyer* and *terminer* relating to crimes committed against Cornwall.[23] Sir Henry de Shottesbroke, Cornwall's steward at Berkhamsted at one point and one of his closest associates, was sheriff of Hampshire in 1273–4 and then of Oxfordshire and Berkshire between 1274 and 1278.[24] Sir John Wyger, mentioned as Cornwall's knight in 1272, was sheriff of Devon from 1274 until shortly before his death in 1277.[25] Sir Robert Malet was briefly sheriff of Bedfordshire and Buckinghamshire during the summer of 1285 and was a tenant and frequent witness of Cornwall's and also his steward at Wallingford at one point.[26] There is also some evidence of association between Cornwall and other local officials beside the shrievalty. Peter Becard, another tenant by knight service of the earl and frequent charter witness, held several temporary government posts in the north midlands and Yorkshire in the late 1290s.[27] Edmund de Wedon was a coroner in

[21] Page, 'Cornwall', 28, 31.

[22] *List of Sheriffs*, 112. For Russell's witnessing, see *CChR 1257–1300*, 208, 240–1, 349, 443; *CChR 1300–1326*, 189, 490; *Eye Priory Cartulary and Charters*, ed. V. Brown, 2 vols., Suffolk Record Society, Suffolk Charters 12, 13 (1992–4), I, no. 109; E 36/57, nos. 131, 197, 284.

[23] *CPR 1272–1281*, 178, 238; *List of Sheriffs*, 95.

[24] *List of Sheriffs*, 54, 107. For his witnessing Cornwall's charters, see *CChR 1257–1300*, 331, 339, 349, 405–6; *CChR 1300–1326*, 189, 490, 490–1, 491; *CChR 1341–1417*, 21; E 36/57, nos. 30, 43, 48, 53, 82, 131, 151, 198, 222, 223 240; *CPR 1281–1292*, 133–4.

[25] *CFR 1272–1307*, 90; *CPR 1266–1272*, 706; *List of Sheriffs*, 34.

[26] *List of Sheriffs*, 1. For his witnessing, see *CChR 1257–1300*, 208; *CChR 1300–1326*, 490; TNA E 36/57, nos. 12, 70, 116, 197 (where he is mentioned as steward).

[27] For charter witnessing, see *CChR 1257–1300*, 240–1; *CChR 1300–1326*, 189; *CPR 1281–1292*, 133–4; *Cartulary of the Cistercian Abbey of Fountains in the West Riding of the County of York*, ed. W.T. Lancaster, 2 vols. (Leeds: J. Whitehead and Sons, 1915), II, 725–6; E 36/57, nos. 48, 107, 121. For office-holding, see *CPR 1292–1301*, 171 (tax collector in Lincolnshire), 338 (commission to inquire into abuses by royal officials, Yorkshire, Lancashire, Nottinghamshire and Derbyshire), 517 (commissioner for upkeep of Magna Carta, Yorkshire).

Buckinghamshire in 1284 and left office in 1286, and was coroner of Bedfordshire from an unknown date until 1300.[28]

Why were there more examples of associations between Cornwall and royal officials, particularly sheriffs, than there were in the case of any other earl in Edward I's reign? The most obvious reason is that Cornwall had the largest estate in England and the sheer extent of his landholding would have brought him into close contact with more officials than almost anyone else. Second, as hereditary sheriff of both Cornwall and Rutland, he had more opportunity than most to influence office-holding and, in Cornwall at least, he seems to have taken advantage of this opportunity to appoint his own men as under-sheriff and had inherited a tightly controlled administrative system from his father. Third, as has been seen, for a man as rich and closely related to the king as he was, he spent a surprisingly small amount of time in the king's company, particularly compared to the other earls.[29] Cornwall obviously spent more time on his estates than many other earls and was therefore in contact with local officials more often, but with the added advantage of being a man of immense wealth and influence and known to be close to the king, which may have made it easier for him to establish links with royal officials since he was known to have the king's confidence.[30]

Despite this, it should be emphasised that Cornwall's links with local officers, though more extensive than those of his contemporaries, were not as widespread and consistent as can be seen among successful 'bastard feudal' lords in the later fourteenth and fifteenth centuries. Aside from Cornwall itself, which should be regarded as a special case given the position of the earldom within the shire, the earl made no attempt consistently to dominate the shrievalty of any other county, even that of Rutland where he was also hereditary sheriff and the greatest landholder. Only in Oxfordshire/Berkshire did more than one of his associates act as sheriff in Edward I's reign. It is interesting, moreover, that most of his associations with sheriffs outside Cornwall come from the first few years of his cousin's reign. It may be that the regency government at the start of the reign, and then the king himself after his return, were prepared to utilise Cornwall's position in the localities to bolster royal authority, but as the reign went on, this was no longer considered necessary. This may also help to explain Guy Beauchamp's control of the Warwickshire shrievalty in the last years of Edward I's reign. The earl was high in the

[28] *CCR 1279–1288*, 440; *CCR 1296–1302*, 371; *CIM*, I, nos. 2271, 2394.

[29] See above, 48.

[30] Cornwall was one of his cousin's principal creditors and was also chosen by Edward as regent in both 1278 and 1286.

king's favour and his control over local administration seems to have helped to calm what had previously been one of England's more disordered counties. That this was done with royal approval, perhaps even royal encouragement, is further suggested by the fact that under Edward II, a king for whom Warwick became a major opponent, the earl's officials were removed from local public office.[31]

The picture of what is largely comital indifference towards local office holding is mirrored in studies of other followings from the thirteenth century. Maddicott found little evidence of office-holding among Simon de Montfort's *familia*, though, as Montfort was an imported noble, this might be expected, but Marc Morris' study of the more territorially rooted Bigod earls of Norfolk has also revealed relatively few Bigod associates being involved with local government, even finding evidence that many of Roger III Bigod's men actively avoided government office-holding by obtaining exemptions from office-holding.[32] This is an important, and very common, phenomenon – something Maddicott has described as a general 'retreat from office holding' – that casts doubt on the whole 'bastard feudal' paradigm in the thirteenth century as it suggests that neither magnates nor the gentry were particularly enthusiastic about the latter holding public office.[33] The general attitude of the earls in the thirteenth century towards their men doing royal work was perhaps summed up by the release obtained by the earl of Hereford in 1300 for his man, Roger Damory, who was due to serve as a commissioner for the upholding of Magna Carta in Oxfordshire. The chancery relieved Damory from the office, noting that 'his lord has need of him'.[34] Magnates generally did not want their men to be distracted or compromised by serving the crown at a local level, not when they were able to protect their interests in other ways.

Such an attitude was mirrored by the crown and the government, which generally frowned upon royal officers moonlighting in magnate administration, wanting their full attention to be on their duties.

[31] Burt, '"Bastard Feudal" Affinity', 178.

[32] Maddicott, *Simon de Montfort*, 61–74; Morris, *Bigod Earls*, 63, 71–3, 138–53. In 1254 Montfort did obtain a grant from Henry III, covering several midland counties, ensuring that no sheriff in these counties would be appointed without Montfort's agreement; Maddicott, *Simon de Montfort*, 122–3. Given the connection of the grant to Montfort's continuing financial wrangles with the king it seems to be evidence more of the earl's mounting distrust of Henry's goodwill than of a real attempt to control local administration.

[33] J.R. Maddicott, 'Magna Carta and the Local Community, 1215–1259', *Past and Present* 102 (1984), 45. See also S.L. Waugh, 'Reluctant Knights and Jurors: Respites, Exemptions, and Public Obligations in the Reign of Henry III', *Speculum* 58 (1983), 937–86.

[34] *Calendar of Chancery Warrants, 1244–1326*, 111–12. There is a similar case involving one of the coroners for Sussex, who was a household knight of Sir Walter de Teye and who was removed from his office in order to join Teye in Scotland; ibid., 146.

Luke de Gare, for example, was removed from his post as commissioner of walls and dykes in Sussex because of his absence on the affairs of the earl of Gloucester.[35] Alexander de Lucas was told that he could not be steward of Wakefield for Earl Warenne and coroner of Lincolnshire simultaneously, and he appears to have chosen to continue in royal office.[36] A more general prohibition against 'double-hatting' was issued to the sheriff of Gloucestershire in 1287 when he was told not to employ seigniorial officials as hundred bailiffs.[37] From the evidence presented above, however, the king and his central officials appear to have been barking at shadows. It is a trap into which some historians have fallen as well. They have taken isolated examples of royal officials in magnate service and extrapolated from them to fit an idea of 'bastard feudalism' operating in the thirteenth century. Huw Ridgeway, for instance, feels that the employment of the sheriff of Yorkshire, Richard de Crepping, as William de Valence's estate steward in Northumberland was 'in true bastard feudal fashion'.[38] What he overlooks, however, is that Valence held no land in Yorkshire and therefore Crepping's position as sheriff there could offer him no benefit, while his own appointment of Crepping was in a different county altogether from where the latter held public office. This is hardly synonymous with the network of local control operated by, say, Richard Beauchamp, earl of Warwick, or Richard, duke of Gloucester, in the fifteenth century.[39]

For most magnates in Edward I's reign, their followings seem to have served more a military than a domestic purpose, ensuring that their members were less likely to be available for local office. Scott Waugh has argued that the Barons' Wars and Lord Edward's crusade 'reinvigorated the martial aspect of seigneurial retaining in the next decades', and this is certainly borne out by the evidence for several of Edward I's earls.[40] The *milites strenui* were conspicuous in comital followings in Edward's reign. Nearly all of Edmund of Lancaster's close followers performed military service for him, often very frequently, and many of these flowed seamlessly into the military retinue and domestic following of his son.[41] Lincoln's following, too, had a strong military flavour to it: nearly all were expected to serve the earl on campaign, and one finds the same names

[35] *CPR 1292–1301*, 152.

[36] *CCR 1279–1288*, 404; *CCR 1288–1296*, 437. A William Rouleby was in post as steward of Wakefield in July 1293; *Early Yorkshire Charters: the Honour of Warenne*, eds. C.T. Clay and W. Farrer, Yorkshire Archaeological Record Series, Additional Series 8 (1949), 250.

[37] Cam, *Hundred Rolls*, 149. [38] Ridgeway, 'William de Valence', 251.

[39] Carpenter, 'Beauchamp Affinity'; Horrox, *Richard III*, chapter 1.

[40] Waugh, 'Third Century', 51. [41] See above, 133; Spencer, 'Earls', app. C.

at the core of his military retinue year after year.[42] John Pecche, John Hamlyn and John de Clinton, all important associates of Guy Beauchamp, earl of Warwick, were also prominent members of the Beauchamp military retinue.[43]

Taking all this evidence together, individual instances of magnate links with royal officials cannot be used to claim that 'bastard feudalism' was already in existence. If, in Coss' view, it is 'the invasion and subversion of law courts and administration which … lies at the heart of bastard feudalism', then, in the case of local administration at least, 'bastard feudalism' had not developed by the time Edward I died.[44] It is not enough, however, merely to say this. Two further questions immediately present themselves: why not, and how then did lords exercise power at a local level? These questions will now be addressed before looking at the role Edward I's reign did play in the development of late medieval 'bastard feudalism'.

The answer as to why 'bastard feudalism' had not developed by the end of Edward I's reign is essentially twofold. First, royal government was not yet extensive or pervasive enough to make 'bastard feudalism' necessary for the crown, nobility or gentry. Second, in the thirteenth century, magnates had more effective ways of protecting their interests than inserting their followers into royal office. The techniques of late medieval 'bastard feudalism', therefore, were neither effective nor necessary.

England was a highly governed society by medieval standards and was growing ever more so as the crown's demands for money and its subjects desire for access to the king's courts grew inexorably from at least the reign of Henry II onwards. Despite this, it was still just about manageable from the centre in the late thirteenth century. During Edward I's reign, the government, particularly Chancellor Robert Burnell, kept a close eye on appointments and cultivated office-holding elites within the counties.[45] As Gerald Harriss has demonstrated, however, royal government and law expanded in response to pressure from both above and below.[46] The result was the development of the gentry as a magistracy and expansion of the reach of royal government but of a royal government that was to become, at its best, a partnership between crown, nobility and gentry. Magnates, like the king and gentry, had to adapt their methods to this changing society and, as Harriss puts it, 'to run with the grain of political

[42] Ibid., 94. William Vavasour and William Stopham, who each served seven times with Lincoln on campaign, are the most conspicuous examples of such men but there were many others. See, for example, ibid., app. D.

[43] For Pecche and Hamlyn, see Burt, '"Bastard Feudal" Affinity', 176. For Clinton see ibid., 176, and C 67/10, m. 2d; C 67/13, mm. 2, 9d; C 67/14, m. 11.

[44] Coss *et al.*, 'Debate', 193. [45] Burt, 'Governance', 73–4, 118, 180.

[46] Harriss, 'Political Society'.

society', while maintaining their own interests.[47] The expansion of royal government was to make engagement with it a necessity by all landowners rather than an optional extra, which it had threatened to become at times in the thirteenth century.

Magnates in this period, by contrast with the later middle ages, made strenuous efforts to keep royal officials out of their lands when their presence was regarded as a threat to the free exercise of their own authority. The most obvious example of this was the battle over franchises that was discussed on the national scale in Chapter 3 but must now be seen at a local level.[48] Magnates' use and abuse of franchises to exclude royal officials was one of the reasons why Edward I and his lawyers were so determined to ensure recognition of the supremacy of royal authority and to defeat conquest theory during the *quo warranto* campaign. In Henry III's reign, and well into Edward I's, lords systematically attempted to exclude royal officials from their lands and, wherever possible, to withdraw their tenants from royal jurisdiction through, for example, preventing the sheriff from holding his yearly tourn in their lands. The results of the Hundred Rolls Inquiry preserve hundreds of examples of this from all over England.[49] Earl Warenne's behaviour in Yorkshire, detailed in the Hundred Rolls, provides a good example of the type of obstruction occurring in the late 1260s and early 1270s. It was alleged that Warenne had withdrawn vills that used to be geldable, had appropriated the franchise of return of writs and was refusing to 'allow the king's bailiffs to carry out any office in [his] lands'.[50] He claimed that neither he nor his tenants at Wakefield owed suit to the county court and, as late as 1303, long after the end of the *quo warranto* campaign, to show that his attitude had not changed, the earl's bailiffs refused to allow the king's commissioners to take an inquest into knights' fees.[51] Warenne's attitude was hardly unique: in just one Yorkshire wapentake, Ryedale, no fewer than ten lords were accused in 1274–5 by the jurors of obstructing the king's bailiffs in their lands.[52]

The Hundred Rolls Inquiry made it clear to both oppressed and oppressing that the open season under Henry III was now closed. For the earls, however, if not for those lords below them, it was still possible to ignore royal officials and even royal law, provided that the king did not become personally involved. Earl Warenne again provides another good example. During the dispute over return of writs in Stamford and Grantham, the sheriff of Lincolnshire complained that he would need

[47] Ibid., 55. See Carpenter, 'War, Government and Governance', 22, on the effects of both royal need and consumer demand.

[48] See above, 71–6. [49] *Rotuli Hundredorum*.

[50] *Yorkshire Hundred and Quo Warranto Rolls*, 93, 110.

[51] Ibid., 140; *Feudal Aids*, VI, 129. [52] *Yorkshire Hundred and Quo Warranto Rolls*, 66.

5,000 men at his back if he were to attempt to enforce a royal writ in the towns in the face of the earl's opposition.[53] In Lancashire in 1276, Gilbert de Clifton, the fiery official of the earl of Lincoln, warned the sheriff that, if he tried to distrain tenants to force suit to the county court within the earl's fee of Rochdale, then he, Clifton, would '*poneret posse contra posse*'.[54]

It was not always necessary, however, for earls to adopt such obviously aggressive methods to gain the desired effect of excluding the king's officials. Simple bribery was always an option, as used by the earls of Norfolk and Cornwall in the 1290s to reduce their tax liability. For those in especial favour with the king, it might be possible to obtain a royal dispensation to keep unwanted officials out of their lands.[55] In June 1271, Edmund of Lancaster obtained a grant from his father, Henry III, that ordered all the sheriffs in counties where Lancaster held lands pertaining to the honour of Leicester that they were 'not to intermeddle with the said honour or with the men or with anything belonging to it'.[56] He obtained a confirmation of this grant from his brother in 1292, illustrating how importantly he regarded it.[57] Thomas of Lancaster, in response to unwelcome action by the sheriff of Wiltshire, obtained a further order for this grant to be observed in 1303, demonstrating again how highly the earls of Lancaster prized this exemption from royal interference and how apparently easy it was for them to obtain it given their intimate relationship with Edward I.[58]

Thus, until royal government and law became more pervasive to the point where the king and gentry would not tolerate nobles excluding it and nor would nobles wish to do so, the great magnates could protect their interests much of the time by ignoring or buying off royal authority when the king saw no need to intervene. This does not mean that they were detached from royal government, more that, to a certain extent, they could deal with it on their terms. Indeed, they often provided the sheriff with aid in law enforcement and their prolonged absence from a locality when on campaign was always a cause for concern because of its effects on the king's peace.[59] The county court was one of the principal ways in which the nobility engaged, at one step removed, with royal law and administration. Even by the early twelfth century, magnates were no

[53] See above, 74; Palmer, *County Courts*, 265.

[54] Ibid., 82. TNA KB 29, 29/21, m. 8. For more of Clifton's attitude to royal officials, see below, 156–7.

[55] E. Miller, 'War, Taxation and the English Economy in the Late Thirteenth and Early Fourteenth Centuries', in J.M. Winter (ed.), *War and Economic Development: Essays in Memory of David Joslin* (Cambridge University Press, 1975), 15; Morris, *Bigod Earls*, 162.

[56] *CPR 1266–1272*, 544.

[57] *CPR 1281–1292*, 467.

[58] *CCR 1302–1307*, 58–9.

[59] *CPR 1272–1281*, 67; *CPR 1292–1301*, 629.

longer attending the county court in person but were sending their seneschals in their stead to act as their attorneys.[60] By the reign of Edward I the county courts had come to be dominated by the seneschals of the nobility on the one hand and the king's officers, the sheriff, under-sheriff and coroners on the other.[61] This, then, was engagement with royal law and administration but on the magnates' own terms. They sought to ensure that their seneschals did the necessary suit at the county court not just for their lords but for their lords' tenants as well.[62] Some magnates may have sought to dominate the county court further by retaining many of those who still did suit at the court, as Henry II, earl of Warwick, had done in the 1220s, but it is notable that none of those whom Warwick recruited in this way were significant landed figures, holding as they did barely a single manor each.[63] These were not the greater gentry of the county whom one finds in the affinities of late medieval magnates, and it emphasises how the county court was being hollowed out as early as this in the thirteenth century, a process that only accelerated as the century progressed.[64] By 1270, or shortly after, the king's government seems to have given up the fight and largely stopped trying to enforce knightly suit at the county court. With these developments and the removal of so much litigation from the county to the central courts, the county court gradually lost most of its power during the thirteenth century and it served the magnates' interests to keep it that way since it allowed them to restrict and control the access of king's law and government within their lands and lordships. As will be suggested at the end of this chapter, however, there were signs that Edward I was not going to allow this happy state of optional engagement on the part of the earls to continue.[65]

The earls were not, however, uninterested in the workings and personnel of the king's courts, to which so much litigation now flowed from the county court. Engagement with royal law by magnates has always been recognised as a crucial part of late medieval 'bastard feudalism'. The importance of successful engagement was just as great to thirteenth-century magnates but they sought the same end through different methods. Magnates could and did manipulate juries in the thirteenth century, just as their successors in the fifteenth century did, but they also had more powerful weapons at their disposal. By the fifteenth century, these had been removed from their arsenal and, with the removal of so much of the administration of the central courts and pleas to the localities, had effectively become redundant.

[60] Palmer, *County Courts*, 113. [61] Ibid., 136. [62] Ibid., 114–16.
[63] Crouch, 'Local Influence', 13. [64] Palmer, *County Courts*, 80–1.
[65] See below, 170–2.

It has long been recognised, thanks to John Maddicott's work, that great lords, lay and ecclesiastical, sought links with central royal justices for legal advice, counsel and, perhaps, to secure favourable verdicts.[66] David Carpenter has shown that reformers in Henry III's reign complained bitterly that great men were able to avoid verdicts against them in court because of their relationship with royal justices.[67] Associations between royal justices and the earls in Edward I's reign were ubiquitous.[68] Edmund of Lancaster had very close links with two royal justices, Roger Brabazon and Walter de Helyun, who also served on his council, of whom Brabazon became chief justice of King's Bench.[69] The earl of Lincoln had strong bonds with five royal justices, John Bek, Peter Malore, Thomas Fishburn, Robert de Hertford and Roger de Cubbeldyk.[70] Gloucester, likewise, was associated with several justices, including Hervey de Borham, Geoffrey de Leukenore and Gilbert de Thornton.[71] Thornton also acted for the earl of Norfolk in Ireland in the 1280s.[72] Henry de Enfield was closely associated with the earl of Hereford, acting as his attorney on several occasions.[73] Master Roger de Seyton, chief justice of Common Pleas from 1274 to 1278, witnessed two charters of Edmund of Cornwall, and Seyton's brother and heir, Richard, was the earl's steward and sheriff of Cornwall.[74] Towards the end of his life, Cornwall was also closely linked with William de Bereford, justice of Common Bench from 1292, who was one of his executors.[75]

As the extent of such links make clear, these men were of immense importance to their lords. It is important to note that this was not just so that their lords could influence justice: they also acted as councillors and legal advisers, for this was a time before the emergence of a fully fledged legal profession. They could therefore be the agents of the king's law on behalf of their lords in both legitimate and illegitimate ways.[76] Some were

66 Maddicott, 'Law and Lordship'. 67 Carpenter, 'King, Magnates and Society', 47–8.

68 See, for example, Morris, *Bigod Earls*, 139–40; Burt, '"Bastard Feudal" Affinity', 172.

69 Maddicott, *Thomas of Lancaster*, 19; Spencer, 'Earls', app. C, nos. 1, 6.

70 Spencer, 'Earls', app. D, nos. 1, 9, 4, 5. For Fishburn, see also *Earliest English Law Reports*, ed. P.A. Brand, 2 vols., Selden Society 111–12 (1996), II, 264. Cubbledyk witnessed five charters and was also Lincoln's steward. Appendix B; DL 25/2523.

71 For Boreham: Altschul, *Baronial Family*, 227–8. Leukenore was a bailiff of the earl in 1265; *CIM*, I, no. 666. Thornton was acting as the earl's attorney in the Dorset eyre of 1279–80; SC 1/25/39.

72 P.A. Brand, 'Thornton, Gilbert of (*b.* in or before 1245, *d.* 1295)', in *ODNB*.

73 *CPR 1272–1279*, 170, 249; *CPR 1281–1292*, 164, 262.

74 P.A. Brand, 'Seaton, Roger of (*c.*1230–*c.*1280)', in *ODNB*; *CChR 1257–1300*, 208 (*bis*); E 36/57, m. 6d no. 19.

75 P.A. Brand, 'Medieval Legal Bureaucracy: the Clerks of the Courts in the Reign of Edward I', in Brand, *The Making of the Common Law*, 166.

76 P.A. Brand, *The Origins of the English Legal Profession* (Oxford: Blackwell, 1992); P.A. Brand, 'The Professionalisation of Lawyers in England', *Zeitschrift Für Neuere Rechtsgeschichte* 28 (2006), 7–19.

accused of unduly favouring their patron when hearing cases involving them. This was often in pleas held under commissions of *oyer* and *terminer*, which magnates were able to obtain perfectly legitimately from the government on demand. These were immensely powerful and, by medieval standards, fast-moving legal commissions to hear and determine individual cases and whose judges could be nominated by the plaintiff himself.[77] Naturally, earls often sought to have their feed justices appointed to such commissions and, in such hands, they could be a devastatingly effective legal weapon. Such appointments included Roger Brabazon and Walter de Helyun for Edmund of Lancaster,[78] Henry de Shotbroke, Master Thomas de Soddington and William de Bereford for Cornwall,[79] Peter Malore for Lincoln[80] and Nicholas de Warwick for the earls of Warwick.[81] Some earls also tried to get their own administrators as well as their lawyers named on such commissions. Thomas de Bray, Ranulph Dacre, Hugh de Vienna and William Wyther were among the associates of Edmund of Lancaster appointed to commissions relating to his lands.[82] *Oyer* and *terminer* commissions were a legitimate, if highly favourable, way for people to defend their interests and they were particularly open to abuse if the plaintiff was influential enough to get his feed justices appointed. There were, however, other more sinister ways for a great lord to use his influence. During the king's absence in Gascony, it was alleged that the earl of Gloucester had conspired with an eyre justice, Richard Boyland, to extort 200 marks from a Gloucestershire knight, William Dernford, with whom the earl was in dispute, by holding him against his will and even threatening his life.[83] Around the same time, as part of the so-called 'State Trials', Chief Justice Thomas Weyland was retrospectively accused of bringing in biased judgments favouring his patron, the earl of Norfolk.[84]

The influence of feed justices may also help to explain why the earls appear so infrequently in royal legal records. It is striking just how little legal pressure the earls were put under during Edward I's reign. Taking two five-year periods (1276–81 and 1289–94) as samples, it is possible to see that between Michaelmas term 1276 and Trinity term 1281, the earl of Lincoln, for instance, does not appear in a single case in King's Bench, save for once where the sheriff of Wiltshire was ordered not to avoid the

77 Kaeuper, 'Law and Order', 750–74.

78 *CPR 1272–1281*, 182; *CPR 1281–1292*, 207, 208, 279, 282, 400 (3), 455–6; *CPR 1292–1301*, 164 (*bis*).

79 *CPR 1272–1281*, 409; *CPR 1281–1292*, 70, 91, 92 (*bis*), 141, 515; *CPR 1292–1301*, 215 (*bis*), 217, 468, 553.

80 *CPR 1292–1301*, 356, 380, 544.

81 *CPR 1292–1301*, 218; *CPR 1301–1307*, 281, 343, 478.

82 *CPR 1272–1281*, 118, 347, 406, 411; *CPR 1281–1292*, 207, 209.

83 *State Trials of the Reign of Edward the First, 1289–1293*, eds. T.F. Tout and H. Johnstone, Camden Society, 3rd Series 9 (1906), 5–11.

84 Morris, *Bigod Earls*, 139–40.

earl's lands in a distraint upon one Peter Fitz Waurin, itself an interesting order as it suggests that the sheriff had to be particularly reminded to attend to this and that the court worried that the sheriff's natural response would be not to enter the earl's lands.[85] Gloucester appears as a defendant on just five occasions in this period and as a plaintiff only twice.[86] On three occasions when he was defendant, the other plaintiffs were persons of consequence, respectively the bishop of Hereford, Agatha Mortimer and the prior of Goldcliff, while on another occasion the plaintiff was the king himself, who was seeking to recover two manors in Dorset from the earl. One of the earl's own cases also involved the king: his unsuccessful attempt to regain the town of Bristol for the earldom. The only man of lesser standing to bring a case against Gloucester during this period was John de Langport, a Dorset parson, who claimed that the earl was denying him a free chace within the earl's chace of Cranborne.

Earl Warenne was defendant in four cases and a plaintiff three times.[87] Three of the four cases brought against him involved the Aguillon dispute in Sussex, where he was taking on a local knight of considerable standing.[88] The only case in which the earl of Hereford was involved in these years was a dispute with a fellow Marcher baron, Roger Mortimer, another example where the high status of an earl's opponent gave the opponent the necessary confidence to bring charges in the king's court.[89] No one felt confident enough to bring a case against the king's own brother, Edmund of Lancaster, in this period, while the earl himself brought seven cases of trespass in his woods, chaces and properties.[90]

The same is true regarding Lancaster for the second sample period between Michaelmas 1289 and Trinity 1294, when the only person to bring a plea in King's Bench against Edmund of Lancaster was the king himself, in a case of *quo warranto* in Lancaster's town of Newcastle-under-Lyme.[91] Lancaster acted as plaintiff on nine occasions, again nearly always involving cases of trespass by minor persons.[92] Lincoln again was almost entirely absent from King's Bench, appearing as plaintiff in just a single case.[93] Gloucester and Hereford, on the other hand, appeared more

[85] KB 27/57, m. 36d.

[86] Defendant: KB 27/27, mm. 5, 7, 8d; 27/47, m. 33d; 27/49, m. 50. Plaintiff: 27/27, m. 8d; 27/49, m. 42.

[87] Defendant: KB 27/31, m. 20 (x3); 27/43, m. 11. Plaintiff: KB 27/33, mm. 11, 20d; 27/52, m. 29.

[88] This case is discussed in more detail below, 162–9.

[89] KB 27/45, m. 19.

[90] KB 27/37, m. 34; 27/39, m. 20 (*bis*); 27/41, mm. 29, 32d; 27/47, m. 38d; 27/55, m. 12.

[91] KB 27/136, m. 38.

[92] KB 27/127, m. 15; 27/128, mm. 6, 9; 27/130, m. 10; 27/132, m. 29d; 27/134, mm. 17, 34d; 27/138, m. 2; 27/141, m. 20.

[93] KB 27/136, m. 17d.

frequently, though still not with any great regularity.[94] Many of their appearances concerned their infamous and violent dispute on the Welsh March and the king's subsequent involvement in it. In addition to this, Gloucester was also still in dispute with the prior of Goldcliff and now additionally with the earl of Norfolk, while Hereford's dispute with the Mortimers had sprung into life once again. As in the earlier period, if a case were brought against an earl, it was likely that the plaintiff was himself a man of high status, for only such a man could feel any confidence of success. The plight of the humbler petitioner for royal justice can be illustrated by the case of Master John Mortimer.[95] Mortimer brought a plea against Earl Warenne and a number of his men in Easter term 1292 complaining of an illegal distraint by the earl's men from Stamford (Lincs.) of his corn and livestock on 14 August 1291. In a rare example of relatively swift justice, Warenne's attorney came before King's Bench at Trinity to answer the plea and the jury heard the case at Michaelmas 1292. Three of the accused were found guilty but the earl and his steward, Sir Peter de London, were acquitted and Master John found himself in mercy for a false plea. As is notoriously the case with the Mafia, the little people got the blame while the boss walked away. The only other person who saw fit to bring a case against the notoriously high-handed Warenne for criminal activity was Edward I himself, when the earl was foolish enough to try to make claim to the custody of the archbishop's manors in Sussex after the death of Archbishop Pecham while the manors were in Edward's hands.[96]

The retaining of royal justices has been seen by Coss as evidence that 'bastard feudalism' had developed by the thirteenth century, but retaining of central justices was not a hallmark of 'bastard feudalism' in the late fourteenth and fifteenth centuries.[97] The potential for corruption from such intimate relationships between lords and justices is obvious and Maddicott shows that, as the fourteenth century progressed, the retaining of central justices by magnates became increasingly controversial, and, by the century's end, in response to powerful and repeated complaints by the parliamentary commons, the practice had virtually ceased.[98] Lords

[94] Gloucester appeared as defendant in four cases: KB 27/123, m. 1 (*bis*); 27/124, mm. 10d, 36d. He appeared as plaintiff in three cases: KB 27/123, mm. 15, 55, 56. Hereford appeared as defendant in six cases: KB 27/121, m. 5d; 27/123, mm. 54d, 55; 27/124, m. 78d; 27/127, m. 27; 27/139, m. 33; 27/140, m. 42d. He appeared as plaintiff twice: KB 27/126, mm. 4d, 8.

[95] KB 27/131, m. 20; 27/132, mm. 19, 30.

[96] KB 27/139, mm. 18–19. The only other case brought against Warenne during this period was a debt case where he was being pursued for 91 marks by the executors of John Adrian the younger: KB 27/123, m. 49.

[97] Coss, 'Bastard Feudalism Revised', 51; Coss, 'From Feudalism to Bastard Feudalism', 91–2.

[98] Maddicott, 'Law and Lordship', 42–3, 60–1, 66, 68, 70, 72–4, 79.

had not lost interest in manipulating the law but this was now done at the local level, through the justices of the peace and the sheriff rather than through intrusive commissions originating from the centre. The aims remained the same in some respects but the methods in the thirteenth century and the fifteenth century were clearly different and there was not the same concern to manipulate the law on behalf of their followers as was a key element of fourteenth- and fifteenth-century 'bastard feudalism'. Coss rightly recognises the direction of travel, if not the spirit in which it was undertaken, when he writes that in the age of 'bastard feudalism', '[t]he subversion of public office begins in the provinces and passes from there to Westminster, in order to control, if possible, the central courts', but it is the opposite that seems to be occurring in the thirteenth century.[99] Lords sought influence at the centre and used that to control events in the provinces. To see how this was done and the king's reaction to it, it is necessary to turn once again from the general to the particular, to look at two case studies examining how the earls of Lincoln and Warenne exercised power within their ancient centres of power.

CASE STUDY: THE EARL OF LINCOLN IN SOUTH YORKSHIRE

The honour of Pontefract in south Yorkshire had been in the Lacy family since the 1080s and was a compact but extensive lordship that stretched across seven wapentakes.[100] By the time the Lacy tenure of the honour came to an end in 1311, the wapentakes of Osgoldcross, Staincross and Staincliffe were held at fee farm by the earl, who also had the castle and town of Pontefract itself, ten manors in demesne, the vills of Bradford and Leeds and numerous other lands, rents and advowsons in the area.[101] Pontefract was one of the earl's seven treasuries and seems to have been his most important residence and the centre of his administration in the north.[102]

The ancient nature of the Lacy honour of Pontefract meant that Lincoln was able to create a very tight-knit dominance over the lordship. Lincoln's methods were largely traditional and seem to have relied upon his position as the honorial lord. The core of the earl's following had its origins within the bounds of the honour of Pontefract. These included his two longest-serving followers: Sir William Vavasour and Sir William de Stopham. Both were in the earl's service from at least 1277 when they

[99] Coss, 'Bastard Feudalism Revised', 60–1.

[100] Dalton, *Conquest*, 20–1, 39. The seven wapentakes were Osgoldcross, Staincliffe, Barkston, Staincross, Agbrigg, Skyrack and Morley.

[101] *CIPM*, v, no. 279. [102] Baldwin, 'Household Administration', 183, 186.

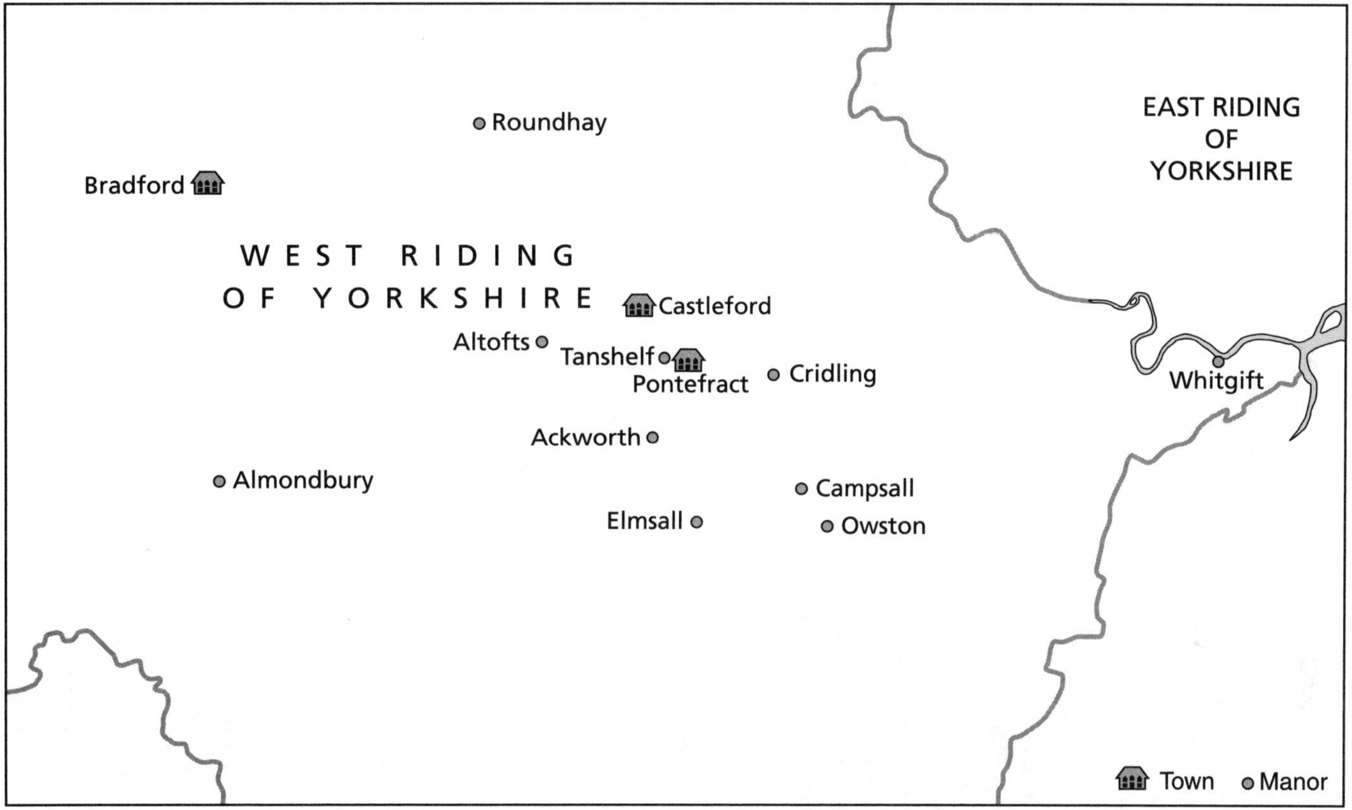

Map 6.1 Lands of the earl of Lincoln in south Yorkshire

were in his military retinue for the First Welsh War.[103] Vavasour was a major landholder in his own right with lands all over Yorkshire but he was an important tenant of the Lacy family, holding the manor of Cocksford near Tadcaster of the honour of Pontefract as well as his chief manor in Lincolnshire, Cockerington.[104] Stopham was lord of Towton within the honour and also of Baildon and Weston near Lincoln's vill of Bradford.[105] Another tenant in his following was John Newmarch, who held the manor of Bentley near Doncaster of the earl.[106] Two non-tenants among his followers with estates near the lordship of Pontefract were Robert de Roos, lord of Gedney in Lincolnshire and also of Brighton in Herthill Wapentake, fewer than four miles from Lincoln's town of Bradford, and Alexander de Leeds.[107] Other Yorkshire knights in Lincoln's following, Miles and John de Stapleton, John Spring and Robert de Hertford, all had lands elsewhere in the county and were not tenants of the earl. Of these Yorkshire knights, only Vavasour and Stopham were associated with Lincoln before the 1290s. The rest became linked with him during the years of intense warfare in the 1290s, and their utility to the earl appears to have been more their military abilities than their local connections. It was natural for such men to look to Lincoln as a military commander, given that he, together with Earl Warenne at nearby Wakefield, was one of the two most powerful lords in south Yorkshire.

As has been shown above, Lincoln does not seem to have paid much attention to controlling local royal administration either in south Yorkshire or elsewhere.[108] Moreover, it seems that he was still able to dominate areas without the formal or informal partnerships with the local gentry that were a hallmark of late medieval 'bastard feudalism'. Lincoln's personal relations with local knights seem to have been incidental rather than essential to his lordship over the area around Pontefract and certainly not mutually beneficial. Rather, he relied on feudal lordship and the assertion of both ancient and newly claimed authority to promote a lordship that can be characterised as powerful, harsh and confident. This is revealed by the returns from the Hundred Rolls Inquiry of 1274–5. Lincoln had built upon long foundations of family rule within the area: for eighty years, so the jurors of Skyrack Wapentake reported, the earls of Lincoln had allowed the sheriff's tourn to be held at Leeds but now the present earl was no longer allowing any of the king's officials to enter his liberty or

[103] *CPR 1272–1281*, 189. For further details of their associations with Lincoln, see Spencer, 'Earls', app. D, nos. 17, 19.

[104] *CIPM*, V, no. 395.

[105] *CIPM*, II, no. 792; *Feudal Aids*, VI, 19, 23; 'Towton: the Battlefield Village (1461)'.

[106] Moor, *Knights of Edward I*, III, 263.

[107] *CIPM*, V, no. 252; *Feudal Aids*, VI, 18.

[108] See above, 138.

to exercise their office without the earl's own bailiffs.[109] The retreat from royal authority under Henry III, seen elsewhere in the Hundred Rolls, is very evident in the lordship of Pontefract. For instance, the jurors of Staincliffe complained that 'the sheriff makes no tourn in this wapentake whence the country is the worse'.[110] In Agbrigg Wapentake, the jurors alleged that the earl's bailiffs were holding a tourn once a year and were fining those who refused to attend, while, since 1269, they had appropriated judgments on felonies and were preventing the king's bailiffs from carrying out their offices.[111]

The earl was also using financial means to mark out and strengthen his lordship. The jurors of the city of York complained that their toll of 100*s* p.a., taken at the point where the Rivers Ouse and Aire meet near Howden, had been appropriated by the earl, while he was also imposing tolls on them throughout his lands.[112] In his vill of Bradford, although Lincoln had many legitimate liberties there, the jurors of Morley Wapentake stated that the bailiffs of the earl and his mother before him had 'used the liberty other than they should have done' by introducing a new toll at the market and were fining those who refused this affront to the 'ancient use', an accusation repeated against both Lincoln and Warenne by the Agbrigg jurors.[113]

The crown's inability or unwillingness to respond to usurpations during the 1260s and earlier may have encouraged the high-handed and arrogant attitude of the earl's steward, Gilbert de Clifton, when Edward I's commissioners arrived in Yorkshire.[114] The lead commissioner, William de Chatterton, told the jurors of Staincliffe Wapentake that they were to speak the truth without fear of the earl of Lincoln's bailiffs; not a point of view with which Gilbert de Clifton had much sympathy. Upon hearing of Chatterton's speech, he insulted him 'with very bad words and offered threats', warning the commissioner that had he, Clifton, been present when these words were spoken, 'he would have dragged him by the feet'. He added that, 'before half a year, he would wish he had not made these inquiries through the whole of his land'.[115] If this in itself were not enough, Clifton offered further offence to the commissioners when Richard Blanchard of Waddington took Chatterton's promise at face value and appeared before the Staincliffe jury to tell of the offences that he and others had suffered at the hands of the earl's bailiffs. When Clifton learned of this, he seized Blanchard's goods in retribution, refusing to

[109] *Yorkshire Hundred and Quo Warranto Rolls*, 33. [110] Ibid., 52.
[111] Ibid., 110. [112] Ibid., 73, 75–6. [113] Ibid., 95–6, 111.
[114] For Henry's attitude towards magnate liberties in the 1240s and 1250s, see Carpenter, 'King, Magnates and Society', 49–52.
[115] *Yorkshire Hundred and Quo Warranto Rolls*, 50.

release them at the commissioners' command, telling them that 'if they should come within the liberty of his lord, he would seize their bodies and all their goods, unless they professed to come in the name of the earl his lord'.[116] This remarkable attitude expresses, in an extreme form, how far Henry III had withdrawn from using his power in the localities and the extent to which some lords were prepared to go to keep the king's officials out of their business. It also provides a glimpse into the attitudes of comital officials, and perhaps of the earls themselves, regarding the inviolability and independence of their lands and traditional lordships. While Clifton's attitude was potentially inflammatory, his actual offences and those of the earl's other officials in Yorkshire were relatively minor compared to some of the others recorded on the Hundred Rolls. Perhaps this, together with the close friendship between Edward I and Lincoln, was why the king seems to have been quite sanguine about the powers Lincoln was wielding in south Yorkshire and the manner in which he was doing it. Moreover, Yorkshire in the 1270s was a long way away from the heartlands of the English monarchy, for the north had yet to assume the strategic importance that it would following the outbreak of the Anglo-Scottish wars. Edward's laissez-faire attitude to Yorkshire may be contrasted with the much greater concern he showed about the egregious behaviour of Earl Warenne in Sussex, a county much closer to the centre of royal authority.[117]

Lincoln's exclusion of royal officials also extended to the law. Even when the eyre came to Yorkshire in 1279, the justices did nothing about Lincoln's exclusion of royal officials from Bradford, nor about the new toll he was levying at Eland.[118] Lincoln escaped judicial aggression almost entirely in the eyres of 1279 and 1293–4, which was surprising given the number of disseisins the earl seems to have committed.[119] Following Thomas of Lancaster's fall in 1322, many petitions appeared in parliament complaining of such disseisins committed by the earl of Lincoln during Edward I's reign.[120] Of course, such petitions, made when the most recent holder of the earldom was dead and disgraced, must be regarded with caution, especially given the period of time that had lapsed between the alleged offence and the bringing of complaints. However, Lincoln's influence with Edward I, and the power of his successor, Thomas of Lancaster, until 1322, may have meant that petitioners felt their grievances would not be heard before this point.

[116] Ibid., 50. [117] See below, 165–9.
[118] JUST 1/1057, mm. 7, 15. [119] JUST 1/1057; 1/1101.
[120] SC 8/74/3664; 8/69/3406; 8/80/3986; 8/260/12976; 8/160/7989; 8/161/8040; 8/201/10047; 8/163/8120; 8/55/2727; 8/12/553; 8/159/7904; 8/159/7902, 7903.

Such petty disseisins and the complaints of the Hundred Rolls' juries aside, Lincoln's rule over the Pontefract area does seem to have been accepted with relative equanimity by locals. He needed only two commissions of *oyer* and *terminer* in Yorkshire during Edward I's reign.[121] His near neighbour, Earl Warenne, by contrast, required five Yorkshire commissions.[122] Undoubtedly, Lincoln's relations with some local knights helped create acceptance of his lordship, as did his generally excellent relations with most of the local ecclesiastical houses, but he achieved his dominance in a very different way from what might be expected under classic 'bastard feudalism'. Lincoln's lordship had a distinctly traditional flavour to it, based as it was on the territorial, administrative and judicial integrity he attempted to impose on the area of ancient Lacy influence. His relations with the Cluniac priory of Pontefract provide an indication of this. The priory had been founded by his ancestor, Robert de Lacy, in about 1090 and the lords of Pontefract had jealously guarded their rights ever since.[123] A dispute emerged in the early 1280s between the earl and the priory of La Charité-sur-Loire, the senior Cluniac daughter-house in France, which had rights of presentation to Pontefract. Lincoln objected to the appointment of a foreigner, William de Bruges, as prior and refused to allow him to be admitted. Eventually, in January 1285, an agreement was hammered out whereby a foreign appointment would always be followed by an English one.[124] From this it is clear that Lincoln was determined to maintain his rights of supervision over the prior's appointment. The earl, being on the spot, would be able to influence the election of the prior when it was the turn of an English appointment much better than the prior of La Charité hundreds of miles distant on the Loire. By 1299 the earl, acting in his traditional role as protector and patron, was able to tell the king that the priory had no foreign monks and had not had any for some time and therefore to prevent the priory from having its revenues confiscated by the crown.[125] He had protected his family's traditional stake in the doings of the priory and his influence over it was recognised by both the priory itself and the central government.

Lincoln's position in south Yorkshire was so strong because of the family's ancient roots there. Elsewhere his control was less effective, particularly on the estates he held in right of his wife in the south-west. It is

[121] *CPR 1301–1307*, 79, 541. One in 1301, when his men were assaulted and robbed while carrying victuals to the Scottish campaign, and the other, in 1307, concerning the breaking of two parks in Yorkshire.

[122] *CPR 1272–1281*, 469; *CPR 1281–1292*, 402, 407; *CPR 1301–1307*, 94, 277.

[123] DL 42/1, fol. 404. Robert de Lacy had removed a prior for having entered the office without his consent during the third year of Pope Innocent III (1200).

[124] DL 27/216. [125] *CCR 1296–1302*, 252.

hard to imagine, for instance, that any Lacy manor in Yorkshire would have come under siege for four days and nights before being ransacked, as happened to his isolated manor of Cowling in Suffolk while the earl was absent fighting in Gascony.[126] Nor is it easy to envisage the earl's men being attacked while going about their business in Pontefract or Bradford, as three of his men were attacked in Shaftesbury (Dorset) in 1278, or while they were holding his fair, as happened at Blandford in Dorset.[127] In Yorkshire, the earl was able to get away with disseisins without fear of being brought to trial, whereas even a very minor landholder in Somerset felt brave enough to accuse him of disseisin of a messuage and a virgate of land before the justices in eyre in Somerset and was able to win his case.[128] In the south-west, in contrast to Yorkshire, Lincoln had to obtain five commissions of *oyer* and *terminer*, suggesting that people there felt more able to defy his authority and that he was less able to exert it than he was in the heartland of his power and inheritance, Pontefract.[129] Such a suggestion is hardly surprising and reinforces David Carpenter's idea that there was a 'kaleidoscopic' pattern of local rule ranging across the different parts of the country.[130] Even the greatest lords could not exercise dominance everywhere on and around their estates. What this case study of Lincoln's power in south Yorkshire reveals, however, is that, where it was possible, the earl promoted an aggressive, assertive and traditional type of lordship that was able to win the acquiescence of both the king and local landed society. A very different story occurred when Earl Warenne tried the same thing in Sussex.

CASE STUDY: EARL WARENNE IN SUSSEX

Earl Warenne's lordship in Sussex can be characterised in a very similar way to Lincoln's in and around Pontefract, but Edward I's handling of them involved significant differences. Essentially, while in Yorkshire Lincoln's rule appears to have caused few ructions among local society, Warenne's stirred up considerable resentment and led to violent disturbances in the county, forcing the king to become involved and leading to a reduction in the earl's power and freedom of action.

Sussex had a unique pattern of tenurial geography. Shortly after 1066, the county was divided into six vertical strips of land known as rapes, each

126 *CPR 1292–1301*, 378. 127 *CPR 1272–1281*, 263, 346.

128 *Somersetshire Pleas from the Rolls of the Itinerant Justices (for the Years 1 to 7 of the Reign of Edward I Inclusive)*, ed. L. Landon, Somerset Record Society 41 (1926), 8–9.

129 See above, 157. *CPR 1272–1281*, 263, 346 (*bis*); *CPR 1281–1292*, 458; *CPR 1292–1301*, 162–3; *CPR 1301–1307*, 544.

130 Coss *et al.*, 'Debate', 184.

of which was given to a single lord who was the only tenant-in-chief in the rape. All of the rest of the land in the rape was held of the lord, giving him tenurial and jurisdictional control. By the start of Edward I's reign, John de Warenne, lord of the central rape of Lewes, had been the dominant figure in Sussex for many years. On Christmas Eve 1263, with civil war on the horizon, Warenne was appointed keeper of Sussex and Surrey, with command of the whole *posse comitatus*.[131] At Easter 1264, Warenne was the royalist constable of Rochester Castle during the short siege by the earls of Leicester and Gloucester.[132] Under his command were John Fitz Alan and William de Braose, lords of the rapes of Arundel and Bramber in Sussex respectively, and their subordination to Warenne strongly suggests he was accepted as the principal lord in Sussex at this time.

During the reign of Henry III, Warenne did not need the influence of royal officials to exercise power in Sussex. He was perfectly capable of doing so in direct opposition to the sheriff's authority. A clear example of this took place in October 1257 when it was alleged that the earl's steward of Lewes, John de la Warre, had impounded 200 sheep belonging to Robert of Cliffe, who complained twice to the sheriff in an attempt to get his goods replevied.[133] The sheriff appears to have been willing, but could not deliver the sheep 'on account of the might and power' of the earl and his steward. Cliffe went over the sheriff's head and took his case to the exchequer and was rewarded with an order from the barons instructing the sheriff to distrain Warre, which was duly done. It is significant that it was only by going directly to central government that Cliffe was able to get movement. This was not the end of the matter, however, and in December 1257 Cliffe's groom and his horse were seized in Lewes and detained in the castle. When Cliffe came to set them free, Warre seized him, 'beat him monstrously' and put him in the stocks at Lewes Castle for five days before bearing him away in a blanket, having first relieved him of his horse, which was worth 10 marks, and an additional 40*s* in cash. Such was the regard the officials of Earl Warenne had for the orders of the sheriff. Their contempt illustrates the kind of self-confident lordship that came with six generations and two hundred years of Warenne rule in the rape.

However, Warenne's authority and prestige took a severe blow following the disastrous defeat at Lewes. He fled abroad and his Sussex lands were entrusted to two Surrey knights, John Abernun and

[131] *CPR 1258–1266*, 357. [132] *Gervase of Canterbury*, II, 235.

[133] *Select Cases of Procedure without Writ under Henry III*, eds. and trans. H.G. Richardson and G.O. Sayles, Selden Society 60 (1941), 126.

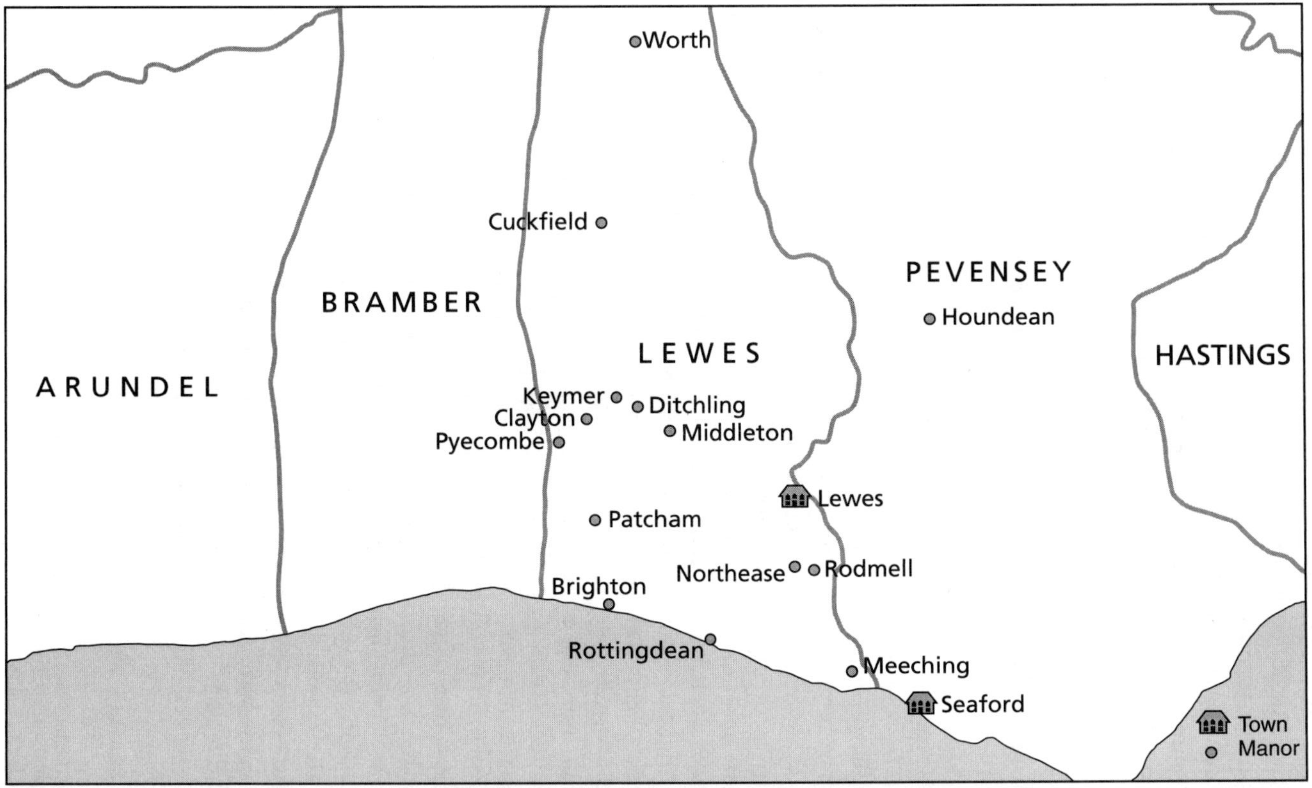

Map 6.2 Lands of Earl Warenne in Sussex

John de Wauton.[134] Following the royalist victory at Evesham in August 1265, however, Warenne was able to set about reconstituting his authority in the most direct manner possible. He was very active in confiscating rebel properties in Sussex in the days and weeks after Evesham. He spared neither great nor small in his reprisals: in the town of Lewes he seized the tenements of two rebels with a combined annual value of just 35*s*.[135] He took the manor of Portslade from his tenant, the minor baron John de Burgh, but his purpose was symbolic not financial; he did not take the Michaelmas rents but wasted the manor.[136] Even some non-rebels were disseised of their lands by Warenne.[137] The fine details of individual allegiance were of little concern to Warenne in his determination to restate his authority. Some of Warenne's authority in the years immediately after Evesham came from association with the royal government, such as the reappointment of his former steward, Roger de Loges, as sheriff in 1266 and 1268, and Warenne's command of 300 Sussex archers raised by the sheriff to 'vex the king's enemies' in Essex during 1266.[138] Mostly, though, as his confiscations made clear, the restitution of his fortunes and power was due to his own direct methods. But the earl was capable of employing more subtle means to extend his power in the county. In September 1268 he married his eldest daughter, Eleanor, to Henry Percy.[139] Percy was lord of Topcliff in Yorkshire, close to Warenne's own estates in the West Riding, but was also lord of the honour of Petworth in the rape of Arundel. With his new son-in-law one of the leading lords in western Sussex, the earl's influence spread westwards. Intermarriage with the leading lords of Sussex was in fact a pastime the Warennes had been indulging in for generations.[140] The extensive building work on Sandal Castle in Yorkshire, going on at least as early as 1270, is another example of how Warenne sought to restore his prestige and authority within his lands, while the earl also rebuilt the town walls of Lewes, another prestige project to emphasise his return to power.[141]

Warenne's control over his lordship of Lewes around 1270 was powerful but not without chinks in it. Robert de Cliffe's successful complaint to the exchequer in 1257 shows that *in extremis* central royal authority

[134] *CPR 1258–1266*, 323. [135] *CIM*, I, no. 919.

[136] Ibid., no. 918. [137] Ibid., no. 918.

[138] *CLR*, v, 244; *List of the Sheriffs*, 135.

[139] Blaauw, 'Early History of Lewes Priory', 26.

[140] For other examples of this practice, see *Early Yorkshire Charters: the Honour of Warenne*, 21, 22–3; K. Thompson, 'Lords, Castellans, Constables and Dowagers: the Rape of Pevensey from the Eleventh to the Thirteenth Century', *Sussex Archaeological Collections* 135 (1997), 214; *CPR 1301–1307*, 11.

[141] 'The Hundred Roll for Sussex Part Two', 51; L. Butler, *Sandal Castle, Wakefield: the History and Archaeology of a Medieval Castle* (Wakefield: Wakefield Historical Publications, 1991), 35.

could penetrate even the oldest and most compact of lordships but, as the aftermath of Cliffe's appeal showed, once the gaze of central government was no longer fixed upon Lewes, the earl and his officials could punish Cliffe with impunity and without fear of reprisal. The Hundred Rolls of 1274–5 illustrate the extent to which Warenne's lordship was largely traditional in nature. The repair of the town walls of Lewes, for example, was partly paid for by the earl taking from each knight's fee in his lordship 100*s*. He also forced 'free men and bond to follow him with arms wherever he goes, without the king's order at his own pleasure'.[142] This remarkable exercise of his traditional seigniorial military authority reveals the extent and nature of Warenne's power within his lordship in this period. Furthermore, he made strenuous efforts to exclude royal officers from his lands. He prevented Matthew de Hastings, the sheriff, from holding his twice-yearly tourn in his lordship and he was prepared to take even more direct action to obstruct the sheriff in the prosecution of his office.[143] On one occasion, when the sheriff had attached a widow and was bringing her to Westminster to take part in a lawsuit, 'certain foresters of Earl Warenne' abducted the lady and, adding insult to injury, even stole the sheriff's horse from him.[144]

Warenne's fortunes took a turn for the worse in 1270 when he became entangled in a dispute with the midlands baron and royal steward, Alan la Zouche, over the profits of war, which ended with a murderous assault on Zouche in Westminster Hall and a humiliating public penance and huge fine being imposed on the earl.[145] While he only ever paid 1,850 marks of that fine, the whole affair forced Warenne to take a much lower profile, and he disappeared from the royal court for the remainder of Henry III's reign.[146]

But while Warenne was relatively marginalised between 1270 and 1272, the same could not be said of another Sussex lord, Sir Robert Aguillon. Aguillon, lord of the manor of Perching in Lewes Rape and also of several other manors in the south-east and East Anglia, was another household steward of Henry III, a member of the king's council and a former sheriff of Sussex.[147] Aguillon's power was growing as a result of royal favour: he

[142] Ibid., 52. [143] Ibid., 50, 53. [144] Ibid., 67.

[145] For the details of the case, see G.T. Lapsley, 'John de Warenne and the *Quo Warranto* Proceedings of 1279', *Cambridge Historical Journal* 2 (1927), 116–20. See below, 180–1, for a full discussion.

[146] In 1306 the debts of the new Earl Warenne were pardoned by the crown; of this 10,000-mark fine, 6,800 marks was still owing (*CPR 1301–1307*, 496–7). A further 1,350 marks had been pardoned previously, meaning that Warenne had paid a total of 1,850 marks in thirty-four years (*CPR 1266–1272*, 545; *CPR 1272–1281*, 146). Warenne witnessed only three charters in the last two years of Henry III's reign; *The Royal Charter Witnesses Lists of Henry III*, 192, 193, 199.

[147] *CPR 1266–1272*, 25, 114; L.F. Salzman, 'The Family of Aguillon', *Sussex Archaeological Collections* 79 (1938), 55–6.

was granted the ransom of William Marmion's lands in Gloucestershire, Lincolnshire and Sussex under the Dictum of Kenilworth;[148] a licence to crenellate at Perching in 1268;[149] and the wardship of the heir of the Sussex and East Anglian knight Richard de Plaiz.[150] All three of these would have been disturbing to Warenne: he had originally seized Marmion's manor of Berwick, only to see the ransom granted instead to Aguillon.[151] The building of fortifications within his rape of Lewes would have been an alarming development for the lord of any fee, no matter one as sensitive of his dignity as Warenne, while Richard de Plaiz was a major tenant of the earl and he might have expected the wardship to come to him.[152] Aguillon's greatest prize, however, came in April 1272 with the wardship of the rape and honour of Arundel.[153] The grant of the wardship of a Sussex rape to a mesne tenant in another rape was irregular, and must have caused Warenne some consternation.[154] Aguillon had been steadily growing in power and influence, both in Sussex and at court. Since the Zouche incident, Aguillon had eclipsed Warenne at court, and now, with the custody of Arundel Rape, this parvenu knight was a definite rival to Warenne and the other great lords of Sussex. Even as late in the reign as this, and perhaps because of the absence of the more judicious rule of his son, Henry III's patronage of Aguillon was another example of the disastrous favouritism that had blighted his reign, in this case serving only to disturb the delicate balance in Sussex.[155] With Henry III's death, and the new king absent on crusade, Warenne saw his chance to cut Aguillon down to size.

The regency government found it extremely difficult to control violence in the shires, and this was certainly the case in Sussex.[156] The sheriff on the spot and the government at Westminster found that, without the authority of an attendant king behind them, it was difficult to restrain the excesses of so powerful a lord as John de Warenne. By June 1273, only eight months after Henry III's death, violence was already out of control in Sussex. The sheriff, Matthew de Hastings, was ordered to preserve the

148 *CPR 1266–1272*, 115; *Close Rolls 1268–1272*, 128. 149 *CPR 1266–1272*, 189.

150 Ibid., 348. 151 *CIM*, I, no. 925.

152 *Book of Fees*, II, 690, 905. 153 *CPR 1266–1272*, 641.

154 He may possibly have wanted the lordship for himself but more likely he would have expected the wardship to go to the heir's mother, Isabelle, or perhaps Isabelle's father, Roger Mortimer of Wigmore, who had obtained the heir's marriage and his extensive lands on the Welsh March. D. Greenhalgh, 'The Fitzalan Family, 1101–1415: a Study in the Development of a Noble Medieval Dynasty', unpublished MPhil thesis, University of Wales, Bangor (2003), 42–3.

155 For other examples, see Carpenter, 'King, Magnates and Society'; H.W. Ridgeway, 'The Lord Edward and the Provisions of Oxford (1258): a Study in Faction', *TCE* I (1986), 89–99; Ridgeway, 'Foreign Favourites'.

156 For contrasting views of the success of the regency government, see J.R. Maddicott, 'Edward I and the Lessons of Baronial Reform: Local Government, 1258–80', *TCE* I (1986), 1–5; Huscroft, 'Robert Burnell and the Governance of England'.

peace in the county, lest it be thought he was conniving at the violence being perpetrated.[157] Names were not given in the writ but the primary cause of disturbance in Sussex at the time was a dispute between Earl Warenne and Robert Aguillon, and it is clear that Warenne was seriously hampering the sheriff in the operation of his duties. Violence erupted when Sir Richard de la Vache and Walter Dragun, both high in the earl's service, seized 146 draught animals from Aguillon's manor of Perching.[158] This was just the first of a series of outrages that Warenne ordered against Aguillon.[159] It was only with great difficulty, and a personal appearance at Lewes, that the sheriff was able to replevy Aguillon's goods and servants taken hostage by the earl.[160] By March 1274, Warenne's archers and men-at-arms were stationed at Perching, causing great damage and refusing to move even at the sheriff's command.[161]

His ancient pedigree and comital title gave Warenne an informal suzerainty over the other lords of Sussex. This was demonstrated by his command of Rochester Castle during the First Barons' War in 1264, among whose garrison were the Sussex lords William de Braose and John Fitz Alan.[162] This position within the county gave him the muscle to bring others to his side when he took on an opponent like Aguillon. Again, this was not a new tactic and had been used by lords for generations.[163] Warenne employed it to counter Aguillon. The Hundred Rolls show clearly that the earl had allied with the lord of Bramber, William de Braose, against Aguillon.[164] Further west, the custody of the lands of his infant grandson, Henry Percy,[165] an alliance against Aguillon with the lord of Midhurst, John de Bohun,[166] and the presence of the earl's widowed sister, Isabella, dowager countess of Arundel, further strengthened the earl's position.[167] Another potential Warenne ally, or at least another Aguillon antagonist, was Robert Kilwardby, archbishop of Canterbury, who was in violent dispute with Aguillon over the wardship of Richard de Plaiz.[168] Aguillon was clearly building an impressive array of enemies in the county.

157 *Report of the Deputy Keeper of the Public Record Office* 42 (1881), 666.
158 JUST 1/915, m. 9.
159 Ibid., m. 9; KB 27/20A, m. 7; 'The Hundred Roll for Sussex Part Two', 50.
160 'The Hundred Roll for Sussex Part Two', 50.
161 *CCR 1272–1279*, 116.
162 *Gervase of Canterbury*, II, 235.
163 Crouch, *William Marshal*, 157–68; Dalton, *Conquest*, 178–84.
164 'The Hundred Roll for Sussex Part Two', 50; 'The Hundred Roll for Sussex Part Three', ed. and trans. L.F. Salzman, *Sussex Archaeological Collections* 84 (1945), 79.
165 *CIPM*, III, no. 214; 'The Hundred Roll for Sussex Part Three', 70.
166 *CPR 1266–1272*, 624; KB 27/11, m. 37d; KB 27/18, m. 39d; KB 27/20A, m. 1d, 7; 'The Hundred Roll for Sussex Part Two', 53.
167 *CIM*, I, no. 470.
168 SC 8/30/1477.

The violence engendered by the dispute between Warenne and Aguillon was not a situation that Edward I could accept upon his return from crusade. Through studying Edward's actions in Sussex, and particularly in relation to the Warenne–Aguillon dispute, it is possible to appreciate the king's success in restoring royal authority, which has long been recognised by historians, and, as one of the main themes of this work, his subtlety, which has not always been.[169] When characterising relations between Henry I and an earlier Earl Warenne almost two centuries earlier, Warren Hollister described it as the 'taming of the turbulent earl'.[170] The same label might be applied to relations between Edward I and John de Warenne in the first decade of Edward's reign. Edward established his authority over Warenne without alienating him. This episode had a distinctly Anglo-Norman feel to it, with both sides flexing their muscles to see whose will was stronger.

On his return to England, but before his coronation, Edward stayed with Warenne at Reigate and no doubt learned the earl's version of the dispute.[171] Whether he was influenced by this we cannot tell, but he certainly recognised the underlying cause of the problem and that the heat needed to be taken out of the situation. Hence, on 28 October 1274, Aguillon was ordered to hand over custody of Arundel Castle and honour to the new sheriff, William de Hevere, a Kentish knight.[172] Hevere's appointment as sheriff a few days earlier, as part of a general replacement of sheriffs, also illustrated Edward's desire to reinvigorate royal lordship both in Sussex and throughout England and reflected the fact that the previous sheriff, Hastings, had lost control of the county.[173] The reduction of Aguillon's fortunes, coupled with the attempted reinvigoration of the Sussex shrievalty under Hevere, an outsider, illustrates nicely Edward's even-handed attitude towards Warenne in the first years of his reign. He was prepared to give ground on the specific point of Warenne's grievance but was determined to re-establish the general principle of royal authority.

Aguillon was not prepared to give up so easily and decided to pursue Warenne through the courts. It was rare for earls to be chased in the courts by those of knightly status and Aguillon's efforts perhaps reflect his lingering influence as a former royal steward and councillor.[174] For all this, however, the legal route did not prove a success. Less than two

[169] Maddicott, 'Lessons of Baronial Reform'; Prestwich, *Edward I*, 91–107.

[170] C.W. Hollister, 'The Taming of the Turbulent Earl: Henry I and William of Warenne', *Historical Reflections* 3 (1976), 83–91.

[171] *Flores Historiarum*, III, 43. [172] *CFR 1272–1307*, 33.

[173] Ibid., 31. For general replacement of sheriffs, ibid., 30–4.

[174] For a discussion of this see above, 149–51.

months after Edward reached England, the dispute first appears in King's Bench, with accusations of abduction, assault and robbery committed by Warenne, his allies and officials.[175] Warenne adopted the simple delaying tactic of refusing to come to court. For six years the case returned repeatedly to King's Bench, while the justices grew increasingly frustrated but nothing and no one could induce the earl to defend himself against the charges.[176] It would have taken direct pressure from the king to force him to answer, something Edward did not exert. The extent of Aguillon's marginalisation under Edward is illustrated by a glance at the index for the Patent Rolls. There are sixty references to Aguillon between 1258 and 1272 and only four from 1272 until his death in February 1286.[177] In Henry III's reign, men sought out Aguillon to obtain royal grants for them;[178] by 1280 he was forced to rely on the intervention of the queen mother to prevent harassment at the hands of the forest justices.[179] During 1279, in the Aguillon cases, specific rather than general distraints were ordered against the earl to try to force his attendance.[180] Emery de Cancellis, the new sheriff, unlike his predecessors, attempted to enforce one of these distraints by sending two men into the earl's liberty to levy it. They were intercepted by servants of Warenne, who recovered the distraint and sent them back empty-handed. These events demonstrated the determination of both the court to have its authority recognised and the earl to prevent the intrusion of royal officials into his domains.[181]

At this point, the earl's authority was still holding, but gradually the sheriff was able to extend his authority into the rape and even into the town of Lewes itself.[182] Despite this, Warenne's position in Sussex remained strong enough to protect his interests there. A Sussex jury pronounced in favour of his claim to hold free warren throughout the whole of the barony of Lewes and also upheld his claim to other liberties in the rape.[183] In a petition to the king, Robert Aguillon complained that, although the juries of all the hundreds in the rape of Lewes had pronounced against the earl's claims to free warren, Warenne had been cleared by the verdict of a single twelve who were his friends and tenants and whom he had corrupted, a complaint with some basis to it.[184]

[175] KB 27/12, m. 28d, 29.

[176] KB 27/12, m. 28d, 29; 27/16, m. 18; 27/18, m. 39, 39d; 27/20A, m. 2, 4d, 7, 8; 27/21, m. 14d, 18d, 20; 27/24, m. 20d, 23; 27/31, m. 20; 27/33, m. 18, 18d; 27/37, m. 11, 18d, 21, 21d; 27/39, m. 13d, 17; 27/41, m. 33d; 27/43, m. 15, 15d; 27/45, m. 21d, 22, 26; 27/47, m. 6d, 8, 13d.

[177] *CPR 1258–1266*; *CPR 1266–1272*; *CPR 1272–1281*; *CPR 1281–1292, passim.*

[178] *CPR 1266–1272*, 111, 164, 219, 233, 245, 325. [179] *CCR 1279–1288*, 15.

[180] KB 27/47, m. 6d, 8, 13d. [181] JUST 1/921, m. 11d.

[182] Ibid., m. 11d. [183] *Placita de Quo Warranto*, 750.

[184] SC 8/276/13780; *Victoria County History for Sussex*, I, 504. The jury included William Maufe, a long-time associate of Warenne; the former sheriff John de Wauton, who had links with the earl;

Thus, though Warenne's position in Sussex was under some pressure, it seems that he was still strong enough to manipulate the judicial system to ensure a favourable verdict. That Edward allowed the verdict to stand, in spite of complaints by Aguillon and 'the community of the barony of Lewes', again shows his willingness to give ground where necessary in order to avoid alienating so important a lord as Warenne. That Edward felt himself able to make concessions, however, illustrates the success of his policy of reasserting royal authority in Sussex. The king could have overturned the jury's verdict, had he been so minded: that he did not was an act of grace, predicated on the strength of his position, not weakness, as had been the case with his father.

Edward demonstrated his strength to Warenne elsewhere, during the *quo warranto* hearings over Stamford and Grantham. These nearly led to violence between the sheriff of Lincolnshire, acting on behalf of the king, and the earl's officials.[185] Warenne's defeat at law in 1281 over Stamford and Grantham vividly illustrated to the earl the king's power and the limits of the extent to which Edward's patience was prepared to stretch. This episode began when, possibly emboldened by the idea that the *quo warranto* campaign was going to humble the power of the great lords, while Warenne's attentions were diverted by the First Welsh War, his enemies in Sussex, led by Aguillon, decided to take the initiative with some direct action of their own. As a result of this, in January 1278 Warenne was granted a commission of *oyer* and *terminer* to investigate an attack upon his large free chase at Cleres.[186] A petition to parliament by Aguillon in that year provides the result. Aguillon and a number of his men had been accused of hunting in the earl's free chase and, despite providing evidence that he and his ancestors had hunted in the area from time immemorial, the jury, instructed to ignore Aguillon's evidence, had found him and his men guilty, leading to his men being imprisoned.[187] The earl's enemies had clearly underestimated the resilience of his power and influence.

The results of another commission into trespass in the earl's hunting grounds, two years later, survive in full on the rolls of King's Bench and further demonstrate the extent of Warenne's continuing ability to harass his foes.[188] The justices heard the case at Croydon in January 1281, where a jury from Sussex and one from Surrey gathered to determine

Richard de Pevensey, steward of the neighbouring rape of Pevensey who was claiming the same right of warren for his lady, and Robert de Esseburn, who would shortly act as a pleader for Warenne in a legal case against poachers in Sussex.

[185] See above, 145–6. [186] *CPR 1272–1281*, 284.

[187] 'Edward I: Petition 1, Text and Translation', in *PROME*.

[188] *CPR 1272–1281*, 414; KB 27/64, mm. 57–8.

the guilt of around seventy men who had previously been accused.[189] The accused included not only Sir Robert Aguillon and his servants, but also Sir Simon de Pierpoint, a member of a prominent local family who were tenants of Warenne. Most of the rest of the accused were men of no political consequence but their names suggest that they were minor tenants of the earl from all across the rape of Lewes, and particularly from Fletching, Oakfield and Ifield, all near important hunting grounds of the earl.[190] Warenne had been fortunate enough to secure not just a commission from the king but also his active support in pursuing the perpetrators. The case was prosecuted by the king's pleader, Robert de Esseburn, who was also Warenne's attorney, and he acted in the king's name as well as in Warenne's.[191] The king's involvement clearly frightened many of the defendants into presenting themselves in court, admitting their guilt and making fine with the justices.[192]

Edward, however, avoided pressing Warenne's case to the bitter end as the earl might have wished. Several of those accused, including Aguillon and Pierpoint, had their names crossed through on the rolls of King's Bench, indicating that the pursuit of them was not carried to a conclusion.[193] Here again the even-handedness and subtlety of Edward's behaviour towards his friend Warenne is revealed. He had granted the commissions, had prosecuted one of the suits himself, imprisoned Aguillon's men and had even allowed the justices to exceed their brief, but he had not allowed Warenne the complete victory he craved. In response to Aguillon's petition against the commission of 1278, the king permitted him to sue the justices for going beyond their remit, while in 1281 Aguillon's name had been expunged from the list of those indicted. Edward's backing of Warenne only went so far. A situation that created untrammelled power for Warenne in Lewes Rape was not one that he seems to have wanted to prevail.

The second commission was the culmination of the Warenne–Aguillon dispute, which had disturbed the peace in Sussex for the best part of a decade. The embers of the dispute continued to burn but, in the wake of the Croydon hearings, the fight appears to have left Aguillon. He brought a case against Warenne in King's Bench the following term, Hilary 1282, for illegal detention of goods and animals by the earl and his bailiffs, but this plea was delayed by the Second Welsh War, which began in March 1282 and during which Warenne was granted respite from it.[194] The

[189] KB 27/62, m. 29. [190] KB 27/64, m. 59.
[191] Ibid., m. 57. [192] Ibid., mm. 57, 57d, 58. [193] Ibid., m. 58.
[194] KB 27/66, m. 9; 27/71, m. 10d.

case never returned to King's Bench and Aguillon died on 15 February 1286.[195]

Warenne's attacks on Aguillon eventually destroyed the latter's position in Sussex but, by attracting the king's attention, they also diminished Warenne's own freedom of action. His attempts to withdraw his lordship from royal authority were partially reversed, as distraints against him were first attempted and then carried through.[196] His withdrawal of his tenants from the sheriff's tourn led to him being placed in mercy by the justices in eyre in 1279, and by the early 1280s the sheriff was able to act once again in Lewes Rape, even in the town of Lewes itself, with relative freedom, in stark contrast to the situation a decade earlier.[197] As the reign wore on, Edward grew more confident in stamping on any pretensions Warenne had in Sussex. Following the death of Archbishop Peckham in 1292, Warenne audaciously sought to establish seisin over the archbishop's Sussex properties by sending his bailiffs to hunt in the archbishop's parks and fisheries. The king responded by imprisoning Warenne's men in the Tower of London, heavily distraining the earl and bringing a case against him for £20,000-worth of damages. The charges were dropped but Edward had made his point.[198]

In this old-fashioned battle of wills, it was Edward's will to reimpose royal authority that proved stronger than Warenne's desire for a free hand in his lordship. Warenne was sensible enough to realise that, in a head-on clash with a king as determined and capable as Edward I, there would be only one winner. Warenne's vigorous defence of his traditional methods of lordship was, in the end, no match for the changing administrative methods of a king who was determined that his writ would run everywhere in his kingdom. Unlike Lincoln in Yorkshire, the earl had made little effort to build relationships with his gentry tenants, relying rather on the support of the other lords of the Sussex rapes, and was in direct conflict with several of them, including Aguillon, Pierpoint and Burgh. Warenne had exposed the limits of traditional lordship. As one of Edward's most trusted and loyal nobles, he had attempted to take advantage of this to confirm and strengthen his position in a region where his family had long held sway and had received something of a bloody nose from the king. If magnates were to retain their dominance over local society in the face of a rising gentry and an assertive crown, they would

[195] *CIPM*, II, no. 604.

[196] By 1288 the sheriff was able, in Warenne's absence in Wales, to carry through a massive distraint on the earl, worth almost £150, including 110 oxen and well over 2,000 sheep. SC 8/200/9970; JUST 1/924, m. 38d.

[197] JUST 1/921, mm. 10d, 59d.

[198] KB 27/139, mm. 18–19.

need to find new methods of exercising lordship in the future that would reconcile both king and gentry.

CONCLUSION: THE ORIGINS OF 'BASTARD FEUDALISM'?

Until royal government became more pervasive it was possible for the great nobles of the thirteenth century to protect their own interests by ignoring royal authority when it suited them to do so. It was only when the king became personally interested in a situation that resistance to local royal officials was no longer effective. Similarly, it was possible for the earls to influence the operations of royal law by their links with feed justices. Earls were able largely to avoid legal pressure in the king's courts unless that pressure was being brought to bear by the king himself or by a fellow magnate.[199] This, together with their ability to mitigate many of the intrusions of royal government, gave magnates sufficient protection for their interests that it was not necessary for them to develop the techniques of 'bastard feudalism'. There are signs, however, in Edward I's reign that the situation was beginning slowly to change, a process that would eventually create the circumstances where 'bastard feudalism' was both necessary and effective.

A king as committed to the restoration of royal authority and as jealous of royal power as Edward I could not regard with equanimity a state of affairs in which his greatest subjects could ignore the king's officials with impunity. Henry III had adopted a hands-off approach with his magnates before 1258, while the Barons' Wars had only further weakened the ability of central government to assert royal authority in the face of magnate resistance.[200] Edward was determined to reverse this situation and, as argued in Chapter 3, the Hundred Rolls Inquiry and the *quo warranto* campaign were part of a policy to reassert the theoretical supremacy of royal authority and to stop the rot of practical seepage of royal jurisdiction thanks to magnate usurpations of franchises.[201] Edward intervened against magnates much more often than his father when he felt that the royal dignity had been compromised and he was not afraid to make examples of the most mighty in the land when he felt the need. The most famous example, of course, is that of the dispute between the earls of Gloucester and Hereford, discussed in detail below, but it was far from unique.[202] Richard Fitz Alan's lordship of Oswestry in 1299 and Bishop Bek's palatinate of Durham in 1302 were both temporarily confiscated by Edward, while William de Braose's insolence

[199] See above, 149–51. [200] Carpenter, 'King, Magnates and Society', 62, 69–70.
[201] See above, 71–6. [202] See below, 217–19.

towards Justice Hengham landed him in hot water over his lordship of Gower in 1305.[203] There are further examples, however, that are less well known but are equally illuminating of Edward's attitude towards magnate indifference to royal authority. In 1278, for instance, the young Roger de Mowbray found himself imprisoned temporarily in Windsor Castle 'for certain trespasses charged against him and for a contempt done to the king'.[204] In March 1297, the chancery sent a furious letter to Anthony Bek, bishop of Durham, accusing his officials of 'manifest contempt' against the king for confiscating the property of prominent Scottish rebels in the palatinate of Durham for the bishop's use, against the terms of a royal ordinance that Bishop Bek had himself helped to draw up as a member of the king's council. He was told that 'the king will not leave such a trespass and contempt unpunished, more especially as other ministers of the realm may thence take a pernicious example', and was ordered to produce his bailiffs at the next parliament 'to answer to [the king] for the trespass and contempt and for other things that he will say against them in the premises'.[205] As the chancery warned Bishop Bek, those closest to the king should expect to be held to the same standard as everyone else. How Edward applied this to the power in Sussex of his close friend, Earl Warenne, has already been shown.[206] There were no longer to be places where the king's agents would not or could not go.

Given Edward's hostile attitude towards open defiance of royal authority and the increasingly pervasive nature of royal government in his reign, particularly from the 1290s onwards, it may be that Caroline Burt's suggestion that the last years of Edward I's reign perhaps see the onset of 'bastard feudalism' comes into its own.[207] The great strength of the English nobility over the centuries was its ability to adapt to survive. Perhaps the earl of Warwick had seen the way the wind was blowing and sought to offer himself and his followers as agents of royal authority while at the same time ensuring his own interests were protected. Warwick and others like him may have decided that they could no longer rely so completely on the king's indifference to their contempt for his officials. They may have come to the conclusion that royal officials were no longer something with which only other people had to deal but that their own interests might be best served by paying closer attention to who did what in the king's name in their neighbourhood. That said, the evidence presented here does not suggest that the other earls had yet grasped the

[203] C.M. Fraser, *A History of Anthony Bek, Bishop of Durham, 1283–1311* (Oxford: Clarendon Press, 1957), 181–2; Davies, *Lordship and Society*, 260; Prestwich, *Edward I*, 538–9.

[204] *CCR 1272–1279*, 471. [205] *CCR 1296–1302*, 23–4.

[206] See above, 165–9. [207] See above, 138.

lesson as quickly as Warwick may have done. It may be safer to say that the restoration of royal authority under Edward I watered some of the seeds for the development of a 'bastard feudal' society where there was a partnership between crown, nobility and gentry but that they were not yet ready to germinate. The sharp frost of Edward II's reign may have hampered its flowering further as royal authority withered again for much of this period.

While the crown and the nobility, and the nature of the relationship between them, were vital planks of late medieval 'bastard feudalism', perhaps the most important piece of the jigsaw was the gentry, for without their involvement the whole system of late medieval government would have been impossible. The growth of government and the law in the thirteenth and fourteenth centuries necessitated devolution to the localities and for the gentry to take the principal role. If the nobility were to continue to exercise extensive power at a local level, then they needed to reinvent themselves as the bridge between the centre and the localities. They could ignore no longer either royal authority within their lands or the needs and concerns of their gentry neighbours as the latter became increasingly subject to the king's demands and customers of the expanding royal law. Under 'bastard feudalism' they could offer themselves to the centre as the principal royal agent in their locality and to their neighbours they could present themselves as protectors and catalysts for advancement, something they were not doing in the thirteenth century.[208] These mutually reinforcing elements helped to build, protect and develop their command of their 'country' and ensured the continuation of noble power in the localities in a different form from that which they had exercised during the thirteenth century.[209] The nobility encountered in this chapter were not in a position to offer these elements to either the crown or the gentry: indeed in the thirteenth century they were fighting two losing battles, to maintain their control and restrict the gentry through traditional methods on the one hand, and to control the access of the king's law and administration within their lands on the other. What was needed for the crown to trust devolved power to the nobility was the nobility's recognition that these were fights they could not win and the concomitant development of a nobility of service that would tie them more closely into the crown's purposes and allow them to act as the link between the centre and localities, thus enabling the fully fledged affinities of the later middle ages to come into being.

[208] See above for discussion of magnates' role in obtaining royal favour, 131–2.

[209] Carpenter, *Wars of the Roses*, 6.

The legal, social and political developments that allowed such a society to emerge were by no means smooth, uniform or linear, for such things rarely are, but Edward I's reign marks a significant stage in the emergence of a 'bastard feudal' society. When they finally all came together lies beyond the scope of this study, though the latter half of Edward III's reign seems most likely, a time when the nobility were providing the king with an unprecedented level of political, administrative and military service, and law and administration was being further devolved to the localities. One should not, of course, try to paint too rosy a picture of 'bastard feudalism': the nobility were not paragons of public-spirited virtue and it is foolish to pretend that they were, but a craftsman can only work with the tools he is given and the late medieval state was, and had to be, a partnership between crown, nobles and gentry: an imperfect and fragile partnership that could and did break down at times, but a partnership nonetheless that could also, under the right circumstances, benefit all three estates immensely. Under Edward I, the circumstances that made it possible were simply not there yet.

PART III

Politics and the earls

Chapter 7

THE MAKING OF EDWARDIAN POWER, 1265–1286

Having examined the nature of the relationship between the king and the earls and the earls' local power thematically, it is possible now to bring those findings to bear upon the politics of the reign of Edward I and to try to offer an analytical narrative from the perspective of the earls. This will not be a blow-by-blow description of the reign or of the lives of Edward or the individual earls themselves. Such a task would necessitate a much longer and a fundamentally different book. Instead this will be a political narrative built on the king's relations with the earls. This will, on occasion, necessitate a certain amount of repetition from earlier chapters but overall it will add new angles and depth to our understanding of English politics in the late thirteenth century.

EVESHAM TO CORONATION, 1265–1274

The events and characters of Edward I's reign cannot properly be understood without reference to the aftermath of the Barons' Wars. The experience of these years shaped the attitudes of the king and of many of his earls and a number of the themes of Edward's reign were set during the late 1260s. Henry III and Lord Edward faced numerous problems following the royalist victory at the Battle of Evesham. First, they needed to reassert royal authority after the humiliations imposed upon it since 1258. Second, they had to decide whether to adopt a policy of reconciliation or extirpation of the remaining rebels. Third, a settlement was needed with Llywelyn ap Gruffydd, prince of Gwynedd and de facto ruler of much of the rest of Wales. Fourth, a personal concern for Edward was the prospect of a new crusade. Finally, a consequence of Edward's decision to take the cross was the need to make arrangements for the possibility of the king's death during his son's absence.

These were great tasks facing the old king and the now mature prince. The earls with whom they were left were as divided and fractious as the country at large. Richard of Cornwall and his son Henry of Almain had, like the king and his son, been imprisoned after Lewes by the Montfort regime.[1] John de Warenne had escaped from Lewes and fled abroad, but had subsequently landed in Pembrokeshire with his brother-in-law, William de Valence, and linked up with Lord Edward.[2] The earl of Norfolk had acquiesced in Montfort's victory, while Hereford had been captured at Lewes and imprisoned.[3] Gilbert de Clare, the young earl of Gloucester, had fought with Montfort at Lewes and was one of the ruling triumvirate before falling out with Earl Simon, switching sides and playing a crucial role in the Evesham campaign.[4] Robert de Ferrers, earl of Derby, had initially joined the Montfortians in 1264, the better to conduct his private feud against Lord Edward, but did not fight at Lewes and quickly fell foul of Montfort too, finding himself imprisoned until after Evesham.[5] Simon de Montfort himself and his heir had died at Evesham but he had three sons still alive and at liberty, while Robert de Vere, earl of Oxford, had been a dedicated Montfortian.[6]

This was hardly encouraging from the crown's perspective. Cornwall, Hereford and Norfolk, while supportive, were all ageing and unable to engage with the more vigorous aspects of reasserting royal authority. Gloucester and Derby would need careful handling and their consent to royal policy could not be guaranteed. Of the remainder, Warenne, Henry of Almain and William de Valence could be regarded as generally reliable but, as has been seen, men like Warenne had their own agendas too, and the reassertion of their own authority and interests was often conducted with a vigour that could run counter to royal wishes for a restoration of peace and order.[7] While the attitude of the earls would be crucial to any restoration of royal authority, it cannot be assumed that this alone would be enough to guarantee peace. It was the gentry who had supported Montfort most enthusiastically and they had the most to lose if the restoration of royal authority meant a return to the oppressions that had afflicted the knights before 1258. The Statute of Marlborough, promulgated in 1267, addressed some of the concerns of the 'reform programme'

[1] Maddicott, *Simon de Montfort*, 272, 280. [2] Ibid., 333.

[3] R.C. Stacey, 'Bigod, Roger (III), Fourth Earl of Norfolk (*c.*1217–1270)', in *ODNB*; N. Vincent, 'Bohun, Humphrey (IV) de, Second Earl of Hereford and Seventh Earl of Essex (*d.*1275)', in *ODNB*.

[4] Altschul, *Baronial Family*, 103–10.

[5] For Ferrers' career during the Barons' Wars, see Golob, 'Ferrers Earls', 323–42.

[6] *GEC*, x, 216. [7] See above, 161.

and was a crucial element in regaining some of the confidence of the gentry.[8]

Despite the somewhat unpromising starting position in 1265 from the crown's perspective, the earls did proceed to play important roles in support of the royal objectives of promoting conciliation and restoring order and authority. Several were prominent in the reconciliation of former rebels. For instance, the earl of Norfolk in East Anglia and Edmund of Lancaster in the counties of Derbyshire, Staffordshire and Lancashire were each given authority to receive rebels back into the king's peace.[9] Two earls, Gloucester and Hereford, were on a committee of twelve chosen on 31 August 1266 to bring about the 'reformation of the peace of the land' whose deliberations led to the Dictum of Kenilworth two months later.[10] Earls had the moral and political authority to undertake reconciliatory acts, since they were able to act on behalf of both the king and the 'community of the realm' and represent each to the other, in an effort to heal the terrible wounds inflicted on the body politic by the events of the past few years.

But, while earls could act for the king as the velvet glove, they were also employed as the mailed fist, and, interestingly, it was those earls not engaged in the processes of reconciliation who took on this more direct role. Earl Warenne was probably the most conspicuous earl in the more forceful aspects of restoring royal authority. Following the Battle of Evesham, he was important in the mopping-up operations: at Dover in August 1265,[11] at Chesterfield and Bury St Edmunds in 1266[12] and on the Isle of Wight in the summer of 1267.[13] Warenne's role, in keeping with his character, was as the royalist big stick, to be employed on rebels who had not yet seen the wisdom of falling in line. Other members of comital families were also employed in this active role, including William de Valence and Henry of Almain, who took part in the attacks on Bury and Chesterfield respectively.[14]

Earl Warenne, as has been seen, was not a simple royalist pawn who could be pointed at a problem and then let loose. He was more complex than that. Determined to pursue his own interests, he was willing to risk

[8] *EHD 1189–1327*, 384–92; Maddicott, 'Lessons of Baronial Reform', 5, on the success and limitations of the statute.

[9] *CPR 1266–1272*, 203; Morris, *Bigod Earls*, 96.

[10] *CPR 1258–66*, 671–2; Robert of Gloucester, *The Metrical Chronicle of Robert of Gloucester*, ed. W.A. Wright, 2 vols., Rolls Series (1887), II, lines 1378–94.

[11] SC 1/12/12.

[12] For his being given military command, see *CLR*, V, 244. For his descent on Bury St Edmunds, see *The Chronicle of Bury St Edmunds*, 34–5. For the Battle of Chesterfield, see *Robert of Gloucester*, II, lines 1287–90.

[13] *CPR 1266–1272*, 156. [14] See note 12, above.

the fragile peace to do so, even if it meant conflict with fellow royalists like Sir Robert Aguillon in Sussex.[15] This attitude was replicated outside Sussex and his two most serious disputes in other counties were also with royalists rather than rebels. First, in 1269 he became involved in an 'exceedingly violent' dispute with Henry de Lacy, heir to the earldom of Lincoln, over some pasture land in Yorkshire.[16] The Warennes and the Lacys had been rivals in west Yorkshire for generations, thanks to the proximity of their respective lordships of Wakefield and Pontefract, and it seems possible that Warenne had taken advantage of Lacy's long minority to appropriate a disputed area on the borders between their lands, while Lacy, now approaching his majority, was determined to reassert his rights. The case went to court, where Lacy won, which put a stop to any further violence, though relations between the two men's lordships remained strained for years afterwards.[17]

Warenne's second dispute was even more serious and was with Sir Alan la Zouche, who, like Robert Aguillon, was a former steward of the royal household.[18] Unlike the Yorkshire quarrel, which was almost certainly based on the traditional rivalry of long-standing neighbours, this was a dispute over the spoils of war, in particular the tangled inheritance of Isabella de Ashby. The case rested on whether her grandfather, David de Ashby, had fought willingly for the rebels at Lewes or not. Interestingly, for the debate on the continuing relevance of the feudal bond, it was claimed by Warenne on Isabella's behalf that Ashby had been forced to appear alongside his feudal lord, Henry de Hastings, at Lewes. If Warenne could prove this, then he would secure Isabella's wardship and marriage, for he had been granted Hastings' lands and rights in the wake of Evesham. If not, then the prize would go to Alan la Zouche, the man who had originally been granted Ashby's property. A special commission in the winter of 1269–70 made judgment in favour of Warenne, but Zouche appears to have frustrated the earl's attempts to get an execution of this judgment. His response was characteristically violent and, as has been seen, culminated in the murderous assault on Zouche and his son in Westminster Hall in front of the king's justices on 1 July 1270.[19]

The heinousness of his offence quickly dawned on Warenne and he fled Westminster immediately, making for his castle of Reigate in Surrey, whither he was pursued by Lord Edward.[20] Understanding that resistance

[15] See above, 162–9. [16] *Flores Historiarum*, III, 17–18.

[17] For evidence of continuing poor relations between Wakefield and Pontefract, see *Court Rolls of the Manor of Wakefield*, I, 150, 308; II, 2, 45.

[18] For the details of the case and for unsubstantiated statements in the following paragraph, see Lapsley, 'John de Warenne', 116–20.

[19] See above, 162. [20] *Robert of Gloucester*, II, line 1462; *Flores Historiarum*, III, 18.

was futile, Warenne wisely offered none and threw himself on his friend's mercy.[21] Just over a month later, his punishment, a fine of 10,000 marks, was handed down at Winchester.[22] There were complaints that Warenne got off lightly, and it is true that most of the fine was never paid, but the whole affair was a serious blow to Warenne's prestige and future freedom of action.[23] The barefoot walk of penance from Temple to Westminster was the sort of public humiliation that no earl could view with equanimity. The use of heavy financial penalties on troublesome members of the nobility was a tactic used by King John, the logic being that the financial Sword of Damocles would provide the king with a means of asserting political control.[24] The difference here is that the expectation was that Warenne would be reassimilated rather than destroyed, as might have happened under John. Warenne's long-standing intimacy with both the king and his eldest son undoubtedly helped to ensure that the punishment was not heavier nor more stringently enforced but he was also aided by the support he received from the rest of the political community. At Winchester, twenty-five knights, including Henry of Almain and the earl of Gloucester, swore that Warenne had not acted premeditatedly.[25]

The Warenne–Zouche case offers a number of revealing insights. First, it showed just how intractable the settlement after Evesham had become, to the extent that two men with strong royalist credentials could end up in a murderous feud. Second, it indicated that even royalists were willing to risk the fragile peace to pursue their own interests. Third, it showed Edward's determination to defend royal dignity and authority, even to the extent of humiliating a close friend and loyal supporter. Finally, it demonstrated that, when an earl found himself in difficulties, it was important to have powerful friends at the apex of the political community on whom to call for aid.

While Warenne's first reaction to opposition was often to go for his sword, that of Richard of Cornwall was to reach for his cheque-book. Earl Richard had never paid a great deal of personal attention to the comings and goings of the county from which he took the title of his earldom but it has been argued that he was alarmed by his difficulty in influencing events in Cornwall after 1258.[26] Upon his release from prison after Evesham, the earl decided that the best way to strengthen his position

[21] *Flores Historiarum*, III, 18. [22] *CPR 1266–1272*, 451, 621–2.

[23] *Liber de Antiquis Legibus: Cronica Maiorum et Vicecomitum Londoniarum*, ed. T. Stapleton, Camden Society, Old Series 34 (1846), 81. Warenne only ever paid 1,850 marks before his death in 1304 when 6,800 marks remained outstanding. *CCR 1272–9*, 218; *CPR 1266–72*, 545, 621–2; *CPR 1272–81*, 146; *CPR 1301–07*, 496–7.

[24] Holt, *Magna Carta*, 109–10, 190–2. [25] *AM*, IV, 234; *Robert of Gloucester*, II, lines 1465–7.

[26] Page, 'Cornwall', 25–31.

in the county was to get his hands on two strategically important castles in Cornwall. In 1268 he purchased the barony of Cardinan from Isolda de Cardinan, which included the castle of Restormel and the town of Lostwithiel. Two years later, he bought the small barony of Trematon in south-east Cornwall from Roger de Valletort for £300. Valletort's heirs claimed that Valletort made the deal when not of sound mind, and certainly Earl Richard paid less than the going rate for an estate that consisted of Trematon Castle and its manor, the borough of Saltash by the River Tamar and the manor of Calstock.[27] In the space of two years, the earl had extinguished two of the most ancient knightly families in Cornwall and used the proceeds to strengthen his own landed position and grant manors to two Devon knights who had remained loyal to him.[28]

If even royalist earls like Warenne and Cornwall were prepared to put at risk public order in the pursuit of their private grievances, or to upset established patterns of landholding, an even more pressing problem facing the government after Evesham was how to deal with the remaining rebels. There was fissure between the king and his son on this point. While Edward played little part in the grab for land after Evesham, Henry III soon decided on a policy of disinheritance for all rebels.[29] This proved unworkable and eventually a compromise was reached in the Dictum of Kenilworth in November 1266, which allowed rebels to buy back their lands at a stiff penalty.[30] The earls also differed in their response to the question of disinheritance for rebels. Some, like Warenne and Gloucester, had been among the most conspicuous participants in the seizure of rebel properties, only for Gloucester subsequently to reinvent himself once more in the following year, this time as the champion of the 'Disinherited'. The elderly earl of Hereford, on the other hand, was on the committee that produced the dictum, where he was joined by Gloucester, newly conciliatory but not yet aggressive in defence of the Disinherited's rights.[31]

The most prominent rebel still alive after Evesham was Robert de Ferrers, earl of Derby. Ferrers had not had a good war.[32] Even his time spent under arrest on Montfort's orders earned him little sympathy from the royalists, thanks to his previous quarrel with Lord Edward.[33] The heir to the throne was not one to forget a slight to his dignity: Ferrers' card

27 Ibid., 32–3; R.J. Burls, 'Society, Economy and Lordship in Devon in the Age of the First Two Courtenay Earls, c.1297–1377', unpublished DPhil thesis, University of Oxford (2002), 157.

28 Ibid., 157.

29 *CPR 1258–1266*, 490–1. For Edward's restraint after Evesham, see Wait, 'Household and Resources', 102, 124.

30 *EHD 1189–1327*, 380–4.

31 See above, 179.

32 See above, 178.

33 See above, 178.

was marked and an example was to be made of him. In October 1265 Ferrers was forced to purchase a royal pardon for the hefty price of 1,500 marks.[34] Royalist vindictiveness towards the earl served only to drive him into the hands of the remaining rebels. In May 1266 he was at Chesterfield with a number of the Disinherited.[35] Stricken with gout, Ferrers was unable to escape when the royalist force, led by Warenne and Henry of Almain, descended upon them. He was captured and found himself returned to the Tower.[36] On 15 August 1266 all Ferrers' lands were granted to Henry III's son, Edmund, a grant that was confirmed in January 1267, despite Ferrers' inclusion in the Dictum of Kenilworth.[37]

Ferrers' turbulent behaviour and the obvious enmity between him and the king and his sons left the earl with few friends to speak for him. Edmund may have felt, however, that Ferrers' inclusion in the dictum meant that his hold over the latter's estates might yet be broken if Ferrers could find the money from somewhere or someone. More drastic measures were needed. In May 1269, Ferrers was swindled out of his inheritance by Edmund of Lancaster and Lord Edward. On 1 May Ferrers was released from custody and his lands restored on payment of a fine to Lancaster of 50,000 marks.[38] Such a fine, though crushingly heavy, was essentially within the system envisaged by the dictum. What happened next, however, certainly was not. Ferrers was taken from Windsor to Chippenham where he was forced to put his seal to a charter that decreed that the fine should be made in one payment, that Lancaster's possession of Ferrers' lands could not be set against the sum and that, until the payment was made, the king's son was to have possession of all the Ferrers estates.[39] McFarlane saw Ferrers as a victim of Lancaster's 'lawless greed' and Edward's 'willingness to be his brother's accomplice in the act'. However, when one considers who else was involved in Ferrers' disinheritance, one can see that this was not mere 'crude high-handedness' by the royal brothers but a calculated act involving many of the leading men in the land.[40] The forced charter had been written at Chippenham, Richard of Cornwall's manor, and Richard's son, Henry of Almain, was one of eleven manucaptors for Ferrers' fine. Among the others were the earls of Warwick and Warenne, William de Valence and Thomas de Clare, brother of the earl of Gloucester.[41] Ferrers had forfeited the support of

34 Golob, 'Ferrers Earls', 343–4. 35 *Robert of Gloucester*, II, lines 1287–90.

36 Ibid., lines 1291–314.

37 *CPR 1258–1266*, 672; *CPR 1266–1272*, 22; *EHD 1189–1327*, 383 (chapter 14 of the dictum).

38 *CPR 1266–1272*, 336; *Close Rolls 1268–1272*, 126.

39 'Extracts from the Plea Rolls, 1272 to 1294', 62–4; Golob, 'Ferrers Earls', 362.

40 McFarlane, *Nobility*, 255.

41 'Extracts from the Plea Rolls, 1272 to 1294', 62.

many of his fellow magnates and found himself helpless to deflect the wrath of his royal foes. He was not only an enemy of Lord Edward but, unlike Warenne, had no support among the royalist establishment. No one was willing to speak for him, as they were to do for Warenne the following year. Not yet, anyway.

Ferrers had been Lord Edward's enemy and, although Henry III had acquiesced in the earl's disinheritance, it is clear that the driving force behind it came from Edward and his brother. Edward's dignity had been affronted by Ferrers' prosecution of private war against him, and the earl, together with the surviving members of the Montfort family who had also participated in Edward's humiliation, was the first to suffer at the hands of a new policy of extirpation aimed at those members of the titled nobility who seriously opposed the crown. This was to last until 1330 and was, or was intended to be, the fate of the earldoms of Norfolk, Lancaster, Hereford, Carlisle, Winchester and Arundel in the later years of Edward I, the reign of Edward II and the rule of Mortimer and Isabella.[42] Only the earl of Oxford, a Montfortian in 1265, escaped this punishment.

Like most of Montfort's supporters, Oxford was able to take advantage of the terms of the Dictum of Kenilworth but even this mechanism was regarded as deficient by many among the Disinherited who chafed at its harsh terms. The man who now emerged as their principal supporter among the royalists was the earl of Gloucester. Although he had served on the committee that produced the dictum, he was evidently unhappy with its outcome and completed his journey from rapacious looter to defender of the Disinherited, having previously switched from Montfortian to royalist with equally startling rapidity.[43] His grievances with Henry III and Lord Edward were both private and public. He was concerned that little had been done to implement Edward's promise to remove aliens and that Henry had been sympathetic to those wanting a policy of total disinheritance of former rebels.[44] His personal grievances included a feeling that he had not been adequately rewarded for his role in Montfort's downfall and that the government was being particularly unhelpful in a territorial dispute with his mother. This went as far as taking Glamorgan into royal hands for six months during 1266, a move bound to offend the sensitivities of this most powerful and prickly of the Marcher barons.[45]

[42] This is argued in more detail in an article on royal policy towards earldoms between 1265 and 1337, which is being prepared for publication in a book on medieval earls edited by David Crouch and Hugh Doherty.

[43] *Robert of Gloucester*, II, lines 1378–94; Altschul, *Baronial Family*, 115.

[44] Altschul, *Baronial Family*, 114–16.

[45] Altschul, *Baronial Family*, 117; Prestwich, *Edward I*, 58.

By April 1267 Gloucester's frustrations had boiled over and, following Henry's refusal to restore all the lands of the Disinherited, the earl joined forces with rebels from the Isle of Ely and descended upon London, where the citizens overthrew the ruling oligarchy and installed a commune.[46] This was a highly volatile situation and the threat of renewed civil war was very real. Fortunately, however, war did not materialise. Instead, a negotiated settlement was reached and further bloodshed avoided. On 13 May Gloucester and his supporters withdrew from the city and, by mid-June, a final settlement with the Disinherited was achieved.[47]

Why had Gloucester avoided the fate of Montfort or Ferrers, despite openly siding with enemies of the king? Three reasons stand out. First, simple necessity. As the greatest Marcher baron, Gloucester was needed to defend Wales and the March against further encroachments by Llywelyn ap Gruffydd. So weak was royal power there after the Barons' Wars that Henry and Edward simply could not risk removing Gloucester, even if they had wanted to. Second, the king and his son may have come to the conclusion that they had mishandled Gloucester since Evesham; certainly Edward's attitude towards the earl for most of his reign demonstrated an understanding that Gloucester needed delicate attention.[48] Finally, the earl retained the goodwill of many of those who mattered in political society. The papal legate, Ottobuono, Richard of Cornwall and Philip Basset were key figures in bringing about a negotiated settlement with him, but others were also in favour of conciliation.[49] The agreement by which Gloucester withdrew to Southwark was witnessed by, among others, William de Valence and the earls of Hereford, Norfolk and Warenne.[50] Even had the government wished to proceed against Gloucester, it would have been difficult, with so many in favour of negotiation. As with Warenne three years later, and in stark contrast to Ferrers, Gloucester was protected by a combination of magnate solidarity and royal common sense. As it turned out, as Altschul noted, the earl's actions had 'hastened, rather than prevented, the pacification of the realm', shocking the government into an acceptable compromise.[51]

As has been suggested, a key reason for leniency towards Gloucester was his position as a bulwark in Wales against Llywelyn. The period of Reform and Rebellion had left the crown in no fit state to overturn Llywelyn's success of the 1250s and early 1260s. Edward had suffered humiliating reverses at the prince's hands in 1257 and again in 1262 but he was shrewd enough to realise that English exhaustion meant that a

46 Altschul, *Baronial Family*, 118. 47 Ibid., 119.

48 See below, 200–1, 220–2. 49 *CPR 1266–1272*, 55.

50 TNA C 47/16/6, no. 4. 51 Altschul, *Baronial Family*, 120.

semi-permanent accommodation needed to be reached with Llywelyn that would go some way to acknowledging the extent of his achievements. The result was the Treaty of Montgomery, sealed on 29 September 1267, which ceded suzerainty over all native Wales to Llywelyn, recognised some of his gains from the Marcher lords and made official his self-styled title of 'prince of Wales'.[52] Even before this, Edward had tacitly acknowledged the magnitude of his defeat in Wales by withdrawing from it personally, surrendering all his castles and lands there to his brother Edmund of Lancaster in the autumn of 1265.[53]

While the treaty was a humiliation for both Henry III and Edward, the latter knew that he had time on his side and in the meantime he had other more pressing concerns facing him, like the restoration of royal authority in England and the increasingly powerful draw of the crusade. Edward was never one to forget an injury but, as many would discover, he was also patient. There would be a reckoning but Llywelyn could wait until Edward was cloaked in the full majesty and authority of kingship. In the meantime, he was happy to let the Marcher barons do his dirty work for him and chip away at the treaty.

This the Marchers were only too happy to do, for they, unlike Edward, did not have the luxury of time and distance. Llywelyn had made extensive inroads into their territory and the treaty threatened to crystallise their position of disadvantage, something they were not prepared to tolerate. The Marchers' determination to unpick the Treaty of Montgomery one castle and valley at a time destroyed any prospect of lasting peace between the king of England and the prince of Wales and made the resumption of war inevitable at some point in the not too distant future. Edward almost certainly appreciated this and would not have been overly disturbed by the prospect.[54]

One of the foremost pressure points on the March in these years was the lordship of Brecon, one of the largest, wealthiest and most important in south Wales. The lordship was ostensibly disputed between Llywelyn and the under-age Humphrey de Bohun, grandson, namesake and heir of the earl of Hereford.[55] Of more import for the purposes of English politics, however, the situation in Brecon was complicated by the covetous attitude of Bohun's near neighbours, the earl of Gloucester and Roger Mortimer of Wigmore. Young Bohun rose to the challenge of maintaining control over Brecon but it was in these years that the seeds of tension

[52] *Littere Wallie Preserved in Liber A in the Public Record Office*, ed. J.G. Edwards (Cardiff University Press, 1940), no. 1.

[53] Prestwich, *Edward I*, 59–60. [54] Davies, *Conquest*, 321–3.

[55] See above, 81, for Bohun's successful struggle to regain control of Brecon from Llywelyn.

were sown between him and Gloucester, the harvest of which would be reaped nearly a quarter of a century later.[56] The origins lay in the grant to Gloucester of the wardship of Brecon and the marriage of the young heir.[57] Although Llywelyn had largely overrun the lordship, Gloucester, who had his own problems with Llywelyn in Glamorgan, made no effort to aid Bohun in Brecon's recovery and was concerned only for his rights over the marriage. There can be little doubt that Bohun resented his guardian's lack of help.[58] Bohun bought the rights to his own marriage from Gloucester in 1270 at the cost of £1,000.[59] By the summer of 1273, however, Gloucester was claiming that he had yet to pay this debt.[60] It is unlikely to be coincidence that, when he married the queen's cousin in the summer of 1275, Bohun was given £1,000 by the queen mother, Eleanor of Provence, and indeed the debt case disappears from King's Bench at around this time, suggesting that he paid the money to Gloucester.[61] This was but the opening salvo in the dispute between the two earls.

Of more immediate concern to Gloucester was his struggle with Llywelyn for supremacy in south Wales. These two most powerful men in Wales clashed repeatedly in the years following the Treaty of Montgomery: over Gloucester's construction of Caerphilly Castle, over his imprisonment of the native lord, Gruffydd ap Rhys, and over Llywelyn's attempts to enforce his perceived rights in Glamorgan.[62] Edward made attempts to intercede between them but they proved heavy-handed and unproductive.[63] He was determined that Gloucester should accompany him on crusade but the earl was naturally reluctant to leave his Marcher estates unprotected, and it took further arbitration by Richard of Cornwall to produce terms acceptable, if not agreeable, to both Llywelyn and Gloucester.[64] Another crisis on the March, precipitated by the prince's attack on Caerphilly on 13 October 1270, ensured that Gloucester never set sail.[65]

With Edward abroad and Henry III fading fast, there was little anyone could do to prevent the escalation of hostilities in Wales and it would remain the most pressing and intractable problem facing the government for the next few years. Men like Gloucester, Bohun, Roger Mortimer and the other Marchers were too concerned with protecting and furthering their own interests to see any profit in ceasing their attacks on Llywelyn,

[56] See below, 214–5, 217–19. [57] *CPR 1258–1266*, 495.
[58] Altschul, *Baronial Family*, 116–17. [59] Ibid., 146. [60] KB 27/5, m. 11.
[61] Jones, 'Bohun Earls', 91. The debt case appears in King's Bench for the last time at Michaelmas 1274; KB 27/12, m. 14.
[62] Altschul, *Baronial Family*, 124–6. [63] Ibid., 126–7.
[64] Lloyd, 'Gilbert de Clare'. [65] Ibid., 62; Altschul, *Baronial Family*, 129.

particularly when, from 1273 onwards, they began to make tangible progress in eroding the prince's power.[66] On the Welsh side, Llywelyn saw no imperative to moderate his behaviour in the face of Marcher provocation and was contemptuous of the regency government's attempts to urge peace upon him after Henry III's death.[67]

The delicate situation in Wales was made worse by the Marchers' quarrels with each other and the absence of effective royal authority to arbitrate and adjudicate between them. The debt case between Bohun and Gloucester, for example, rumbled on until 1275, after Edward had returned. Bohun was also in dispute with William de Valence over the homage due for Haverford to Valence, as lord of Pembroke, and Valence did not return Haverford to Bohun until after Edward's return.[68] In Haverford, Bohun claimed he held the lordship direct from the king in chief but in Brecon he found himself on the other side of a similar dispute with Roger Mortimer. In February 1275 a commission was appointed to decide whether the manor of Glasbury was in Herefordshire, as Mortimer claimed, or within the lordship of Brecon as Humphrey maintained.[69] Again, it was not until Edward reached England that some progress was made on the case. That the magnates needed the king to arbitrate in their disputes with each other, otherwise they soon descended into spirals of violence that dragged other lords and neighbours into the disputes, is a key theme of medieval political history and is clearly highlighted during the periods of Edward I's absence from England.[70] This specific argument was the beginning of a long-running and violent dispute between the Bohuns and the Mortimers. It is typical of one of the many boundary disputes on the March and also of the inconsistency of the Marcher lords. As seen in Part I, they asked for royal intervention in one case and sought privilege of the March in another.[71]

In some senses Edward had only himself to blame for the continuing problems in Wales and the March. His decision to go on crusade, while that of a good Christian prince, left uncertainty behind him. This was not the best time for Edward to leave the country and it illustrates just how important the crusade was and would remain to him.[72] He took the cross amid great ceremony at Northampton around midsummer 1268 and the oath was also sworn by, among others, Edmund of Lancaster, William de Valence, Henry of Almain, Earl Warenne and the earl of Gloucester.[73] In

[66] *CAC*, 10–11, 57–8, 92–3, 109–10; *CPR 1272–1281*, 48; Altschul, *Baronial Family*, 132–3.

[67] See, for instance, *CAC*, 86.

[68] *Select Cases in the Court of King's Bench*, I, 2–4; *CPR 1272–1281*, 54, 56.

[69] *CPR 1272–1281*, 116–17. [70] See above, 66; see below, 213–15. [71] See above, 61–70.

[72] For the re-emergence of the crusade in Edward's priorities and its effect, see below, 224–6.

[73] *AM*, IV, 217–18.

the end, of these, only the three members of the royal family actually joined the crusade. These three could be certain that their interests would be guaranteed during their absence; the other two earls could not be so sure. Gloucester had too much to lose in south Wales to risk a protracted absence in the Holy Land. Warenne may have had second thoughts when his disputes mounted between 1268 and 1270.[74] For the non-royal earls, domestic concerns were more pressing than foreign adventures and they were unwilling to compromise their interests at home, even if that meant reneging on a sacred oath. This reluctance by the non-royal earls to join Edward's crusade was to be reflected again in their attitude to Edward's crusading plans from the mid-1280s.[75]

Before leaving, Edward had made clear arrangements for the disposition of his own affairs during his absence. He created a committee, headed by Richard of Cornwall and including Walter Giffard, archbishop of York, Robert Burnell, his chancellor, and two staunchly royalist barons, Philip Bassett and Roger Mortimer.[76] Should Henry III die while Edward was still abroad, then Richard of Cornwall or his son, Henry of Almain, was to act as regent. If both were unavailable, then power was reserved to the remaining members of the committee to appoint one of their number or someone else to be regent.[77] When Henry III died, during the evening of 16 November 1272, his son's instructions were changed in favour of a more collegiate response to the situation of a kingdom without a king. The *Flores Historiarum* reports that, after Henry's body had been interred, the earl of Gloucester and Earl Warenne 'and all the clergy and laity, proceeded without delay to the great altar [of Westminster Abbey], and there swore fealty to Edward, the eldest son of the late king, though they were ignorant whether he was alive'.[78] These two earls were 'conspicuous beyond all the other nobles of the country' and it was clearly thought proper that they should take leading parts in the proclamation of the new king's authority.[79] But they did more than this. After the funeral, the nobles retreated to the New Temple, where the government was entrusted to Edward's deputies, principally Walter Merton, bishop of Rochester, who became chancellor of England, and Edward's own chancellor, Robert Burnell, who emerged as the dominant figure in the government.[80] While the administrative duties fell on Merton and Burnell, in the view of the Bury chronicler, 'the keeping of

[74] See above, 179–81. [75] See below, 224–6.

[76] Prestwich, *Edward I*, 72–3.

[77] R. Huscroft, 'The Political Career and Personal Life of Robert Burnell, Chancellor of Edward I', unpublished PhD thesis, University of London (2000), 26, 31.

[78] *Flores Historiarum*, III, 28. [79] Ibid., 43.

[80] Ibid., 28; Huscroft, 'Political Career', 62.

the peace and care of the royal authority' was in the hands not of clerics, but of the great nobles.[81] According to the Lewes Chronicle, the earls of Gloucester, Cornwall and Warenne, together with the archbishop of York, were appointed guardians of the realm 'by the assent of all the magnates'.[82]

By choosing corporate governance rather than a single regent, the community of the realm in the aftermath of Henry III's death significantly deviated from what Lord Edward had envisaged. Why was Edward in favour of a regency and why did the nobility reject it? Edward's initial choices for regent were Richard of Cornwall and his eldest son, Henry of Almain. As senior members of the royal family who were both personally close to Edward, he would have trusted them to guarantee his interests and those of the crown during his absence. In 1270, it was only a dozen years since a baronial council had emasculated the power of the king and only five years since Montfort had co-opted royal authority for his own purposes. Richard of Cornwall and Henry of Almain were safe pairs of hands. It is entirely possible that, had either man been alive in November 1272, the community of the realm would have been happy to accept one of them as regent. With both of them dead, however, men shied away from appointing an alternative regent, despite Edward's instructions to his administrative committee to choose one of their number, or someone else, to be regent. Of his original committee, the two most obvious candidates for regent among the laymen, Cornwall and the former justiciar Philip Basset, were both dead and the only other layman on the committee, Roger Mortimer of Wigmore, was not of sufficient status to act as regent. So soon after civil war it may have seemed injudicious to appoint a cleric as regent, even one as senior as Archbishop Giffard of York, and certainly there appears to be no hint that any of the three clerics on Edward's committee were prepared to take on the formal role as regent or considered for it. They had been granted the power, however, to appoint someone from outside their number to act as regent. This they did not do, perhaps because the number of potential candidates was neither very long nor very inspiring. Among the earls only three might be considered as serious candidates.

The most obvious was Edward's younger brother, Edmund of Lancaster. Lancaster, however, was in the East with his brother until May 1272 and does not seem to have returned to England before his father's death.[83]

[81] *The Chronicle of Bury St Edmunds*, 53.

[82] Blaauw, 'Early History of Lewes Priory', 30.

[83] It is not known for certain when Lancaster reached England, but the chroniclers who describe Henry III's death and the events following it make no mention of him, which strongly suggests he was not there.

He was back in England by February 1273, however, but the evidence of his behaviour after his return hints at his unsuitability for the regency. He wrote to the chancellor, Walter Merton, requesting armed assistance in the siege of Chartley Castle, part of his continuing feud with Robert de Ferrers, the dispossessed earl of Derby.[84] A regent more concerned with establishing his own private authority, in the face of continuing resistance from those he had displaced, than with the stability of the realm was not a viable option. The second potential candidate, Edmund of Cornwall, was too inexperienced. He was just twenty-three and had only become heir to the earldom when his half-brother, Henry of Almain, was murdered at Viterbo in March 1271, forcing the young Edmund to abandon the crusade he had joined before he even got to the East.[85] He had only been earl since his father's death in April 1272, seven months before Henry III's own death. His youth and inexperience, together with the fact that he had spent considerable time since 1265 out of England (with his father in Germany and then at the start of the crusade), must all have militated against the idea of his becoming regent. The final potential candidate may have been the earl of Gloucester. Gloucester was powerful and experienced enough to command respect across the community of the realm but his relations with Edward before the latter's departure on crusade had been strained and he had held London in defiance of the king just five years before Henry III's death. It is unlikely that Edward would have welcomed a decision by the committee to appoint Gloucester as regent, nor, given his concerns on the Welsh March, is it certain that he would have wanted such a task anyway.

This last point needs a little more consideration. There are reasons for thinking that the nobility themselves were wary, for several reasons, of the idea of appointing a regent. For anyone appointed it would mean, first, time away from protecting and promoting his own interests, not things any sensible magnate wished to neglect. Second, it was extremely difficult for a magnate to act effectively as a regent. One of the prime characteristics of kingship, which a regent would be expected to imitate, was impartiality. A magnate was, by his very nature, partial. He had his own interests to pursue and his own men to reward and support. If he followed his instincts as a magnate and used the resources of the crown to promote his own interests and those of his friends and supporters, then he laid himself open to charges of abusing the royal authority with which he had been entrusted. If he sacrificed his own interests on the altar of impartiality, he potentially did immense damage to his own position after he laid down the responsibilities of regency. Although the position was

[84] SC 1/7/85. [85] Vincent, 'Edmund of Almain'.

superficially attractive, an intelligent magnate knew that the regency was a poisoned chalice. If, however, the burdens and obligations of regency were to be avoided for oneself, it was equally important, if not more so, to ensure that a rival magnate would not become regent instead. The example of Simon de Montfort stood before the magnates as a warning of what damage an ambitious magnate with access to royal authority could cause. Montfort had pursued his own interests, and those of his family, against several prominent magnates and even against Lord Edward himself, and his example may have made the magnates in 1272 wary of investing vice-regal authority in the hands of a single magnate. Much safer, they may have reasoned, for a regency committee to run the day-to-day administration of the realm, while a group of prominent magnates took corporate responsibility for the general direction of policy and for the keeping of the king's peace. A fear of regency was to become a feature of the English political elite for the rest of the middle ages: whenever possible they chose corporate over individual responsibility.[86] As well as showing their practical concerns about the implications of a regency, the decision to choose earls as three of the four guardians of the realm offers a revealing insight into the political mindset of the earls. Corporately they saw themselves as responsible for 'the care of the royal authority', as the Bury chronicler puts it: the natural repository for the crown's authority in the king's absence.[87] Such a robust view of their own authority was at odds with Edward's views as expressed in his dispositions of 1270, which expressed the belief that he could determine in advance and effectively from afar the arrangements to be followed in the event of his absence upon his accession. How he reconciled such conflicting positions as king would do much to define how successful his reign would be.

For the meantime, however, the nobility would have to cope as best they could without a king. Edward's initial absence at the start of his reign set the pattern of conflict among the nobility during his subsequent absences from England. Without the king, disputes flourished, became violent, dragged in others and were very hard to eradicate. The most conspicuous example of this in the early 1270s was the dispute between Edmund of Lancaster and Robert de Ferrers. Ferrers had regrouped after his humiliation of 1269, and in February 1273 he took revenge. Taking advantage of Roger Lestrange's absence on crusade, Ferrers stormed his own former castle of Chartley, which Lestrange had seized in the aftermath of the Barons' Wars.[88] Lestrange was a knight of

[86] See Watts, *Henry VI*, 111–22, for the events and thinking of the magnates about regencies and royal authority during Henry VI's minority.

[87] *The Chronicle of Bury St Edmunds*, 53.

[88] Golob, 'Ferrers Earls', 348, 373.

Lord Edward's household and his younger brother, Hamo, was a close associate of Lancaster, who as the holder of the greater part of the Ferrers' inheritance was now feudal overlord of Chartley.[89] As has been seen, Lancaster, who had himself only just returned from the Levant, wrote to the chancellor on 17 February asking for aid in the recapture of the castle.[90] Another letter to Chancellor Merton two days later, this time from Gloucester, indicates how such disputes could encompass other people who were initially seemingly unconnected, further undermining public order. Gloucester expressed his concerns to Merton and Burnell about Lancaster's plans to attack Chartley without recourse to law.[91] At first glance, Gloucester's intervention might be regarded as that of a disinterested and even-handed observer concerned about preserving the king's peace, but subsequent events suggest that the earl may already have decided to support Ferrers. In May 1273, Ferrers and Gloucester entered a remarkable pact, whereby Ferrers agreed to surrender his stake in a considerable proportion of his lost estates to Gloucester in return for the latter's help in securing the return of the remainder from Lancaster.[92] The agreement was witnessed by, among others, Earl Warenne, John Fitz John and the substantial Staffordshire baron, James de Audley. This, and the presence with Lancaster at the siege of Chartley of the earl of Lincoln and Reginald de Grey, shows that important people were taking sides in this dispute, making it a delicate issue for the regency council to handle and one with potentially devastating consequences for order in the midlands and beyond.[93] The best the council could manage was to put the affair into stasis, ordering Chartley to be handed over to the king's escheator 'so that no contentions may arise among the magnates'.[94] The dispute was not resolved until after Edward's return but it possessed a number of classic features of disputes between the nobility in the king's absence: neither side showed much inclination to take the case to court with the king away; it quickly turned violent; and it spread to involve other important members of local and even national political society. Such features were to repeat themselves later in Edward's reign and to underline the nobility's need for the crown as mediator.[95]

The siege of Chartley was the most serious dispute in this twilight period between Henry III's death and Edward I's coronation, but violence was widespread.[96] Caroline Burt has shown that the scars of the Barons' Wars ran deep. Violence was endemic between the knightly

89 For Roger Lestrange, see Moor, *Knights of Edward I*, IV, 299–301. For Hamo's association with Lancaster, see Appendix B, nos. 2, 5, 6, 10.

90 SC 1/7/85. 91 SC 1/22/26. 92 Golob, 'Ferrers Earls', 37; DL 25/2267.

93 *CPR 1281–1292*, 53. 94 *CPR 1272–1281*, 9. 95 See below, 213–15.

96 Maddicott, 'Lessons of Baronial Reform', 1–9.

inhabitants of Warwickshire, while in Kent criminal activity flourished in the absence of effective royal authority.[97] Earl Warenne's clash with Robert Aguillon helped create something approaching chaos in Sussex, leaving the sheriff all but powerless to intervene.[98] Many lords took advantage of weakened royal authority to appropriate franchises and withdraw themselves and their men from royal jurisdiction.[99] Violence and appropriation, which the earls had done little to stop and much to propagate, would be two of the most pressing issues facing the new king when he returned. It is significant that Warenne and Gloucester, the two most senior earls remaining in England, and two of three nominated as guardians in 1272, were among the most egregious in their troublemaking. On his return, Edward had to balance his response to their wrongdoing against their importance and the role they had played in securing his authority following Henry III's death. What made the balancing act so delicate for Edward was that it was not easy to categorise some earls as troublemakers and others as peacemakers: quite often, as in the cases of Gloucester and Warenne, they could be both simultaneously, combining a sense of corporate responsibility to maintaining order and the crown's authority with a ruthless determination to uphold and extend their own interests. Unfortunately, the latter helped to undermine the former, for one could not afford to neglect one's own interests when others were determined to pursue their own ends.

The years 1265–74 provide a context for much of what followed in Edward's reign and it is possible to identify many of the themes that would shape that reign. The pacification of England after the Barons' Wars taught Edward the need to balance reconciliation with a firm hand. The weakening of the crown's authority in the years after 1258 was something he was determined to reverse and never allow to happen again. He was haunted by the humiliations of 1264–5 and this may explain his ferocious responses to subsequent slights against his authority, whether they came from Wales, Scotland or within England itself. In Wales, the Treaty of Montgomery resolved little but Edward knew that the time for a full-scale confrontation with Llywelyn, although not yet reached, was approaching. The crusade also figured large in Edward's imagination in these years. His desire to return to the East at the head of a pan-European army shaped many of Edward's actions in the middle and later years of his reign.

These crucible years of 1258–74 also helped define his relations with his earls. With the exception of Henry de Lacy, earl of Lincoln (who had

[97] Burt, 'Governance', 49–52, 56–7. [98] See above, 162–9.
[99] Burt, 'Governance', 41–3, 57–8.

nevertheless grown up at Henry III's court), the dominant comital figures of the first twenty-five years of Edward's reign were those whom he had known intimately in these years of strife. John de Warenne and William de Valence had been two of Edward's closest companions, while Gloucester had been both an enemy and an ally, and this complex legacy shaped their relations for the rest of their lives. Edmund of Lancaster was Edward's brother and proved his worth by accompanying Edward on crusade. It is interesting to note that Edward's two opponents in 1297, the earls of Hereford and Norfolk, came of age during Edward's absence on crusade and had not taken part in the Barons' Wars.[100] As has been shown above by their charter-witnessing, neither of them ever established the kind of intimacy with Edward of those who had fought beside him on the fields of Evesham or in the Holy Land.[101] Similarly, Edward never had the same close relationship with Edmund of Cornwall as he had had with Edmund's older brother, Henry of Almain, before the latter's murder at Viterbo.[102] The friendships Edward formed in these years with those earls closest to him helped him project his authority as king when the time came to do so.

The earls, too, learned lessons from these years that they carried forward. They had used the weakness of the crown in the years after 1258 to extend their local control, particularly through the usurping of franchises, and they would be reluctant to relinquish such gains. On the other hand, they had witnessed first hand the disintegration of order and stability between 1258 and 1267 and had seen the fragile peace threatened again during Edward's absence. By 1274 England had not seen effective government for at least sixteen years and arguably a great deal longer than that. Having seen the results of this, the earls, and political society more broadly, were willing to allow the new king considerable room for manoeuvre: room that Edward lost little time in exploiting.

MAKING HIS MARK, 1274–1286

Edward I reached England on 2 August 1274 and was crowned at Westminster Abbey on 19 August.[103] The new king had three major concerns facing him in this first part of the reign. There was, first, to complete the pacification of England and establish his authority, particularly by ending the quarrels and strife that had emerged during his absence. Second, he needed to strengthen the rights of the crown by recovering

[100] Jones, 'Bohun Earls', 87; Morris, *Bigod Earls*, 101.
[101] See above, 47–8. [102] Powicke, *Henry III*, II, 609.
[103] Prestwich, *Edward I*, 89. See above, 37–8.

what had been lost and by initiating new reforms. Third, he had to address the running sore of Llywelyn ap Gruffydd. All three were themes at the coronation itself. At the banquet, the king of Scots, five earls and all their retinues came before Edward and released their horses for anyone to catch and keep.[104] This story nicely encapsulates the comradeship and sense of a new beginning that Edward wished to foster. The king's determination to establish his authority was shown during the ceremony itself when, having had the crown placed on his brow by Archbishop Kilwardby, Edward removed it and set it aside, reportedly saying that he would not wear it again until he had recovered all that he had lost.[105] All those who had profited from royal weakness were put on notice. Finally, the absence of Prince Llywelyn, despite a personal invitation to attend and pay homage, was a slight not likely to go unnoticed.[106]

The sense of a new beginning was aided by a further changing of the comital guard during the king's four-year absence. As king, Edward inherited a generation of earls of a roughly similar age. The king was thirty-five years old at the time of his coronation. Only William de Valence, in his late forties, and Earl Warenne, at forty-three, were significantly older than the king and both were old and trusted friends. Between 1270 and 1274, Richard of Cornwall had died and had been succeeded by his son, Edmund, aged twenty-five in 1274. Henry de Lacy had come of age and inherited the earldom of Lincoln and was now twenty-four, and Roger Bigod had become earl of Norfolk and was twenty-nine. William Beauchamp was thirty-six, having succeeded to the earldom of Warwick in 1268, while Humphrey de Bohun, aged twenty-four, was shortly to become earl of Hereford on the death of his grandfather in 1275. This left Edward's own brother, Edmund, who was twenty-nine, Gilbert de Clare, earl of Gloucester, aged thirty-one and, finally, Robert de Vere, earl of Oxford, who was thirty-four. As noted before, it is remarkable that between 1275 and 1295 not a single earl died.[107] This uniquely long period of continuity at the top of English society, together with their similarity in age and shared military experiences in two Welsh campaigns, helped to create a largely, though not entirely, harmonious relationship among them, and between themselves and the king.

This was not inevitable, however, and things seemed far from rosy in 1274. As has been demonstrated, there had been a great deal of disorder recently and a number of destabilising and violent quarrels had arisen, involving several earls. The king needed to promote both harmony and his own authority, something that it was by no means certain that he

[104] Richardson, 'Coronation', 98. See above, 38. [105] Prestwich, *Edward I*, 91.
[106] Morris, *GTK*, 130. [107] See above, 30.

could do. Edward's record during the period of Reform and Rebellion was not one that could inspire complete confidence in his competence or trustworthiness and there was no guarantee that the quarrels of the 1260s might not surface once more.

Edward had been out of England for four years by the time of the coronation and of the earls only his brother, Edmund of Lancaster, and uncle, William de Valence, had spent any significant time with him. As has been seen, things had changed during his absence, and it would take time for all the earls and Edward to get used to the king's return and his new rule. Table 7.1 shows that this was indeed the case. One way of exploring Edward's relations with the earls in this period is to return to the question of charter witnesses. Charter-witnessing has been discussed in general terms about the implications for Edward's kingship in Part I but in this part the overall figures will be broken down and discussed for each period of Edward's reign and what they can reveal about politics.[108] Only one earl witnessed any of the five royal charters issued between August and November 1274 (the remaining months of regnal year 2 Edward I), while between November 1274 and November 1275 only the two crusading earls, Lancaster and Valence, witnessed significant numbers of royal charters. It was not until regnal year 4 Edward I (1275–6) that other earls started to witness royal charters regularly. Table 7.1 shows that it was after the First Welsh War that one finds the earls regularly in the king's company and witnessing his charters. The experience of that first campaign together had, perhaps, helped to forge a real sense of partnership and togetherness in a way that nothing else could.

In the meantime, however, a number of pressing problems faced the new king, particularly those concerning law and order, and he tackled them with considerable skill. Almost immediately, the king's presence acted as a naturally calming influence. Caroline Burt has observed that it was common for people to delay bringing cases to court while the king was absent from the realm.[109] Edward's return in 1274 was the signal for a number of simmering disputes to be brought to court. The most important, as they were the most potentially combustible, were the cases Robert de Ferrers brought against Edmund of Lancaster and Roger Lestrange, which came before King's Bench at Michaelmas 1274.[110] In this instance justice certainly was not blind, since the court's judgment in Lancaster's favour was no doubt reached with the king's connivance, but it did at least bring to an end one of the most destabilising and dangerous disputes of the previous few years. As a sop to Ferrers' dignity, his case

[108] See above, 45–51. [109] Burt, 'Governance', 107.
[110] 'Extracts from the Plea Rolls, 1272 to 1294', 62–4; Golob, 'Ferrers Earls', 382–6. See above, 192–3.

Table 7.1 *Comital witnesses to royal charters, 2–14 Edward I*[a]

Regnal year	Total charters	Gloucester	Hereford	Lancaster	Lincoln	Warenne	Norfolk	Cornwall	Valence	Warwick
2	5	0	0	0	1	0	0	0	0	0
3	16	1	0	5	1	1	1	2	9	1
4	22	0	7	0	9	1	0	0	18	2
5	24	3	2	0	8	5	3	0	8	3
6	25	5	1	3	9	3	5	1	11	1
7	38	3	5	4	5	0	3	2	7	2
8	89	18	9	66	45	14	0	11	14	9
9	108	35	33	26	40	25	21	31	34	3
10	24	5	6	3	17	9	9	3	11	5
11	47	29	2	22	31	14	21	5	5	7
12	57	4	3	0	16	1	0	0	0	0
13	151	94	0	77	47	90	76	68	48	54
14	49	33	15	29	23	12	8	42	24	10
Total	655	230	83	235	252	175	147	165	189	97

[a] These figures are taken from my own study of comital witness found in *The Royal Charter Witness Lists of Edward I*. Royal charters are only recorded from Edward's return in 1274, in the regnal year 2 Edward I.

against Roger Lestrange for the return of Chartley Castle was allowed to stand and the castle was restored to him in 1275.[111] By ensuring that Ferrers retained a landed stake and was not permanently ruined, thereby discouraging him from any further direct action against Lancaster by giving him something to lose, Edward I demonstrated a delicate subtlety.

In Sussex, the king's return meant Earl Warenne scaled back his violence against Robert Aguillon and for several years afterwards the dispute was conducted, or rather, given Warenne's continual non-appearance, not conducted, through King's Bench.[112] As the case study of Sussex in Chapter 6 shows, Edward again showed a subtlety and sophistication of approach not usually ascribed to him. He re-established royal authority in the county while preserving the peace and sacrificed Aguillon to keep Warenne content while also reducing the earl's power.[113] Humphrey de Bohun, earl of Hereford from 1275, was also able to get royal arbitration and adjudication in some of his disputes. The queen appears to have resolved the debt dispute between him and Gloucester during the winter of 1274–5, while, less to Hereford's liking, in Easter term 1276 the dispute over Haverford was settled in favour of William de Valence.[114]

Edward's presence in England oiled the wheels of law, arbitration and adjudication that had to some extent seized up during his absence. This offered the nobility non-violent ways to resolve their quarrels, and the king's involvement prevented bilateral disputes escalating into ones that divided large sections of political society. The non-reaction to the overwhelmingly partial judgment in the Lancaster–Ferrers case illustrates how easily Edward had established his authority. The acceptance with which this verdict was met was in stark contrast to what happened in 1258, when Henry III's court gave a similarly biased judgment in favour of *his* brother against a significant member of the nobility.[115]

Returning to the royal charter witness lists, most of the earls witnessed between a quarter and a third of all royal charters during this period, a figure that, as has been demonstrated, was high by the standards of the thirteenth and early fourteenth centuries.[116] It is not surprising to see members of Edward's family among those earls who witnessed most frequently, nor to see his friends, Lincoln and Warenne, also often in the king's presence. What may need more explanation, given assumptions of tension between the two men, is why the earl of Gloucester appears as the third most frequent comital witness in this period.[117]

111 Ibid., 392–3. 112 See above, 165–6. 113 See above, 165–9.
114 See above, 188; KB 27/21, m. 30. 115 Carpenter, *Reign of Henry III*, 192–3.
116 See above, 45–50.
117 See, for example, Prestwich, *War, Politics and Finance*, 247; Lloyd, 'Gilbert de Clare', 48.

Gloucester's frequent presence at court raises questions about these assumptions. The earl may well have seen the start of Edward's reign as a fresh start. He took seriously the oath to protect the kingdom that he swore at Henry III's bedside, as his quashing of disturbances in London immediately after Henry III's death and his letter of concern to Burnell over the Chartley affair demonstrate, despite his personal stake in the latter case.[118] Once back in England, Edward showed his appreciation of Gloucester's actions in his absence. He stayed with the earl at Tonbridge immediately upon his return and he gave Gloucester the right to carry the blunted sword *Curtana* at the coronation, in preference to the claims of Edward's own brother.[119] Both men were clearly attempting to put the past behind them. Further efforts were made in 1275. Three manors, two in Bedfordshire and one in Hertfordshire, had been taken into the king's hands for a default on the earl's part and in April 1274 an attempt by Gloucester to replevy these manors from the regency government had been unsuccessful.[120] In May 1275, however, Sutton (Bedfordshire) was returned to Gloucester.[121]

Edward made two grants of deer to Gloucester in 1275 and also a gift of his own goshawk, valuable both financially and symbolically.[122] These were perhaps rewards for Gloucester's diplomatic activity on the king's behalf in the summer of 1275.[123] He was shown additional favours in 1276, including a respite of debts due at the exchequer for rent he had seized illegally after Evesham and for which he had never accounted.[124] However, that year also saw the king's stance towards Gloucester harden a little, perhaps as the extent of the earl's usurpations, as recorded in the Hundred Rolls, became clearer. Around this time a list of Gloucester's alleged usurpations was drawn up in the exchequer and Edward clearly had it in mind to make an example of the earl when he came to start his *quo warranto* campaign in earnest two years later.[125] He was still prepared to show Gloucester some goodwill, however. In June 1276 the earl was given licence to go abroad, thereby missing a court date to answer charges brought by several foreign merchants, who claimed that he owed them more than £750.[126]

The relationship of king and earl took another upswing in the aftermath of the First Welsh War in 1277. Gloucester's activities, though 'not especially remarkable', obviously pleased the king, for he dispensed

[118] Altschul, *Baronial Family*, 131; see above, 193.
[119] *Flores Historiarum*, III, 43; Prestwich, *Edward I*, 1, 90.
[120] *CCR 1272–1279*, 119. [121] Ibid., 167.
[122] Ibid., 207, 216, 220. [123] *CPR 1272–1281*, 94.
[124] *CPR 1272–1281*, 274. [125] Sutherland, *Quo Warranto*, 146–7; E 163/2/30. See above, 74.
[126] *CCR 1272–1279*, 338, 344.

several favours to the earl over the next year.[127] In October 1277, he was granted receipts in Ireland dating back to the time of his father's death.[128] In January 1278 Justice John Bek was ordered not to proceed against Gloucester on behalf of the foreign merchants he had avoided in 1276, in order to allow the earl time to make his own agreements with them, because he had 'served the king laudably' in Wales 'not without immense labours and expenses'.[129] Gloucester received a further grant of deer in 1278 and a respite of his debts at the exchequer.[130] Although Gloucester was indeed targeted during the *quo warranto* campaign in 1278 and 1279, it is interesting that, in response to the earl's petition in the parliament of 1278 that he should not be arbitrarily singled out, Edward seems to have taken care not to alienate Gloucester further, offering him another small tranche of favours in 1279 and 1280.[131]

Conciliation of Gloucester continued in the early 1280s. Edward made him another five grants of deer between 1281 and 1284, together with a gift of twelve oaks in 1282.[132] Gloucester was also given permission to establish a market in Bletchingley (Surrey) and, in a sign that the king was easing the pressure of *quo warranto* against him, in November 1281 Edward withdrew a *quo warranto* plea for the park of Eastwood (Cambridgeshire), allowing the earl to hold it in peace.[133] A further concession on *quo warranto* was made in February 1285, when a number of liberties in Somerset, previously confiscated, were returned to Gloucester by the king's command.[134] Around this time negotiations were already under way for Gloucester to marry the king's second daughter, the thirteen-year-old Joan of Acre. Gloucester's divorce from his first wife, Alice de Lusignan, was a necessary first step and this was concluded in Easter term 1285.[135] All that remained now was for a papal dispensation, but such things were frustratingly slow, and this delay, combined with the king's absence from England between 1286 and 1289, meant it was not until 1290 that the wedding finally happened.[136] The good relations between Edward and his prospective son-in-law at this time are confirmed by the fact that, between November 1284 and June 1286, when the king sailed for France with Gloucester in tow, the earl witnessed 127 out of 200 royal charters, more than any other earl.[137]

[127] Altschul, *Baronial Family*, 136. [128] *CCR 1272–1279*, 406.

[129] Ibid., 435. [130] Ibid., 474, 462.

[131] 'Edward I: Petition 1, Text and Translation', in *PROME*; *CCR 1279–1288*, 1; SC 1/45/2; *CPR 1272–1281*, 404.

[132] *CCR 1279–1288*, 93, 143, 146, 208, 248, 280. [133] *CChR 1257–1300*, 268; *CPR 1272–1281*, 463.

[134] *CCR 1279–1288*, 314. [135] KB 27/90, m. 38.

[136] See below, 217. [137] See above, Table 7.1.

Edward's relationship with Gloucester stands as a microcosm of his relations with the earls in this period. The king had shown great political skill in pressing his own agenda of restoring royal authority, while reconciling and rewarding a potentially awkward noble in return for the valuable service he rendered during Edward's absence and in Wales. Similarly, it has been shown how Edward established his authority over Earl Warenne, while ensuring that the earl was not unnecessarily alienated, and Marc Morris has shown that Edward used a similar tactic of carrot and stick in his behaviour towards the earl of Norfolk in these early years of his reign.[138] The one earl whose relations with Edward were not so harmonious for most of this period was Humphrey de Bohun, earl of Hereford.

Hereford was one of the least frequent witnesses of comital charters during these years, though the earl's attempts to win back and retain his family's lands in Wales, in the face of fierce native opposition, probably goes part of the way towards explaining this. However, Hereford's experiences in Wales probably also help to explain the relative coolness between the two men in the first part of Edward's reign.[139] Hereford may have felt that he had received little support from the crown in his struggles for Brecon and he had reason to feel sore at the distribution of lands in the wake of the conquest of Wales. In west Wales, his plea to hold the town of Haverford directly from the crown was thrown out in 1276 and it was probably William de Valence's oppressions as his lord there that drove Hereford to sell Haverford to the queen in 1286.[140] There may also have been an element of personal resentment towards Edward. After all, Hereford's father had been fatally wounded fighting alongside Montfort at Evesham. This is, of course, speculation, but it cannot be simply set aside, especially when one considers Hereford's poor relations with Gloucester, William de Valence and the Mortimers, who were all prominent royalists in 1265.[141]

Whatever the truth of this, Edward seems to have made some efforts to reconcile Hereford. In 1275, the earl married the queen mother's cousin, Maud de Fiennes, while Edward made several gifts of deer to him in the decade following.[142] Towards the end of this period, Edward's attempts to reconcile him appear to have been paying dividends. Hereford was abroad for much of the second half of 1285 but, by the time Edward himself left England in May 1286, the two were on seemingly good

[138] See above, 165–9; Morris, *Bigod Earls*, 114–18, 125–8, 131–5. [139] See above, 81–2.

[140] KB 27/21, m. 30; SC1/10/111; J.C. Parsons, *Eleanor of Castile: Queen and Society in Thirteenth-Century England* (London: Macmillan, 1994), 187.

[141] See above, 188.

[142] *CChR 1257–1300*, 191–2; *CCR 1272–1279*, 399, 472; *CCR 1279–1288*, 21, 270.

terms.[143] Hereford accompanied the king to the coast and was granted six deer just four days before Edward embarked.[144]

If Edward was able to establish good relations with his earls and complete the pacification of England with relative ease, it was a much harder proposition to win back some of the ground the crown had lost in the localities during Henry III's personal rule and since 1258.[145] Such a policy would bring him into conflict with the earls and other magnates, for it could be achieved only at the expense of some of the gains made by the nobility. Here, however, Edward was helped by his generally excellent personal relations with individual earls. This helped to neutralise the possibility that one or more would emerge as leader of a noble opposition to an assertive policy of royal restitution. By courting the gentry as assiduously as he did, Edward further strengthened his hand against any potential grumbling by the nobility that the restoration of royal power was coming at their expense. By conciliating the earls and courting the gentry, Edward was able to bind the earls into recognising that the restoration of the power and authority of the crown was for the common good of the whole realm while reducing their potential for finding allies among the gentry.

The first step was to gather information, and so on 11 October 1274 the Hundred Rolls Inquiries were launched.[146] Despite the grumblings of the Dunstable Annalist that 'no good came of it', there can be little doubt that the inquiry was, as Burt says, a 'major public relations victory', for it showed the lesser landholders that here at last was a king serious about tackling the corruption and usurpations from which they had suffered for years.[147]

For the nobility, however, the Hundred Rolls Inquiry was both uncomfortable and unwelcome. An extreme example of this, as seen in Chapter 6, was the attitude of Lincoln's steward at Pontefract.[148] His threats and warning to the commissioners not to return 'unless they professed to come in the name of the earl his lord' show how far some lords and their officials regarded such matters as beyond the crown's concerns and illustrate just what an immense task Edward was facing if he was to reverse such attitudes.[149] For the time being, the king did not act systematically against individual abuses but the Statute of Westminster I in 1275

143 *CPR 1281–1292*, 161.

144 *Royal Charter Witness Lists of Edward I*, nos. 14.24, 14.18, 14.17, 14.12–10, 14.07, 14.03; *CCR 1279–1288*, 394.

145 Carpenter, 'King, Magnates and Society', 40, 44–6, 49–52, 65–70.

146 *CPR 1272–1281*, 59.

147 *AM*, III, 263; Maddicott, 'Lessons of Baronial Reform', 11; Burt, 'Governance', 39.

148 See above, 155–6.

149 *Yorkshire Hundred and Quo Warranto Rolls*, 50.

flowed directly from many of the findings contained within the Hundred Rolls, providing tangible evidence of Edward's reforming principles, and included several clauses aimed at rectifying some of the baronial abuses contained in the Hundred Rolls.[150] Several of these had been live issues since 1258–9.

It quickly became clear, however, that Edward's weapon of choice in this fight to restore royal authority was to be the writ of *quo warranto*. At the Gloucester parliament of August 1278, it was decided that *quo warranto* cases would be heard principally before the eyre.[151] The legal arguments used by both sides in the *quo warranto* campaign and the long-term political and constitutional implications of the campaign have been discussed in detail above, but the key questions to be addressed here are how much resentment did the campaign create among the earls and did it have a negative long-term impact on the relationship between Edward I and his earls?[152]

There is little doubt that the campaign did cause a good deal of annoyance and frustration among the magnates, and Edward may have been fortunate, as Prestwich notes, that the campaign's general 'ineffectiveness ... meant that a policy which could have provoked a serious confrontation with the magnates did not destroy the essential harmony that existed in the late 1270s and in the 1280s between the king and his greater subjects'.[153] There is evidence to suggest, however, that this was not mere accident. It is worth re-emphasising just how little the earls were actually affected by *quo warranto*.[154] Edward and his justices, again demonstrating the king's subtlety, were careful not to press their cases against the earls too far, apart from a few targeted exceptions. Gloucester and Warenne were made examples of because they had been identified as notorious usurpers, and both made their feelings at such treatment quite clear.[155] However, as has just been seen, with regard to Gloucester, Edward took care to ensure that neither earl was excluded from royal favour. Set against Gloucester's huge liberties, his actual losses were very minor and Edward was able to handle the difficult earl with some skill in these years, but there are also several instances of Edward's generosity towards Warenne in this period. In February 1281, the king gave him respite for three years from paying

[150] *EHD 1189–1327*, 396–410; Prestwich, *Edward I*, 96. Chapter 31, for example, legislated against lords charging excessive tolls in their market towns, while chapter 35 sought to prevent magnates from arresting men who were not of their fee in order to answer in their private courts. Chapter 36 prevented magnates from charging too much from their tenants for the knighting of their eldest son or the marriage of their eldest daughter.

[151] Sutherland, *Quo Warranto*, 23. [152] See above, 71–6.

[153] Prestwich, *Edward I*, 264. [154] See above, 75.

[155] Sutherland, *Quo Warranto*, 146–7, 149; JUST 1/1340; See above, 74–5.

instalments of the fine for the Zouche affair because of the expense the earl had gone to in paying for the marriage of his eldest daughter, while in June he was given twelve bucks by the king.[156] Just a few months after losing return of writs in Stamford, and Grantham, Warenne received the infinitely more valuable grant of Bromfield and Yale in north-east Wales for his services against Llywelyn.[157] Edward had made his point over Stamford, and elsewhere Warenne was given a fairly easy ride.[158] In most cases when the eyre justices came into a county, it was only the earls who were allowed to claim their franchises by prescriptive right.[159] This happened so often that it must have been a conscious policy on the part of the king and his lawyers. The policy ensured that general resentment against the whole *quo warranto* project did not find coherent and powerful leadership from the very top of political society.[160]

Despite the obvious unpopularity of the *quo warranto* campaign, it does not seem to have had a greatly negative effect upon the earls' relationships with the king. The proceedings did not diminish their willingness to fight in Wales or the amount of time they spent at court. Although the king's assault on private liberties was cited by the opposition in 1297 to try to garner support, it was very much a subsidiary complaint to the more pressing complaints about novel demands for military service and taxation.[161] *Quo warranto* was a potentially explosive issue, as Edward sought to reverse sixty years of royal retreat in the teeth of a confident nobility used to riding roughshod over local royal officials. That it did not lead to a conflagration in the way that it might have done is due, in part, to the length of the campaign and its very ineffectiveness, which prevented it from becoming more than an irritation. But the king also knew when to compromise and when he had pushed things as far as they could go. Edward was playing a subtler game over *quo warranto* than either the nobility at the time or many more recent historians realised.

Edward's plans to restore royal authority were by no means restricted to *quo warranto* and confrontations with franchise holders. The dozen years between Edward's coronation and his long visit to France constituted the most creative reforming period of the reign. What role, if any, was played by the earls in the framing and implementing of the eleven statutes passed in these years?[162] Legislation was often prefaced with phrases indicating that the king had taken counsel from the earls and others but it is hard to know whether there was anything behind these platitudes.[163]

[156] *CCR 1279–1288*, 75–6, 89. [157] Davies, *Conquest*, 363.
[158] *Placita de Quo Warranto*, 191, 421, 429–30, 485, 498, 751. [159] Sutherland, *Quo Warranto*, 83.
[160] See above, 75–6. [161] *EHD 1198–1327*, 472.
[162] *Statutes of the Realm*, I, 26–102. See above for general discussion on earls and counsel, 51–60.
[163] See, for example, the preamble of the Statute of Westminster I, *EHD 1189–1327*, 397.

Charter-witnessing may be of some help in demonstrating which earls were present when statutes were enacted. Few earls witnessed charters during the spring parliament of 1275, when the Statute of Westminster I was passed: only William de Valence and Edmund of Lancaster can be definitely shown to have been present.[164] There was a better turnout of earls at the Gloucester parliament of August 1278, perhaps because this was where legislation related to *quo warranto* was passed. William de Valence and the earls of Lancaster, Gloucester, Hereford, Warenne and Norfolk were all at Gloucester.[165] When Westminster II was enacted in May 1285, eight out of the ten earls were present at the parliament and a slightly different eight were at Winchester a few months later when the eponymous statute was promulgated there.[166] Whether this increased comital attendance at the enacting of important legislation is symptomatic of an enhanced involvement or interest in the detail of legislative reform is impossible to say but it is worthy of note nonetheless. There are some parts of Edward's legislation that deal with magnate grievances, and these are likely to have been included in response to representations by the earls and other great lords. Chapter 11 of Westminster II, for instance, protected lords against corrupt or unreliable officials and was used extensively by them.[167] As Prestwich points out, this clause was considered partial towards the lords, for the author of the *Mirror of Justices* commented that bailiffs had no recourse against lords or their 'tortious auditors'.[168] The two most obvious examples of magnate influence on Edwardian legislation, however, are *De donis conditionalibus* from the Statute of Westminster II, which established the law of entail protecting the rights of donors, and the Statue of *Quia Emptores* (1290), which protected lords against subinfeudation.[169] The latter statute was expressly passed 'at the instance of the magnates of [the] kingdom'.

With respect to the implementation of Edwardian reforms, the earls appear not to have played much of a part. The reforms to peacekeeping initiated by the Statute of Winchester, for instance, led to the appointment of keepers of the peace in each county but no earl took the office, and only one known comital associate was appointed.[170] As was argued in Chapter 6, the earls' attitude to royal government in the localities was

[164] *Royal Charter Witness Lists of Edward I*, nos. 3.13–11. [165] Ibid., p. 13.

[166] Ibid., nos. 13.121–029, 13.17–04. The eight earls at Westminster were Gloucester, Lancaster, Warenne, Norfolk, Lincoln, Cornwall, Warwick and William de Valence, while the eight at Winchester were Lancaster, Valence, Cornwall, Norfolk, Warenne, Warwick, Oxford and Gloucester.

[167] *EHD 1189–1327*, 438–9; Denholm-Young, *Seignorial Administration*, 158–9; T.F.T. Plucknett, *The Legislation of Edward I* (Oxford: Clarendon Press, 1949), 153–6; Prestwich, *Edward I*, 275.

[168] *The Mirror of Justices*, 164–5; Prestwich, *Edward I*, 275. [169] *EHD*, III, 428–9, 466.

[170] *Parl Writs*, I, 388–90. Sir William Vavasour in Yorkshire was an associate of the earl of Lincoln.

indifference at best and opposition when it went against their interests.[171] As was indicated there, there is no evidence to suggest that the earls acted in any way as 'the essential political and governmental link between centre and localities', as it has been argued they were in the fifteenth century.[172] The earls should not be seen as roadblocks to reform, but they seem to have been largely incidental to the programme of reform during this period.

But if the earls were not deeply involved in implementing the king's reforming legislation, the same cannot be said of the Welsh wars, which were the other great occupation of this first period of Edward's reign. Their military service has already been discussed in general terms.[173] The important questions for the purposes of this particular discussion are what does the earls' service say about their attitude, how did Edward reward such service and what does this relate about his attitude to their service?

Nine earls fought in the first Welsh campaign and eight in the second.[174] Such a high turnout is a powerful testament to the unity of purpose Edward had created. Self-evidently, the Marcher earls had vested interests in cutting Llywelyn down to size but the others were no less keen to fight in Wales. Warwick and Lincoln, neither of them Marchers, were even commanding royal troops well before the main campaign started.[175] The circumstances of the summons to the second war in 1282, however, show that, as already observed, while the earls were eager to fight, they would do so on their terms and not the king's. The council at Devizes, where the earls led the opposition to the king's plans for a fully paid army and sought to ensure military commands for themselves, demonstrates their essential conservatism.[176]

While the Devizes Council shows that the earls still saw military service as a right and a duty, this does not mean that they did not expect to be compensated and rewarded for their efforts. The First Welsh War was not one of conquest, so there was no land to be redistributed in the wake of Llywelyn's submission.[177] The rewards for their service were consequently small but not non-existent. Several received grants of deer during or shortly after the war, including Hereford in July 1277, Warwick in February and July 1278 and Hereford, Gloucester and Lincoln in

[171] See above, 144–6. [172] Carpenter, 'Midlands', 12.

[173] See above, 76–86. [174] See above, Table 3.1.

[175] *CPR 1272–1281*, 171; Morris, *Welsh Wars*, 300. Lincoln did not become a Marcher lord until 1282.

[176] See above, 83.

[177] The four cantreds were taken back into crown hands and two were granted to Dafydd ap Gruffydd, Llywelyn's brother. Prestwich, *Edward I*, 181, 183.

August 1278.[178] Lincoln, who performed conspicuous service in the middle March in 1277, obtained a number of rewards, including help with his creditors and the grant of money owed to him by the exchequer.[179] Warwick, another major commander in 1277, was also given rewards and concessions as part of Edward's usual pattern of remunerating conspicuous service. In addition to the deer noted above, Warwick was allowed to recover his position as chamberlain of the exchequer, which had recently been confiscated because of a trespass by the earl's clerk. This concession, it was specifically noted, was being made 'in consideration of his good service'.[180]

If good service was, as has been argued earlier, Edward's primary criterion for dispensing patronage, his attitude to military service is encapsulated by the way he rewarded it.[181] He, like the earls, regarded military service as a duty that was to be expected but conspicuous service would be duly rewarded. This is further evident in the land grants he made after the conquest of Wales in 1282–3.[182] Nonetheless, Edward did not forget the efforts of those earls not rewarded with land and they received more routine rewards. No fewer than seven earls were given gifts of deer between 1283 and 1286.[183] Other favours were not slow in coming: Warwick was pardoned £250 of his debts;[184] Norfolk was granted 1,000 marks to help cover his expenses during the Welsh war;[185] Edmund of Cornwall was given licence to hunt in the king's forests and Lincoln was granted permission to sport along rivers in the south-west.[186]

Regardless of Edward's success against Llywelyn, he was unable to prevent the Marchers from engaging in their traditional occupation of quarrelling with each other, several examples of which have already been encountered.[187] The king's return had helped to calm the disputes that had arisen during his absence but these further clashes illustrate two important things about medieval politics. First, that even a king as determined and skilful as Edward I could not prevent tensions developing between his greatest subjects but that, second, the intervention of a king with an authority such as Edward's was enough to prevent disputes escalating out of control.

178 *CCR 1272–1279*, 399, 440, 469, 471, 472, 474.

179 *CCR 1272–1279*, 462; *CPR 1272–1281*, 228, 303.

180 Ibid., 486.

181 See above, 87–93. 182 See above, 90. Davies, *Conquest*, 363.

183 Norfolk, *CCR 1279–1288*, 212; Cornwall, *CCR 1279–1288*, 77; Lincoln, *CCR 1279–1288*, 278; Warwick, *CCR 1279–1288*, 207, 269; Gloucester, *CCR 1279–1288*, 248, 280; Hereford, *CCR 1279–1288*, 270, 394; Oxford, *CCR 1279–1288*, 25.

184 *CPR 1281–1292*, 150. 185 Morris, *Bigod Earls*, 131.

186 *CCR 1279–1288*, 69; *CPR 1281–1292*, 134. 187 See above, 68–70, 188.

The earl of Hereford was central to a number of these disputes. He continued his quarrels with Gloucester, Valence and Mortimer and began a new one with John Giffard. The rekindling of hostility between Hereford and Gloucester needed the arbitration of the queen mother to bring about a truce in August 1278.[188] At Easter 1279, Roger Mortimer brought a case in King's Bench against Hereford, alleging that the earl had committed transgressions against him in his forest of Penklyn in the March, in defiance of the king's order not to harm Mortimer.[189] It is likely that this was connected to the argument between Mortimer and Hereford over whether the former's lands were in Brecon or not.[190] Although Hereford did not appear in court, the case did not return to King's Bench, so it may be presumed that arbitration of some sort, perhaps instigated by the king, who had already taken an interest, helped to calm the situation. Just to show that fighting the Welsh did not entirely occupy the attention of the Marcher lords, Hereford and William de Valence were in violent dispute over Haverford during the war of 1282–3 itself.[191] Hereford's grievance with Giffard was over the lordship of Iscennen, which he had conquered in 1282, only to see it granted to Giffard in the aftermath of the conquest of Wales.[192] Fighting broke out between the men of Giffard and the earl and in December 1284 a high-level commission, including both chief justices, was appointed to look into the affair.[193]

Such arguments were inevitable on the March, given the custom of settling disputes by violence and the indistinct nature of boundaries between lordships but, while the king was available to act as umpire, they were unlikely to get out of hand. Edward was planning to go abroad for some considerable time, however, and, without his calming and authoritative presence, tempers on the March and elsewhere could get very heated very quickly, and there was little anyone could do about it.

Edward's three-year absence marks an obvious break and provides an opportunity to assess his achievements in this period, generally regarded as the most successful and constructive in his reign.[194] That this is so was due in no small part to his ability to create a successful partnership with his earls. The scale of this achievement should not be underestimated. How was Edward able to manage this? Partly it was because of his already established reputation by the time he became king. He had defeated Simon de Montfort, one of the most famous soldiers in Christendom, had been the driving force of the restoration of royal power in the aftermath of Evesham and had been on crusade. Unlike Henry III, here was

[188] *CCR 1272–1279*, 504–5. [189] KB 27/45, m. 19.
[190] See above, 188. [191] *CPR 1281–1292*, 60; SC 1/10/111.
[192] Jones, 'Bohun Earls', 98. [193] *CCRV*, 297.
[194] Prestwich, *Edward I*, 266.

a king of whom the earls could be proud and with whom they would wish to be associated. But Edward was also able to create a virtuous circle whereby he reinforced the sense of partnership he forged at his coronation. This was done through tournaments and Round Tables, like the one at Kenilworth in 1279;[195] through ceremonies such as the laying of the foundation stone of Vale Royal in 1277, witnessed by four earls;[196] and most of all, of course, by the two Welsh wars.

Edward's success in creating comradeship and purpose among his titled nobility gave him the freedom of manoeuvre to launch an extensive reform programme aimed at correcting abuses and regaining ground lost to the crown under Henry III. Edward's good relations with the most powerful earls, Lancaster, Gloucester, Warenne, Lincoln and Cornwall, meant that cohesive opposition to his plans from the top of political society was never forthcoming during these years. Besides, Edward's reforms were generally popular with the knights, answering many of their complaints of 1258–65 against the king and their lords, and successful opposition to the crown usually needed a coalition of magnates and gentry.[197] Nor is there any evidence that the earls opposed any of the king's major legal reforms of these years; after the Westminster parliament of 1275 they certainly attended the others parliaments at which statutes were promulgated in large numbers and prompted certain of the most important legislation themselves.[198] The king was able largely to circumvent the main point of friction between him and his earls in these years, that is *quo warranto*, by a combination of good luck and good judgement. Magnate opposition to *quo warranto* never crystallised into anything coherent or serious until the parliament of 1290, after the campaign had entered a new and more severe phase. Before then, Edward was slowly killing 'conquest theory' with kindness, while all the time reinforcing the idea of royal supremacy over franchises, meaning that, when the crisis over *quo warranto* did come in 1290, he was able to ensure the victory of his theory over that of the nobility.[199]

This first phase of Edward I's rule was one of remarkable success. This has been generally acknowledged, but what has not been demonstrated is the degree to which it rested on his relationship with his earls and the subtlety with which this relationship was forged. By harnessing his earls as he did, Edward was able to expedite and reinforce his domestic reforms and his military victories. This was McFarlaneite 'unite and rule'; a model of what McFarlane called 'the essence of late medieval government at

[195] See above, 38–9. [196] Prestwich, *Edward I*, 113.
[197] Maddicott, 'Lessons of Baronial Reform', 9–30.
[198] See above, 206. [199] See above, 73–6, and below, 216.

its best'.[200] That Edward had created this sense of unity around a programme of restoring the rights of the crown and had persuaded the earls and the rest of the nobility that they could gain more from supporting royal power under him than they had by usurping it under his father underlines the scale of his achievement. For the first time since before the accession of King John, there was a real partnership between king and nobility. Moreover, thanks to Edward's inquiries and reforms, the lesser landholders were now an essential part of the partnership in political society and this augmented the power of the crown immeasurably. Edward I was finally showing that Magna Carta need not mean the crown had to be weaker: under the law the crown could be just as strong as it had been before it was placed there by the Charter, providing that it listened to the concerns of the nobility and gentry, even if not necessarily doing what they wanted unless it suited the king. However, what Edward had achieved in the dozen years since his coronation would be put to the test during a three-year sojourn on the continent that would bring to the surface old and new tensions among his earls and other magnates.

[200] McFarlane, *Nobility*, 121.

Chapter 8

THE TESTING GROUND, 1286–1307

THERE AND BACK AGAIN: 1286–1294

Edward I had plenty of reasons to be satisfied as he left for France in May 1286: England was better governed than at any time in the last century and it seemed as if he had indeed successfully learnt the lessons of the period of Reform and Rebellion. He had vigorously reasserted the power and authority of the crown and, through reform, parliaments and war, had forged a unity across the body politic that had not been known for generations. His three-year absence revealed both the strength and the fragility of his achievements. On the positive side, public order did not collapse and government carried on pretty much uninterrupted in the king's absence. The regency was also able to cope with two emergencies within Britain, a revolt in Wales and the sudden death of King Alexander III of Scots, without Edward feeling the need to return to England precipitously. More negatively, however, Edward was never again to have the time to devote to the harmonious governance of England, in large part because 1286 marks the moment when his mind became increasingly preoccupied with matters beyond the borders of England: his relations with France, the disposition of Scotland and, closest of all to his heart, the possibility of leading a new crusade. Moreover, in the years between 1286 and 1289 many of his nobles fell back into traditional habits of quarrelling and usurpation of each other's and the king's rights. Angered by this and by what he perceived to be failures on the part of his officials, soured perhaps by the deaths of his wife and mother in 1290 and hampered by the loss of Bishop Burnell in 1292, as time went on Edward's mood worsened. Increasingly, he found himself in positions where too often he was forced to react to events rather than controlling them himself. Edward was a man who demonstrated considerable political skill when his back was to the wall but it tended to bring out his less attractive characteristics. Edward's skills in political management were still often on display, but increasingly it was masterfulness that was often his first reaction in this period rather than the last resort it had been before 1286.

As he had done during his brief visit to France in 1279, Edward appointed Edmund of Cornwall to act as regent in his stead and he made some attempts to ensure that existing disputes between his nobility did not get out of hand.[1] For example, he had appointed his household knight, Grimbald Pauncefoot, to the custody of the parts of Malvern Chase that were in dispute between the earls of Warwick and Gloucester.[2] But he could not legislate for the unexpected. Although four earls had gone abroad with the king, with Edward gone, arguments between the nobility could no longer be so easily restrained and a number flared up.[3] Earl Warenne's son, William, was killed at a tournament in Croydon in December 1286, murdered, so the gossips said, by his enemies.[4] That such rumours gained currency, despite no corroborating evidence, demonstrates how nervy the atmosphere could become in the king's absence. William de Warenne's death threatened even graver consequences for public order. As a matter of course, on his death his lands were taken into the king's hands.[5] William's father had granted his son the Marcher lordship of Bromfield and Yale that Edward I had given to him in 1282, and this was now taken into the king's hands by the justice of Chester, their Marcher neighbour Reginald de Grey.[6] Earl Warenne claimed that William had held the lordship directly from him and not in chief from the king. It was not until a council meeting in London at Candlemas 1287 that Warenne was given seisin until the king's return and Grey was forced to release the lordship.[7]

Matters did not end there, however, and by August 1288 Warenne was writing to the earl of Warwick complaining that Grey had occupied a 'great part' of Bromfield and Yale and asking Warwick for his assistance as his friend.[8] Despite Warenne's assurances to Warwick that the issue did not 'in any way touch the king', the latter felt compelled to write to Edward's regent urging him to 'strictly forbid persons from stirring at all'.[9] Cornwall responded by issuing a general prohibition against military activity on 22 August 1288, to the earls of Gloucester, Warwick and Norfolk, Hugh le Despenser, William de Braose and Richard Fitz John, while three days later Warenne and Grey were issued with the

[1] *CPR 1272–1281*, 310–11; *CPR 1281–1292*, 248. [2] *CPR 1281–1292*, 247.

[3] The four earls were Gloucester, Lincoln, Lancaster and William de Valence. Although the latter three were abroad for the whole time that Edward was, Gloucester appears to have returned shortly after Edward paid homage to Philip IV in Paris. *CPR 1281–1292*, 238–41.

[4] *Chronicle of Bury St Edmunds*, 87. [5] *CFR 1272–1307*, 232.

[6] *CAC*, 134–5, 137. [7] Ibid., 135; *CFR 1272–1307*, 234.

[8] *CAC*, 170–1. [9] SC 1/29/183.

same order.[10] Warenne regained all of Bromfield and Yale but it is not clear whether this was achieved through force or negotiation.[11] Whether Cornwall's prohibition was simply a general one, or was based upon intelligence about who might be involved in the dispute, it again demonstrates how bilateral disputes could escalate into extremely serious threats to public order by dragging in other nobles on one side or the other.[12]

Cornwall was successful in this instance but there was one case which emerged during Edward's absence that the regent could not contain: the quarrel between the earls of Gloucester and Hereford. This has been touched on previously but will now be addressed in more detail.[13] Ill-feeling between the two men stretched back over twenty years, but it was the revolt in Wales of Rhys ap Maredudd in 1287 that precipitated the violent feud that now erupted. While Hereford was helping to suppress Rhys' revolt elsewhere, a serious disturbance broke out within his own lordship of Brecon and Gloucester was ordered to put it down.[14] Gloucester used this as cover to try to extend his own lordship of Glamorgan into the southern parts of Brecon and began building a new castle there.[15] The affront to Hereford was blatant and Gloucester's grab for power naked. Given Hereford's disappointments with the landed settlement after the conquest of Wales, it must have been particularly galling for him to see Gloucester eating into the southern border of Brecon.

Fighting broke out some time in late 1288 or early 1289, and in February 1289 the first attempt at mediation was made by the queen mother.[16] This appears to have failed and Hereford went to Abingdon to complain in person to the regent. He then went to Westminster, where he pleaded with Cornwall, in the presence of the archbishop of Canterbury and the bishop of Durham, for a remedy. This is known from a letter sent by Archbishop Peckham to Gloucester shortly afterwards, in June, urging him to amend his behaviour and to settle the matter before the king's return.[17] On 26 June 1289, Cornwall wrote to Gloucester ordering him to cease construction of the castle until the return of the king.[18] Cornwall realised that only the king could achieve a settlement and that the best he

[10] *CCR 1279–1288*, 547. [11] Rogers, 'Marcher Lordship of Bromfield and Yale', 60.

[12] See above, 192–3. [13] See above, 70–1, 186–8.

[14] *CCRV*, 308; Jones, 'Bohun Earls', 99–101; Morris, *Welsh Wars*, 208.

[15] Morris, *Welsh Wars*, 224; Altschul, *Baronial Family*, 147; Prestwich, *Edward I*, 348, all state that Morlais was the castle, but Jones, 'Bohun Earls', 108–9, makes a convincing case that this accepted view is incorrect. She points out that Morlais was under construction in 1271 but that the castle in dispute was clearly being newly constructed. Also Morlais lies *south* of the Taff Fechan and therefore in Glamorgan and not Brecon.

[16] TNA C 49/2/13.

[17] *Registrum Epistolarum Johannis Peckham*, ed. C.T. Martin, 3 vols., Rolls Series (1882–4), III, 960–2.

[18] *CCR 1288–1296*, 47.

could hope for at present was to hold the matter over. The failure of the regent, the queen mother and the archbishop of Canterbury to mediate successfully between the feuding earls again emphasises just how indispensable the king was in cases like this. Only he had the supreme authority to bring an end to violence between the parties. Widespread violence across much of England during this period underlines this point.[19] As noted already, the workings of the king's law, often the most effective way to ensure successful settlements of disputes, also tended to seize up when the king was absent, as people preferred to wait for his return before bringing lawsuits.[20] Moreover, as Burt has shown, several Marcher lords had taken advantage of the king's absence to press their claims of jurisdiction against weaker opponents.[21]

How one judges the earls' behaviour during the king's absence depends upon one's vantage point. There seems little doubt that Edward was angered by the disorder he found on his return and he probably felt let down in that, despite all his efforts to create unity among his nobles, they had, from almost the moment his back was turned, quickly degenerated into their old ways of dispute and violence. His mood would hardly have improved on hearing, at the beginning of 1289, that Gloucester had spearheaded the refusal to grant a tax to Edward while he remained out of England.[22] Edward had acquired considerable debts during his absence and was also turning his mind towards a new crusade that would need considerable funds. On the other hand, Gloucester, Hereford and Warenne might easily have pointed out that they were pursuing their legitimate interests and following traditional Marcher methods and that Edward's demand for taxation in his absence was highly irregular. The earls had rallied to defend the king's interests (and their own) in Wales during Rhys' rising in 1287; they obeyed Cornwall's prohibition against military activity in August 1288; and Warwick had gone to some lengths to warn the regent of the threat posed to order from Warenne's dispute with Reginald de Grey.[23]

Despite all this, Edward did not return to England in a good temper. At first, he turned the heat of his anger on the judiciary. He appointed a high-ranking commission, including the earl of Lincoln, to hear complaints and grievances against many royal officials during the king's absence.[24] Several high-profile judges, including both chief justices, were dismissed and heavily fined, something that helped to improve his finances if nothing else.[25]

[19] Burt, 'Governance', 99, 107, 111–14, 120–1. [20] See above, 197.

[21] Burt, 'Governance', 107–8. [22] *AM*, IV, 316. [23] See above, 213.

[24] *CCR 1288–1296*, 55; *State Trials of the Reign of Edward the First, 1289–1293*.

[25] Prestwich, *Edward I*, 339–42. See also P.A. Brand, 'Edward I and the Judges: the "State Trials" of 1289–93', *TCE* I (1986), 31–40, for a reinterpretation of the so-called 'State Trials'.

This provided Edward with an opportunity to appoint new men and to take a firmer line on *quo warranto* cases; an attitude perhaps stimulated by anger at further magnate usurpations of liberties in the previous three years. The appointment of Gilbert de Thornton, principal prosecutor of *quo warranto* cases in the 1280s, as chief justice of the King's Bench was a powerful message that Edward was hardening his stance on this issue. Thornton proved himself resolved to make a reality of the king's claims not to be bound by prescription in *quo warranto* cases, the groundwork for which had been put in place by the tactics used by the king and his pleaders over the past decade.[26] Long tenure pleas were no longer to be permitted and two high-profile cases precipitated a minor crisis at the Easter parliament of 1290.[27]

All the matters preoccupying the king and his subjects came to a head at this parliament. It is a testament to the success of Edward's rule thus far that a parliament that had the potential to be extremely difficult ended with just about everyone, except the Jews, satisfied with the result. Edward's primary concern was money; he owed his Italian bankers almost £110,000.[28] What he needed was a grant of general taxation. The parliament assembled on about 28 April but it was not until 21 May that Edward acted to redress the magnates' principal grievance: *quo warranto*.[29] On that day he compromised on *quo warranto*, issuing the eponymous statute.[30] Further concessions to the magnates were made in the form of the Statute of *Quia Emptores*, which protected tenants-in-chief against the sometimes deleterious consequences of subinfeudation.[31] The magnates on their own, of course, could no longer grant permission for a tax to be levied; the consent of the gentry was needed.[32] To get what he wanted, Edward played on the prejudices of his subjects. When parliament resumed in July 1290, Edward ordered the expulsion of all Jews from his kingdom and, in return, the knights consented to the grant of a fifteenth on movables, the most valuable tax of the whole reign, bringing in £116,346.[33]

The events of this parliament meant that king, magnates and knights all left with something they wanted but the sequence of events seems to

[26] See above, 72–3.

[27] Prestwich, *Edward I*, 347. The cases involved the barons Robert Fitz Walter and Henry de Grey.

[28] Morris, *GTK*, 223.

[29] P.A. Brand, 'Edward I: Parliament of Easter 1290, Introduction', in *PROME*, I, 49; *EHD 1189–1327*, 464–6.

[30] Ibid., 464–6. See above for discussion of implications, 74.

[31] Plucknett, *Legislation*, 102–8; Prestwich, *Edward I*, 274.

[32] Maddicott, *Origins*, 206–7.

[33] Prestwich, *Edward I*, 343, 569; R.R. Mundill, *England's Jewish Solution: Experiment and Exlusion, 1262–1290* (Cambridge University Press, 1998), chapter 8.

suggest that, in this case, Edward dealt with the grievances of both groups separately. The magnates were appeased during the first session and the knights when parliament resumed in July. That there was no coalescence of magnate and knightly grievances at this parliament suggests there was, as yet, no sense that the earls were providing political leadership for the knightly class to force the king to provide redress. This is in keeping with findings so far in this book about the nature of magnate–gentry relations during most of Edward I's reign: thus far Edward had proved himself a more reliable ally than the magnates for advancing the gentry's interests.[34] The parliament turned out to be a triumph of compromise, demonstrating Edward's political skill in extracting a massive tax in return for limited concessions on his part: at least one of which, over *quo warranto*, was as much a victory for the crown as for the magnates.

The parliament had been called initially to coincide with the marriage of the king's daughter, Joan of Acre, to the earl of Gloucester, which took place on 30 April 1290.[36] Two weeks before the marriage, Gloucester had surrendered his lands to the king and received them back on 27 May to hold jointly with Joan with reversion to her of twenty-five of his manors.[37] By the time the marriage took place, the high point in the relationship between Edward and Gloucester had already passed. Gloucester's behaviour during Edward's absence, and particularly his dispute with Hereford, was the cause of the problem. That Gloucester had headed those magnates who had refused the king a tax grant during his absence undoubtedly further piqued Edward.[38] In addition to the Hereford case, Gloucester was involved in at least two other disputes on the March, with the earl of Norfolk in Chepstow and the prior of Goldcliff in Caerleon.[39]

The Gloucester–Hereford case provided an excellent opportunity for Edward to extend royal authority over the Marchers. It is important to remember, however, that he did not initiate proceedings. This case was begun, like so many others on the March, by a Marcher lord.[40] Hereford brought his case to King's Bench on 20 January 1290.[41] In response, the king issued a proclamation on 25 January forbidding private warfare on the March.[42] Gloucester reacted to each of Edward's interventions with calculated defiance. On 3 February 1290, barely a week after the king's

[34] See above, 172, for conclusions on this issue.

[36] Brand, 'Edward I: Parliament of Easter 1290, Introduction', in *PROME*.

[37] *CChR 1257–1300*, 350–1; *CFR 1272–1307*, 274–5; McFarlane, *Nobility*, 260. See above, xxx.

[38] *AM*, IV, 316.

[39] For the Norfolk case, see KB 27/123, m. 1. For the Goldcliff case, see KB 27/124, m. 36d; 27/129, m. 12. See above, 70, 150–1.

[40] See above, 69–70. [41] KB 27/122, m. 1. [42] *CCRV*, 334.

proclamation, Gloucester's men, bearing the banner of their lord, entered Brecon, killing some of Hereford's men and carrying off livestock and other goods.[43] A second raid occurred in June, shortly after Gloucester's lands were returned following his marriage, perhaps as an attempt to restate his lordship over Glamorgan.[44] A third and final attack happened in November 1290, again just after a royal intervention in the March. Gloucester had been claiming traditional custody of the temporalities of Llandaff during vacancies of the see and one such vacancy had occurred in 1290. Edward, in belligerent mood since his return, responded that all Welsh episcopal temporalities belonged to the crown and forced the acceptance of this by the lords of Brecon and Gower.[45] Gloucester was not so easily cowed and it was not until the case came before parliament in October that he was forced to concede the king's right.[46] Having made his point, Edward was prepared to compromise and, on 2 November, of 'his special grace', he granted Gloucester and Joan a life interest in the temporalities during vacancies.[47] Despite Edward's face-saving gesture, it was a serious blow to the independence of the earl's position as a Marcher lord. Gloucester's response was swift and defiant, launching a third attack on Brecon on 27 November.[48]

Edward assured Hereford of his continuing support by granting him fifteen deer on 7 November 1290, and on 18 January 1291 the king took his first positive action in the case, appointing William de Valence, the bishop of Ely and two royal justices to hear the case on 12 March at Brecon.[49] The king was concerned that Hereford's resolve might be weakening in the face of criticism from his fellow Marchers at his flouting of Marcher custom by calling in the king, and so he ordered the commissioners to proceed even if either earl attempted to withdraw.[50] This case was no longer just Hereford vs Gloucester but was increasingly Rex vs Gloucester as well. Hereford was seemingly encouraged by the king's actions and on 12 February 1291 renewed his protest against Gloucester.[51] Valence's commission was a humiliating failure, however, for neither Gloucester nor the jury of Marcher lords turned up.[52] Two days later, on 14 March, seven Marchers appeared at Llanddew and were

[43] Morris, *Welsh Wars*, 225–6; Altschul, *Baronial Family*, 147–8.

[44] Ibid., 148–9.

[45] The earl of Hereford and William de Braose, respectively. *CFR 1272–1307*, 269; Davies, *Lordship and Society*, 254, 265.

[46] 'Edward I: Michaelmas Parliament of 1290', in *PROME*.

[47] *CChR 1257–1300*, 372. [48] Altschul, *Baronial Family*, 149–50.

[49] *CPR 1281–1292*, 452, 454. [50] Ibid., 452. [51] Morris, *Welsh Wars*, 227.

[52] Details of the case in the next paragraph can all be found in 'Edward I: Epiphany Parliament 1292', in *PROME*, item 1.

ordered to 'put their hand on the Bible to do what they will be instructed to do on the lord king's behalf', to which they indignantly and correctly replied that such a demand directly contradicted Marcher custom.[53] Edward's position was restated but when each was offered the Bible in turn, they all refused. This was now becoming a case of not just Rex vs Gloucester, but Rex vs the custom of the March. Undeterred, and under prior instructions from the king, the commissioners proceeded with an English jury from Herefordshire and Gloucestershire, supplemented by men from Edmund of Lancaster's Welsh lordship and men from west Wales brought by the justiciar Robert Tiptoft. This carefully picked jury enunciated the catalogue of attacks on Brecon by Gloucester's men and the justices then reported their findings to the king.

A new jury was now summoned before the king himself at Abergavenny in October. By the time it assembled, though, both earls were in the dock, for now Hereford too stood accused. Between the hearing at Llanddew and the parliament at Abergavenny, there had been a number of incidents of retaliatory action by the men of Brecon. Two of these were responses to direct provocation by men from Glamorgan. In these instances, the men of both lordships acted without the consent or knowledge of their lords and Hereford had moved quickly to disavow any association with the actions. On a third occasion, however, on hearing a rumour that men from Glamorgan were grazing cattle in the disputed region between the two lordships, the constable of Brecon led a large force down to the area and chased the offending parties off the land. This force pursued them into Glamorgan before catching up with them and impounding the cattle, after a struggle during which some Glamorgan men were killed. The cattle were taken to Brecon and given to Hereford, making him an accessory after the fact. At Abergavenny, both earls were found guilty of contempt of the king's command not to wage private war. Both were imprisoned briefly and then bailed to appear before the king at Westminster, in a parliament called for January, to hear their punishment. The original sentences were crushing in their severity: both earls were to lose their Marcher lordships for life, with Gloucester being fined 10,000 marks and Hereford the sum of 1,000 marks, reflecting his lesser crimes. On 19 February 1292 both lordships were taken into the king's hands. However, having made his point, Edward restored both lordships a few months later.[54]

[53] The seven Marchers were John de Hastings, John FitzReginald, Edmund Mortimer, Roger Mortimer, Theobald de Verdun, John Tregoz and Geoffrey de Camville.

[54] *CPR 1281–1292*, 478, 489, 501.

The fallout from this case was serious, particularly in Gloucester's case: it permanently soured his relationship with the king. He was with the king at Berwick during the Great Cause in the autumn of 1292 but after 25 October 1292 he witnessed only one other royal charter in the three years before his death.[55] In May 1293, Gloucester retired to Ireland to lick his wounds and deal with a rebellion in Kilkenny.[56] He was still there in April 1294 but returned before another revolt broke out in October, this time in Wales.[57] The revolt was a general one but, in Glamorgan, the leader, Morgan ap Maredudd, claimed that his rebellion was not against the crown but against Gloucester alone.[58] Edward's reaction to Morgan's plea serves only to emphasise the extent to which his relations with Gloucester had deteriorated. He accepted Morgan's surrender, against Gloucester's wishes, and in order to calm the situation in Glamorgan, he took the lordship back into his hands, a further humiliation for the earl.[59]

The deterioration in the relationship, however, was not all due to Edward. In one of the few examples of joint magnate and gentry opposition to the king's plans thus far in the reign, Gloucester had reduced the war tax granted to Edward at the Michaelmas parliament of 1294 and angered the king by failing to restore the temporalities of Llandaff to the new bishop, despite being ordered to do so in April 1295.[60] To be fair to the earl regarding the latter case, he was preoccupied with the rebellion, and large parts of Glamorgan were not in his possession, but Edward was not in the mood to sympathise, reissuing the order on 24 August with the stark warning that Gloucester ought to 'conduct himself in such manner herein that it may not be necessary for the king to apply his hand to this in another manner'.[61] Perhaps fortunately for Gloucester, he did not live long enough for the king to carry out this threat, since he died on 7 December at Monmouth, probably en route to parliament.[62]

It is not easy to come to a quick judgement on the relationship between Edward and Gloucester. It is commonly assumed that they got on poorly throughout the reign but, as has been demonstrated, the situation was by no means so clear-cut.[63] In order to come to a more satisfactory conclusion, it is necessary to pose a few questions. How did Edward use the earl? What was Gloucester willing to do and not do for his king?

[55] *Royal Charter Witness Lists of Edward I*, nos. 20.04, 21.03.

[56] *AM*, IV, 336; *CPR 1292–1301*, 11.

[57] Altschul, *Baronial Family*, 154.

[58] *AM*, III, 387; Altschul, *Baronial Family*, 154–5; Prestwich, *Edward I*, 220.

[59] *AM*, IV, 526; Altschul, *Baronial Family*, 155.

[60] *CPR 1292–1301*, 132; Prestwich, *Edward I*, 457.

[61] *CCR 1288–1296*, 453–4.

[62] Altschul, *Baronial Family*, 155.

[63] See above, 199–201.

And how important was the relationship between the two men for the politics of the reign? Edward employed the earl in a number of ways. The most obvious of these was militarily. Although Gloucester had a distinctly mixed military record, his status as the most powerful Marcher lord, and the number of men he could bring to the muster, made him an essential element in all the Welsh campaigns and Edward recognised this with certain rewards.[64] His prestige as the premier non-royal earl before his marriage to the king's daughter in 1290 made him useful to Edward diplomatically. He sent Gloucester abroad on diplomatic business early in the reign, had him accompany Alexander III of Scotland on progress to Westminster and persuaded Gloucester to accompany himself as far as Paris in 1286 to add lustre to his entourage when doing homage to Philip IV of France.[65] As one of the most frequent witnesses to Edward's charters before 1292, Gloucester was one of the king's intimates and close counsellors. He was obviously willing to carry out each of these acts for the king and they all added to his own prestige and, as is shown by his actions on Edward's accession, the earl saw it as his duty to help secure the realm in the king's absence. However, there were limits to his acquiescence. For instance, he appears to have demanded command of the English forces in south Wales for himself in 1282, being unwilling to serve under the administrator Robert Tiptoft.[66] His protest in parliament about his treatment over *quo warranto* demonstrates that he was unhappy at being made a scapegoat for the extensive usurpation of liberties that had occurred across the length and breadth of England.[67] As the dispute with Hereford showed, Gloucester, like the king, was not willing to compromise where his own vital interests were at stake. This case became a struggle of wills between a king and an earl who had each staked their prestige and authorities on the outcome. That was Gloucester's mistake and hubris, for Edward demonstrated he was easily strong enough to humiliate comprehensively the man some believed to be the next most powerful man in the kingdom.[68] It would be wrong, however, to think of Gloucester as only concerned with his own self-interest to the exclusion of all else. His early career had shown that he had political ideas beyond his own aggrandisement and this attitude reappeared in the late 1280s and early 1290s.[69] His opposition to Edward's taxation demands in 1289 and 1294 were motivated in the first instance by a sense of propriety, that a king could not obtain taxation in his absence, and in the second instance by a differing assessment of the level of the king's necessity.[70] In

[64] See above, 200–1. [65] *CPR 1272–1281*, 94, 268; *CPR 1281–1292*, 247.
[66] Morris, *Welsh Wars*, 155, 158. [67] See above, 75. [68] *AM*, IV, 323.
[69] For his earlier political ideas, see Altschul, *Baronial Family*, 109, 113–16, 120–1.
[70] See above, 215.

the Hereford dispute, too, Gloucester saw himself as defending not only his own interests but also those of Marcher privilege more generally.[71]

Edward invested a great deal of time and effort on his relationship with Gloucester, ensuring that the earl was supportive and remained so as far as possible. This meant for the most part that the two had a positive relationship that only helped enhance Edward's authority, but their relationship was clearly disintegrating in the final years and months of Gloucester's life. The blame for this falls on both sides and lies in the fact that each misunderstood the other's position and underestimated the other's resolve. Gloucester, puffed up by his newly acquired status as the king's son-in-law, was determined to continue on the March as if nothing had changed since the Welsh conquest, while Edward was always going to call the tune in his relationship with the earl, and his dignity would not allow anyone, especially not Gloucester himself, to think otherwise. It was perhaps fortunate for the king that the earl died when he did and was not around when general resentment towards royal policies burst forth in 1297. If Gloucester had been alive, his power and resentment might have made the crisis even more serious than it was.

But, if Gloucester was drifting away from Edward, what of the other earls? Where did they stand in relation to the king as, unknown to the participants, the years of peace began to draw to a close? Again, the witness lists of royal charters provide some help in assessing the state of the relationship between Edward and his chief subjects, in this case shortly before he would have his greatest need of them and their support.

Table 8.1, showing the charter witness lists for the years 1289 to 1293, demonstrates a somewhat greater disparity in witnessing than in earlier years. The earls of Lancaster and Lincoln, William de Valence and, at least until 1292, Gloucester all remained very close to the king in these years and there can be little surprise in this. The witnessing evidence also suggests that, in contrast to Gloucester, Edward was successful in rehabilitating the earl of Hereford after the latter's humiliation in 1292, which is important when considering Hereford's reasons for opposition to the king in 1297.[72] Hereford witnessed ten charters in 1293, attended the June parliament and was with the king at Bristol in September and Westminster in early November.[73] Further evidence that he had put his humiliation behind him for the time being came in April 1294, when he headed the train of Eleanor, the king's daughter, when she sailed to Brabant to meet her husband.[74] The other earls all witnessed charters relatively frequently and

[71] See above, 219. [72] See below, 235–6.

[73] *Royal Charter Witness Lists of Edward I*, nos. 21.23–17, 21.15, 21.03–02.

[74] *CPR 1292–1301*, 65.

Table 8.1 *Comital witnesses to royal charters, 17–21 Edward I*

Regnal year	Total	Gloucester	Hereford	Lancaster	Lincoln	Warenne	Norfolk	Cornwall	Valence	Warwick
17	12	1	4	3	5	9	0	0	11	1
18	104	64	32	46	75	33	14	32	73	7
19	68	21	9	37	38	12	10	0	29	2
20	68	31	24	31	52	14	9	0	22	3
21	32	1	10	8	12	12	12	10	19	3
Total	284	118	79	125	182	80	45	53	154	16

Edward had little reason to doubt their support. Although the proportion of charters witnessed by Norfolk, Cornwall and Warwick was lower than in the period before 1286, there is no evidence that this represented a general cooling of relations. Norfolk, for instance, was granted ten bucks from Pember Forest in August 1290 and successfully enlisted the king's help in his dispute with the exchequer over the matter of his debts.[75] Following the death of Queen Eleanor, Edward spent several weeks of mourning at Edmund of Cornwall's manor of Ashridge and, in June 1291, granted the earl custody of Eleanor's county of Ponthieu in northern France while Prince Edward, Eleanor's heir, was a minor.[76] Warwick received three grants of deer from the king between 1290 and 1293 and was also acquitted a debt of £240, 'for his good service' at the time of the First Welsh War.[77] Less frequent personal attendance on the king by these three earls, therefore, did not mean they were beyond the king's good offices. Thus the relations between Edward I and his earls remained strong right up to the outbreak of war with France in 1294.

A defining feature of these years was Edward's diplomatic manoeuvres in Scotland, in France and for a new crusade. What part did he expect the earls to play in these ventures? In Scotland, certainly, the earls were active both diplomatically and politically. Diplomatic engagement with Scotland was principally undertaken by Earl Warenne and the bishop of Durham, together with the earl of Lincoln, William de Vescy and the dean of York.[78] They negotiated the Treaty of Birgham in 1290, which agreed the marriage between Edward of Caernarfon and Margaret of

[75] *CCR 1288–1296*, 97; Morris, *Bigod Earls*, 159–60.

[76] *CPR 1281–1292*, 435; *The Itinerary of Edward I, 1272–1290*, List and Index Society 103 (1974), 298; *The Itinerary of Edward I, 1290–1307*, List and Index Society 132 (1976), 2–3. The grant of Ponthieu may have been in lieu of repayments for Edward's debts to his cousin but, even so, it was still a very generous and prestigious grant.

[77] *CCR 1288–1296*, 79, 110, 242, 296.

[78] *CPR 1281–1292*, 372, 386.

Norway, heiress of Scotland, aborted on Margaret's death that year.[79] When Margaret died, diplomacy ground to a halt and politics took over. Edward, asked by the Scottish guardians to judge between the various contenders for the Scottish crown, was determined to extract the maximum concessions from the Scots.[80]

His position as arbiter was indirectly helped by the interests of his own earls in the Scottish succession. The earl of Gloucester was supporting the cause of his uncle by marriage, Robert Bruce, while Warenne pressed the claims of his son-in-law, John de Balliol.[81] There is no indication that the two earls fell out over this issue, or that their support made any difference to the resolution, but it may indirectly have aided Edward in presenting himself as a non-partisan figure. When Edward met the Scots at Norham Castle in June 1291 for preliminary discussions of 'the Great Cause', he issued a military summons to ensure that the English political and military hierarchy was there in force.[82] The earls responded to their king's call for a show of English military strength. Six of them were at Norham with Edward in June 1291 and another, Hereford, arrived at Berwick-upon-Tweed at the beginning of July.[83] Two of them, Norfolk and Lincoln, were appointed among the twenty-four auditors to hear the Great Cause.[84] The following summer five earls were again on the Scottish border.[85] In October 1292, when Edward announced his decision in favour of John Balliol, there were once more five earls present.[86] That Edward was able to drag his most important earls up to the Scottish border on three occasions in just over a year to take part in what was essentially political theatre is further evidence of his ability to deploy his nobility in support of his political aims.

In one matter of great importance to Edward, however, he and the earls do not appear to have been in such close accord. This was his renewed fervour for crusading. Ensuring peace in Europe was the essential precondition for any successful crusade and had been one of the primary objectives of Edward's three-year stay on the continent.[87] He took the

[79] *EHD 1189–1327*, 467; *CPR 1281–1292*, 386; Prestwich, *Edward I*, 362.

[80] Prestwich, *Edward I*, 362–9.

[81] Sir Thomas Gray, *Scalacronica, 1272–1363*, ed. and trans. A. King, Surtees Society 209 (2005), 33.

[82] *Parl Writs*, I, 256.

[83] *Royal Charter Witness Lists of Edward I*, nos. 19.47, 19.45, 19.29. The six earls were Gloucester, Lancaster, Warenne, Lincoln, Norfolk and Valence.

[84] Morris, *Bigod Earls*, 154.

[85] *Royal Charter Witness Lists of Edward I*, nos. 20.29, 20.28, 20.16. The five earls were Gloucester, Hereford, Warenne, Lincoln and Norfolk.

[86] Ibid., nos. 20.06–04. The five earls were Gloucester, Hereford, Warenne, Lincoln and Valence.

[87] For Edward's attempts to secure peace and to organise a second crusade, see Morris, *GTK*, 196–7, 203, 205, 209, 211, 228.

cross while in France, reportedly saying that he had 'no other thought than this affair'.[88] On his return to England, he secured a grant of crusading taxation from Pope Nicholas IV and was much involved in continuing diplomatic preparations for the new crusade.[89] Edward's redecoration of his chamber in the Palace of Westminster with scenes from the Book of Maccabees, a clear allusion to the sufferings of the Christian communities in the Holy Land, was a graphic call to arms and a statement of intent.[90] Indeed, it can be said that this was the main ambition of his later years and it is impossible to assess his actions in this period fully without acknowledging this.

It does not seem, however, that many of his earls shared his enthusiasm. Lincoln was with Edward when he took the cross and, given his close relationship with the king, it is almost certain he was one of those who took the cross with his lord.[91] At the wedding of Princess Margaret to the duke of Brabant in July 1290, Archbishop Peckham preached the crusade, and the earl and countess of Gloucester, the former perhaps swept along by a combination of his wife's desire to return to the Holy Land, the place of her birth, his own unfulfilled vow from 1268 and the fervour of the archbishop's sermon, also took the cross.[92] His ardour appears to have quickly cooled, however, for he does not seem to have made many preparations to fulfil his vow. No other earl is mentioned as having taken the cross at the wedding, even though six of them were there and had they done so, it would probably have been noted.[93]

What of the others then? Lancaster had gone east in 1271 and he took the cross again some time before December 1289.[94] William de Valence had also been on Edward's first crusade and might be expected to have gone again but by the early 1290s he was in his late sixties and may well have decided that he was too old to join it. It is more likely that he would have sent his heir, Aymer, in his stead had the crusade materialised. Warenne may also have felt himself too old. He had taken the cross in 1268 but never fulfilled his vow.[95] He would probably have remained

[88] Ibid., 211. [89] Prestwich, *Edward I*, 328–32.

[90] M. Reeve, 'The Painted Chamber at Westminster, Edward I and the Crusade', *Viator* 37 (2006), 189–221.

[91] *CChR 1427–1516*, 303. Lincoln witnessed a charter of Edward's to Robert Burnell on 5 August shortly before Edward took the cross at St Sever. Morris, *GTK*, 211.

[92] R.C. Stacey, 'Parliamentary Negotiation and the Expulsion of the Jews from England', *TCE* 6 (1997), 90–1.

[93] Cotton, *Historia Anglicana*, 177. They were Lancaster, Gloucester, Warenne, Norfolk, Lincoln and Oxford. The other named lay crusaders, Robert Tatershale and his son and Otto de Grandisson, were not of the same rank as the earls present.

[94] *Calendar of Papal Letters*, 20 vols. (London: HMSO, 1893), I, 506; S.D. Lloyd, *English Society and the Crusade, 1216–1307* (Oxford: Clarendon Press, 1988), 243.

[95] See above, 188–9.

behind once again to protect his interests in England. Given his notorious harshness as a landlord, these would have come under threat during any prolonged absence.[96] Edmund of Cornwall had set out on the crusade in 1270, though he was forced to turn back by his father's death, but he would be the obvious choice for regent again. Warwick may have chosen to go, though it is possible that he may not have been able to afford it.[97] This is also likely to have been the case for the young earl of Arundel.[98] Hereford had, as a younger man, gone on pilgrimage to Santiago, and so may have been tempted to make the even more spiritually meritorious journey to Jerusalem.[99] However, it is unlikely that he would have gone unless Gloucester went too and there is no evidence to suggest that Hereford made any preparations to join the crusade. This leaves just Norfolk and Oxford. The Bigods had no history of crusading and the current earl of Norfolk showed no inclination to break with this tradition, while Oxford was probably too poor.[100] Of the ten English earls, therefore, it is possible to state with reasonable certainty that two would have gone (Lancaster and Lincoln). Beyond that one can only speculate but it seems unlikely that more than four would have set out.

What reasons might be found for their seeming lack of enthusiasm? Obviously, campaigning in the Holy Land was an entirely different prospect from fighting a war in Wales and the expense and dangers of crusading must be the main reason why the earls appear not to have shown much interest. They had displayed little enthusiasm for Edward's first crusade and the protection and pursuit of their interests at home must have been a more attractive and urgent prospect than the arduous journey east with little hope of success at the end of it. It may also have worried them that their king, having just returned from three years abroad that had threatened to destabilise the realm, was planning another protracted absence of at least two years, and probably much longer, to fight thousands of miles away in a campaign from which he might never return, leaving only a young child as his heir. In this, the earls may have had more concern for the welfare of his kingdom than Edward himself.

[96] His harshness as a landlord is very plain from encounters with his methods in this book but it was also commented upon by the archbishops of both York and Canterbury; *Registrum Epistolarum Johannis Peckham*, I, 38; *The Register of Walter Giffard, Lord Archbishop of York, 1266–79*, ed. W. Brown, Surtees Society 109 (1904), 227–8.

[97] For Warwick's financial difficulties, see Denton, 'Evesham Chronicle', 576.

[98] For Arundel's financial problems, see *Documents Illustrating the Crisis of 1297–8*, no. 132.

[99] *CPR 1272–1281*, 249.

[100] My thanks to Dr Marc Morris for this information about the Bigods.

In Edward's dealings with France in these years, there was markedly less involvement from the earls, probably because they had less to offer him than they did in Scotland, since the power relationship between England and France was very different from that between England and Scotland, and also fewer earls had a direct interest in what happened in France. Ostensibly, the diplomacy with France of 1293 and 1294 was not about the crusade directly but over a naval dispute and the status of Gascony.[101] Edward knew, however, that he could not depart while there were grounds of dispute between him and Philip IV and his eagerness to reach a settlement may have temporarily blinded him to the potentially disastrous consequences of his actions. The two earls he did appoint to deal with Philip, Lancaster and Lincoln, were the natural choices.[102] Through his wife, the French king's mother-in-law, Edmund of Lancaster was well connected at Philip's court, was a frequent visitor there and, as the king of England's brother, was of the right status to head the negotiations. Lincoln, as Edward's most intimate friend and counsellor and also someone familiar with France and French politics after spending three years there with Edward, was likewise a natural choice. Both were also probable crusaders. That Edward kept the details of his negotiations secret from the rest of his nobility may have been because of the leeway he gave his negotiators to reach a settlement with Philip over Gascony, a settlement that would free him to depart on crusade. This proved foolhardy. Lancaster, overestimating his influence in Paris, was comprehensively duped by Philip and the anti-English faction and effectively ended up surrendering Gascony to the French king without a fight.[103] Philip's confiscation of the duchy made war inevitable, destroyed Edward's plans for a second crusade and opened a new and crucial phase of the reign.

WAR AND CRISIS: 1294–1301

The years between 1294 and 1301 placed sustained pressure upon the relationship of Edward I and his earls for the first time. The historiography has naturally tended to focus on the opposition to the king from the earls and magnates and has rather neglected those earls who gave unstinting support to their king and those who were stuck in the middle, uncertain which way to jump.[104] In the end, it should be remembered

[101] Prestwich, *Edward I*, 377–8. [102] *CPR 1292–1301*, 15.

[103] Prestwich, *Edward I*, 378–80.

[104] See, for example, Michael Prestwich's chapter on the 1297 crisis in *War, Politics and Finance*, 247–61, which gives considerable space to the opposition of Norfolk and Hereford but does not mention the attitude of the other earls. The best account of the crisis of 1297 and its causes remains Harriss, *King, Parliament, and Public Finance*, chapter 3.

that, though these were years of crisis, the political community did not break apart as it had done under Henry III after 1258 and was later to do under Edward II. The bonds that Edward I had created over the previous twenty years were now tested and strained but did not shatter. A comprehensive understanding of the role played by the earls in these years will help illuminate the true nature of the events. By focusing on the individual grievances of the opposition leaders, modern historiography has not fully explored the possibility that magnate grievances might not have been the driving force behind a movement that brought England close to civil war in 1297.[105]

In order to understand better the crisis of 1297 and the role played in it by the earls, it is necessary first to examine their attitude to the king's military and financial demands between 1294 and 1296, which provide the backdrop for the events of 1297, and to ask to what extent the earls were in step with broader public opinion on these issues. Most of the earls had been excluded from the disastrous negotiations over Gascony and, when parliament met at the end of May 1294, it took a public act of contrition on Edward's part to change the atmosphere of anger at the king's folly and lack of consultation.[106] It was the nobility who sustained him in his hour of need. Pierre Langtoft, the chronicler, says that in this time of crisis Edward turned for advice and support to Anthony Bek, bishop of Durham, and to 'his earls and barons who had good will to him'.[107] The earls at this parliament were those closest to the king: Lancaster, Valence, Cornwall, Warenne and Lincoln, together with Norfolk.[108] Of the other major earls, Hereford and Gloucester were both abroad but the whereabouts of the more minor earls, Warwick, Arundel and Oxford, are unknown. Edward must have been pleased at the response of his earls. They rallied to their king, demonstrating that, despite his catastrophic errors during the negotiations with the French, the unity of purpose created earlier in his reign had not been broken.

Nor were they merely prepared to offer words of support; they were willing to lead by example and join the king's expedition to Gascony. The earls of Lancaster and Lincoln were appointed to lead one of the contingents but other earls were not backward in coming forward. Significantly for what happened later, both Hereford and Norfolk agreed to serve.[109] A generous grant of deer made to the earl of Warwick at Portsmouth

[105] See below, 235–7, 240–3.
[106] *Langtoft*, II, 201–3; *Guisborough*, 243; *Chronicle of Bury St Edmunds*, 120.
[107] *Langtoft*, II, 201.
[108] *Royal Charter Witness Lists of Edward I*, nos. 22.27–26.
[109] Morris, *Bigod Earls*, 155; *CPR 1292–1301*, 84.

on 3 July suggests that he also had agreed to accompany the king.[110] Earl Warenne and William de Valence were with the king at Fareham, near Portsmouth, at the end of July and the beginning of August, suggesting that they too were preparing to sail.[111] There is good evidence, therefore, that seven earls were prepared to countenance service overseas; a high level of concrete support. What is equally striking, however, is that the earls' enthusiasm was not matched further down the social hierarchy, suggesting that where the earls led, the knights did not necessarily follow any longer.[112] This cleavage between the attitude of the high nobility and the gentry is significant for the events of 1297. The weather prevented the main fleet from sailing in the summer of 1294 but, when news of another Welsh rebellion arrived at the end of September, the earls proved no less eager to fight there than in Gascony.[113] Every earl turned out for the final Welsh campaign of Edward I's reign.[114]

Once the Welsh were defeated, Edward turned his attention once more to Gascony and came up against the first comital opposition to overseas service. On 23 August 1295, during a parliament at Westminster, Edward ordered the exchequer to distrain fourteen barons and knights, including Richard Fitz Alan, earl of Arundel, who had refused to go to Gascony.[115] Edward had allowed Arundel to inherit his earldom in 1291 but the earl was heavily encumbered by debts to the crown in excess of £5,000.[116] He was not particularly wealthy for an earl and drew much of his income from his Marcher estates, whose value would probably have been reduced during the Welsh rebellion. It was poverty that Arundel and his fellow recalcitrants pleaded, but Edward was not prepared to listen to excuses and on 3 September ordered an even harsher distraint.[117] Despite these protests, a considerable force, numbering around 200 knights, did eventually sail to Gascony in January 1296 under Lancaster and Lincoln.[118] An invasion scare in the late summer of 1295 led Edward once again to turn to his earls. Warenne, Norfolk and Hereford were appointed in August and September 1295 to be custodians of the coast in various parts of the country.[119] A month later, Warenne was given command of all the counties north of the Trent, in preparation for an invasion of Scotland the following year.[120] At the end of 1295, therefore, eighteen months after the outbreak of war, the earls remained overwhelmingly supportive, with Arundel's complaints of poverty the only foreboding of what was to

[110] *CCR 1288–1296*, 355. [111] *Royal Charter Witness Lists of Edward I*, nos. 22.13–12.
[112] For knightly reluctance, see Morris, *GTK*, 273–4.
[113] Ibid., 273, 275; Morris, *Welsh Wars*, 242. [114] See above, Table 3.1.
[115] Fryde, 'Magnate Debts', 262. [116] Ibid., 263–4. [117] Ibid., 262.
[118] Prestwich, *Edward I*, 384. For the number of knights, see *Rôles Gascons*, III, *passim*.
[119] *CCR 1288–1296*, 455; *CPR 1292–1301*, 147. [120] *CPR 1292–1301*, 151, 152.

come. However, had Edward been more sensitive to what was happening and not exclusively focused on achieving his war aims, he might have noticed that his military and financial demands were, as Arundel's reluctance shows, beginning to squeeze even the bottom rung of the earls. Only the super rich were still avoiding pain from the king's measures.

The invasion of Scotland in 1296 was again the occasion for the earls to turn out in force. Norfolk, Hereford, Warenne and Warwick all fought in Scotland.[121] Of the remaining earls, Lancaster and Lincoln were in Gascony, and Valence, Gloucester and Oxford had died.[122] This leaves Arundel. He does not seem to have sailed for Gascony even after Edward's pressure, for in January 1296 he was in charge of ensuring that all those with land worth £40 or more p.a. were ready to join the king's service.[123] This is interesting in two respects. First, it seems that Edward had quickly patched up their quarrel and was employing Arundel once more in a military capacity despite the earl's evident failure to obey Edward's command to serve in Gascony. Pleas of poverty notwithstanding, Arundel certainly joined the king in Scotland.[124] Second, the order states specifically that 'some persons have not obeyed the king's former mandate' to be ready to set out at three weeks' notice, signs of a growing reluctance among the gentry to perform military service, which was the result of the financial burdens being placed on them.

This was one of the most sustained and intensive periods of financial demands on the laity and clergy in the whole middle ages. Edward's necessity was made more acute by the collapse of the previously reliable Riccardi banking firm, which, like Edward himself, was completely unprepared for the sudden outbreak of war.[125] The Riccardi failure forced Edward to turn to his subjects for immediate cash. His financial demands took three forms, all of which fell more heavily upon the gentry than the magnates. The first was on England's most lucrative export, wool. After an aborted seizure of wool, Edward devised, in liaison with England's wool merchants, a massive increase in customs duty, raising it from 6*s* 8*d* a sack to 40*s*.[126] This caused a drop in prices of around 25 per cent across England and it quickly became known as the *maltolt*.[127] Big producers of wool, such as the earl of Norfolk, were able to hold back some of their

[121] See above, Table 3.1.

[122] See above, Table 3.1. See above, 220, for Gloucester's death; see Morris, *GTK*, 293, for Valence's death; for Oxford's death, see *GEC*, x, 218.

[123] *CPR 1292–1301*, 182.

[124] *Royal Charter Witness Lists of Edward I*, nos. 24.13–10, 24.8.

[125] The reasons for the Riccardi failure are discussed in R.W. Kaeuper, *Bankers to the Crown: the Riccardi of Lucca and Edward I* (Princeton University Press, 1973), 209–20.

[126] *EHD 1189–1327*, 469. [127] Miller, 'War, Taxation and the English Economy', 14.

crop and wait for prices to rise but this was not an option for those for whom the wool crop represented a greater part of their income.[128]

The second financial demand, again non-consensual, was the numerous prises of foodstuffs levied for the use of royal armies.[129] Some earls were fortunate in avoiding having their victuals seized. Lincoln, for example, along with many others serving in Gascony, was granted exemption from having his corn taken by royal officials and permitted to send it instead to Gascony.[130] Edmund of Lancaster was even more generously treated in March 1295, when royal officials were ordered not to take victuals from him or any of his tenants.[131] For an earl, a prise would be inconvenient but he would have reserves elsewhere to call upon and would probably be first in the queue for payment. The same was not true of a knight with only one or two manors, for whom the loss of provisions or marketable produce could have a devastating short-term impact and then involve a long wait to be compensated. In an age of high-farming, prises were potentially ruinous for those with small estates. There appears to have been some resentment directed at the earls for their escape from the worst burdens of prises. While Aymer de Valence was in Flanders with the king in the autumn of 1297, men allegedly broke into one of his manors and stole a large quantity of corn.[132] It is tempting to believe that the perpetrators had themselves recently been the victims of one of the king's prises.

The third and most crushing financial demand was the three taxes on lay movables and the two on clerical temporalities between 1294 and 1296. The extent to which these taxes sapped the wealth of the kingdom can be seen not just in the amounts but also by the diminishing returns.[133] This suggests a draining of wealth of course, but also widespread avoidance. Again, the earls could insulate themselves from the worst effects. Most had received a respite from the tenth granted in 1294 because of their service in Wales, and in September 1295, in a concessionary move, Edward turned many of these respites into full pardons.[134] Perhaps most indicative is the evidence of tax evasion. The excellent surviving accounts for the earldom of Norfolk show that the earl was able to reduce his payments to the 1295 tax by bribing royal officials, a tactic likely to have been repeated elsewhere.[135] It was the gentry and not

128 Ibid., 14. 129 Prestwich, *Edward I*, 407–10.

130 *CCR 1296–1302*, 5–6. 131 *CPR 1292–1301*, 131.

132 *CPR 1292–1301*, 378.

133 Prestwich, *Edward I*, 569. The lay tenth of 1294 was assessed at £81,838, but the lay twelfth granted just two years later was assessed at less than half that level, just £38,870.

134 *CCR 1288–1296*, 456; Morris, *GTK*, 281. 135 Morris, *Bigod Earls*, 162.

the earls who were really suffering. A good example of this comes from Sussex. There, Earl Warenne, with a lordship of fifteen manors and two towns worth around £1,000 p.a., paid £23 8*s* 5½*d* towards the eleventh of 1295, barely 2 per cent of his income.[136] The Etchingham family, a leading knightly dynasty in Pevensey Rape, paid £13 1*s* 11*d* from their four manors.[137] At Beddingham, the family was paying *c.*10.5 per cent of gross income.[138] With part of his estate held in dower by his mother, and in debt for 200 marks by 1300, it is not surprising that, with the added burden of sustained taxation, Sir William de Etchingham refused three separate summonses to Flanders in 1297.[139]

It was not just that earls were better able to protect their income, it was that they, or most of them, do not seem to have realised the resentment these taxes were causing. It is significant that it was Gloucester, by 1294 the most isolated politically and physically of the earls from Edward, who spoke out most strongly against Edward's original demands for a tax of a third from the laity.[140] Edward eventually accepted a tenth and, after Gloucester died in 1295, he encountered little opposition from the magnates in obtaining further lay taxes in 1295 and at the Bury St Edmunds parliament in November 1296.[141] Of course, lay taxes were granted by the Commons as well as the magnates but without the support of at least one major earl to rally around there would be little that the knights of the shires could do to resist the king's demands.

Why were the earls isolated from the growing sense of anger and desperation in the localities at the king? Obviously the fact that they were not as seriously affected by the king's measures as those further down the scale was a factor. Also, as Part II has suggested, the earls were not as integrally involved in local affairs as they were in the late middle ages, so they would have had less sensitive antennae for trouble than their late fourteenth- and fifteenth-century successors might have. Their extended military service also meant that they were simply not in a position to hear the level of complaints emanating from their tenants and neighbours. It was probably not until he returned home from Bury St Edmunds in November 1296, having granted another lay tax without much argument, that the earl of Norfolk first became aware of the level of resentment building against the king's policies. Prior to this, he had been almost constantly in the king's service in one capacity or another

136 *The Three Earliest Subsidies for the County of Sussex*, ed. W. Hudson, Sussex Record Society 10 (1909), *passim*.

137 Ibid., 10, 11, 15, 21, 25, 76, 80.

138 Saul, *Scenes from Provincial Life*, 117; *Three Earliest Subsides*, 25.

139 Moor, *Knights of Edward I*, I, 299–300.

140 Prestwich, *Edward I*, 404.

141 Ibid., 405.

Table 8.2 *Comital witnesses to royal charters, 22–4 Edward I*

Regnal year	Total	Gloucester	Hereford	Lancaster	Lincoln	Warenne	Norfolk	Cornwall	Valence	Warwick
22	51	0	1	13	32	17	9	18	36	1
23	22	0	6	16	15	10	1	0	5	0
24	24	0	6	0	0	13	14	0	2	10
Total	97	0	13	29	47	40	24	18	43	11

for two-and-a-half years.[142] This might explain the remarkable change in attitude on the part of Norfolk and some other magnates, from the pliancy at Bury St Edmunds in November 1296 to outright defiance at Salisbury in February 1297.

Table 8.2 illustrates the isolation of Gloucester after 1292 but it also brings into focus an important change in the composition of the comital elite, which had an important impact on the events of 1297. After twenty years when no earl had died, four perished between December 1295 and the following Christmas. The least significant of these was Oxford, who died in September 1296.[143] Given the significant deterioration in their relationship since 1292, Gloucester's death in December 1295 may have come as something of a relief to the king.[144] Edward was already developing plans to bestow the earl's widow, his own daughter Joan, upon one of his closest foreign allies, Count Amadeus of Savoy, when at the beginning of 1297 she stunned everyone by announcing that she had married one of her household knights, Ralph de Monthermer.[145] Edward's anger was initially fierce but he may have come to realise that, in the hands of a man entirely dependent upon his goodwill, the earldom of Gloucester was of considerable use.[146] The other two deaths would have affected him most acutely for they were those of his uncle, William de Valence, and his brother, Edmund of Lancaster.[147] These two had for decades been men he could count on unquestioningly and Edward would have felt their loss most keenly, both personally and politically. The words he used to request prayers for his brother's soul reflect this: 'by [Lancaster's] death the king and his realm is left desolate.'[148] Both Lancaster and Valence left adult heirs, but neither yet had the experience or standing that their fathers

[142] The earl had been preparing to go to Gascony in the summer of 1294, fought on the Welsh campaign of 1294–5, attended the 1295 parliament, was appointed to guard the East Anglian coast against French invasion in the autumn of 1295, served in Scotland in 1296 and then attended the Bury St Edmunds parliament in November 1296.

[143] *GEC*, X, 218. [144] Altschul, *Baronial Family*, 155.

[145] Ibid., 157. [146] Ibid., 157–8.

[147] *CFR 1272–1307*, 376; *CIPM*, III, no. 423. [148] *CCR 1288–1296*, 512.

had been able to place at Edward's disposal. A further problem was that, following the loss of these three senior earls, the two earls who remained closest to the king he had sent away: Lincoln to Gascony and Warenne as guardian of Scotland. Edward still had no reason to doubt the loyalty of those earls he summoned to the Salisbury parliament in February 1297, but the five most prominent earls of the past twenty-five years would not be present for one reason or another and, though he had not yet realised it, as the fateful year of 1297 dawned, the king was more isolated politically and physically than at any previous point in his reign.[149] The death of Queen Eleanor in 1290, the chancellor, Robert Burnell, in 1292, and now the loss of some of those earls closest to him robbed Edward of the support of those he could rely on unfailingly and whose advice he tended to take.

Until the Salisbury parliament assembled, it had been the clergy, not the laity, that had proved most problematic. So much so that on 30 January 1297, when faced with a refusal by the clergy to grant him a tax, Edward responded by outlawing them as a body and forcing them to pay him for re-admission to his peace.[150] The English church had been leaderless in 1294 and therefore unable to resist the king's outrageous demand for a moiety of their temporalities. Now, however, with Archbishop Winchelsey at their head, and armed with the papal bull *Clericis Laicos*, the clergy presented a much more united and formidable opposition, at least until Edward used the nuclear option of outlawry.[151] The gentry had been similarly leaderless but they now found a champion in the earl of Norfolk, and he would soon be joined by others. Edward's key mistakes were that he presumed too far upon his subjects' goodwill and displayed a total inability to see their point of view. In 1297, the irresistible force of popular discontent met the immovable object of Edward I's will. It is testament to Edward's previous successes that, in the aftermath of this clash, his authority remained intact, whereas, faced with similar circumstances, his father's and son's crumbled entirely.

For Edward, the years between 1294 and 1296 had been largely ones of frustration. His schemes for crusade had been overtaken by events: poor weather had prevented him from sailing for Gascony in the summer of 1294; he had then been forced to waste a year putting down rebellion in Wales; and finally he had spent another campaigning season in Scotland crushing the apparently pathetically weak Scottish resistance. Edward's

[149] *Parl Writs*, I, 51–2. The English earls summoned were Cornwall, Norfolk, Warwick, Oxford and Arundel.

[150] J.H. Denton, *Robert Winchelsey and the Crown, 1294–1313* (Cambridge University Press, 1980), 107–8.

[151] Ibid., 69–76.

attitude towards his excursion into Scotland is summed up by his reputed remark to Earl Warenne, when handing over to him the great seal of Scotland, that '[h]e does good business, who rids himself of a shit'.[152] It was not conquering Scotland that was Edward's principal concern but recovering Gascony. He had spent all this time, and nearly £300,000, fighting in Britain while making little progress in the prime aim of the war.[153] Edward wanted this war out of the way so he could go on crusade again. All these things were merely getting in his way. Nor did matters look as if they were improving. His brother had died in Gascony in June 1296, while, in January 1297, Lincoln, Lancaster's successor as commander, was ambushed and badly mauled by the French at Bellegarde.[154] The Salisbury parliament, with no gentry or clergy present, was supposed to provide him with a platform to lay out to his nobles his military plans for the coming year, when, finally, he would be able to go to the continent himself. But these plans proved too ambitious for those magnates who gathered there. The king proposed leading a force to Flanders himself, while also sending reinforcements to Gascony.[155] Guisborough reports that opposition was widespread but it was the king's confrontation with Norfolk that caught the chronicler's attention.[156] For the first time since the war began, a senior earl spoke out against the king's military plans. Previously, Edward would have been able to rely on his brother, Lincoln, Valence or Warenne to speak in his support and bring any reluctant magnates round to his point of view, but none of those men were there. Instead, for the first time in his reign, Edward encountered open and face-to-face defiance from one of his earls on a strategic issue and Guisborough memorably records the anger he felt, reportedly telling the earl that he would either go or hang.

Norfolk was soon joined by Hereford. Together they spearheaded the lay opposition to Edward I in 1297. What was their motivation and what position did the other earls take in response to this development? In his most recent account, Michael Prestwich has stated that the events of 1297 were not 'a crisis born of personal grievances'.[157] His previous work, however, and that of some other historians, strongly emphasise the personal element in the opposition of the earls of Hereford and Norfolk. In his *DNB* article on Norfolk, for example, Prestwich states that 'the

[152] Gray, *Scalacronica*, 39. For Edward's subsequent neglect of Scotland and the problems it caused for the English administration, see Spencer, 'John de Warenne'.

[153] Edward's wardrobe accounts indicate that he spent £289,730 in the regnal years 22–4 Edward I (November 1293–November 1296). By comparison, in the three years previously he spent £129,917. Prestwich, *Edward I*, 570.

[154] Ibid., 384–5. [155] *Guisborough*, 289–90.

[156] *Guisborough*, 290. [157] Prestwich, *Plantagenet England*, 169.

combination of grievances over his debts, and anger at the way his rights as hereditary marshal had been disregarded, led to the earl playing a leading role in the opposition to the king in 1297'.[158] Equally, Scott Waugh, in the *DNB* article on Hereford, writes that 'Bohun's sensitivity about his rights, and the rebuffs that he received at Edward's hands, explain why he became such a staunch opponent of the king during the crisis of 1297'.[159]

The principal rebuff Waugh refers to was, of course, the infamous dispute between Hereford and Gloucester on the March, but in itself this is not an adequate explanation for Hereford's opposition. His relations with the king had been largely repaired by 1294 and they continued to improve right up until the start of 1297.[160] Edward did not intervene decisively in Hereford's territorial dispute with Roger Mortimer on the March, even though, on this occasion, the earl had been the aggressor.[161] Hereford was in fact one of the first Marchers to grant Edward a fifteenth in his Marcher lordship in July 1292.[162] He had fought without complaint in Wales and Scotland and had been prepared to go to Gascony in 1294.[163] Possibly in connection with this, he was granted twelve deer in August 1294 as a sign of the king's approbation.[164] In November 1296, Hereford was able to secure two commissions of *oyer* and *terminer* for himself into hunting and fishing offences on his Essex estates and in January 1297 he was given the honour of leading the train of the king's daughter, Margaret, to her husband in Brabant.[165] In short, when Hereford sailed for Brabant, it was by no means obvious that within a few weeks he would be leading the opposition to Edward's military and financial plans.

Norfolk's grievance, Prestwich suggests, emanated from his treatment over his debts to the crown.[166] However, Marc Morris has shown that Edward's interventions in Norfolk's disputes with the exchequer were at the latter's own instigation.[167] A more serious issue between the men was the question of the office of marshal in both peace and war. There had been arguments over the rights of the marshal, particularly his financial rights, in wartime in both 1282 and 1287, and the broader issue emerged again during the Welsh rebellion of 1294–5, in this case over whether the marshal had a right to refuse to serve in person except with the

158 Prestwich, 'Bigod, Roger (IV)'. For an earlier example of Prestwich's focus on the personal motives of Norfolk and Hereford, see Prestwich, *War, Politics and Finance*, 249.

159 Waugh, 'Bohun, Humphrey (VI)'.

160 See above, 222.

161 KB 27/127, m. 27; KB 27/138, m. 32d; KB 27/139, mm. 6d, 8d; KB 27/141, mm. 32–32d; KB 27/142, m. 16d; KB 27/147, m. 13; *CPR 1281–1292*, 515; *CPR 1292–1301*, 108.

162 *CPR 1281–1292*, 502.

163 See above, 228–30.

164 *CCR 1288–1296*, 363.

165 *CPR 1292–1301*, 220, 226, 259.

166 Prestwich, 'Bigod, Roger (IV)'.

167 Morris, *Bigod Earls*, 157–60.

king himself.[168] In November 1294, Edward appointed Norfolk as joint commander in south Wales but the earl ensured that this would not be made into a precedent and that his right to personal attendance upon the king in wartime would be preserved.[169] Once this promise was secured, Norfolk served happily and successfully in south Wales and received the money due to him as marshal.[170] As Morris makes clear, relations between the earl and Edward I were on a good footing right up to the end of 1296, Norfolk serving with the king in Scotland with full accordance of his rights as marshal.[171] As with Hereford, then, it was events in 1297 itself that drove Norfolk into opposition against his king, not any long-standing personal grievance.

What caused their volte-face? It was probably a combination of the king's military demands and their realisation of the strength of feeling in the country stirred up by the king's financial exactions. Norfolk and Hereford, as hereditary marshal and constable, were uniquely well qualified to express their reservations, and those of others, to the king's policies. It was Edward, and not the earls, who made things personal, as his targeted attacks on Norfolk and his family in the wake of the Salisbury parliament and his attempts to destabilise Hereford's lordship in Brecon in July show.[172] That, even then, Norfolk remained reconcilable is demonstrated by an indenture he made with John de Segrave on 9 June. Its provisions for service overseas suggest that the earl was still contemplating serving with the king in Flanders.[173] His objections at Salisbury and, later, when the muster for Flanders assembled on 7 July appear to have been based on genuine principle rather than personal grievances. As the Norwich chronicler, Bartholomew Cotton, made clear, Norfolk and Hereford saw themselves as acting 'on behalf of the commonalty of the kingdom' when they objected to the king's summons, on the grounds that Edward was demanding service overseas without pay and had not even stipulated in the summons where the campaign was due to take place.[174] Guisborough was even more explicit about their motivation, saying that 'the cause they were striving for was not only their own, but also that of the whole community'.[175]

But what of the other earls? Their attitude and actions will illuminate the crisis and its implications more than just looking at the motives and actions of the leaders of the opposition. At least two other earls seem to have flirted with opposing the king before thinking better of it.

168 Morris, *Bigod Earls*, 157. 169 *CPR 1292–1301*, 126.
170 Morris, *Bigod Earls*, 156–7. 171 Ibid., 160–1.
172 Ibid., 164; *Documents Illustrating the Crisis of 1297–8*, no. 90.
173 Denholm-Young, *Seignorial Administration*, 23–4.
174 Cotton, *Historia Anglicana*, 325. 175 *Guisborough*, 291.

Around Easter, a meeting was held in the Wyre Forest attended by four earls – Norfolk, Hereford, Warwick and Arundel – as well as the Marcher barons, Edmund Mortimer and John de Hastings.[176] According to the Evesham Chronicle, they agreed that they could not serve the king overseas because, whether speaking for themselves or for the broader political class, perhaps both, they claimed to be impoverished by a combination of frequent campaigning and royal taxes. Whatever was agreed in the Wyre Forest did not hold for very long. Norfolk was preparing in June to serve overseas, while Edward sought to assuage the money worries of Warwick, Arundel and Hastings. The Evesham chronicler sourly noted that Warwick was bribed into submission by the king but it is doubtful that either of them saw it this way; Warwick was far from being the wealthiest earl and Edward was merely ensuring that one of his most able commanders was able to accompany him.[177] By July, Warwick had returned to his natural position of support for the king and, although he was prevented by illness from sailing to Flanders himself, he sent his son and his military retinue with the king and himself served on Prince Edward's regency council.[178]

Arundel, too, had retreated from opposition by July and was making ultimately fruitless efforts to raise the necessary money to join the king's expedition to Flanders.[179] Although he did not go himself, he did provide 100 infantry from his Marcher lordship of Clun, showing that he had committed himself to the king, if rather half-heartedly.[180] Hastings did serve in Flanders with the king and without pay, although he did receive a £20 loan from the exchequer, which would have helped defray the expense of yet another campaign.[181] Mortimer, on the other hand, was cowed into submission. Using complaints against him by his Welsh tenants, Edward forced Mortimer to appear in parliament to defend himself and then made him grant concessionary charters to the Welsh.[182] In the face of this display of ruthlessness, Mortimer decided that discretion was the better part of valour and, although he did not go to Flanders himself, he clearly believed, like Arundel, that it was prudent to send men from his Marcher estates.[183]

Part of the reason Edward was so intransigent in 1297 was that he was an old man in a hurry. This feeling was doubtless exacerbated by the

[176] Denton, 'Evesham Chronicle', 576.
[177] Ibid., 576. [178] E 101/6/37, m. 7; *CCR 1296–1302*, 130.
[179] *CPR 1292–1301*, 289; *Documents Illustrating the Crisis of 1297–8*, no. 132.
[180] N.B. Lewis, 'The English Forces in Flanders, August–November 1297', in R.W. Hunt, W.A. Pantin and R.W. Southern (eds.), *Studies in Medieval History Presented to F.M. Powicke* (Oxford: Clarendon Press, 1948), 317.
[181] Ibid.; *Documents Illustrating the Crisis of 1297–8*, 7, no. 106.
[182] *CCR 1296–1302*, 107; *CPR 1292–1301*, 290–1. [183] Lewis, 'English Forces', 317.

deaths and illness of several of his earls in the previous two years: a point rammed home by the funeral of Edmund of Lancaster in Westminster Abbey during the middle of his dispute with Hereford and Norfolk in July 1297.[184] In addition to the comital deaths of 1295 and 1296, the earls of Cornwall, Warenne and Warwick were all in poor health in 1297. Both Cornwall and Warenne received grants from the king to be enacted in the contingency of their deaths, strongly suggesting that both men believed themselves to be gravely ill.[185] In Warenne's case, such an idea is backed up by Guisborough's report that he had failed to carry out his duties as guardian of Scotland because he felt unable to remain there on account of his health.[186] Despite his apparent illness, Cornwall lent his support to the regency council and was one of a select group of loyalist lords who were summoned on 5 September to a Michaelmas parliament.[187] Cornwall was also one of the government's chief creditors, having lent the king £6,560 by 1299.[188] Warenne, on the other hand, was more energetic. He was ordered to join Edward in Flanders and was negotiating to relinquish his office of guardian of Scotland in order to free himself for service overseas.[189] However, the deteriorating situation in Scotland forced Warenne to march north to put down the rebellion of William Wallace, which he signally failed to do. His failure, however, does not detract from the fact that Warenne was unequivocally in the king's camp during the crisis. Lincoln was fighting in Gascony and, though not available for service in Flanders, was anything but dissident.

By the end of July, then, while Norfolk and Hereford had taken up a hardening opposition stance, Edward had retained or regained the support of Cornwall, Warenne, Warwick and Arundel. But, while Edward had backing from these four earls, they all, for various reasons, were unable to join his expedition to Flanders. What the king really needed was concrete assistance to bolster numbers for an expedition for which he was finding it hard to recruit. Pierre Langtoft noted that no earls accompanied Edward to Flanders, but this does not tell the whole story.[190] Better still than the efforts made by Warenne, Warwick and Arundel to join the expedition was the fact that the heirs to three earldoms did actually go to Flanders, the first indication that Edward had little reason to fear a changing of the comital guard.[191] Of the ten men of comital status in 1297, Edward had the firm support of seven and was opposed by two, which leaves one, Oxford. He had only inherited his father's earldom in September 1296 and had been serving in Gascony at the time. He did not

[184] Trivet, *Annales*, 358. [185] *CPR 1292–1301*, 241, 300.
[186] *Guisborough*, 294. [187] *Parl Writs*, I, 55. [188] Prestwich, *Edward I*, 522.
[189] *Documents Illustrative of the History of Scotland*, II, no. 465; Spencer, 'John de Warenne', 47.
[190] *Langtoft*, II, 297. [191] E 101/6/37, mm. 5, 7, 8.

serve in Flanders, perhaps because he had already gone to the expense of serving in Gascony, but appears to have been supportive of the regency government during the crisis.[192] Thus, whatever else 1297 was, it was not a revolt of the king's leading subjects, as was the case in 1258 or 1311. At the outset of the baronial reform movement in 1258, only two earls had supported Henry III, while, at the time of the Ordinances of 1311 in the reign of Edward II, eight earls were in open opposition to the king.[193] The extent of Edward I's support is probably explained by the continuing sense of personal loyalty these men had to their king; others, not of comital rank and who knew the king only from a distance, might not have this. Moreover, several earls were isolated from complaints about Edward's policies by absence on military service or by illness and, when they did become aware of complaints, may have felt that their loyalty to the king and the justness of his cause outweighed other complaints. Edward's pleas of necessity to justify his demands, made on several occasions in 1297, were powerful arguments.[194]

So, how was Edward forced into concessions in 1297, if not by the earls? It has been suggested that opposition came principally from the Marchers. Both Rees Davies and Michael Prestwich have emphasised this element.[195] This argument is founded upon four points. First, that Hereford and Norfolk were Marcher lords; second, the meeting of disaffected Marcher lords at Easter in the Wyre Forest; third, that no important Marcher lord joined the Flanders expedition; and finally that the Remonstrances, the opposition's statement of grievances, included a complaint about violation of ancient franchises, something close to the heart of the Marchers.[196]

However, all these statements can be easily countered. First, the credentials of the two opposition earls as Marcher lords were ambivalent. Norfolk was lord of Chepstow, quite a small lordship worth only about £150 p.a., barely a tenth of the value of the greatest lordships.[197] Hereford's lordship of Brecon was much more valuable but, in the course of his quarrel with Gloucester, he had incurred the displeasure of other Marcher lords by breaking with the custom of the March and appealing directly to the king for justice.[198] Such a man could hardly portray himself as a convincing defender of Marcher liberties. Second, whatever was agreed at the Wyre Forest meeting, it quickly fell apart, with all those present, bar Hereford, making some preparations for

[192] *GEC*, x, 219. [193] *EHD 1189–1327*, 362; McKisack, *Fourteenth Century*, 10n.
[194] *EHD 1189–1327*, 477–80, 480–1, 482–3.
[195] Prestwich, *War, Politics and Finance*, 234; Davies, *Lordship and Society*, 268.
[196] *EHD 1189–1327*, 472. [197] Davies, *Lordship and Society*, 196.
[198] Altschul, *Baronial Family*, 150. See above, 218.

going to Flanders.[199] Third, the complaint in the Remonstrances about the violation of liberties was hardly specific to the Marches. Finally, Prestwich's claim that 'no important Marcher accompanied the king to Flanders' cannot be justified.[200] Of twenty-one active lay Marcher lords in 1297, only Norfolk and Hereford were in opposition to the king. The loyalty of three lords is uncertain, though, of these, both Edmund Mortimer and the earl of Arundel sent troops to Flanders. The remaining sixteen were certainly loyal to the king. Earl Warenne was in Scotland and the earl of Lincoln in Gascony. Also in Gascony was Roger Mortimer of Chirk.[201] Beyond this, Reginald de Grey, Guy de Brian and John Giffard were prominent loyalists in England.[202] This leaves nine lords, all of whom were in Flanders, including several of the greatest Marcher lords such as Henry of Lancaster, William de Braose, Peter Corbet and John de Hastings.[203] It is clear that, far from being a hotbed of opposition, the March of Wales was, as it had been for Edward since the 1260s, the bedrock of his support. Should one doubt the level of Edward's Marcher support, one only needs reflect upon the fact that, as well as providing almost 70 per cent of the infantry in Flanders, the Marchers furnished the king with his lieutenant in Gascony, his guardian of Scotland, the head of his regency council in England and the marshal of his army in Flanders.[204]

The groundswell of opposition to the king came not from the earls, the Marchers or the bulk of the baronage but from the English shires and the church. Prestwich has strongly disagreed with Bertie Wilkinson's observation that the language of the Remonstrances 'seems to be that of the smaller landholder rather than the earl'.[205] But, as G.L. Harriss points out, the Remonstrances, the opposition's propaganda statement produced in July, combined the grievances over taxation, military obligation and prise that had been building up over the previous three years, and represent 'an articulated attack on the doctrine of necessity'.[206] These were, he believed, the grievances of 'the generality of the knightly class',

[199] See above, 238. [200] Prestwich, *War, Politics and Finance*, 234.

[201] L. Smith, 'Mortimer, Roger (IV), First Lord Mortimer of Chirk (*c.*1256–1326), in *ODNB*.

[202] *Parl Writs*, I, 55, 296,

[203] Henry of Lancaster (C 67/12, m. 3); Hastings, Braose and Corbet (*CPR 1292–1301*, 314). The other lords were Geoffrey de Geneville of Ewyas Lacy (E 101/6/28, m. 1), William Fitz Martin of Cemais (*CPR 1292–1301*, 314), Ralph de Tony of Elfael (C 67/12, m. 9d), Geoffrey de Camville (*CPR 1292–1301*, 325) and Aymer de Valence, heir to Pembroke (E 101/6/28, m. 2).

[204] Lewis, 'English Forces', 317. Lincoln was the lieutenant of Gascony, Warenne was guardian of Scotland, Grey was head of the regency council and Geoffrey de Geneville was Edward's marshal in Flanders.

[205] B. Wilkinson, *Constitutional History of England, 1216–1399*, 3 vols. (London: Longman, 1948–58), I, 196; Prestwich, *Edward I*, 421.

[206] *EHD 1189–1327*, 469, 472; Harriss, *King, Parliament, and Public Finance*, 61.

and the evidence laid out above about where the king's demands fell heaviest tallies with this view.[207] It also mirrors the situation among the clergy, where it was the lower clergy and not the prelates who were most robust in their opposition to Edward's financial demands.[208]

Direct evidence of opposition in 1297 comes most strongly from the gentry, rather than the earls and other magnates. The muster of 7 July, to which all £20 landholders had been summoned, was a failure, and even Edward's offer of pay does not seem to have greatly broadened the appeal of service in Flanders. Only sixty-three men were added to the payroll in this way.[209] What transformed the opposition from passive resistance to active hostility was the eighth of 30 July 1297 that, according to one chronicler, was granted only by 'people standing round in his chamber'.[210] Prestwich has argued that it was the level of taxation and not its nature that aroused opposition but the anger that exploded when this tax was announced cannot simply be explained by the cumulative effect of Edward's other financial demands, though doubtless this was important.[211] The taxes of 1294–6 caused resentment but there was no undue opposition because they had been granted by the proper procedures and in full parliament. It can be no coincidence that widespread and open resistance to the king's financial demands came only when he had ignored the proper constitutional channels for obtaining the necessary consent.

Hereford, Norfolk and a group of their supporters appeared at the exchequer on 22 August in an attempt to prevent the collection of the tax and Hereford is reported to have said that the community of the realm would not accept being tallaged as though they were in bondage.[212] As Prestwich says, historians have been puzzled by the opposition's terminology of 'tallages', but Hereford's statement at the exchequer explains this.[213] Hereford called the eighth a tallage: a tax levied without consent like those upon serfs. Both the Remonstrances and *De Tallagio* (the opposition 'manifesto' at the Michaelmas parliament) make it clear that it was those burdens that had not been consented to that roused the most resentment: the prises of foodstuffs and wool, the *maltolt* and, above all, the eighth.[214] That Edward was aware that the collection of the eighth might be frustrated in the shires is clear from his appointment of outsiders to collect the tax in each county, unlike his practice for all previous

[207] Harriss, *King, Parliament, and Public Finance*, 60; see above, 230–2.

[208] Denton, *Winchelsey*, 74–5, 102–5. [209] *Documents Illustrating the Crisis of 1297–8*, 7.

[210] Ibid., no. 95; *Flores Historiarum*, III, 296.

[211] *Documents Illustrating the Crisis of 1297–8*, 9; Prestwich, *Edward I*, 421.

[212] *EHD 1189–1327*, 482. [213] Prestwich, *Edward I*, 421.

[214] *EHD 1189–1327*, 472, 486.

taxes.[215] By doing so, he was tacitly admitting the possibility that local opinion would pressurise local assessors into not collecting the tax properly, a damning self-assessment from the king of the level of support for his policies that he was expecting. Even such precautions did not prevent failure; on 9 September, the exchequer ordered the seizure of the goods of one of the collectors of Bedfordshire who, fully six weeks after his appointment, had still not taken up his duties.[216] When the two assessors attempted to collect the eighth in Worcestershire, the county community assembled at the county court informed them that they would grant no money until they received the liberties to which they were entitled under Magna Carta and the Forest Charter.[217] The writ for the eighth had included a promise to confirm the Charters but the reaction of the Worcestershire county court shows how far trust in Edward among lesser landholders had sunk by the early autumn of 1297. Edward's dissatisfaction with the performance of local officers in mobilising support for him is clear from the fact that eighteen out of the twenty-eight sheriffs were replaced during 1297–8, four of them twice, a rate of turnover greater than at any other time during the reign.[218]

At this point it is necessary to return to the earls' role in the opposition. What had given the gentry the will openly to oppose the king's policies was the leadership offered by the earls of Norfolk and Hereford. As with the clergy, without high-level leadership there could be no effective lay opposition. There is a similarity here with the situation in 1258. The grievances of the knightly class against Henry III's government were long-standing but Henry had succeeded in keeping a lid on magnate opposition by his laxity towards them until his support for the Lusignans, his hare-brained Sicilian scheme and his failure to contain the Welsh rebellion finally alienated a substantial proportion of his nobility, who began to give voice to the concerns about Henry's rule of the wider political community. Just as in 1297, gentry grievances could only be answered when there was leadership from the nobility. When that leadership was not there, or was taken away, as happened after 1302, the crown was able, if it wished, to ignore the grievances of the gentry, though in the long term such a policy was unwise. What is interesting for ideas about the development of the gentry as a political force, however, is that the lesser landholders in 1297 were so self-conscious and confident in their demands that they were able to press their demands with minimal magnate leadership, unlike in 1258 when it was not until virtually the

[215] *Parl Writs*, I, 53–4. [216] *Documents Illustrating the Crisis of 1297–8*, no. 136.
[217] Prestwich, *Edward I*, 426. [218] Evidence is taken from *List of Sheriffs*.

whole political establishment turned against Henry III and the Poitevins that the grievances of the gentry could be addressed.[219]

News of an opposition 'parliament', to be held at Northampton on 21 September, persuaded the regency council that civil war was probable and they made frantic preparations to face a force that Guisborough estimated at 1,500 mounted men.[220] Ironically, they were saved by Earl Warenne's defeat at Stirling Bridge on 11 September. This reminded everyone that there was a greater enemy to be confronted. Unlike his father or son, Edward I had many years of good governance to fall back upon and still maintained the support of much of his nobility. Military disaster at Stirling thus helped to prevent a political crisis, whereas Henry III's disasters in Wales in 1257 and Edward II's humiliation at Bannockburn in 1314 precipitated political crises.

This did not mean, of course, that grievances were forgotten but the earls on both sides helped to calm the situation sufficiently to achieve a compromise. Norfolk and Hereford secured pardons for themselves, their followers and all those £20 landholders who had ignored the muster of 7 July.[221] They also won considerable concessions, including the confirmation of the Charters, the abolition of the *maltolt*, promises that prises would not become customary and that taxes would not be levied without 'the common assent of all the realm', and that there would be a perambulation of the royal forests.[222] It was the royalist earls and councillors around Prince Edward, the nominal regent, who recognised that concessions were necessary, and presented the absent king with a fait accompli that spared his blushes. They helped to smooth things over again in the coming months. In January, Warenne secured the support of Norfolk and Hereford to join his campaign against the Scots by agreeing that the bishop of Carlisle should pronounce excommunication on all those who might infringe Magna Carta.[223] After Edward returned, the royalist earls again helped to bring the king and his opponents together for the benefit of the kingdom. The muster at Roxburgh was held in an atmosphere of mutual suspicion, it being the first time the king had seen the opposition earls since he had summarily dismissed them the previous July. They demanded that he immediately and publicly keep the promises he had made while in Flanders but Edward was unwilling to allow

[219] See D.A. Carpenter, 'What Happened in 1258?', in Carpenter, *Reign of Henry III*, 183–97.

[220] *CCR 1296–1302*, 59, 61; *Parl Writs*, I, 296–7; *Guisborough*, 290. Unfortunately, there is no direct evidence of who might have been at this parliament, but an indication of the magnates present may be forthcoming from the list of opposition lords summoned by the government to a Michaelmas parliament. *Parl Writs*, I, 56.

[221] *EHD 1189–1327*, 487. [222] Ibid., 486–7; Prestwich, *Edward I*, 427–9.

[223] *Langtoft*, II, 307–9; *Guisborough*, 314.

Table 8.3 *Comital witnesses to royal charters, 26–9 Edward I*

Regnal year	Total	Gloucester	Hereford[a]	Lancaster	Lincoln	Warenne	Norfolk	Cornwall	Valence	Warwick
26	13	0	1	3	6	5	1	1	0	1
27	35	0	6	6	21	15	11	0	5	8
28	41	2	5	24	29	31	12	0	0	4
29	54	3	0	16	4	41	14	0	19	39
Total	143	5	12	49	60	92	38	1	24	52

[a] From 27 Edward I the earl of Hereford was Humphrey III de Bohun (d. 1322).

himself to be held to ransom. It took the intervention of the royalist earls, Lincoln, Warenne and the new earl of Gloucester, to ensure that the campaign could proceed. They swore that, if victory was obtained, then the king would grant the opposition's demands.[224] They seemed to realise what was best for the king, even if he did not see it himself.

The three years after Falkirk demonstrate that, as in 1297, Edward retained the loyalty and support of most of the earls but faced opposition, resistance and recalcitrance from those further down the social scale and from the clergy. That the opposition remained coherent was because of the leadership of Norfolk and Archbishop Winchelsey. Table 8.3 shows that Edward maintained close contact with several earls during these difficult years, particularly with the old guard of Warenne and Lincoln, but also with the younger generation such as Lancaster and Warwick. However, also among the younger generation was Hereford's heir who, apparently urged on by his dying father, gave his backing to Norfolk and the opposition when he inherited the earldom at the beginning of 1299.[225] This may explain his infrequent witnessing in this period. More concrete examples of comital support for Edward can also be found. Following the Falkirk campaign, the king attempted to regain the initiative by launching a commission of inquiry into abuses committed by royal officials, a recycling of tactics that had been effective earlier in the reign, and Warenne and Lincoln were two of those appointed.[226] Valence and Lincoln were both involved in diplomatic missions to the king of France and the pope in 1299 and 1300.[227] Edmund of Cornwall demonstrated his continuing support for his cousin with loans totalling almost 12,000 marks in 1298 and 1299.[228]

[224] *Guisborough*, 324; Prestwich, *Edward I*, 518. The earl of Gloucester was Ralph de Monthermer; see above, 233.

[225] *Guisborough*, 329–30. [226] *CPR 1292–1301*, 373–4.

[227] Ibid., 415, 538. [228] *CPR 1301–1307*, 463.

Why, then, with only Norfolk and young Hereford among the earls still in opposition to the king between 1298 and 1301, was the king so much on the defensive during these years, and why was he forced to make further concessions in both 1300 and 1301? The answer is the fierce opposition he still faced from the clergy and the gentry. Archbishop Winchelsey, stubborn in his defence of clerical liberties, was a constant thorn in Edward's side. Once the Scots were expelled from England, Winchelsey refused to countenance any further collection of the clerical tenth, judging that the necessity to defend the realm had already been met.[229] Denton has shown just how 'closely and directly' Winchelsey and the clergy were involved in the 'struggle for the charters' in these years and they doubtless gave spiritual and moral support to the king's lay opponents.[230] Like Norfolk, Winchelsey seems to have seen himself as 'defending the common interests of the realm' against the king's excesses: saving the king from himself.[231]

The key issue of contention in these years was that of the royal forest, an issue that vexed the gentry far more than the magnates. At the parliament of March 1299, the king's opponents, led by Norfolk, and numbering, it was estimated, as many as a thousand horsemen, demanded that the king confirm the charters, something he made every effort to avoid.[232] When finally he did so, Edward caused outrage by omitting a whole section of the Forest Charter, including the part dealing with a perambulation.[233] The *Articuli Super Cartas*, issued on 28 March 1300, did not serve to resolve the tension between Edward and the gentry because he maintained stipulations on the terms of the perambulation.[234] Edward's tactic of offering inquiries to salve his subjects' grievances, so successful earlier in his reign, was no longer working.

Parliament was only one means for the gentry to register their frustration with the king's continued intransigence. What hurt him most was their refusal to accede to his military demands. Edward had planned a winter campaign in late 1299, setting out for Scotland after his wedding to Margaret of France in the company of most of the earls. His design was scuppered, not by them, for even Norfolk sent John de Segrave to act in his stead, but by the gentry. They neither came themselves nor helped to raise sufficient numbers of infantry and the whole campaign was humiliatingly cancelled.[235] The contrast between the continuing support the king had from his earls and the complete lack of aid from the gentry is stark and reveals just how detached many of the earls were from

[229] Denton, *Winchelsey*, 173–4. [230] Ibid., 188–92.
[231] Ibid., 192. [232] *Guisborough*, 329–30; *Chronicle of Bury St Edmunds*, 151–2.
[233] *Guisborough*, 330. [234] Morris, *GTK*, 322–3. [235] Ibid., 321.

the sentiments of most of their gentry neighbours. Edward experienced similar problems raising knights and infantry for the Scottish campaign of 1300, which achieved little more than the capture of Caerlaverock Castle.[236] The earls too were struggling to find men-at-arms. Between the seven earls on campaign, only 101 men-at-arms are known to have been in their retinues.[237] This compares poorly to the 250 and 264 men-at-arms in comital retinues in the campaigns in Wales during 1294–5 and Falkirk in 1298 respectively.[238] Across the country, participation rates among the gentry fell sharply after the Falkirk campaign.[239] The concessions wrung from Edward in 1301 demonstrate again that those he needed to conciliate were not his greatest subjects but the gentry. These concessions, on the king's right of prise, to increments above the county farm and the perambulation of the forest, were overwhelmingly their concerns, not those of the magnates.[240]

This was the low point in Edward I's reign but it is clear that, although the years 1294–1301 had severely strained the king's relations with his subjects, almost to breaking point, he had, for the most part, been much more successful in retaining the backing of his earls. No others had joined Norfolk and Hereford in open opposition. For the most part, the earls, both young and old had clung to the king. Personal affection and loyalty to Edward undoubtedly played their part in this, and for the younger earls probably a sense of awe towards a king who was already a legendary figure, but there was also a real sense of dislocation between most of the earls and the gentry's concerns. As noted above, their frequent military, diplomatic and administrative service for the king kept them away from their estates and neighbours for long periods of time, so they may not have been aware of the extent of the resentment Edward's policies had built up. The fact that very few of their *familiares* held local public offices would also have meant that they had no direct knowledge of the resentment and resistance the king's officials were coming up against.[241] Furthermore, their wealth insulated many of them from the worst financial effects of Edward's demands and, when some of them felt the pinch, they were able to gain concessions.[242]

[236] Morris, *GTK*, 323–4. [237] C 67/14, mm. 8–15.

[238] C 67/10; *Gough, passim*. The surviving records for the Caerlaverock campaign are not particularly extensive and the number of men-at-arms in comital retinues is consequently somewhat understated: indeed the numbers enrolled with letters of protection for service with the earls of Lancaster and Gloucester seem particularly low, but the shortfall in the 1300 numbers is too great to be explained by simple under-reporting.

[239] Spencer, 'Warlike People', 98, 100, 101.

[240] Harriss, *King, Parliament, and Public Finance*, 104–6; Prestwich, *Edward I*, 525–6.

[241] See above, 136–43. [242] See above, 230–2.

Norfolk and the elder earl of Hereford, although by no means excluded, had not been in the king's company earlier in the reign as frequently as many of the other earls and therefore, perhaps, had a sense of detachment that these others did not. Also their hereditary offices gave them a different perspective on the novelty of some of Edward's military demands and provided them with a sense of duty to make representations on behalf of the community of the realm. By alienating them in the way he did, by attacking them personally, he fostered their sense of importance and provided totemic figures for the gentry to gather around to express their discontent. Leaderless, the gentry were unable to resist the king's majesty but, through Norfolk and Hereford, their complaints could be funnelled, magnified and addressed, as could those of the clergy through Winchelsey.[243] The royalist earls helped to prevent civil war by mediating between the king and his opponents, upholding royal authority on the one hand, and making concessions the king could not or would not make on the other. As for Edward himself, his crusading ambitions had been temporarily thwarted, though they remained very much in his mind, but his immediate concerns in 1301 were to reverse the concessions he had been forced to make since 1297, to regain possession of Gascony and to complete the conquest and pacification of Scotland.[244] These would provide the battlegrounds for the last conflicts of Edward I's life.

AN OLD MAN IN A HURRY: 1301–1307

Little had gone right for Edward I in the five years following his easy victory over King John Balliol of Scotland in 1296, but in 1301 the obstacles to success one by one began to be reduced or dissipated altogether. Power started to flow back to the king. The significant concessions he had made in 1301 seem to have appeased the gentry and Edward's financial demands slackened following the grant of the fifteenth in 1301.[245] The difficulties he had in obtaining this tax appear to have persuaded him that it was not worth the effort to try to extract parliamentary taxes on the scale he had between 1294 and 1297. Although the campaign against the Scots in 1301 had ended in another frustrating stalemate, the king's diplomatic efforts were beginning to bear fruit. The ever-trustworthy Lincoln headed an important embassy to the king of France in October 1301, which secured a truce with the French that excluded the Scots, effectively giving Edward a free hand in Scotland.[246] The catastrophic French

[243] For the importance of leadership among the clergy, see Denton, *Winchelsey*, 70, 95.
[244] For his continuing crusading ambitions, see Morris, *GTK*, 353.
[245] Prestwich, *Edward I*, 528–9. [246] *CPR 1292–1301*, 608; Morris, *GTK*, 336.

defeat at Courtrai the following summer crushed any lingering Scottish hopes that the French would come to their aid and obviated the need for Edward to spend money on further expeditions overseas.[247]

The Scots were not alone among those the king counted as his enemies to find themselves isolated after 1301. Edward's appeasement of gentry grievances in 1301 deprived those who had led the lay opposition of much of the support that had made them such formidable opponents since 1297. Archbishop Winchelsey retained, at least for the time being, strong support within the church for his defence of ecclesiastical rights but the noble leaders of the gentry opposition found their position undercut by Edward's concessions.[248] The king's handling of the two earldoms that had led the opposition, Hereford and Norfolk, reveal both his political skill and his vindictiveness towards those who opposed his will, two defining characteristics of his reign.

Most vulnerable was Norfolk. Since the death of Hereford in December 1298, Norfolk had been the undisputed leader of the lay opposition. He had spent large amounts of money in maintaining his stance and, by the end of 1301, seems to have financially and politically exhausted himself.[249] In April 1302 a deal was struck between Norfolk and the king, whereby, in return for a life grant of lands and rents worth £1,000 p.a., the earl surrendered the reversion of his entire inheritance, save a few manors he could bestow at will, to the crown.[250] It has recently been argued by Morris that this was not an example of an earldom being 'murdered' by the crown but was a mutually satisfactory accommodation between the two parties.[251] He suggests that both men needed to make the deal, Norfolk to restore his finances and Edward to provide for the future demands of his growing family. Certainly both these motives must have been part of the impetus behind the events of April 1302 but the naked reality was less consensual. While both sides played nice in public, what actually seems to have happened was that Edward took advantage of Norfolk's financial problems and political isolation to take his revenge and appropriate the earldom of Norfolk in the interests of the crown. The *Flores Historiarum* goes as far as to say that Edward summoned Norfolk to Westminster and accused him of treason, forcing him to sign away his earldom or face the consequences.[252]

[247] *Langtoft*, II, 341. [248] Denton, *Winchelsey*, 204.

[249] McFarlane, *Nobility*, 251, 262; Morris, *Bigod Earls*, 175–9.

[250] *CPR 1301–1307*, 29–30. [251] Morris, 'Murder'.

[252] *Flores Historiarum*, III, 125. There is some confusion about to which earl the chronicler was referring, but it is clear from the context that it was Norfolk and not Warwick as mentioned in some manuscripts.

There are problems with the account in the *Flores* but it is hard to credit that a great earl would sign away his family's inheritance, painstakingly built up over two-and-a-half centuries, purely in response to short-term financial difficulties, particularly when his eventual heir, John Bigod of Stockton, was a close member of his entourage. John Bigod was compensated with the manor of Settrington in Yorkshire and was a witness to the agreement, but it can have caused him little satisfaction given the scale of the inheritance that was being snatched from him.[253] Much of the detail of the *Flores* story is wrong, not least the fact that the author places the events in 1305, around the time the deal was re-confirmed, rather than 1302, when it actually took place.[254] It may be, however, that the Westminster monk placed the story in 1305 because he linked it with the suspension of Archbishop Winchelsey, which did take place in that year.[255] The two events were of a piece in his mind, both examples of the king's revenge on his enemies of 1297, and therefore he related them both at the same point. The author's Westminster base weighs heavily in favour of his account and it seems to fit the 'court' view of events. This view, that Norfolk was forced into it, is implicit in the *Annals of London*, which makes the king's future inheritance of the earl's estates the condition by which '*facti sunt amici*'.[256] Writing a few years later, the well-connected author of the *Vita Edwardi Secundi* had no doubt why Norfolk, whom he brackets with Robert de Ferrers and Simon de Montfort, made the deal. 'Each of these resisted the king', he wrote, 'and each of them in the end succumbed.' Reflecting on Thomas of Lancaster's opposition to Edward II, he warned that '[i]t is not safe to rise up against the king, because the outcome is often likely to be unfortunate'.[257] It is not surprising that this court view quickly became established, given the pains Edward went to in publicising Norfolk's surrender of his estates. The escheator was ordered to take all Norfolk's castles, manors and lands into his possession and to 'take the fealties of the free tenants and others thereof', while the justiciar in Ireland was told to retain Norfolk's estates there for forty days so that the king's possession of them 'be notorious' before restoring them to the earl.[258] Norfolk, and everyone associated with him, was to be left in no doubt who was the master now.

[253] Morris, 'Murder', 95. [254] Ibid., 92–3, 96.

[255] *Flores Historiarum*, III, 125–6.

[256] *Chronicles of the Reigns of Edward I and Edward II*, I, 127. Morris argues that the chronicler believed that 'the deal was an amicable one', but though the outcome may have been friendly relations between the two men, the conditional nature of the chronicler's words suggests that the impulse for it was not.

[257] *Vita Edwardi Secundi*, 77. [258] *CFR 1272–1307*, 452.

Edward certainly murdered the Bigod earldom of Norfolk in an expression of authoritarian vindictiveness of which his Angevin forebears would have been proud. By contrast, his treatment of the earldom of Hereford shows the kind of deft political management that McFarlane believed he eschewed. On 9 October 1302, the young earl surrendered his estates to the king, receiving them back the next month, following his marriage to Edward's daughter, Elizabeth.[259] McFarlane saw this of a piece with the king's other transactions in providing for his relatives at the expense of the relatives of his earls.[260] As argued above, however, there is no need to see the marriage in such a negative light and it can be seen rather as evidence of reconciliation between Edward and the Bohuns.[261] Given that Elizabeth was just twenty, the risk of the marriage not producing children was relatively low, but the rewards for Hereford were potentially great: by becoming the king's son-in-law he enhanced his standing and his potential to receive rewards from the king.[262] Relations between the two men improved greatly after the marriage and Hereford became one of the earls closest to Edward. The charter witness lists demonstrate this point vividly: Tables 8.3 and 8.4 show that in the four years between 27 and 30 Edward I, Hereford witnessed 16 out of 181 charters (8.83 per cent), while in the last five years of the reign, he witnessed 237 of 346 charters (68.5 per cent), a quite remarkable turnaround. Hereford's greatest reward came in 1306 with the grant of the lordship of Annandale in Scotland, which was confiscated from Robert Bruce following his rebellion, and it is unlikely that such a prize would have been given had he not been the king's son-in-law.[263] Both sides must have regarded the marriage as an unqualified success and, rather than view it as an attack on the earldom, it should be seen as a masterstroke of conciliation on Edward's part.

Is it possible to reconcile the contrasting treatment meted out by Edward to the earls of Norfolk and Hereford as part of a consistent strategy on the part of the king? The answer should be yes. Edward's policy towards earldoms is clear and consistent: they should be used to strengthen the interests of the crown. Norfolk and the older earl of Hereford had, from Edward's perspective, failed to do this. Norfolk's circumstances, his straitened finances and lack of an heir of his body, provided the king

[259] Ibid., 458–9; *CChR 1300–1326*, 33.

[260] McFarlane, *Nobility*, 261. [261] See above, 42.

[262] Of course, Elizabeth's youth did mean that there was the chance of her marrying again should Hereford die young. If Hereford and Elizabeth had no children then she would have passed part of the Bohun inheritance to her children by a third marriage. The Bohuns were a fecund family, however, and Humphrey must have felt the risk was a calculated one.

[263] *Calendar of Documents Relating to Scotland*, IV, 473.

with the opportunity to divert the resources of the earldom in another direction, that of Edward's son Thomas of Brotherton. In the hands of a member of the royal family, such as Thomas, the earldom would, Edward assumed, given the exemplary record of his own brother, cousin and uncle, be employed to bolster the interests and policies of the crown under Edward II. Young Hereford's situation, on the other hand, was more complicated. He was undoubtedly his father's heir, so there was no way in which Edward could legitimately deny him the earldom. A different tactic would have to be employed if the resources of the earldom of Hereford were to serve the crown's purposes better. Reconciliation was the tactic Edward chose in this instance to further his overall strategy and there is no doubt that it worked. His ability to use different tactics, depending upon circumstances, to achieve similar ends in these two cases is a perfect illustration of the fusion of masterfulness and political management that embodied Edward I's kingship and made it so successful in restoring royal authority.

It was a challenge to an earlier manifestation of this policy that helped to undermine the position of Archbishop Winchelsey. John de Ferrers was the son and heir of the unfortunate Robert de Ferrers, earl of Derby, who had been disinherited by Edmund of Lancaster in 1269, with the connivance of Lord Edward and much of the royalist establishment. Robert de Ferrers had tried, without success, to obtain justice through the king's courts in 1275 but Lancaster's extortion was upheld and the prospects of restoration seemingly closed off.[264] There was, however, one possible route still open to them and in 1300, encouraged by his 'special friend' Archbishop Winchelsey, John de Ferrers appealed to the pope for the restoration of his inheritance.[265] This was, of course, at the height of the king's political difficulties and Ferrers, aided by Winchelsey, seems to have viewed this as the best chance he would get to overturn the injustices of 1269 and 1275. The man who possessed Ferrers' estates at this time was the king's nephew, Thomas of Lancaster. In the spring of 1301 Lancaster was summoned by Winchelsey to be at St Paul's on 24 April to defend himself before the archbishop's deputies, to whom Winchelsey had, in turn, delegated the sole authority granted to him by the pope to hear the case. John de Ferrers was claiming that, by extracting more from the Ferrers' lands than the original debt of £50,000, Edmund and Thomas of Lancaster were guilty of usury, a crime pursuable in the church courts. Lancaster immediately sought, and obtained, his uncle's aid, and a royal

[264] See above, 197, 199.

[265] *Registrum Roberti Winchelsey*, ed. R. Graham, 2 vols., Canterbury and York Society (1952–6), II, 566–7; Denton, *Winchelsey*, 205–6.

prohibition against hearing a case affecting lay fees in church courts was handed to Winchelsey by the earl's messenger on 26 May. Despite this, hearings took place at St Paul's on 30 May and 27 June 1301, before the case was referred back to Rome. This defiance of a royal prohibition was a grave error on the part of both Ferrers and the archbishop, as it laid them open to charges of contumacy against the king. Lancaster duly brought just such a case against Winchelsey in King's Bench. Ferrers was warned by Edward not to proceed 'on the pain of all he can forfeit' in August 1301, and in December the sheriff of Northamptonshire was ordered to produce Ferrers before the king to explain why he had done so.[266] In Trinity term 1302 Ferrers was left with no choice but complete surrender: accepting that the papal bull against Lancaster had no force and claiming that he had not known that by acquiring the bull he had acted against the king's dignity. In return for this comprehensive retreat, Ferrers obtained a pardon of the king's special grace.[267] Edward had proved determined to uphold the judgment of his courts regarding the Ferrers inheritance and ensured that the earldom's resources remained firmly in the hands of his nephew. The moves by Ferrers and Winchelsey to undo this threatened not only the royal dignity, something always likely to inflame Edward's ire, but also his policy, hence his swift and decisive response.

As well as deepening the hostility between the king and his archbishop, the Ferrers case only served to isolate Winchelsey from the nobility. It had threatened to set a dangerous precedent whereby cases concerning lay fees might be heard in church courts, and the nobles doubtless would have been pleased that the king saw fit to prohibit this. As well as offending the nobility in the general sense, Winchelsey had particularly offended Thomas of Lancaster, of course, but also probably Lincoln, who was Lancaster's father-in-law and would certainly have been concerned about the diminution of his daughter's estate. In February 1299 Winchelsey had described Lincoln as his 'most special friend' ('*amico specialissimo*') but in 1305 the earl was part of the embassy to the pope that secured the archbishop's suspension from office as well as the revocation of the *Confirmatio* and *Articuli*.[268] Winchelsey had also incurred the wrath of Guy Beauchamp, earl of Warwick, over interference in the question of the latter's marriage.[269] Winchelsey was building up a formidable array of enemies among the high nobility and it comes as little surprise that, when the king moved against him in October 1305, not a single earl spoke up for him.

[266] *CCR 1296–1302*, 496, 571. [267] KB 27/168, m. 10; 27/169, m. 24d.

[268] *Registrum Roberti Winchelsey*, I, 306; *CPR 1301–1307*, 380, 387.

[269] Denton, *Winchelsey*, 207.

Moving to the larger issue, Edward had painstakingly ensured that all the earls were on board at the moment he threw off the *Confirmatio*. In this he had learned from his father's mistakes. Henry III's restoration of power and overthrow of the Provisions of Oxford in 1261, although ultimately successful, was clumsy, drawn-out and provoked widespread baronial opposition (not least from Lord Edward himself) that nearly tipped the country into civil war in the late autumn of that year.[270] There was no repeat of this in 1305. Lincoln was, as has been related, part of the embassy that sought to undo the *Confirmatio* and *Articuli*. As early as March 1305 Edward had taken steps to ensure that Norfolk would not resume his opposition. Having broken Norfolk's will through his masterfulness in 1302, Edward was now prepared to use a little political management to ensure that the earl remained pliant. On 14 March 1305 Edward pardoned all Norfolk's considerable debts to the exchequer, thereby resolving an issue that had long vexed the earl and at the same time confirmed the arrangements made in 1302.[271] This seems to have been enough to keep the earl happy and he even condescended to attend the autumn parliament at Westminster, at which the embassy to the pope was commissioned, where he witnessed his last royal charter, on 20 October 1305, the first he had witnessed since November 1302.[272]

Once again the charter witness lists provide further evidence for those earls around Edward at this crucial time and they show how effectively he had worked. Hereford witnessed twenty-five of the twenty-nine royal charters issued between the end of May and early November 1305, further emphasising the success of Edward's policy of reconciliation towards him.[273] In the same period, Aymer de Valence witnessed twenty-one charters;[274] Ralph de Monthermer, earl of Gloucester, six.[275] Warwick witnessed only three, but around this time he is mentioned as a member of the king's council and so was almost certainly aware of the king's plans.[276] All the politically active earls were thus in close touch with Edward during the summer and autumn of 1305, the months during which he was planning to overturn his concessions of 1297 and 1301. The only exception was Thomas of Lancaster, who was distracted by a violent dispute with the prior of Tutbury but whose loyalty the king had no reason to doubt.[277]

But, while Edward had learned the lesson of his father's mistake in 1261 of trying to undo unwanted reforms without first securing the

[270] For an overview of these events, see Maddicott, *Simon de Montfort*, 210–15.

[271] *CPR 1301–1307*, 317.

[272] *Royal Charter Witness Lists of Edward I*, nos. 33.15, 30.01.

[273] Ibid., nos. 33.29, 28, 25–14, 12–1.

[274] Ibid., nos. 33.29–26, 20–17, 14, 12–1.

[275] Ibid., nos. 33.14, 12–10, 7, 4.

[276] Ibid., nos. 33.23–1; *CCR 1302–1307*, 334.

[277] *CPR 1301–1307*, 353, 405–6; SC 1/21/17.

Table 8.4 *Comital witnesses to royal charters, 30–5 Edward I*

Regnal year	Total	Gloucester	Hereford[a]	Lancaster	Lincoln	Warenne	Norfolk	Valence	Warwick
30	51	8	5	13	13	43	10	32	3
31	49	20	36	29	5	40	0	4	26
32	109	97	98	91	49	25	0	54	88
33	78	26	67	11	48	0	1	53	22
34	39	10	24	20	25	1	0	23	5
35	71	3	11	22	54	6	0	9	30
Total	397	164	241	186	194	115	11	175	174

[a] From 27 Edward I the earl of Hereford was Humphrey III de Bohun (d. 1322).

consent of the high nobility, he appears to have forgotten the lessons that he himself had learned from the years of Reform and Rebellion. Whereas in the early years of his reign Edward had adopted much of the rhetoric and substance of the reformers and, in doing so, had strengthened the relationship between the crown and the gentry, now he desired nothing less than the complete overthrow of the concessions he had made to the gentry opposition of the years 1297 to 1301.[278] While the nobility were carefully brought to his side by the king, the gentry, now stripped of essential magnate leadership, were abandoned and their resentments left to fester. This pool of unresolved grievances, poisoned further by the king's perfidy, was Edward's most toxic legacy to his son: even more than the unfinished war in Scotland, which the nobility at least had no qualms about continuing. Once Edward had been replaced by a successor with a fraction of his ability, the gentry did not have to wait long for new leaders to emerge among the nobility, men who had become dissatisfied with Edward II's kingship. The programme they adopted was that of the opposition of 1297–1301: seven of the eleven clauses of the Statute of Stamford in 1309 were taken directly or indirectly from the *Articuli* of 1300.[279]

It was not just the support of the nobility, however, that gave Edward the confidence to seek to overturn his concessions to reform. By 1305 it seemed as if he had finally overcome Scottish resistance and established himself as the true master of Britain. It is not surprising that, once he had done so, he sought to restore his untrammelled authority within

[278] Maddicott, 'Lessons of Baronial Reform'.

[279] Maddicott, *Thomas of Lancaster*, 97–8. For the text of the articles, see *Select Documents of English Constitutional History, 1307–1485*, eds. S.B. Chrimes and A.L. Brown (London: A and C. Black, 1961), no. 5.

England. The earls had already proved vital in his efforts to bring Scotland to heel in the long campaign of 1303–4, where six had served.[280] When war restarted in 1306, after Robert Bruce's murder of John Comyn in Dumfries, the earls again turned out in force for their king: seven of them participated in the campaign of 1306.[281] In keeping the earls committed, Edward demonstrated his skills with the tools of patronage, though, as often, at no great cost to himself. Their efforts were rewarded with lavish grants of land in Scotland, particularly after 1306.[282] In addition to this, between 1305 and his death in July 1307, the king also pardoned all the debts of the earls of Norfolk, Lancaster, Arundel and Warenne, as well as the Anglo-Irish earl of Ulster.[283] It is possible to interpret these pardons as evidence of the weakness of Edward's position: that he needed to make them to shore up support for his unending war in Scotland. There is certainly evidence that Edward was struggling to maintain service in Scotland on the part of the gentry, as will be discussed shortly, but this does not seem to be the case regarding the earls. The pardoning of Norfolk's debts was done from a position of political strength, while Lancaster's pardon came specifically in return for good service already done in Scotland.[284] In the cases of Warenne and Arundel, these pardons were clearing the financial decks at the beginning of the earls' careers to allow them to provide military service unencumbered by debt. This had, in the case of Arundel's father in particular, been a significant restraint on service in the past.[285]

But, while the earls remained committed to the Scottish war, thanks, in part, to the landed stake the king had given many of them in it, the same cannot be said of the gentry. Recent work has shown that Edward found it hard to maintain gentry enthusiasm for his campaigns in Scotland after the Falkirk campaign in 1298, in large part because of the huge demands of cash, resources and men he made of them.[286] Although Edward managed to arrest the decline somewhat for his monumental campaign of conquest in 1303–4, participation all across England showed an alarmingly steep decline when he raised forces to fight Robert Bruce in 1306 and 1307.[287] The earls too were again finding it hard to recruit as many men for their retinues as they had before. The number of men who can be definitely shown to be in comital retinues for the years 1303–4 and

[280] See above, Table 3.1.
[281] For Bruce, see G.W.S. Barrow, *Robert Bruce and the Community of the Realm of Scotland*, 3rd edn (Edinburgh University Press, 1988), 146–8; see above, Table 3.1.
[282] See above, 90. [283] See above, 92. [284] *CPR 1301–1307*, 468.
[285] See above, 229–30, 238 [286] Spencer, 'Warlike People'.
[287] Ibid., 98, 100, 101.

1306 was well below that for the campaign of 1295 in Wales and the Falkirk campaign, for instance.[288]

Noel Denholm-Young wrote that Edward II 'sat down to the game of kingship with a remarkably poor hand, and he played it very badly', and there is much truth to this.[289] Edward left debts in excess of £200,000, a war in Scotland with no end in sight and a deeply impaired relationship with the wider community of the realm. All this had been manageable while the old king was alive, in large part simply because of who he was and the fierce strength of his personality, will and political skill: it was not a situation that could last much beyond his death. This is not to say, however, that Edward II's situation was quite as hopeless as Denholm-Young believed, particularly in the case of the crown's relations with the nobility. John Maddicott made the point in his biography of Thomas of Lancaster that 'in 1307 the baronage was very largely loyal to the Crown'.[290] Time and again in the 1290s and early 1300s Edward I had been able to rely on his earls and barons when he was in political difficulties and the earls were as loyal to him in 1307 as their fathers had been at any time over the previous thirty-five years. Table 8.4 demonstrates that no fewer than six earls witnessed over 44 per cent of royal charters in the last half-dozen years of Edward's reign, a remarkably high level of attestation. For the king to have forged links with the new generation of earls so successfully was a rare achievement: kings from William the Conqueror to Richard II often ran into difficulty when they were dealing with nobles who were predominantly of a different generation from their own. Through symbolic events like the Feast of the Swans, Edward had tried to foster a sense of comradeship between his heir and his nobles, but he had also tried to develop more prosaic links with the nobility for his son by appointing young Edward to military command, while surrounding him with a mixture of experienced soldiers from among the nobility, like Lincoln, and men nearer his own age, like Hereford.[291]

As his strength began to fail him, Edward relied increasingly on his earls to conduct the war in his absence. The earl of Richmond was appointed guardian of Scotland in 1306, while the earls of Gloucester and Hereford, together with Aymer de Valence, commanded the royal army in Scotland during the winter of 1306.[292] The trust Edward I retained in

288 The seven comital retinues in 1303–4 had 84 known men-at-arms in them, while in 1306, the seven comital retinues had 115 men-at-arms. This compares to 313 men-at-arms in comital retinues at Falkirk.

289 *The Life of Edward the Second*, ed. N. Denholm-Young (London: Nelson Press, 1957), ix.

290 Maddicott, *Thomas of Lancaster*, 68.

291 Phillips, *Edward II*, 88.

292 Watson, *Under the Hammer*, 217; *CCR 1302–1307*, 524.

his earls and those magnates who had served him so faithfully in Scotland is demonstrated by the story in the *Brut* chronicle describing his deathbed. The king called to his bedside the earls of Lincoln and Warwick, Aymer de Valence, Henry Percy and Robert Clifford and entrusted them with the welfare of his son and heir.[293] Whether the story has any basis in fact cannot be known but it has the ring of truth about it. These five men had been among the most important figures in the Scottish wars but, while the story shows clearly the bonds of trust between them and Edward I, it also hints at the fears the dying king may have had about his son's willingness and ability to complete the work the old king was leaving unfinished. Perhaps part of Edward II's problem, however, was that the earls and nobles bequeathed to him by his father, although they were mostly of his own generation, were never truly *his* nobles: they would always remain in awe of Edward I and his achievements, and they grew ever more frustrated at Edward II's inability and unwillingness to finish the job in Scotland and his reliance on the one man who really was his: Piers Gaveston. This is speculation beyond the limits of what the sources say but it is surely significant that so many Ordainers were among Edward I's most trusted lieutenants and counsellors.[294] Robert Clifford, Hugh de Vere and six of the eight earls who were Ordainers were among Edward I's closest associates before 1307.[295] These were not potential dissidents who had been held in check only by Edward I's domineering personality: they were the Edwardian establishment. They were all ready to serve another king like Edward I. Instead, they saw Edward II squander his father's legacy and their own prospects in Scotland. In his last years Edward I had an old man's urgency; Edward II proved to be a young man lacking such urgency and he incurred the wrath and intense frustration of his earls accordingly.

[293] *The Brut*, vol. 1, ed. F.W.D. Brie, Early English Text Society, Original Series 131 (1906), 202–3.

[294] McKisack, *Fourteenth Century*, 10n.

[295] Lincoln, Lancaster, Richmond, Warwick, Hereford and Aymer de Valence, now earl of Pembroke.

CONCLUSION

> When even they [the earls and barons], like the king, are without bridle, then will the subjects cry out and say 'Lord Jesus, bind fast their jaws in rein and bridle.'
>
> Bracton, *De Legibus Et Consuetudinibus Angliæ*[1]

In his reign Edward I did indeed seek to bridle his nobility, and they, shocked by the events of Lewes, Evesham and elsewhere, saw the wisdom of renewed royal authority wielded by a man who had learned the lessons of his father's mistakes. Edward bridled his earls not through 'confrontation and compulsion' but by the simple, though skilful, application of carrot and stick.[2] He rewarded good service, he sought their counsel and their company, he offered them internal peace, justice and arbitration in their quarrels and he strove to bind them more closely to the crown and its purposes. In this he presaged the policy and achievements of his grandson and laid the foundations for the service nobility of the fourteenth and fifteenth centuries. Under a less skilful monarch than Edward I, the combination of a vigorous king with powerful ideas about the nature and scope of royal authority and nobles used to throwing their weight about and getting their own way could have been an explosive cocktail. Edward's great achievement was to avoid this and to co-opt his earls so successfully. In his famous 'rusty sword' outburst, Earl Warenne articulated the comital vision of the earls' role in society as the king's 'partners and co-workers'.[3] Edward I's greatness lay in offering them partnership with him, while ensuring that, at the same time, in *Bracton*'s phrase, 'qui socium habet, habet magistrum'.[4] In his reign, Edward ensured that it was he who was the master carrying his partners' bridle and not vice versa.

[1] *Bracton*, II, 110. See above, 8–9. [2] Prestwich, *Edward I*, 562.
[3] *Guisborough*, 216. [4] *Bracton*, II, 110. 'He who has a partner, has a master.'

Having thus summarised the relationship between Edward and his earls, it is worth reflecting again on the challenges facing both nobility and kingship at the start of Edward I's reign and asking how both of them stood at the end of his life.[5] Taking kingship first, it is safe to say that Edward I was not a complex man but, rather, one possessed of plentiful common sense, intelligence, energy and an almost unshakeable determination. He applied all these to his one big idea: the restoration of the power and authority of the English monarchy on every front at home and abroad. Through this determination he did indeed meet and overcome many of the challenges facing him at the outset of his reign. By the end of his life, however, new challenges had replaced the old, challenges he had not been able to surmount and which would test his successors for decades, even centuries, to come.

His determination to restore the crown's authority was felt most painfully and obviously by the people of Wales and Scotland, who found their own interests and rights sacrificed in the face of what Edward perceived as the greater rights of the English crown. Edward's rights found a more harmonious channel down which to flow in England where, for most of his reign, he was able to forge a mutually beneficial accommodation between the rights and purposes of the crown and the interests and desires of the nobility and gentry.[6] Through parliaments Edward was able not only to foster a sense of political unity and promote the image of a listening and responsive monarchy but also to solve the chronic financial problems of Henry III's reign by his own much better financial management and by obtaining regular parliamentary taxation to pay for the crown's military and diplomatic policies.[7] Edward's legislation, agreed and promulgated in these parliaments, was not just restorative but expansionist, extending the reach and authority of the crown in all sorts of different directions. Likewise, the financial, material and manpower needs of the crown after the outbreak of war with France in 1294 began a further expansion of the role and reach of royal government, which was to have profound consequences for English law and government in the later middle ages.[8] By strengthening the relationship between the crown and the gentry, by further extending the local reach of the king's government and by investing so much royal capital in parliaments in return for regular supply, Edward I was laying the foundations of the late medieval English monarchy, even if he would not have approved of some of its features, notably the devolution of so much governance to the localities.

[5] See above, 6–9. [6] Maddicott, 'Lessons of Baronial Reform'.

[7] Harriss, *King, Parliament, and Public Finance*, chapters 2 and 3; Carpenter, 'Plantagenet Kings'; Maddicott, *Origins*, chapters 4–6.

[8] Carpenter, *Wars of the Roses*, 65.

The unfinished war in Scotland, however, is a vivid reminder that these changes were far from complete by the time Edward I died, and the last decade of his reign revealed a whole new set of problems for the English crown. Warfare with Scotland and the unresolved status of Gascony were to dominate English politics for the next two centuries and ended in eventual defeat in both Scotland and France. Edward succeeded in restoring and increasing the authority of the crown, a process aided by the ever-expanding reach of royal government in search of resources to wage war, but imbuing the crown with so much authority paradoxically made individual kings much more vulnerable. As Christine Carpenter has put it, 'a great deal was expected of the king and … failure to do his job had such devastating consequences that some action would have to be taken, perhaps deposition'. England could cope, just about, with an inadequate king like Stephen or Henry III, but not with the failure in different ways of Edward II, Richard II and Henry VI to exercise that mighty authority responsibly.[9]

The harmonious relationship Edward I had enjoyed with the gentry began to unravel in the last decade of the reign under the strain of his military and financial demands.[10] The problem of matching what the crown wanted with what the gentry were prepared to give was not a new one but was now becoming even more acute as the crown was forced to rely ever more upon the gentry for governance, supply and military service. Through his intransigence and duplicity in the last ten years of his reign, Edward I poisoned the well of goodwill that he had created during the previous quarter-century of good rule. It was not until after the crisis of 1340–1 and the further devolution of local power to the gentry over the next few decades, that the unresolved issues of Edward I's final years at last found a workable solution.[11] Edward's reign and the unhappy reign of his son thus marked a period of transition during which the English monarchy solved many of the problems created by Magna Carta and wrestled with new ones, thereby bringing the late medieval English polity into being. One might say that the challenges that had been overcome were those of the high middle ages, those yet to be solved were of the later middle ages. McFarlane may have argued that Edward 'belonged less to the future than to the past' but he seems, from this analysis, to be

[9] Ibid.

[10] Prestwich, *War, Politics and Finance*, chapter 12; Harriss, *King, Parliament, and Public Finance*, chapters 3 and 4; Prestwich, *Edward I*, chapters 16 and 19; Spencer, 'Lay Opposition'; Spencer, 'Warlike People'.

[11] Harriss, *King, Parliament, and Public Finance*, chapters 10–14. Devolution seems to have happened somewhat slower than Harriss believed. See Carpenter, 'War, Government and Governance', 20–1.

standing instead at the very cusp of the past and the future of the English monarchy.[12]

A crucial part of the late medieval polity was, of course, the nobility, and here too Edward's reign marked an important stage in their development. David Crouch has written that the thirteenth century was a time of 'aristocratic self-confidence and strength', and there is much to commend this idea.[13] The nobility had imposed Magna Carta on a reluctant King John and sought to depose him when he repudiated it. Under Henry III, they had been given a largely free hand by a king wary of provoking them as his father had done, and, in 1258, felt confident, and exasperated, enough to reduce the king to a cipher and run the country themselves. Noble confidence in the mid-thirteenth century was perhaps summed up by the reported comment of Roger Bigod, earl of Norfolk, when confronted by Henry III in 1249 for his illegal order to seize the count of Guisnes.[14] Guisnes had previously stopped Norfolk when the latter was passing through his territory and extorted a toll. Norfolk now sought to return the favour with interest and had ordered his men to arrest the count when 'crossing through my land'. His justification was spurious but demonstrates the lofty position he assumed earls held in England at this time: 'Teneo enim terram meam tam libere a vobis, domine mi rex, ut ipse suam a domino suo rege Francorum, et sum comes ut ipse.'[15] Norfolk was claiming equality in terms of tenure and authority with the much more powerful, independent and territorially compact counts of France. His claim to be 'comes ut ipse' was untrue insofar as it related to actual power, as he and everyone hearing it must have known, but that he was proud enough to make it says much about the self-image of the English earls under Henry III.

Such confidence, however, was undoubtedly shaken by the events of 1258–65 that revealed two things to the magnates. First, that they could not run the country themselves. Differing visions about the nature and pace of reform had quickly emerged among the leaders of the 1258 revolution, differences that had eventually released terrifying violence and resulted in the supreme rule of one magnate, Simon de Montfort, as a quasi-king with no respect for his opponents' lands or traditional areas of influence.[16] The internecine quarrels among the nobility and the period of Montfortian rule reminded the magnates why effective royal power was both necessary and desirable. Second, they had been forced to

[12] McFarlane, *Nobility*, 267. [13] Crouch, *English Aristocracy*, 83.

[14] Paris, *Chronica Majora*, V, 85–6.

[15] Ibid., 86. 'For I hold my land as freely from you, O lord my king, as he does from his lord the king of France, and I am an earl as he is.'

[16] Maddicott, *Simon de Montfort*, 309–31.

recognise and address the grievances of the gentry who had felt themselves oppressed by baronial as much as royal officials in the years before 1258. As has been seen, under Edward I things were to change.

While Edward had offered his nobility much in the way of personal and political inducements, this was not free of pain for them. Through the *quo warranto* campaign and the subsequent statute, he forced them to accept that the authority that went with their lands was delegated, as with the land itself, from the crown and did not originate in their ancestors' exploits at the time of the Norman Conquest. On a more practical level, the *quo warranto* campaign and the public examples made of egregious offenders like Warenne and Gloucester broadcast the king's determination to stop the rot of usurpations, withdrawal from royal jurisdiction and private feuding that had characterised the nobility's behaviour during much of both the indulgent years of Henry III's personal rule and the chaos of the period of Reform and Rebellion.

At the same time as they were coming under scrutiny from above, the nobility were also feeling pressure from below, from a gentry who, under Henry III, were finding their political voice and who had many grievances about the behaviour of magnates, particularly their officials. For the time being, the earls of Edward I had been able to rely on the trusted methods of the thirteenth century to bolster and protect their local power by trying to filter the crown's access to the localities and the localities to the crown, but these techniques could not long survive the further expansion of royal government begun after the outbreak of war in 1294. A crown so greatly in need of the resources of its subjects to fight its wars could not permit the restraint or exclusion of its agents by the nobility. If the nobility were to maintain their local power and authority, they needed to engage more closely and more positively with both royal government and their gentry neighbours than they had been accustomed to doing for a long time. By the end of Edward I's reign it was no longer clear that the methods of the thirteenth century would continue to be effective for the nobility. The expansion of the power and influence of both the crown and the gentry as the fourteenth century developed meant that the 'bastard feudal' control of local public offices by the agents of the nobility would begin to become part of the normal functioning of local society.

Is it possible to reconcile the seemingly incompatible views of thirteenth-century and fifteenth-century historians about the nature of bastard feudalism?[17] If the historiography of the nobility in the twelfth and

[17] For representative views, see, for instance, Coss *et al.*, 'Debate', 181; Harding, *England in the Thirteenth Century*, 263; Carpenter, *Wars of the Roses*, 6.

thirteenth centuries and that of the fourteenth and fifteenth centuries are not to drift wholly away from each other, then some attempt must be made. The evidence presented in this book suggests that, though the thirteenth-century nobility were using many of the techniques of 'bastard feudalism' and were no longer restricting their search for service to their feudal tenants, if indeed they ever had, they were emphatically not engaging with royal law and administration in the way in which their successors in the late fourteenth and fifteenth centuries did, or in the way in which thirteenth-century historians of 'bastard feudalism' have assumed they did. The service nobility of the later middle ages was integrated into the systems of royal law, administration and war in a manner unknown in the thirteenth century or, indeed, at any time since the late Anglo-Saxon period.[18] This is not to say, of course, that the nobility had no role in this period. They were always prominent in war and counsel and were expected to help keep order in the localities but their role in supervising local government, so prominent in the late Anglo-Saxon period, was massively restricted within a generation of the Conquest. After a long period of more than two centuries, where the nobility's direct role in local government was, for the most part, limited except for emergencies, things began to change. The nobility in general, and the earls in particular, became an essential component in the late medieval polity, not some malignant force corrupting it from the outside. 'Bastard feudalism' was thus a vital part of the late medieval system of government, not an aberration from it. That is not to say, of course, that the system was perfect by any means. It assuredly was not. For most of the time, however, and in most places it rubbed along reasonably well, which was as much as could be hoped for in a pre-modern (or indeed a modern) world. It is important to emphasise, of course, that in offering themselves as the link between the centre and the localities magnates were not acting disinterestedly or altruistically. They had their own interests to defend. To protect and enhance their power, both locally and at the centre, they needed to demonstrate their indispensability both to the king and to their neighbours.

Conversely, the crown had to delegate (though importantly not reduce) its authority to the localities for law and administration to function effectively and the nobility were able to seize the opportunity to act as the conduit between the centre and the periphery in the way described above, and thereby protect their own position at the same time by promoting the interests of both the crown and the members of their affinity. There were inevitably casualties of 'bastard feudalism', as there are in any

[18] See Baxter, *Earls*, for integration of late Anglo-Saxon earls in the governance of England.

political system, who complained loudly about its obvious failings, and it took a good deal of time for the crown, nobility and gentry to see that such a system was in all their best interests: in many ways, indeed, 'bastard feudalism' was not planned by anyone, all sides rather stumbled into it as the best solution in changed times. The circumstances of Edward I's reign, however, and the decisions he took regarding his nobility were an important staging post in the creation of a new service nobility and in the development of the late medieval polity.

Thus, for both nobility and kingship in England the reign of Edward I was a crucial period of transition. It was, as has been seen, a transition that was for both the king and the earls one that was painful and incomplete. For all this, however, Edward's reign was indeed, as Michael Prestwich has called it, 'a great one', and this was in no small part due to the nature of the relationship between Edward and his earls.[19] For the most part he had met their expectations of good kingship and they had provided him with loyal and steadfast service in war and peace. His reign stands as one of the clearest examples of what a medieval king could achieve when he worked in partnership with his earls. This was not an equal partnership, however, but one that gave Edward, as was only fitting for a king, the last word.

[19] Prestwich, *Edward I*, 567.

Appendix A

CALENDAR OF LANCASTER *ACTA*, 1267–1295

NB: Only charters with witness lists have been included. Transcripts for charters marked with a ★ were kindly provided by Professor David Crouch.

(1) **Grosmont, 29 May 1267:** (Monmouth) Grant to prior of Monmouth not to exact money on change of prior.[1]

(2) ***Inspeximus* dated 7 November 1268:** (Staffordshire) Grant to Hamo Lestrange and his heirs of a half virgate in Penkhull with advowson of Stokes Church.[2]

(3)★ **Grosmont, 1 January 1270:** (Monmouth) Confirms three grants to Cistercian abbey of Dor.[3]

(4) ***Inspeximus* dated 20 February 1270:** (Lancashire) Letters patent to William le Botiller of Warrington that Edmund has received 150 marks which William owed him.[4]

(5)★ **Winchester, 1 August 1270:** (Herefordshire) Grant to Roger Mortimer and his heirs of the manor of Maworthyn in exchange for 1000 marks.[5]

(6) ***Inspeximus* dated 15 October 1270:** (Herefordshire) Grant to Hugh Baldwin of land in the manor of Marden.[6]

(7) **Westminster, 23 October 1270:** (Dorset) Grant to the church of SS Mary and Benedict of Queen's Place upon Trent of the manor of Bere.[7]

(8) ***Inspeximus* dated 2 November 1270:** (Gloucestershire) Grant to Elias de Heydon of land in Rodley at rent of 13*s* 9*d* and suit of court.[8]

(9) **26 December 1270:** (Derbyshire) Grant to the abbot and convent of St Mary de Pratis, Leicester of the manor of Melbourne, for three years in exchange for £120.[9]

(10)★ ***Inspeximus* dated 1270:** (Herefordshire) Grant to Robert and Matilda Walerand of the manor and advowson of Ludwardyn.[10]

(11) ***Inspeximus* dated 1270:** (Warwickshire) Grant to Sir William Bagot, his knight, his heirs and assigns, the manor of Esseby with the rent of Lilleburn.[11]

[1] *CChR 1257–1300*, 150. [2] *CChR 1257–1300*, 114.
[3] Kenneth Spencer Research Library, University of Kansas, MS 191:11.
[4] *CChR 1257–1300*, 135–6. [5] British Library, Ms. Harley 1240, f. 76.
[6] *CChR 1257–1300*, 153. [7] *CChR 1257–1300*, 227–8.
[8] *CChR 1257–1300*, 155. [9] *CPR 1266–1272*, 502.
[10] TNA C 53/59, m. 4. [11] C 53/59, m. 7.

(12) **Westminster, 12 January 1271:** (Nottinghamshire/Berkshire) Grant to Sir Geoffrey de Langley the younger, his knight, the manor of Kingshaugh, and the mills of Hungerford.[12]

(13) **Westminster, 26 January 1271:** (Gloucestershire) Grant to Nicholas de Valers, son and heir of Sir William de Valers, sometime knight of Edmund, for his homage and service all the manor of Donaumeneye, for ½ kt fee.[13]

(14) **Westminster, 1 February 1271:** (Berkshire) Grant to Richard de Fukeram, his knight, of the manor of Ildslegh for ½ knight's fee.[14]

(15) **Westminster, 1 February 1271:** (Gloucestershire) Grant to Robert de Turbeville, his knight, of £20 a year from the manor of Minsterworth because he is about to cross the sea with him.[15]

(16) **Westminster, 2 February 1271:** (Yorkshire) Grant to Sir John de Oketon, for his service, all the town of Easingwald to be held until provided with £30 of land.[16]

(17) **London, 20 February 1271:** (Yorkshire) Grant to the prior of Bridlington peaceable possessions of lands, rents and possessions in Little Kelk.[17]

(18) **Windsor, 3 November 1271:** (Gloucestershire) Grant to Gilbert Talbot and his heirs of his manor of Rodley until he or they shall receive an equivalent in wardships, marriages or escheats.[18]

(19)* **Hungerford, 31 January 1274:** (Nottinghamshire) Confirmation of his grant to Geoffrey de Langley, his knight, of Kingshaugh.[19]

(20) **London, 11 April 1274:** (Herefordshire) Grant to Wormley Priory of an acre in Dilum.[20]

(21)* **Windsor, 24 February 1275:** (Northumberland) Grant to Merton College, Oxford, of the advowson of Embelton.[21]

(22)* **London, 16 August 1275:** (Northumberland) Grant to Sir Ralph de Kirketon of the eastern half of the town of Barton.[22]

(23) **London, 7 August 1276:** (Leicestershire) Quitclaim, for £400 paid over four years, to Sir James de Meynill of his right in the manors of Thornton and Bagworth.[23]

(24)* **Monmouth, 1 December 1276:** (Monmouth) Grant to Dor Abbey the land of Walerand ap Adam.[24]

(25)* **3 March 1277:** Grant to Stanley Abbey in Arden 120 acres of waste in Westwood and Dalley, and three acres of land in Kingshull.[25]

(26)* **Tutbury, 5 November 1277:** (Derbyshire) Grant to Sir Nicholas de St Maur and the heirs of his body for his homage and service all the land he has in the manor of Repton, with the park, fishery, and woods.[26]

(27)* **21 February 1278:** (Monmouth) Exchange of rents between Edmund and Monmouth Priory in Wilton.[27]

[12] *CChR 1257–1300*, 162. [13] *CChR 1257–1300*, 161. [14] *CPR 1266–1272*, 515.
[15] *CPR 1266–1272*, 515. [16] *CChR 1257–1300*, 162. [17] *CPR 1281–1292*, 174.
[18] *CChR 1257–1300*, 162. [19] DL 42/2, f. 71. [20] *CChR 1257–1300*, 250.
[21] Merton College, Oxford, Muniments no. 435. [22] DL 27/300.
[23] DL 27/1791. [24] Kenneth Spencer Research Library, University of Kansas, MS 191:14.
[25] S.B.T. MS DR 10/1406 (Gregory Leger Book), 183–4.
[26] DL 42/2, f. 78. [27] TNA E 210/4545.

(28)* **Monmouth, 13 February 1279:** (Northumberland) Confirmation of above grant to Merton College of advowson of Embelton.[28]

(29) **London, 10 November 1279:** (Derbyshire) Grant to the king of the counties and castles of Cardigan and Carmarthen in exchange for the manors of Wirksworth and Ashbourne, and wapentake of Wirksworth.[29]

(30)* **Newcastle-under-Lyme, 25 March 1280:** (Staffordshire) Agreement with Sir William de Mere over common pasture in Hanchurch.[30]

(31) **London, 9 November 1280:** (London) *Inspeximus* for Aaron son of Vives, his Jew, of his charter to Jews of London to build a synagogue.[31]

(32) **Newcastle-under-Lyme, 28 March 1281:** (Staffordshire) Agreement with Sir John de Swynnerton concerning common pasture.[32]

(33) **London, 20 May 1281:** Ratification of the grant of Simon de Montfort to the hospital of St John of Hungerford.[33]

(34) **Westminster, 24 May 1281:** (Huntingdonshire) Grant to Eleanor, widow of Robert de Ferrers, earl of Derby, the town of Godmanchester for life at a rent of 1*d*.[34]

(35)* **Rhuddlan, 12 August 1282:** Confirmation of three charters by William of Blois, John count of Mortain and Henry III.[35]

(36)* **11 October 1282:** (Gloucestershire) Grant to William de Grandisson of the manors of Rodley and Minsterworth for his 'praiseworthy services'.[36]

(37)* **Ludgershall, 12 April 1284:** (Herefordshire) Grant to William de Grandisson and the heirs of his body of the manors of Ashperton and Stratton.[37]

(38)* **Guildford, 25 April 1285:** (Staffordshire) Grant to the burgesses of Newcastle-under-Lyme letting to farm the borough's mills.[38]

(39) **Amesbury, 15 August 1285:** (Herefordshire) Grant to William de Grandisson and Sybil his wife and their heirs of the manors of Ashperton and Stretton.[39]

(40) **Finkhale, 4 December 1285:** (Northumberland) Grant for his and his wife's soul to the priory of Finkhale of 20*s* rent from the mills of Embleton.[40]

(41)* **Tutbury, 31 December 1285:** (Staffordshire) Grant to Robert Vencitore of Uttoxeter four acres of waste in Tensette park.[41]

(42) **Tutbury, 8 September 1286:** (Derbyshire) Grant to Robert de Creccon of Foston of ten acres of waste in Scropton and Foston.[42]

(43)* **Lancaster, Michaelmas 1286:** (Lancashire) Grant to prior of Boursco of a weekly market in Ormskirk in return for one mark p.a.[43]

(44) **Canterbury, Wednesday after the octaves of Easter 1292:** (Monmouth/Gloucestershire) Release to king of the castle, town and honour of Monmouth, the Three Castles, Rodley and Minsterworth, and all his lands beyond the Severn.[44]

(45) ***Inspeximus* 7 November 1294 of undated charter:** (Nottinghamshire) Grant to Master Walter de Gloucester, clerk, and his heirs of Kingshaugh Manor, in return for £200.[45]

[28] Merton College, Oxford, Muniments no. 415. [29] *CChR 1257–1300*, 218.
[30] DL 42/2, f. 88. [31] *CChR 1257–1300*, 245.
[32] DL 25/1854. [33] *CPR 1272–1281*, 436. [34] *CPR 1272–1281*, 440.
[35] DL 42/1, f. 130v. [36] British Library, MS Lansdowne 229, f. 127v.
[37] DL 25/2340. [38] DL 42/2, f. 89. [39] DL 27/237.
[40] *CChR 1257–1300*, 329. [41] British Library, MS Stowe 666, f. 91.
[42] *Descriptive Catalogue of Derbyshire Charters*, ed. I.H. Jeaves (London: Bemrose, 1906), no. 2100.
[43] DL 42/1, f. 78. [44] *CCR 1288–1296*, 263. [45] *CPR 1292–1301*, 105.

Table A.1 *Knightly multiple witnesses to Lancaster* acta

	Numbers of *acta* witnessed	Total
Richard de Fukeram	3, 4, 9–10, 12–13, 15–28, 31, 33–6, 38–9, 47	28 (1270–85)
Gilbert Talbot	1–3, 6–9, 12–17, 47	14 (1267–71)
Laurence de St Maur	7, 19, 21, 25, 31, 33–6, 38–9, 46, 48	13 (1270–95)
Thomas de Bray	8, 22–3, 25, 27, 30–2, 34, 36, 44, 48	12 (1270–92)
Walter de Helyun	10, 21, 27, 29, 37, 39, 44–6, 48–9	11 (1270–95)
Roger de Somery	2, 4–7, 10, 14–15	8 (1268–71)
Hamo de Aungerville	2, 12–13, 16, 18–19, 47	7 (1268–74)
Geoffrey de Langley the elder	2–3, 9, 22–3, 25	6 (1267–77)
John de Oketon	4, 12–13, 17–18, 47	6 (1270–1)
William Wyther	38, 41–2, 45, 48–9	6 (1285–95)
Geoffrey de Langley the younger	34, 38–40, 46	5 (1281–95)
Roger Brabazon	41–2, 44, 46	4 (1285–95)
Roger de Clifford	5, 6, 10, 29	4 (1270–9)
William de Kugenhoe	33, 37, 39–40	4 (1281–5)
William Bagot	1–2, 40	3 (1267–85)
William de Coleville	24, 27–8	3 (1276–9)
William de Huntley	24, 27–8	3 (1276–9)
Hamo Lestrange	5, 6, 10	3 (1270)
Walter de Percy	2, 14–15	3 (1268–71)
Robert de Stafford	26, 37, 41	3 (1277–85)
Robert de Turbeville	1, 3, 9	3 (1267–70)
Robert de Ufford	19–20, 22	3 (1274–5)
Alan de Waldeshef	33, 37–8	3 (1281–5)

(46)* **Fulham, 23 October 1295:** (Derbyshire) Grant to abbess of St Clare-without-the-walls, London, of 10 acres in Hartingdon.[46]

(47)* **Undated:** (Yorkshire) Grant to prior of Bridlington of the manor of Little Kelk.[47]

(48)* **Undated:** (Derbyshire) Confirmation of a grant to canons of Darley of land in Wigwell.[48]

(49)* **Undated:** (Staffordshire) Grant to William de Sadinton of 9 acres in Uttoxeter in return for 36*s*.[49]

(50) **Undated:** (Lancashire) Confirmation, at the instance of 'the magnificent man' Henry de Lacy, earl of Lincoln, to the abbot and convent of Benedict at Stanlaw of the grant to the abbey of land by Geoffrey de Byron.[50]

[46] LR 14/1173. [47] University of London Library, Fuller Collection, MS 13/8.

[48] *Cartulary of Darley Abbey*, ed. R.R. Darlington, 2 vols. (Kendal: Titus Wilson and Son, 1945), II, 591–2.

[49] British Library, MS Cotton Claudius A xiii, f. 204v.

[50] *Coucher Book of Whalley Abbey*, III, 884–5.

Appendix B

CALENDAR OF LINCOLN *ACTA*, 1278–1308

NB: Only *acta* with witness lists have been included.

(1) **Pontefract, John the Baptist 1278:** (Yorkshire) Settlement of a dispute between Lincoln's house of Pontefract and the house of Monk Bretton.[1]
(2) **Chester, 3 July 1282:** (Lincolnshire) Exchange of manors between earl of Lincoln and Roger de Mowbray.[2]
(3) **21 September 1282:** (Lincolnshire) Grant to William de Louth, dean of St Martin-le-Grand, London of the custody of Ingelby manor and the wardship and marriage of Thomas de Multon.[3]
(4) **Pontefract, 2 February 1283:** (Lancashire) Grant to Stanlow Abbey, Cheshire, of the advowson of Whalley.[4]
(5) **Denbigh, 3 June 1283:** (Cheshire) Grant to Adam son of Adam of land in Congleton.[5]
(6) **Denbigh, 8 June 1283:** (Cheshire) Grant of 10 acres in Congleton.[6]
(7) **Denbigh, 20 July 1283:** (Cheshire) Grant of waste in Halton.[7]
(8) **London, 30 November 1283:** (London) Grant to Stephen Mareschal, Lincoln's armourer, and Maud his wife of land in the parish of St. Stephen, Coleman Street.[8]
(9) **Donington, 14 February 1284:** (Lincolnshire/Rutland) Agreement with Sir Ralph de Trehampton.[9]
(10) **Rothwell near Pontefract, 12 Edward I:** (Yorkshire) Grant for life to Sir William Vavasour rent of 20 marks in Almonbury.[10]
(11) ***Inspeximus* dated 15 July 1285:** (Berkshire) Quitclaim to nuns of Bromhale of 100 acres of waste in Ashridge.[11]
(12) **Halton, Cheshire, 1 October 1285:** (Wales) Grant to burgesses of Denbigh of burgages there.[12]
(13) **Bentley, 9 November 1285:** (Cheshire) Grant in tail to Hugh son of Hugh de Clitheroe, his groom, of land in Cogshall.[13]

[1] DL 25/2189. [2] *CCR 1279–1288*, 191. [3] DL 25/2913.
[4] TNA E 327/447. [5] DL 25/68. [6] DL 25/67.
[7] DL 25/69. [8] DL 36/2/189. [9] DL 25/2364.
[10] DL 25/2174. [11] *CPR 1281–1292*, 185.
[12] DL 27/33. [13] DL 25/2072.

(14) **Bicester, January 1286:** (Oxfordshire) Confirmation of grants to Bicester Priory by Gilbert Basset and William Longsword.[14]

(15) **Kingston, Dorset, 2 March 1286:** (Dorset) Demise of land for life in Wimborne Holt.[15]

(16) **Paris, 12 June 1286:** (Wales) Grant to Richard de Elstane, his cook, of land near Denbigh to hold for life by knight's service.[16]

(17) **St Severum, France, Saturday after St Luke 1287**: (Lancashire, Yorkshire) Agreement between Abbot Hugh of Kirkstall and earl of Lincoln in which Lincoln agrees to pay 80 marks p.a. in return for a quitclaim of lands, tenements and rents in Lancashire and Yorkshire.[17]

(18) **London, January 1290:** (Buckinghamshire) Grant of land and pasture in manor of Holmer.[18]

(19) **Kingston, Dorset, 4 November 1291:** (Dorset) Grant to Henry Caperon and Alice his wife of an assart.[19]

(20) **Kingston, Dorset, 7 November 1291:** (Dorset) Grant to John le Chapman, warrener of Henstridge, Somerset, for life of a tenement formerly held by William le Warrener in Kingston Lacy.[20]

(21) **Alverton, 22 December 1290:** (Nottinghamshire) Letters patent to Blyth Priory that they should have the common fine of the wapentake of Alverton.[21]

(22) ***Inspeximus* dated 24 January 1292 of charter probably dating from February 1291:** (Lincolnshire) Grant to cannons of St Mary Thornton of the manor of Halton-by-Kilvingholm.[22]

(23) **London, 23 January 1292:** (Lincolnshire) Grant for life to Richard Burgellon of a messuage in Donington.[23]

(24) **London, 6 February 1292:** (Somerset) Quitclaim to Henry de Portibus, canon of Wells, of the chapel of Whitchurch within the church of Henstridge.[24]

(25) **Donington, 14 May 1292:** (Northamptonshire) Grant to John son of Philip de Daventry of 5 ½ acres in the moor of Murcott.[25]

(26) **Halton, Cheshire, Friday before St James 1295:** (Yorkshire) Grant of a messuage in Bradford.[26]

(27) **Rhuddlan, 3 Kalends March 1295:** (Cheshire/Lancashire) Grant to Stanlaw Abbey concerning impropriation of the church of Whalley.[27]

(28) **Cowick near Exeter, 25 November 1295:** (Lincolnshire) Grant to 'our dear bachelor', Sir William de Stopham, of the manor of Waddington for his homage and service.[28]

(29) **Bolingbroke, Friday after Pentecost 1301:** (Lincolnshire) Grant for life to Ralph de Freskeney of land in Wrangle and Leake in return for 10 marks p.a. of rent.[29]

(30) **Bolingbroke, 8 May 1301:** (Lincolnshire) Grant in tail of a toft in Bolingbroke in exchange for another.[30]

[14] DL 25/71. [15] DL 25/3442. [16] DL 36/2/248. [17] DL 27/199.
[18] DL 25/3436. [19] DL 25/2338. [20] DL 36/1/108.
[21] *The Cartulary of Blyth Priory*, ed. R.T. Timson, 2 vols. (London: HMSO, 1973), I, A74.
[22] *CChR 1257–1300*, 412. [23] DL 25/3202. [24] *CPR 1281–1292*, 481.
[25] DL 25/2271. [26] DL 25/1878. [27] *CChR 1257–1300*, 460.
[28] DL 25/3249. [29] DL 25/2479. [30] DL 25/2403.

(31) **Altofts, Yorkshire, 20 June 1301:** (Yorkshire) Grant of 1 ½ acres of land in Ackworth.[31]

(32) **Bolingbroke, 23 January 1302:** (Lincolnshire) Grant of a messuage in Boston.[32]

(33) **Eudswelle near Odiham, 1 January 1303:** (Cambridgeshire) Grant to 'our dear bachelor', Sir Baldwin de Manners, of £20 rent in the manor of Grantchester.[33]

(34) **Altoftes, 2 May 1305:** (Yorkshire) Confirmation of a grant by Dame Alice de Lacy, dowager countess of Lincoln, dated 30 Edward I.[34]

(35) **London, 2 November 1308:** (Lincolnshire) Grant of land in Halton and Steeping.[35]

(36) **Undated:** (Unknown) Grant for life to William le Fitz Brian of a messuage in the vill of Pyry.[36]

(37) **Undated:** (Lincolnshire) Grant to Sir Edmund Talbot and his wife of the manor of Rishton in tail male to hold as fully as Adam de Rishton, a bastard, held it.[37]

(38) **Undated:** (Yorkshire) Grant to Robert de Veylly and Joan his wife of a messuage in Owston which Emma de Veylly formerly held of him for her life.[38]

(39) **Undated:** (Cheshire) Grant in tail to 'our beloved sergeant', John le Fauconer, for good service past and future of land in Cogshall.[39]

(40) **Undated:** (Dorset) Grant to Roger de la Hyde and Maud his wife of 40 acres of waste in Wimborne.[40]

(41) **Undated:** (Lincolnshire) Grant in tail to Thomas Sadelbowe of a burage in Wainfleet at a rent of 4*s* p.a.[41]

(42) **Undated:** (Lincolnshire) Grant in tail to Sir Adam de Newmarch and Elizabeth his wife of lands and rents in Saltfleetby.[42]

(43) **Undated:** (Derbyshire) Grant to Rufford Abbey of land in Emton which they hold by the grant of John, constable of Chester, his ancestor, at a rent of 10*s* p.a.[43]

(44) **Undated:** (Yorkshire) Indenture to Sir William Vavasour of £20 annual rent from North and South Elmsall and Moorthorpe.[44]

(45) **Pontefract, undated:** (Yorkshire) Quitclaim to Byland Abbey of lands of his fee.[45]

(46) **Undated:** (Northamptonshire) Grant for life to William and Emma de Paris and Emma his wife of land in Long Buckby.[46]

(47) **Bolingbroke, undated:** (Lincolnshire) Grant to Alan de Claxby, clerk, and Joan his wife of messuages in Bolingbroke.[47]

(48) **Undated:** (Lincolnshire) Grant to the men of Boston of common pasture in his fenland.[48]

(49) **Undated:** (Norfolk) Grant to Wendling Abbey of 4 ½ acres which they have by the gift of Sir William de Wenling.[49]

[31] DL 25/2173. [32] DL 25/2419. [33] DL 25/3421. [34] DL 25/2190.
[35] DL 25/2519. [36] DL 25/63. [37] DL 25/61. [38] DL 25/3628.
[39] DL 25/2074. [40] DL 25/2337. [41] DL 25/2523. [42] DL 26/2565.
[43] DL 27/35. [44] DL 36/1/119. [45] DL 36/2/45. [46] DL 36/2/122.
[47] DL 36/2/210. [48] DL 36/2/257. [49] TNA E 42/199.

Appendix B

Table B.1 *Knightly multiple witnesses to Lincoln* acta

	Numbers of *acta* witnessed	Total
William Vavasour	1–2, 4, 9, 14–16, 18, 23, 25, 27–8, 38, 42, 45, 49–53	20 (1278–95)
Robert Fitz Roger	2, 9, 11–12, 14–16, 18, 23, 27, 35, 42, 44	13 (1282–1308)
William de Stopham	8–11, 14–16, 23, 34, 39, 42, 44, 53	13 (1283–1305)
Robert de Hertford	8, 18, 22, 23, 27–8, 42, 44, 51, 53	10 (1282–95)
James de Neville	4, 8, 27, 33–4, 38–9, 44, 49, 53	10 (1283–1305)
John Bek	1, 4, 9, 43, 4–6, 49–50, 52	9 (1278–84)
Roger de Trumpington	4, 9, 12, 14–16, 46, 50	8 (1283–6)
Peter de Malore	8, 19–20, 22, 24–5	6 (1283–92)
Walter Bek	9, 22–3, 44, 49	5 (1284–92)
Roger de Cubbeldyk	30–1, 35, 41, 47	5 (1301–5)
Thomas de Fishburn	23, 33–4, 41, 47	5 (1291–1303)
Wakelin de Arden	8, 14, 44, 53	4 (1283–6)
Hugh de Dutton	5–7, 13	4 (1283–5)
Adam de Huddleston	22, 28, 44, 53	4 (1291–5)
Robert Shireland	31, 37, 39, 51	4 (1301)
John Spring	28, 31, 39, 51	4 (1295–1301)
Miles de Stapleton	28, 33, 35, 39	4 (1295–1308)
Adam de Blackburn	4, 52, 53	3 (1283)
Richard de Bruce	1, 3, 12	3 (1278–85)
John de Cresacre	11, 46, 49	3 (1285)
Peter de Mauley	2, 11–12	3 (1282–5)
Giles de Trumpington	28, 30, 51	3 (1295–1301)
William de Venables	5, 6, 13	3 (1283–5)
Ralph de Vernon	5, 6, 13	3 (1283–5)

(50) **Undated:** (Berkshire) Confirmation of grant by Robert de Rokeby to canons of Burncestre.[50]

(51) **Undated:** (Lancashire) Grant to 'our dear bachelor' Sir Adam de Huddleston for good service past and future of the manor of Billington for term of life.[51]

(52) **Undated:** (Lancashire) Grant to Henry son of Robert de Bolton of 60 acres of waste in Billington in return for an annual rent of 25*s* 4*d*.[52]

(53) **Undated:** (Lancashire) Remission of suit of court at Clitheroe for Robert Franklin.[53]

[50] E 326/3498. [51] *Coucher Book of Whalley Abbey*, IV, 944–5.
[52] Ibid., 945–6. [53] MS Harley 2074, f. 165r.

Appendix C

CALENDAR OF CORNWALL *ACTA*, 1276–1300

NB: Only *acta* with witness lists have been included.

(1) **Knaresborough, 10 September 1276:** (Yorkshire) Permission to minister and brethren of the Order of Holy Trinity, Knaresborough, to build a watermill within their close.[1]

(2) ***Inspeximus* dated 10 August 1278:** (Hertfordshire) Grant to Hales Abbey of the church of Hemel Hempstead in frank almoin.[2]

(3) ***Inspeximus* dated 10 August 1278:** (Oxfordshire) Grant to Hales Abbey of the church of North Leigh in frank almoin.[3]

(4) ***Inspeximus* dated 10 August 1278:** (Oxfordshire) Grant to the master of the chapel of St Nicholas in Wallingford Castle of £4 rent in Shillingford and Warborough for the support of the master, five chaplains, six clerks and four acolytes.[4]

(5) **Gimingham, 28 August 1279:** (Cambridgeshire) Pardon to William, prior of Eye, for default against him in King's Bench over the advowson of the church of Thornton which Edmund recovered and now grants to the prior in pure and perpetual alms.[5]

(6) **Knaresborough, 29 May 1280:** (Yorkshire) Grant to minister and friars of the Order of Holy Trinity, Knaresborough, of land in Pannal and advowson of the church of Foston in frank almoin.[6]

(7) ***Inspeximus* dated 24 November 1280:** (Yorkshire) Grant to Friar Ralph, minister of the Order of Holy Trinity, Knaresborough, of all his land in Hampsthwaite and Scotton Thorpe and the advowson of the church of Pannal in exchange for the manor of Rotheclyve.[7]

(8) **Berkhamsted, 8 Edward I:** (Cornwall) Grant to Hales Abbey of a meadow and piece of land in the manor of Helston in frank almoin.[8]

(9) **London, 2 June 1280:** (Oxfordshire) Grant to John de la Russe, his beloved servant, of two pieces of land in Wallingford.[9]

(10) **Clerkenwell, 2 November 1281:** (Yorkshire) Grant to the minister and friars of the Order of Holy Trinity, Knaresborough, that their men of Pannal and

[1] *CChR 1300–1326*, 189. [2] *CChR 1257–1300*, 208. [3] Ibid., 208.
[4] Ibid., 209. [5] *Eye Priory Cartulary*, I, no. 109. [6] *CChR 1257–1300*, 240–1.
[7] Ibid., 240. [8] *CChR 1300–1326*, 490. [9] E 36/57, no. 284.

Hampsthwaite should be quit of toll, stallage and other customs in Cornwall's town of Knaresborough and all other places belonging to him.[10]

(11) **Exeter, 25 May 1284:** (Cornwall) Grant to Launceston Priory 20*s* rent annually from the town of Launceston together with freedom from tolls and the assize of bread and ale.[11]

(12) ***Inspeximus* dated 15 August 1284:** (Oxfordshire) Establishment and endowment of Cistercian abbey of Rewley.[12]

(13) **Berkhamsted, 12 July 1285:** (Somerset) Grant to the prior and brethren of the Charterhouse, Witham, of 100*s* rent in Witham.[13]

(14) **Berkhamsted, 20 November 1285:** (Yorkshire) Grant to Fountains Abbey of free transit in the River Ouse between Boroughbridge and York.[14]

(15) **Exeter, 6 January 1286:** (Cornwall) Grant to Launceston Priory of lands of Hollygrove, Cleave and 'Herthyscote'.[15]

(16) ***Inspeximus* dated 17 April 1286:** (Hertfordshire) Grant to rector and brethren Ashridge Priory of a series of franchises in Ashridge, Hemel Hempstead, Gatesden, and Pichelsthorn.[16]

(17) **Berkhamsted, 20 June 1286:** (Cornwall) Grant to Hales Abbey of the church of St Paulin in frank almoin.[17]

(18) ***Inspeximus* dated 16 December 1287:** (Berkshire) Grant to Amesbury Priory of 5*s* rent from township of Chadelworth together with view of frankpledge in frank almoin.[18]

(19) **Clerkenwell, 18 April 1288:** Confirmation, as founder, of a grant by Rewley Abbey to Thame Abbey of 20*s* rent.[19]

(20) **14 February 1289:** (Wiltshire) Grant to dean and chapter of Salisbury Cathedral of a garden and small toft in Mere.[20]

(21) ***Inspeximus* dated 5 June 1290:** (Unknown) Grant to Hales Abbey of manor of Langeberge in frank almoin.[21]

(22) **Restormel, 30 December 1290:** (Cornwall) Confirmation of three charters for Priory of St Michael's Mount.[22]

(23) ***Inspeximus* dated 8 January 1291:** (Hertfordshire) Grant to rector and brethren of Ashridge Priory of all his land in Pichelsthorn and outlying hamlets along with rights of pasture, return of writs and view of frankpledge in frank almoin.[23]

(24) **Restormel, 4 May 1291:** (Cornwall) Confirmation of charters of liberties granted to Launceston Priory in Launceston by Reginald, earl of Cornwall, and Richard, earl of Cornwall.[24]

(25) **24 June 1291:** (Cornwall) Quitclaim to Odo de Branicoyn of 12 acres of land near the waters of Fowey and quitclaim by Odo of 15 acres of woodland in Penlyn.[25]

[10] *CChR 1300–1326*, 189.
[11] *Cartulary of Launceston Priory*, no. 265. [12] *CPR 1281–1292*, 133–4. [13] *CChR 1257–1300*, 330.
[14] *Cartulary of Fountains*, II, 725–6. [15] *Cartulary of Launceston Priory*, no. 398.
[16] *CChR 1257–1300*, 331. [17] *CChR 1300–1326*, 490. [18] *CChR 1341–1417*, 21.
[19] *CChR 1257–1300*, 339. [20] E 36/57, no. 43. [21] *CChR 1257–1300*, 359.
[22] *The Cartulary of St Michael's Mount*, ed. and trans. P.L. Hull, Devon and Cornwall Record Society, New Series 5 (1962), no. 4.
[23] *CChR 1257–1300*, 383–4. [24] *Cartulary of Launceston Priory*, no. 16.
[25] C 36/57, no. 127.

Table C.1 *Knightly multiple witnesses of Cornwall* acta

	Numbers of *acta* witnessed	Total
Walter de Puylle	2–3, 5, 12, 15–19, 21, 27, 32–4	14 (1278–94)
Richard de Cornubia, the earl's brother	2–3, 5–6, 12, 16–19, 21, 27, 33–4	13 (1278–94)
Henry Shotbroke	10–12, 16, 18–21, 26, 32–3	11 (1281–91)
Geoffrey de Russell	2–3, 5–6, 8–10, 21, 27, 34	10 (1278–94)
Reginald de Botreaux	17, 22–6, 28, 35	8 (1286–95)
Thomas de Breauté	6, 8, 10, 12, 16–17, 21	7 (1280–90)
Robert Damory	5, 7–8, 10, 33–4, 36	7 (1279–81)
Peter Becard	1, 6, 11–12, 14	5 (1276–85)
William de Botreaux	11, 22, 24–5, 35	5 (1284–91)
Robert Malet	2–4, 8, 36	5 (1278–81)
Thomas de Kancia	11, 22, 25, 35	4 (1284–91)
Oliver de Dynham	11, 16–17	3 (1284–6)
John de Gatesden	16, 23, 26	3 (1286–91)
Richard de Hiwys	22, 25, 35	3 (1290–1)
John Neyrnuit	4, 16, 26	3 (1278–91)
Robert de Plumpton	1, 7, 14	3 (1276–85)
Seman de Stokes	5, 10, 27	3 (1279–94)

(26) ***Inspeximus* dated 20 September 1291:** (Oxfordshire) Grant to rector and brethren of Ashridge Priory of the manors of Chesterton and Ambrosden in frank almoin.[26]

(27) ***Inspeximus* dated 16 June 1294:** (Yorkshire) Grant to master and brethren of St Leonard's Hospital, York, that they may bring victuals and goods along the rivers Ouse and Ure from Boroughbridge to York without charge.[27]

(28) **Berkhamsted, 3 February 1295:** (Cornwall) Grant to Hales Abbey of a piece of land in Helston.[28]

(29) **Ashridge, 5 October 1296:** (Oxfordshire) Grant to Walter de Aylesbury, his servant, of messuage, land and advowson in Rousham to hold in fee tail by service of ¼ knight's fee.[29]

(30) **Hales, 3 December 1299:** (Middlesex) Grant to the Knights Templar of pasture and heathland between Cranford and Twickenham and Babworth Bridge and Hounslow.[30]

(31) **Rutherfield, 14 September 1300:** (Oxfordshire) Grant to Sir William de Bereford and Lady Margaret, his wife, in fee of the whole of his free fishery, valued at ½ mark, below the bridge of Shillingford on the Thames.[31]

(32) **Undated:** (Suffolk) Grant to Hales Abbey of one acre of land in Haughley.[32]

(33) **Undated:** (Suffolk) Exchange with Hales Abbey of lands in Haughley in frank almoin.[33]

[26] *CChR 1257–1300*, 405–6. [27] Ibid., 443. [28] *CChR 1300–1326*, 490.
[29] *CPR 1292–1301*, 509. [30] *CPR 1292–1301*, 608. [31] Ibid., 574–5.
[32] *CChR 1300–1326*, 490–1. [33] Ibid., 491.

(34) **Undated:** (Cornwall) Grant to Sir Thomas the Archdeacon of the manor of Trebernet at a rent of 13*s* 2 ½*d* at Michaelmas and a rose at Midsummer.[34]

(35) **Undated:** (Cornwall) Grant to John Fitz William of manor of Arworthel, except the advowson, to hold of Sir Oliver Dynham and his heirs by service of ½ knight's fee in exchange for his manor of Penlyn.[35]

(36) **Undated:** Demise, for life, to Christina, widow of Ralph de Cesterton, of the manor of Halghton with reversion to Cornwall.[36]

[34] *Catalogue of Ancient Deeds*, 6 vols. (London: HMSO, 1890–1915), III, D. 1129.

[35] C 36/57, no. 90. [36] Ibid., no. 116.

BIBLIOGRAPHY

MANUSCRIPT SOURCES

KANSAS CITY, KENNETH SPENCER RESEARCH LIBRARY

University of Kansas, MS 191

LONDON, THE BRITISH LIBRARY

MS Additional 43972
MS Cotton Claudius A xiii
MS Harley 1240
MS Harley 2074
MS Lansdowne 229
MS Stowe 666

LONDON, THE NATIONAL ARCHIVES

C 49 – Chancery, King's Remembrancer
C 67 – Chancery, Additional Patent Rolls
C 53 – Chancery, Charter Rolls
C 153 – Chancery, Vetus Codex
DL 25 – Duchy of Lancaster Deeds, Series L
DL 27 – Duchy of Lancaster Deeds, Series LS
DL 36 – Duchy of Lancaster, Cartae Miscellaneae
DL 41 – Duchy of Lancaster, Miscellanea
DL 42 – Duchy of Lancaster, Great Cowcher Book
E 36 – Exchequer, Treasury of Receipt, Miscellaneous Books
E 101 – Exchequer, King's Remembrancer, Accounts Various
E 159 – Exchequer, King's Remembrancer, Memoranda Rolls
E 162 – Exchequer, King's Remembrancer, Minutes of Decrees
E 163 – Exchequer, King's Remembrancer, Miscellanea
E 210 – Exchequer, King's Remembrancer, Ancient Deeds, Series D
E 327 – Exchequer, Augmentation Office, Ancient Deeds, Series BX

E 372 – Exchequer, Pipe Rolls
JUST 1 – Eyre Rolls
KB 27 – Court of King's Bench, Coram Rege Rolls
KB 29 – Court of King's Bench, Controlment Rolls
LR 14 – Land Revenue, Ancient Deeds, Series E
SC 1 – Special Collections, Ancient Correspondence
SC 6 – Special Collections, Ministers' and Receivers' Accounts
SC 8 – Special Collections, Ancient Petitions

LONDON, UNIVERSITY OF LONDON LIBRARY

Fuller Collection, MS 13/8

OXFORD, MERTON COLLEGE ARCHIVES

Muniments no. 415
Muniments no. 435

PRINTED PRIMARY SOURCES

The 1263 Surrey Eyre, Stewart, S. (ed. and trans.), Surrey Record Society 40 (2006)
Annales Monastici, Luard, H.R. (ed.), 4 vols., Rolls Series (1864–9)
Aquinas, St Thomas, *De Regno: On Kingship to the King of Cyprus*, Phelan, G.B. (ed. and trans.) and Eschmann, I.T. (revised), Toronto: Pontifical Institute of Medieval Studies, 1949
Blaauw, W.H., 'On the Early History of Lewes Priory and Its Seals, with Extracts from an MS Chronicle', *Sussex Archaeological Collections* 2 (1849), 7–37
The Book of Fees, 3 vols., London: HMSO, 1920–31
Bracton De Legibus Et Consuetudinibus Angliæ, Thorne, S.E. (ed. and trans.), 2 vols., Cambridge, MA: Harvard University Press, 1968
The Brut, vol. 1, Brie, F.W.D. (ed.), Early English Text Society, Original Series 131 (1906)
Calendar of Ancient Correspondence Concerning Wales, Edwards, J.G. (ed. and trans.), Cardiff University Press, 1935
Calendar of Chancery Rolls Various, 1277–1326, London: HMSO, 1912
Calendar of Chancery Warrants, 1244–1326, London: HMSO, 1927
Calendar of Documents Relating to Scotland, Bain, J. (ed.), 4 vols., Edinburgh: General Register Office, 1881–5
Calendar of Liberate Rolls, 6 vols., London: HMSO, 1916–64
Calendar of Papal Letters, 20 vols., London: HMSO, 1893
Canterbury, Gervase of, *The Historical Works of Gervase of Canterbury*, Stubbs, W. (ed.), 2 vols., Rolls Series (1880)
The Cartulary of Blyth Priory, Timson, R.T. (ed.), 2 vols., London: HMSO, 1973
Cartulary of the Cistercian Abbey of Fountains in the West Riding of the County of York, Lancaster, W.T. (ed.), 2 vols., Leeds: J. Whitehead and Sons, 1915
Cartulary of Darley Abbey, Darlington, R.R. (ed.), 2 vols., Kendal: Titus Wilson and Son, 1945
The Cartulary of Launceston Priory, Hull, P.L. (ed. and trans.), Devon and Cornwall Record Society, New Series 30 (1987)

Cartulary of Lewes Priory: The Portion Relating to Counties Other Than Sussex: Surrey, Sussex Record Society, Extra Vol. (1943)

The Cartulary of St Michael's Mount, Hull, P.L. (ed. and trans.), Devon and Cornwall Record Society, New Series 5 (1962)

Catalogue of Ancient Deeds, 6 vols., London: HMSO, 1890–1915

The Chronicle of Bury St Edmunds, 1212–1301, Gransden, A. (ed. and trans.), London: Thomas Nelson and Sons, 1964

Chronicles of the Reigns of Edward I and Edward II, Stubbs, W. (ed.), 2 vols., Rolls Series (1882)

Chronicon Johannis de Reading et Anonymi Cantuariensis, Tait, J. (ed.), Manchester University Press, 1914

Close Rolls of Henry III, 14 vols., London: HMSO, 1902–38

Cotton, Bartholomew, *Historia Anglicana*, Luard, H.R. (ed.), Rolls Series (1859)

Coucher Book of Furness Abbey, Brownbill, J. (ed.), Chetham Society, New Series 74 (1915)

The Coucher Book of Whalley Abbey, Hulton, W.A. (ed.), 4 vols., Chetham Society, Original Series (1847–9)

Court Rolls of the Manor of Wakefield, vol. i: 1274–1297, Baildon, W.P. (ed. and trans.), Yorkshire Archaeological Record Society 29 (1901)

Court Rolls of the Manor of Wakefield, vol. ii: 1297–1309, Baildon, W.P. (ed. and trans.), Yorkshire *Archaeological Society* 36 (1906)

Descriptive Catalogue of Derbyshire Charters, Jeaves, I.H. (ed.), London: Bemrose, 1906

Documents of the Baronial Movement of Reform and Rebellion, 1258–1267, Treharne, R.F. and Sanders, I.J. (eds. and trans.), Oxford University Press, 1972

Documents Illustrating the Crisis of 1297–8 in England, Prestwich, M.C. (ed.), Camden Society, 4th Series 24 (1980)

Documents Illustrative of the History of Scotland, Stevenson, J. (ed.), 2 vols., Edinburgh: General Register Office, 1870

Earliest English Law Reports, Brand, P. (ed.), 2 vols., Selden Society 111–12 (1996)

Early Yorkshire Charters: the Honour of Warenne, Clay, C.T. and Farrer, W. (eds.), Yorkshire Archaeological Record Series, Additional Series 8 (1949)

Emden, A.B. (ed.), *Biographical Register of the University of Oxford to AD 1500*, 3 vols., Oxford University Press, 1957–9

English Historical Documents, 1189–1327, Rothwell, H. (ed.), London: Eyre and Spottiswoode, 1975

'Extracts from the Plea Rolls, 1272 to 1294', Wrottesley, G. (ed. and trans.), W.M. Salt *Archaeological Society* 6 (1885), 37–300

Eye Priory Cartulary and Charters, Brown, V. (ed.), 2 vols., Suffolk Record Society, Suffolk Charters 12, 13 (1992–4)

Feudal Aids, 6 vols., London: HMSO, 1899–1920

Flores Historiarum, Luard, H.E. (ed.), 3 vols., Rolls Series (1890)

Foedera Conventiones, Litterae, et Cujuscunque Generis Acta Publica, I.ii, Rymer, T. and Sanderson, R. (eds.), London: Record Commission (1816)

Fortescue, John, *The Governance of England: Otherwise Called the Difference Between a Limited and an Absolute Monarchy*, Plummer, C. (ed.), Oxford: Clarendon Press, 1885

Gloucester, Robert of, *The Metrical Chronicle of Robert of Gloucester*, Wright, W.A. (ed.), 2 vols., Rolls Series (1887)

Gray, Sir Thomas, *Scalacronica, 1272–1363*, King, A. (ed. and trans.), Surtees Society 209 (2005)
Guisborough, Walter of, *The Chronicle of Walter of Guisborough*, Rothwell, H. (ed.), Camden Society, 3rd Series 89 (1957)
'The Hundred Roll for Sussex', Salzman, L.F. (ed. and trans.), *Sussex Archaeological Collections* 82: 20–34; 83: 35–54; 84: 60–81 (1943–5)
The Itinerary of Edward I, 1272–1290, List and Index Society 103 (1974)
The Itinerary of Edward I, 1290–1307, List and Index Society 132 (1976)
Langtoft, Pierre, *The Chronicle of Pierre de Langtoft*, Wright, T. (ed.), 2 vols., Rolls Series (1859–68)
Laon, Adalbéron de, *Poème au Roi Robert*, Carozzi, C. (ed.), Paris: Les Belles Lettres, 1979
Liber de Antiquis Legibus: Cronica Maiorum et Vicecomitum Londoniarum, Stapleton, T. (ed.), Camden Society, Old Series 34 (1846)
The Life of Edward the Second, Denholm-Young, N. (ed.), London: Nelson, 1957
List of Sheriffs of England and Wales from the Earliest Times to A.D. 1831, List and Index Society 9 (1963)
Littere Wallie Preserved in Liber A in the Public Record Office, Edwards, J.G. (ed.), Cardiff University Press, 1940
Manners and Household Expenses of England in the Thirteenth and Fifteenth Centuries, Turner, T.H. (ed.), London: William Nicol Press, 1841
Milemete, Walter of, 'On the Nobility Wisdom and Prudence of Kings', in Nederman, C.J. (ed. and trans.), *Political Thought in Early Fourteenth-Century England: Treatises by Walter of Milemete, William of Pagula, and William of Ockham*, Temple, AZ: Arizona Center for Medieval Studies, 2002
Ministers' Accounts of the Earldom of Cornwall, Midgley, L.M. (ed.), Camden Society, 3rd Series 66, 68 (1942–5)
The Mirror of Justices, Whitaker, W.J. and Maitland, F.W. (eds. and trans.), Selden Society 7 (1893)
The Northumberland Lay Subsidy Roll of 1296, Fraser, C.M. (ed.). Society of Antiquaries of Newcastle-upon-Tyne 1 (1968)
Parliamentary Writs and Writs of Military Summons, Palgrave, F. (ed.), 2 vols., London: Record Commission, 1832
The Parliament Rolls of Medieval England, Given-Wilson, C., Brand, P., Curry, A., Horrox, R.E., Martin, G., Ormrod, W.A. and Phillips, J.R.S. (eds. and trans.), Leicester: Scholarly Digital Editions, 2005. Online: www.sd-editions.com/PROME
Paris, Matthew, *Chronica Majora*, Luard, H.R. (ed.), 7 vols., Rolls Series (1872–83)
Paston Letters and Papers of the Fifteenth Century, Davis, N. (ed.), 2 vols., Oxford University Press, 1971–6
Placita de Quo Warranto, Illingworth, W. (ed.), London: Record Commission, 1818
The Pleas of Quo Warranto for the County of Lancashire, Cantle, A. (ed.), Chetham Society, 98 (1937)
'Private Indentures for Life Service in Peace and War, 1278–1476', Jones, M. and Walker, S.K. (eds.), *Camden Miscellany*, Camden Society, Fifth Series 3 (1994)
Records of the Barony and Honour of the Rape of Lewes, Taylor, A.J. (ed.), Sussex Record Society, 44 (1939)
The Register of Walter Giffard, Lord Archbishop of York, 1266–79, Brown, W. (ed.), Surtees Society, 109 (1904)

Registrum Epistolarum Johannis Peckham, Martin, C.T. (ed.), 3 vols., Rolls Series (1882–4)
Registrum Roberti Winchelsey, Graham, R. (ed.), 2 vols., Canterbury and York Society (1952–6)
Report of the Deputy Keeper of the Public Record Office, 42 (1881)
Rishanger, William, *Chronica et Annales*, Riley, H.T. (ed.), Rolls Series (1865)
Rôles Gascons, Bémont, C. (ed.), 3 vols., Paris: Imprimerie Nationale, 1896–1906
The Rolls of the 1281 Derbyshire Eyre, Hopkinson, A.M. (ed.), Derbyshire Record Society 28 (2000)
Rome, Giles of, *De Regimine Principum*, Rome, 1556
Rotuli Hundredorum, 2 vols., London: Record Commission, 1812–18
Rotuli Scotiae, 1291–1377, London: Record Commission, 1814
The Royal Charter Witness Lists of Edward I (1272–1307) from the Charter Rolls in the Public Record Office, Huscroft, R. (ed.), List and Index Society 279 (2000)
The Royal Charter Witness Lists of Edward II (1307–1326) from the Charter Rolls in the Public Record Office, Hamilton, J.S. (ed.), List and Index Society 288 (2001)
The Royal Charter Witness Lists of Henry III (1226–1272) from the Charter Rolls in the Public Record Office, Morris, M. (ed.). 2 vols., List and Index Society 291–2 (2001)
Salisbury, John of, *Policraticus: of the Frivolities of Courtiers and the Footprints of Philosophers*, Nederman, C.J. (ed. and trans.), Cambridge University Press, 1990
Scotland in 1298: Documents Relating to the Campaign of Edward I in That Year and Especially to the Battle of Falkirk, Gough, H. (ed.), Paisley: A. Gardiner Press, 1888
Select Cases in the Court of King's Bench, Sayles, G.O. (ed.), 7 vols., Selden Society (1936–71)
Select Cases of Procedure without Writ under Henry III, Richardson, H.G. and Sayles, G.O. (eds. and trans.), Selden Society 60 (1941)
Select Documents of English Constitutional History, 1307–1485, Chrimes, S.B. and Brown, A.L. (eds.), London: A. and C. Black, 1961
Somersetshire Pleas from the Rolls of the Itinerant Justices (for the Years 1 to 7 of the Reign of Edward I Inclusive), Landon, L. (ed.), Somerset Record Society 41 (1926)
Stamford in the Thirteenth Century: Two Inquisitions from the Reign of Edward I, Roffe, D. (ed.), Stamford: Paul Wilkins, 1994
State Trials of the Reign of Edward the First, 1289–1293, Tout, T.F. and Johnstone, H. (eds.), Camden Society, 3rd Series 9 (1906)
Statutes of the Realm, 10 vols., London: Record Commission, 1810–28
The Three Earliest Subsidies for the County of Sussex, Hudson, W. (ed.), Sussex Record Society 10 (1909)
Three Early Assize Rolls for the County of Northumberland, Page, W. (ed.), Surtees Society 88 (1891)
Trivet, Nicholas, *Annales Sex Regum Angliae*, Hogg, T. (ed.), London: English Historical Society, 1845
Two Compoti of the Lancashire and Cheshire Manors of Henry de Lacy, Earl of Lincoln, 24 and 33 Edward I, Lyons, P.A. (ed. and trans.), Chetham Society, Old Series 112 (1884)
Vita Edwardi Secundi: The Life of Edward the Second, Childs, W.A. (ed. and trans.), Oxford University Press, 2005
Yorkshire Hundred and Quo Warranto Rolls, 1274–1294, English, B. (ed.) Yorkshire Archaeological Society 151 (1994)

Bibliography

SECONDARY SOURCES

Altschul, M., *A Baronial Family in Medieval England: the Clares, 1217–1314*, Baltimore, MD: Johns Hopkins University Press, 1965

Ayton, A., *Knights and Warhorses: Military Service and the English Aristocracy under Edward III*, Woodbridge: Boydell and Brewer Press, 1994

Baldwin, J.F., 'The Household Administration of Henry Lacy and Thomas of Lancaster', *EHR* 42 (1927), 180–200

The King's Council during the Middle Ages, Oxford: Clarendon Press, 1913

Barker, J.R.V., *The Tournament in England, 1100–1400*, Woodbridge: Boydell and Brewer Press, 1986

Barrie, D.A., 'The *Maiores Barones* in the Second Half of the Reign of Edward I, 1290–1307', unpublished PhD thesis, University of St Andrews, 1991

Barrow, G.W.S., *Robert Bruce and the Community of the Realm of Scotland*, 3rd edn, Edinburgh University Press, 1988

Bartlett, R., *England under the Norman and Angevin Kings: 1075–1225*, Oxford: Clarendon Press, 2000

Baxter, S., *The Earls of Mercia: Lordship and Power in Late Anglo-Saxon England*, Oxford University Press, 2007

Bean, J.M.W., '"Bachelor" and Retainer', *Medievalia et Humanistica*, New Series 3 (1972), 117–31

The Decline of English Feudalism, 1215–1540, Manchester University Press, 1968

Bémont, C., *Simon de Montfort*, Jacob, E.F. (trans.), 2nd edn, Oxford: Clarendon Press, 1930

Bennett, M.J., *Community, Class and Careerism: Cheshire and Lancashire in the Age of* Sir Gawain and the Green Knight, Cambridge University Press, 1983

Bothwell, J.S., *Edward III and the English Peerage: Royal Patronage, Social Mobility and Political Control in Fourteenth-Century England*, Woodbridge: Boydell and Brewer Press, 2004

Brand, P.A., 'Brabazon, Sir Roger (*b.* in or before 1247?–*d.* 1317)', in *ODNB*

'Edward I and the Judges: The "State Trials" of 1289–93', *TCE* 1 (1986), 31–40

The Making of the Common Law, London: Hambledon Press, 1992

The Origins of the English Legal Profession, Oxford: Blackwells, 1992

'The Professionalisation of Lawyers in England', *Zeitschrift Für Neuere Rechtsgeschichte* 28 (2006), 7–19

'Seaton, Roger of (*c.*1230–*c.*1280)', in *ODNB*

'Thornton, Gilbert of (*b.* in or before 1245, *d.* 1295)', in *ODNB*

Britnell, R.H. and Pollard, A.J. (eds.), *The McFarlane Legacy: Studies in Late Medieval Politics and Society*, Stroud and New York: Sutton and St. Martin's Press, 1995

Brown, A.L., *The Governance of Late Medieval England, 1272–1461*, London: Hodder Arnold, 1989

Burls, R.J., 'Society, Economy and Lordship in Devon in the Age of the First Two Courtenay Earls, c.1297–1377', unpublished DPhil thesis, University of Oxford, 2002

Burt, C., 'A "Bastard Feudal" Affinity in the Making? The Followings of William and Guy de Beauchamp, Earls of Warwick, 1268–1315', *Midland History* 34 (2009), 156–80

'The Governance of Edward I, 1272–1307, with Special Reference to Shropshire, Warwickshire and Kent', unpublished PhD thesis, University of Cambridge, 2004

Butler, L., *Sandal Castle, Wakefield: the History and Archaeology of a Medieval Castle*, Wakefield: Wakefield Historical Publications, 1991

Cam, H.M., *The Hundred and the Hundred Rolls: an Outline of Local Government in Medieval England*, London: Methuen Press, 1930

Carpenter, D.A., 'The Decline of the Curial Sheriff in England, 1194–1258', *EHR* 91 (1976), 1–32

'Henry III and the Sicilian Affair', *Fine of the Month*, www.finerollshenry3.org.uk, 2012

'King, Magnates and Society: the Personal Rule of King Henry III, 1234–1258', *Speculum* 40 (1985), 39–70

'The Plantagenet Kings', in Abulafia, D. (ed.), *New Cambridge Medieval History, c.1198–1300*, vol. V, Cambridge University Press, 1999

The Reign of Henry III, London: Hambledon Press, 1996

'The Second Century of English Feudalism', *Past and Present* 168 (2000), 30–71

The Struggle for Mastery: Britain, 1066–1284, London: Penguin, 2003

Carpenter, M.C., 'The Beauchamp Affinity: a Study of Bastard Feudalism at Work', *EHR* 131 (1980), 514–33

'England: the Nobility and the Gentry', in Rigby, S. (ed.), *A Companion to Britain in the Later Middle Ages*, Oxford: Blackwell, 2003

Locality and Polity: a Study of Warwickshire Landed Society, 1401–1499, Cambridge University Press, 1992

'Political and Geographic Space: the Geopolitics of Medieval England', in Kümin, B. (ed.), *Political Space in Pre-industrial Europe*, Farnham: Ashgate Publishing, 2009

The Wars of the Roses: Politics and the Constitution in England, c.1437–1509, Cambridge University Press, 1997

'Who Ruled the Midlands in the Later Middle Ages?', *Midland History* 19 (1994), 1–20

Castor, H., *The King, the Crown and the Duchy of Lancaster: Public Authority and Private Power, 1399–1461*, Oxford University Press, 2000

Cherry, M., 'The Courtenay Earls of Devon: the Formation and Disintegration of a Late Medieval Aristocratic Affinity', *Southern History* 1 (1979), 71–97

Chibnall, M., 'Mercenaries and the Familia Regis under Henry I', *History* 62 (1977), 15–23

Chrimes, S.B., *English Constitutional Ideas in the Fifteenth Century*, Cambridge University Press, 1936

Clanchy, M.T., *England and Its Rulers, 1066–1272: Foreign Lordship and National Identity*, Oxford University Press, 1983

England and Its Rulers, 1066–1272, 2nd edn, Oxford University Press, 1998

England and Its Rulers, 1066–1307, 3rd edn, Oxford University Press, 2006

Cockayne, G.E. (ed.), *The Complete Peerage*, 12 vols., London: George Bell and Sons, 1887–98

Coss, P.R., 'Bastard Feudalism Revised', *Past and Present* 125 (1989), 27–64

'Beauchamp, William (IV) de, Ninth Earl of Warwick (*c.*1238–1298)', in *ODNB*

'From Feudalism to Bastard Feudalism', in Fryde, N., Monnet, P. and Oexle, O.G. (eds.), *Die Gegenwart des Feudalismus*, Göttingen: Vandehoeck & Ruprecht (2002), 79–107

Lordship, Knighthood and Locality: a Study in English Society, c. 1180–c. 1280, Cambridge University Press, 1991

Coss, P.R., Crouch, D. and Carpenter, D.A., 'Debate: Bastard Feudalism Revised', *Past and Present* 131 (1991), 165–203

Crouch, D., *The Beaumont Twins: the Roots and Branches of Power in the Twelfth Century*, Cambridge University Press, 1986

The Birth of Nobility: Constructing Aristocracy in England and France, 900–1300, Harlow: Longfield Press, 2005

The English Aristocracy, 1070–1272: A Social Transformation, New Haven, CT and London: Yale University Press, 2011

'The Local Influence of the Earls of Warwick, 1088–1241: a Study in Decline and Resourcefulness', *Midland History* 21 (1996), 1–22

William Marshal: Court, Career and Chivalry in the Angevin Empire, c.1147–1219, Harlow: Longfield Press, 1990

Dalton, P., *Conquest, Anarchy and Lordship: Yorkshire, 1066–1154*, Cambridge University Press, 1994

Davies, R.G. and Denton, J.H. (eds.), *The English Parliament in the Middle Ages*, Manchester University Press, 1981

Davies, R.R., *The Age of Conquest: Wales, 1063–1415*, Oxford University Press, 1987

Lords and Lordship in the British Isles in the Late Middle Ages, Smith, B. (ed.), Oxford University Press, 2009

Lordship and Society in the March of Wales, 1282–1400, Oxford University Press, 1978

Denholm-Young, N., *Richard of Cornwall*, Oxford: Blackwell, 1947

Seignorial Administration in England, Oxford University Press, 1937

Denton, J.H., 'The Crisis of 1297 from the Evesham Chronicle', *EHR* 93 (1978), 560–79

Robert Winchelsey and the Crown, 1294–1313, Cambridge University Press, 1980

Duby, G., *The Chivalrous Society*, Postan, C. (trans.), London: Edward Arnold, 1977

English, B., 'Forz, Isabella de, Suo Jure Countess of Devon, and Countess of Aumale (1237–1293)', in *ODNB*

Farrer, W., *Honors and Knights' Fees*, 3 vols., Manchester University Press, 1923

Fraser, C.M., *A History of Anthony Bek, Bishop of Durham, 1283–1311*, Oxford: Clarendon Press, 1957

Fryde, E.B., 'Magnate Debts to Edward I and Edward III: a Study of Common Problems and Contrasting Royal Reactions to Them', *The National Library of Wales Journal* 27 (1992), 249–88

Fryde, E.B. and Miller, E. (eds.), *Historical Studies of the English Parliament*, Cambridge University Press, 1970

Fryde, N.M., *The Tyranny and Fall of Edward II, 1321–1326*, Cambridge University Press, 1979

Given-Wilson, C., *The English Nobility in the Late Middle Ages: the Fourteenth-Century Political Community*, London and New York: Routledge and Keegan Press, 1987

'Royal Charter Witness Lists, 1327–1399', *Medieval Prosopography* 12 (1991), 35–94

'Wealth and Credit, Public and Private: the Earls of Arundel 1306–97', *EHR* 106 (1991), 1–26

Golob, P.E., 'The Ferrers Earls of Derby: a Study in the Honour of Tutbury, 1066–1279', unpublished PhD thesis, University of Cambridge, 1984

Goodman, A., 'John of Gaunt: Paradigm of the Late Fourteenth-Century Crisis', *Transactions of the Royal Historical Society*, 5th Series 37 (1987), 133–48

Gray-Birch, W. de., *A History of Neath Abbey*, Neath: John E. Richards, 1902

Green, J.A., *The Aristocracy of Anglo-Norman England*, Cambridge University Press, 1997

Greenhalgh, D., 'The Fitzalan Family, 1101–1415: a Study in the Development of a Noble Medieval Dynasty', unpublished MPhil thesis, University of Wales, Bangor, 2003

Gundy, A., 'The Earl of Warwick and the Royal Affinity', *The Fifteenth Century* 2 (2001), 57–70

Hamilton, J.S., 'Bohun, Humphrey (VII) de, Fourth Earl of Hereford and Ninth Earl of Essex (*c.*1276–1322)', in *ODNB*

'Lacy, Henry de, Fifth Earl of Lincoln (1249–1311)', in *ODNB*

Piers Gaveston Earl of Cornwall, 1307–1312: Politics and Patronage in the Reign of Edward II, Detroit, MI: Wayne State University Press, 1988

Harding, A., *England in the Thirteenth Century*, Cambridge University Press, 1993

The Law Courts of Medieval England (London: George Allen & Unwin Ltd, 1973)

Harriss, G.L., *King, Parliament, and Public Finance in Medieval England to 1369*, Oxford: Clarendon Press, 1975

'Political Society and the Growth of Government in Late Medieval England', *Past and Present* 138 (1993), 28–57

Hollister, C.W., 'The Taming of the Turbulent Earl: Henry I and William of Warenne', *Historical Reflections* 3 (1976), 83–91

Holmes, G.A., *The Estates of the Higher Nobility in Fourteenth-Century England*, Cambridge University Press, 1957

The Later Middle Ages, 1272–1485, Edinburgh: Thomas Nelson and Sons, 1962

Holt, J.C., *Magna Carta*, 2nd edn, Cambridge University Press, 1992

Horrox, R., *Richard III: a Study in Service*, Cambridge University Press, 1989

Hudson, J., *Land, Law and Lordship in Anglo-Norman England*, Oxford University Press, 1994

Huscroft, R., 'The Political Career and Personal Life of Robert Burnell, Chancellor of Edward I', unpublished PhD thesis, University of London, 2000

'Robert Burnell and the Governance of England, 1270–74', *TCE* 8 (2001), 59–69

Johnstone, H., *Edward of Carnarvon, 1284–1307*, Manchester University Press, 1946

Jones, G., 'The Bohun Earls of Hereford and Essex, c.1270–1322', unpublished MLitt thesis, University of Oxford, 1984

Jones, M., 'Brittany, John of, Earl of Richmond (1266?–1334)', in *ODNB*

Kaeuper, R.W., *Bankers to the Crown: the Riccardi of Lucca and Edward I*, Princeton University Press, 1973

'Law and Order in Fourteenth-Century England: the Evidence of Special Commissions of Oyer and Terminer', *Speculum* 54 (1979), 734–84

Keen, M.H., *England in the Later Middle Ages: a Political History*, London: Methuen Press, 1973

Nobles, Knights and Men-at-Arms in the Middle Ages, London: Hambledon Press, 1996

Knowles, C.H., 'Clare, Gilbert de, Seventh Earl of Gloucester and Sixth Earl of Hertford (1243–1295)', in *ODNB*

Lander, J.R., *Government and Community: England 1450–1509*, London: Edward Arnold, 1980

Lapsley, G.T., 'John de Warenne and the Quo Warranto Proceedings of 1279', *Cambridge Historical Journal* 2 (1927), 110–32

Lewis, N.B., 'The English Forces in Flanders, August–November 1297', in Hunt, R.W., Pantin, W.A. and Southern, R.W. (eds.), *Studies in Medieval History Presented to F.M. Powicke*, Oxford: Clarendon Press, 1948

'The Recruitment and Organisation of a Contract Army, May to November 1337', *BIHR* 37 (1964), 1–19

Lloyd, S.D., *English Society and the Crusade, 1216–1307*, Oxford: Clarendon Press, 1988

'Gilbert de Clare, Richard of Cornwall and the Lord Edward's Crusade', *Nottingham Medieval Studies* 30 (1986), 46–66

Loomis, R.S., 'Edward I: Arthurian Enthusiast', *Speculum* 28 (1953), 114–27

McFarlane, K.B., *England in the Fifteenth Century: Collected Essays*, London: Hambledon Press, 1981

The Nobility of Later Medieval England, Oxford: Clarendon Press, 1973

McKisack, M., *The Fourteenth Century, 1307–1399*, Oxford University Press, 1959

Maddicott, J.R., 'Edward I and the Lessons of Baronial Reform: Local Government, 1258–80', *TCE* 1 (1986), 1–30

'Law and Lordship: Royal Justices as Retainers in Thirteenth- and Fourteenth-Century England', *Past and Present* supplementary 4 (1978)

'Magna Carta and the Local Community, 1215–1259', *Past and Present* 102 (1984), 25–65

The Origins of the English Parliament, 924–1327, Oxford University Press, 2010

Simon de Montfort, Cambridge University Press, 1994

Thomas of Lancaster, 1307–1322: a Study in the Reign of Edward II, Oxford University Press, 1970

Maitland, F.W., 'History from the Charter Roll', *EHR* 8 (1893), 726–33

Marshall, A., 'An Early Fourteenth Century Affinity: the Earl of Norfolk and His Followers', *Fourteenth Century England* 5 (2008), 1–13

Mason, E., 'The Resources of the Earldom of Warwick in the Thirteenth Century', *Midland History* 3 (1975), 67–75

Miller, E., 'War, Taxation and the English Economy in the Late Thirteenth and Early Fourteenth Centuries', in Winter, J.M. (ed.), *War and Economic Development: Essays in Memory of David Joslin*, Cambridge University Press, 1975

Milsom, S.F.C., *Historical Foundations of the Common Law*, 2nd edn, Oxford University Press, 1981

Moor, C., *The Knights of Edward I*, 5 vols., Leeds: Harleian Society, 1929–32

Moore, T.K., 'Government and Locality in Essex in the Reign of Henry III', unpublished PhD thesis, University of Cambridge, 2006

Morris, J.E., *The Welsh Wars of Edward I*, Oxford: Clarendon Press, 1901

Morris, M., *The Bigod Earls of Norfolk in the Thirteenth Century*, Woodbridge: Boydell and Brewer Press, 2005

A Great and Terrible King: Edward I and the Forging of Britain, London: Hutchinson Press, 2008

'The "Murder" of an English Earldom? Roger Bigod IV and Edward I', *TCE* 9 (2003), 89–99

Morris, W.A., *The Medieval English Sheriff to 1300*, Manchester University Press, 1927

Mundill, R.R., *England's Jewish Solution: Experiment and Expulsion, 1262–1290*, Cambridge University Press, 1998

Orme, N., *Medieval Children*, New Haven, CT and London: Yale University Press, 2001

Ormrod, W.M., *Edward III*, New Haven, CT and London: Yale University Press, 2011

'The Personal Religion of Edward III', *Speculum* 64 (1989), 849–77

Page, M., 'Cornwall, Earl Richard and the Barons' War', *EHR* 115 (2000), 21–38

Painter, S., *Studies in the History of the English Feudal Barony*, Baltimore, MD: Johns Hopkins University Press, 1943

Palmer, R.C., *The County Courts of Medieval England, 1150–1350*, Princeton University Press, 1982

Parsons, J.C., *Eleanor of Castile: Queen and Society in Thirteenth-Century England*, London: Macmillan, 1994

Payling, S., *Political Society in Lancastrian England: the Greater Gentry of Nottinghamshire*, Oxford: Clarendon Press, 1991

Phillips, J.R.S., *Aymer de Valence, Earl of Pembroke, 1307–1324: Baronial Politics in the Reign of Edward II*, Oxford University Press, 1972

Edward II, New Haven, CT and London: Yale University Press, 2010

Plucknett, T.F.T., *The Legislation of Edward I*, Oxford: Clarendon Press, 1949

Powell, E., 'After "After McFarlane": the Poverty of Patronage and the Case for Constitutional History', in Clayton, D.J., Davies, R.G. and McNiven, P. (eds.), *Trade, Devotion, and Governance: Papers in Later Medieval History*, Stroud: Sutton Press, 1994

Kingship, Law, and Society: Criminal Justice in the Reign of Henry V, Oxford: Clarendon Press, 1989

Powell, J.E. and Wallis, K., *The House of Lords in the Middle Ages: a History of the English House of Lords to 1540*, London: Weidenfeld & Nicolson, 1968

Powicke, F.M., *King Henry III and the Lord Edward: the Community of the Realm in the Thirteenth Century*, 2 vols., Oxford University Press, 1947

The Thirteenth Century, 1216–1307, 2nd edn, Oxford University Press, 1962

Powicke, M., *Military Obligation in Medieval England: a Study in Liberty and Duty*, Oxford: Clarendon Press, 1962

Prestwich, J.O., 'The Military Household of the Norman Kings', *EHR* 96 (1981), 1–35

Prestwich, M.C., *Armies and Warfare in the Middle Ages: the English Experience*, New Haven, CT and London: Yale University Press, 1996

'Bigod, Roger (IV), Fifth Earl of Norfolk (*c.*1245–1306)', in *ODNB*

'Cavalry Service in Early Fourteenth Century England', in Gillingham, J. and Holt, J.C. (eds.), *War and Government in the Middle Ages: Essays in Honour of J.O. Prestwich*, Woodbridge: Boydell and Brewer Press, 1984

Edward I, 2nd edn, New Haven, CT and London: Yale University Press, 1997

Plantagenet England, 1225–1360, Oxford University Press, 2005

'Royal Patronage under Edward I', *TCE* 1 (1986), 41–52

The Three Edwards: War and State in England, 1272–1377, London: Methuen Press, 1980

War, Politics and Finance under Edward I, London: Rowman & Littlefield Press, 1972

Rawcliffe, C., *The Staffords, Earls of Stafford and Dukes of Buckingham, 1394–1521*, Cambridge University Press, 1978

Reeve, M., 'The Painted Chamber at Westminster, Edward I, and the Crusade', *Viator* 37 (2006), 189–221

Rhodes, W.E., 'Edmund, Earl of Lancaster', *EHR* 10 (1895), 19–40 and 209–37

Richardson, H.G., 'The Coronation of Edward I', *BIHR* 15 (1937), 94–9

Richardson, H.G. and Sayles, G.O. (eds.), *The English Parliament in the Middle Ages*, London: Hambledon Press, 1981

Richmond, C., 'An English Mafia?', *Nottingham Medieval Studies* 36 (1992), 235–43

Ridgeway, H.W., 'Foreign Favourites and Henry III's Problems of Patronage, 1247–1258', *EHR* 104 (1989), 590–610

'The Lord Edward and the Provisions of Oxford (1258): a Study in Faction', *TCE* 1 (1986), 89–99

'Mid-Thirteenth Century Reformers and the Locality: the Sheriffs of the Baronial Regime, 1258–1261', in Fleming, P., Gross, A. and Lander, J.R. (eds.), *Regionalism and Revision: the Crown and Its Provinces in England, 1250–1650*, London: Hambledon Press, 1998

'William de Valence and His Familiares, 1247–1272', *Historical Research* 65 (1992), 239–57

Rogers, M., 'The Welsh Marcher Lordship of Bromfield and Yale, 1282–1485', unpublished PhD thesis, University of Aberystwyth, 1992

Roskell, J.S., 'The Problem of the Attendance of the Lords in Medieval Parliaments', *BIHR* 29 (1956), 153–204

Ross, J., *John de Vere, Thirteenth Earl of Oxford (1442–1513): 'The Foremost Man of the Kingdom'*, Woodbridge: Boydell and Brewer Press, 2011

Salzman, L.F., 'The Family of Aguillon', *Sussex Archaeological Collections* 79 (1938), 45–60

Saul, N.E., *Knights and Esquires: the Gloucestershire Gentry in the Fourteenth Century*, Oxford: Clarendon Press, 1981

Scenes from Provincial Life: Knightly Families in Sussex, 1280–1400, Oxford: Clarendon Press, 1986

Sayles, G.O., *The King's Parliament of England*, London: Edward Arnold, 1975

Simpson, G.G., 'The *Familia* of Roger de Quincy, Earl of Winchester and Constable of Scotland', in Stringer, K.J. (ed.), *Essays on the Nobility of Medieval Scotland*, Edinburgh: John Donald Publishers, 1985, 102–30

Smith, L., 'Mortimer, Roger (IV), First Lord Mortimer of Chirk (*c.*1256–1326)', in *ODNB*

Somerville, R., *History of the Duchy of Lancaster*, London: Chancellor and Council of the Duchy of Lancaster, 1953

Spencer, A.M., 'The Comital Military Retinue in the Reign of Edward I', *Historical Research* 83 (2010), 46–59

'The Earls in the Reign of Edward I, 1272–1307', unpublished PhD thesis, University of Cambridge, 2009

'John de Warenne, Guardian of Scotland, and the Battle of Stirling Bridge', in King, A. and Simpkin, D. (eds.), *England and Scotland at War, c. 1296–c. 1513*, Leiden and Boston: Brill, 2012

'The Lay Opposition to Edward I in 1297: Its Composition and Character', *TCE* 12 (2009), 91–106

'Royal Patronage and the Earls in the Reign of Edward I', *History* 93 (2008), 20–46

'A Warlike People? Gentry Enthusiasm for Edward I's Scottish Campaigns, 1296–1307', in Bell, A. and Curry, A., (eds.), *England's Wars, 1272–1399: the Soldier Experience*, Woodbridge: Boydell and Brewer Press, 2011

Stacey, R.C., 'Bigod, Roger (III), Fourth Earl of Norfolk (*c.* 1212–1270)', in *ODNB*

'Parliamentary Negotiation and the Expulsion of the Jews from England', *TCE* 6 (1997), 77–102

Politics, Policy, and Royal Finance Under Henry III, 1216–1245, Oxford: Clarendon Press, 1987

Stansfield, M.M.N., 'The Holland Family, Dukes of Exeter, Earls of Kent and Huntingdon, 1352–1475', unpublished DPhil thesis, University of Oxford, 1987

Stenton, F.M., *The First Century of English Feudalism, 1066–1166*, Oxford: Clarendon Press, 1932

Stubbs, W., *The Constitutional History of England*, 4th edn, 3 vols., Oxford University Press, 1906

Sutherland, D.W., *Quo Warranto Proceedings in the Reign of Edward I*, Oxford: Clarendon Press, 1963

Templeman, G., 'Edward I and the Historians', *Cambridge Historical Journal* 10 (1950), 16–35

Thomas, H.M., *Vassals, Heiresses, Crusaders and Thugs: the Gentry of Angevin Yorkshire, 1154–1216*, Philadelphia: University of Pennsylvania Press, 1993

Thompson, K., 'Lords, Castellans, Constables and Dowagers: the Rape of Pevensey from the Eleventh to the Thirteenth Century', *Sussex Archaeological Collections* 135 (1997), 209–20

Tout, T.F., 'The Earldoms under Edward I', *Transactions of the Royal Historical Society*, 2nd Series 8 (1894), 129–55

'Fitzalan, Richard (I), First Earl of Arundel (1267–1302)', Saul, N. (rev.) in *ODNB*

'Towton: the Battlefield Village (1461)'. Online: www.oldtykes.co.uk/towton.htm (last accessed 29 August 2008)

Tuck, A., *Crown and Nobility, 1272–1461: Political Conflict in Late Medieval England*, Totowa, NJ: Barnes and Noble Press, 1985

Victoria County History for Sussex, Salzman, L.F. (ed.), 9 vols., 1905–97

Vincent, N., 'Bohun, Humphrey (IV) de, Second Earl of Hereford and Seventh Earl of Essex (*d.* 1275)', in *ODNB*

'Edmund of Almain, Second Earl of Cornwall (1249–1300)', in *ODNB*

'Lacy, John de, Third Earl of Lincoln (*c.* 1192–1240)', in *ODNB*

Wait, H.A., 'The Household and Resources of the Lord Edward, 1239–1272', unpublished DPhil thesis, University of Oxford, 1988

Walker, S.K., *The Lancastrian Affinity, 1361–1399*, Oxford University Press, 1990

'Yorkshire Justices of the Peace', *EHR* 108 (1993), 281–313

Warren, W.L., *The Governance of Norman and Angevin England, 1086–1272* (Stanford University Press, 1987)

Watson, F.J., *Under the Hammer: Edward I and Scotland, 1286–1306*, East Linton: Tuckwell, 1998

Watts, J.L., 'The Counsels of Henry VI', *EHR* 106 (1991) 279–98

Henry VI and the Politics of Kingship, Cambridge University Press, 1996

The Making of Polities: Europe, 1300–1500, Cambridge University Press, 2009

Waugh, S.L., 'Bohun, Humphrey (VI) de, Third Earl of Hereford and Eighth Earl of Essex (*c.*1249–1298)', in *ODNB*

'The Fiscal Uses of Royal Wardships in the Reign of Edward I', *TCE* 1 (1986), 53–60

'From Tenure to Contract: Lordship and Clientage in Thirteenth-Century England', *EHR* 101 (1986), 811–39

'Reluctant Knights and Jurors: Respites, Exemptions, and Public Obligations in the Reign of Henry III', *Speculum* 58 (1983)

'The Third Century of English Feudalism', *TCE* 7 (1999), 47–59

'Thomas, First Earl of Norfolk (1300–1338)', in *ODNB*

'Warenne, John de, Seventh Earl of Surrey (1286–1347)', in *ODNB*

Weiler, B.K., 'Henry III and the Sicilian Business: a Reinterpretation', *Historical Research* 74 (2001), 127–50

Westervelt, T., 'Royal Charter Witness Lists and the Politics of the Reign of Edward IV', *Historical Research* 81 (2008), 211–23

Whitaker, T.D., *An History of the Original Parish of Whalley and the Honour of Clitheroe*, 4 vols., London: George Routledge and Sons, 1872

Wilkinson, B., *Constitutional History of England, 1216–1399*, 3 vols., London: Longman, 1948–58

Wright, S., *The Derbyshire Gentry in the Fifteenth Century*, Derbyshire Record Society, 1983

INDEX